Chris Stapleton first heard African  where he worked between 1972–4. editor of *Black Music and Jazz R* column, he contributed 'Afroheat', until 1984 and subsequently in *Blu* has written about African pop for magazines from *Africa Music* and *Africa Beat* to *Q*. He has also contributed to the *Independent*, *Marxism Today*, *City Limits* and *Wire*.

Chris May edited the monthly magazine *Black Music and Jazz Review* 1980–4 and has written for a large number of other magazines, including *Melody Maker*, *New Musical Express*, *No. 1* and *Time Out*. A regular broadcaster for the BBC World Service on African music, he is the author of several books on music, including *British Beat*, *Rock and Roll* and *Bob Marley*. Once resident in Nigeria, he now lives in London with his wife and two children.

CHRIS STAPLETON AND CHRIS MAY

African All-Stars

The Pop Music of a Continent

Illustrations by Andy Isham
Photographs by Jak Kilby and David Browne

PALADIN
GRAFTON BOOKS
A Division of the Collins Publishing Group

LONDON GLASGOW
TORONTO SYDNEY AUCKLAND

Paladin
Grafton Books
A Division of the Collins Publishing Group
8 Grafton Street, London W1X 3LA

Published in Paladin 1989

First published in Great Britain by
Quartet Books Ltd 1987

ISBN 0-586-08781-8

Printed and bound in Great Britain by
Collins, Glasgow

Set in Garamond

CONTENTS

INTRODUCTION

This book is the product of the respective enthusiasm of two British writers who, independently, fell in love with the music of Africa in the early 1970s. At that time, one of the authors was working for an international aid agency in Sierra Leone, while the other was indulging in a more marginal existence in Nigeria. Different motives had taken the two to west Africa but, once there, both developed passionate interests in the musics and cultures they found themselves exposed to and involved in.

On returning to Britain, the two — like a succession of other been-to's before them — fell with evangelical zeal to the task of converting anyone within reach to the magic of African music. As media channels through which to achieve this were severely limited at the time (the mid-1970s), it was inevitable that the two would sooner or later converge on one margin or another. This they did via the late specialist music magazine *Black Music and Jazz Review* and its Afroheat column — first put together by Chris May and then, when he took over the editorship of the magazine, taken up by Chris Stapleton.

Although a number of well-informed books on traditional African music have been available in the West since the early 1970s, the two authors feel the need for a basic, yet comprehensive, survey of contemporary styles such as they have attempted to provide here. The book begins with a general picture of the development of urban popular music in Africa. Although the survey ranges from pre-colonial and colonial times to post-independent Africa, unless the context demanded it, the modern country names have been used. The next section, the main body of the book, is taken up by surveys of the multitude of styles of music popular in Africa today, together with portraits of and interviews with the key artists within those styles. Other chapters deal with the history of African music (and musicians) in Britain, and the erratic involvement of the Western recording business with African music both within and outside Africa. The authors hope that the book will serve to provide a more or less detailed and continent-wide primer for the Western listener who is developing an interest in African music and would like to place what he or she is listening to into a wider contemporary context.

The book, however, makes no attempt to cover the whole of modern African music, country by country. Sights have been narrowed to those styles that have been significantly influential in Africa itself and which are now starting to make an impact in the West, to the broad streams of African music, and to the musicians with whom personal interviews have been conducted. A number of the interviews were originally carried out either for *Black Music* or for the Afroheat column which continued, after the demise of *Black Music*, in *Blues and Soul*. Where this has happened, the material has been considerably expanded and revised.

The list of people who have helped in the gestation and finishing of this book is immense. In particular the authors would like to record their gratitude to Lucy Duran, Kwabena Fosu-Mensah and Ben Mandelson for their help, advice and encouragement, to Chris Parker, their editor at Quartet, and to Martin Noble for his Herculean indexing.

And to the following: Abdilatif Abdalla, Otuo Acheampong, Tony and Ebere Amadi, Don Amaechi, Steve Ansah, Herman Asafo-Agyei, Ray Allen, Abdon and Yolande Bayeto, Francis Bebey, Chris Brobby, Matthew Bury, Jenny Cathcart, John Collins, Seke N.Y. Diakondua, Manu Dibango, Charles Easmon, Ruth Edge, Akin Euba, Graeme Ewens, Jim Fish, N'Simba Foguis, Hilton Fyle, Ambrose Ganda, Werner Graebner, Folo Graff, Ronnie Graham, Idris and Kuburat Hameed, Chris Harris, Trevor Herman, Malu Halasa, the late Ginger Johnson, Gerhard Kubik, David Laing, Gasper Lawal, Albert Loudes, Mwana Musa, Mwambay Kalengay, Abdoulaye Kebe, Kufuakunita Petelo, Papa Kodjo, Fela Anikulapo-Kuti, Kwebe-Kimpele, Kwabena Kwarteng, Jacques Massaya, Todd Matshikiza, Ali Mutasa Nkiambi, Famille Ndongala, Nkathazo Ngubo, Lubasa N'Ti Nseendi and Zayiluadi Masala, Anye Ntumazah, Gilles Obrynger, Emil Ogoo, Zembi Okeno, Johnathan and Cheryl Park, David Rycroft, Samuel I. Omoaka, Tunji Omoshebi, Aziz Salim, Sidi Ahmed Siddy, Tshepo Skwambane, Jan Sliwinski, the late Jake Sollo, Sue Steward, Foday Musa Suso, the staff at Sterns, Rufai Thomas, Wala, Abdul Tee-Jay, Jumbo Vanrenen, Mary Vanrenen, Bonny Wanda, Fred Zindi.

Finally, to Eve May and Bryony Howe for their patience and understanding.

Lyrics of Salawa Abeni reproduced courtesy of Leader Records, c/o Sterns, 118 Whitfield St, London W1; Bembeya Jazz c/o Sono Disc, 85 rue de Fondary, 75015 Paris; Youssou N'Dour c/o Jenny Cathcart, London W4; Sery Simplice c/o 15 BP 238 Abidjan 15, Côte d'Ivoire; Franco c/o African Sun Music, Coudenberg 70, 1000 Bruxelles; Tabu Ley c/o Genidia BP 414, Brazzaville, Congo.

Chris Stapleton and
Chris May, 1987

'. . . welding and regeneration will be the pattern for African art. Many of the foreign influences that have penetrated Africa will be incorporated into a new form of black African art. This form of initiation may be deplored by those with deep-seated conservative or racialist tendencies, but far from resulting in a bastardized and damaging modernism, we believe this mutation will breathe new life into African art and will demonstrate the triumph of humanism and universality over esoteric sterility'

(Francis Bebey: *African Music*, Harrap, 1975)

BACKGROUND

URBAN DEVELOPMENT

Africa has produced a range of stunning dance musics. This is the story of some of them: of highlife and juju music, soukous from Zaire, mbaqanga from South Africa and the ancient sounds of the mbira, now brought up to date in independent Zimbabwe. It is also the story of the men and women who make the music.

Each of the styles dealt with here has a distinctive sound and reflects a distinct tradition. But these styles also share a number of common features: nearly all are urban musics; nearly all involve electric guitars and the kind of line-up found in Western pop music; and most reflect a meeting between vibrant traditional roots and the Western music, from hymns to jazz, sea shanties to brass-band music, that flooded across Africa during colonial times. From this meeting has come the mass of African sounds that are slowly beginning to establish themselves in the West.

In a South African dancehall, clipped guitars and a wheezing synthesizer ring out over a bassline thick enough to park a car on. A juju band blows the dust from a Lagos studio with a steel guitar that glides icily over a rich talking-drum groove. In an open-air Kinshasa nightclub, three lead guitarists roar into a full-blooded soukous while the wet-look singers pick up the beat and shout catchphrases at the microphone: 'Mama push, pappa push, mama push, pappa push . . .'

It is thirty years since the electric guitar became an established part of the armoury of popular music, thirty years since Chuck Berry, Bo Diddley and Elvis Presley created a new, crossover city beat. In that time, the electric guitar has played a vital role in moulding urban music across the world, nowhere more forcibly than in Africa. Once associated primarily with ceremonial and social music played on traditional instruments, the continent now boasts an urban culture whose vitality and technical flair is making the world sit up and listen.

One of the first African hits to register on the world market was 'Tom Hark' by Elias and his Zig Zag Jive Flutes. The South African connection continued with Miriam Makeba and the Manhattan Brothers, whose 'Kilimanjaro' gave America possibly its first taste of African pop; Hugh Masekela's 'Grazing in the Grass', which topped the American charts in 1968; and various versions of Solomon Linda's evergreen 'Mbube', also known as 'Wimoweh', some of which were good, some plain awful.

In 1973, Manu Dibango's 'Soul Makossa' brought Cameroonian music to world attention and Africa enjoyed a brief vogue as Western pop stars like Ginger Baker and Paul McCartney recorded in Lagos. But it was left to Ghanaian band Osibisa to bring African music truly into the limelight with a series of Afro-rock fusion albums that sold millions.

In the eighties, interest in the West has again picked up, not through Afro-rock, but through electro and funk fusions and, more encouragingly, on Africa's own terms, with artists like Franco, Youssou N'Dour and Sunny Ade creating a small, but growing audience for African music as it is actually played in Africa. Despite this interest in the authentic product, however, the search for a crossover continues. If imitation is the sincerest form of flattery, Malcolm McLaren, former manager of the Sex Pistols, was positively obsequious with his 1983 'Duck Rock' which laid pallid UK rapping over a series of South African mbaqanga tracks. Higher up the credibility ratings, American funk producer Bill Laswell created a series of 'collisions' between African music, represented by Foday Musa Suso and Fela Kuti, and the whiplash electro funk of the day. 'Don't let him near Youssou N'Dour,' wrote British critic Graham Lock in a letter to Celluloid, the American label which had released Laswell's collisions.

The theme continues: in 1986, Youssou N'Dour recorded and toured America with ex-Genesis singer Peter Gabriel. Paul Simon recorded his chart-topping *Graceland* album with a set of South African musicians, including the top choir Ladysmith Black Mambazo. But possibly the most fertile meeting of musics took place in Paris, where Jacob Désvarieux and Jean-Claude Naimro, of Kassav, worked with artists from M'Pongo Love to Beny Bezy to create a new synthesis of African and Caribbean music. Zouk music, pioneered by Kassav, has become part of the repertoire of a growing number of musicians from Zaire, Cameroon and the Côte d'Ivoire.

Everywhere there is mixture, collision and collusion. Africa 'impacts' on the West; the West on Africa. Pessimists predict that African music will lose its identity as a result of this global give and take. This has not happened yet. Since the 1930s, the forms that have had the biggest impact in Africa have all come from there in the first place: calypso, reggae and, most significantly, rumba. Today's funk and electro music, which are having a strong influence on some of the younger African artists, are the latest in a long line of musics that owe their basic thrust to Africa. The packaging may have changed: syndrums and synthesized bass and drums, horns and guitars reflect a predominantly Western techno-logy; but the 'new-look' African pop and its functions remain firmly rooted in African rhythms and African society.

OLD AND NEW

In its traditional context, African music covers every aspect of life, from recreation and work to religious ceremonies associated with birth, the naming of children, initiation into adulthood, marriage and death. Each occasion has its appropriate music, rhythm and dance.

African pop draws on a variety of such sources. Some of them are recreational, others deeply ceremonial. Mbalax, the sound of Youssou N'Dour and Super Etoile de Dakar, develops from traditional Wolof drumming and dancing that accompanies circumcision, heeling and naming ceremonies. Fuji music, from Nigeria, has its roots in the Muslim festival of Ramadan, while the kora songs of Mory Kante and other top Malian and Guinean musicians rework a tradition of court music, epic and praise song that stretches back over the centuries.

Other forms have different roots. Zairean soukous, mbaqanga from South Africa and Ghanaian dance-band highlife sprang less from ceremonial and religious sources, more from the jostling of African and Western music that has taken place in the streets, bars and dancehalls of twentieth-century Africa.

But no matter how new or recent the style, the link with African traditional music remains. Sometimes it is hard to spot the dividing line. Modern musicians work, for the most part, within established traditions and borrow freely from the earlier music. Sometimes this borrowing is direct and conscious, as in Sierra Leone, where the top rumba band Super Combo Kings cut an electric version of a song connected with Bundu secret society. 'Ngombu' appeared in 1970 and caused a sensation. In a similar vein, the Senegalese crossover band Toure Kunda utilized the music and rhythms connected with Mandinka circumcision rites. In Ghana, the adowa rhythm forms the basis for modern highlife songs recorded by the African Brothers and C.K. Mann.

Apart from specific rhythms, a number of general characteristics also cross over between the ancient and modern forms, the most notable being high levels of activity and a strong rhythmic interest. Western music generally accentuates melody and harmony, keeping the rhythm to a simplistic, time-keeping role. In Africa, no such separation exists: horns, keyboard and stringed instruments are exploited for their full rhythmic potential, while many instruments which Westerners would consider exclusively percussive, such as talking drums or bells, are tuned to different pitches and increase the melodic feel of the music. African music's concept of timing is also completely different from that of Western music, which generally sticks to one common beat, say 4/4 or 3/4. In Africa, a bell player in a percussion group will keep the time-line while the rest of the ensemble creates a complex interplay of different beats, from 3/4 to 6/8, and 6/8 to 2/4, all at the same time.

Some of this complexity passes into various forms of African pop, where the kit drummer will pick out a 4/4 beat on the bass drum and a complementary 12/8 on the hi-hat. Duple and triple times are frequently mixed, giving a rich polyrhythmic flavour. Even when large bands take the stage, the basic minute attention to rhythm remains. When Fela Kuti and his Egypt 80 played at the Brixton Academy in November 1986, it was curious to hear, running through the huge horn and guitar arrangements, a steady *tss-t*, *tss-t* as the kit drummer hit the hi-hat and the shekere player, standing a good thirty feet away, past guitarists, the brass section and the back-up singers, hit the off-beat.

Percussion thus provides an obvious link between the old and the new, but African pop draws on a whole range of other instrumental forms. Stringed instruments such as the xalam and the kora are played by the jalis, or hereditary musicians of west Africa. Xylophones, using small gourds as resonators, are found in many countries, along with flutes and plucked instruments such as the likembe or sanza, which consists of a set of iron keys set across a wooden resonator or calabash. Described by early observers as a 'hand piano', likembe songs and styles have had a big influence on African pop musicians. No one makes the connection more clearly than Thomas Mapfumo, who created a new Zimbabwean style by reproducing the interlinked mbira lines on electric guitar. The likembe is also cited as the father of the guitar by a number of modern Zairean musicians, among them Franco, whose finger-picked style creates a flow of notes similar to that emanating from the likembe.

Unlike their Western colleagues, who separate solo and rhythm parts, today's African musicians strike a more subtle balance. In modern Zairean soukous, the layers of solo, half solo and accompanying guitar set up an interplay that is as shifting and as vivid as any west African percussion orchestra. The music becomes a community, with percussion and guitars playing an equal, carefully balanced role. Melody and rhythm overlap.

EARLY DAYS

African pop music springs from the intermingling of cultures which took place, more or less forcibly, before and during colonization. The European influence started with Christian traders, missions and armies and intensified after the Conference and Treaty of Berlin (1884–5), which precipitated the Scramble for Africa and ushered in the colonial era. Great changes took place. The map of the entire continent was redrawn, new countries conjured into existence. European culture, expressed in Christian education, music, fashion and thought, created a way of life that was at odds with much that had gone before.

Out of this new way of life came a variety of distinctive musical forms. They owed their existence to African traditional music adapted for new instruments: guitars, brass and concertinas; to changing musical fashions: turn-of-the-century ragtime, waltzes and foxtrots, jazz (later swing) and finally, and most significantly, the rumbas and cha chas of the Latin American dance boom that exploded out of Cuba in the fifties. From the early days, church music proved a strong influence, as did sea shanties and calypsos.

But the story of modern African music has little to do with note-by-note imitation of outside forms. Music was never copied as an end in itself. Instead it served as a catalyst for the creation of the new forms, like highlife, soukous and juju, that drew their strength from local as well as foreign music. The early dance orchestras, with their wing collars and violins, may appear to be the last word in cultural capitulation. But it didn't last: the playing of waltzes and foxtrots provided a valuable apprenticeship on imported instruments. Having mastered them, the musicians wasted little time before reworking indigenous music into orchestral or big-band forms.

Modern pop developed at different speeds and with varying intensity in different parts of the continent. The process was rapid in the coastal towns and industrial centres of the western seaboard, where African and outside sounds jostled together, less rapid in east and southern Africa where long-term white settlement had built a solid wall between local and imported cultures. And it was largely absent in the rural areas and in the strongly Islamic states, less susceptible to Western influence.

BRASS BANDS

The introduction of Western music began long before the heyday of European colonization. As musicologist David Coplan records, a 'slave orchestra', composed of musicians from south and west Africa, including some Malays, entertained the Governor of Cape Town in 1676.[1] In 1831, an African orchestra, playing Western instruments, was in residence at Cape Town Castle. On the west African coast, the forts built by the British and Dutch to hold the slaves before their hellish journey west became early centres of European occupation. African brass bands appeared on the west coast as early as 1750. By 1841 a Ghanaian band was playing mazurkas, polkas and marching music for the Europeans at Cape Coast Castle.

The local repertoire expanded as the West Indian Rifles, stationed in Sierra Leone from the 1850s, introduced Caribbean music and a popular version of 'Everybody Loves Saturday Night'. The Royal West African Frontier Force, formed in 1897, capitalized on the growing interest in brass-band and fife-and-drum music with a repertoire that ranged from 'Old Calabar' and 'The Lincolnshire Poacher' to 'The Orangeman', 'South Carolina's a Sultry Clime' and the 'Hausa Farewell', a medley of bugle calls based on traditional Hausa tunes from northern Nigeria.

Brass bands were enormously important in the development of African pop, bringing in new instruments and stimulating African musicians to create their own fusions. In Ghana, slave-fort musicians created a syncopated form of military music that became known as adaha. Musicians carrying their instruments back to the rural areas created a new form of highlife, based on local songs and rhythms. Rural brass bands still exist in Ghana, their trumpets and tubas ('steam bass') and percussion providing the warm-up for football matches and other social events.

Colonial Africa also produced a number of celebrated military and police bands, playing a mixture of marching and dance music. The British South Africa Police Band recorded a version of 'Nkosi Sikelel' iAfrika'. Ghana's Police Dance Band recorded highlife tunes for Decca; Kenya's army band played cover versions of Western songs, while the band of the King's African Rifles played military music alongside local rhythms adapted from the massively popular beni dance, itself a direct response to and imitation of Western military music. In his *Dance and Society in Eastern Africa*, T.O. Ranger explains how beni sprang from European brass-band music in the 1880s and developed into a uniquely African form that spread throughout east Africa and beyond. Adherents wore military uniforms and paraded to the sound of brass-band music. Where the instruments were unobtainable, kazoos and drums were used.[2]

As Ranger points out, the Christian missionaries showed a keen interest in introducing brass bands into east Africa. Their enthusiasm reflected a deep ignorance of the nature and function of African music. For instance, in Zanzibar, the exposure to the regular rhythms of hymns and European band music was thought to be 'an excellent way of introducing freed slave children to the necessities of industrial time'. For the missionaries, European music represented a 'world of order' in contrast to what they saw as 'the inexplicable monotony and sudden passions of African drumming'. Musical ability was taken as 'a sign, a promise of potential for civilization'.

One of the earliest accounts of the arrival of brass-band music comes from James Juma Mbotela, a freed slave who lived in a Church Missionary Society settlement on the Kenyan coast near Mombasa. He explains how drums and traditional songs were forbidden by the European missionaries and how they helped in the organization of local singing groups and in the formation of a band to play Christian music. Choirs sprang up all along the coast – indeed, in 1903, Mbotela's group won a cup presented by Bishop Peel.[3]

MISSIONS

The zeal of the Mombasa missions repeated itself in other parts of Africa. The original concern was to save the souls of freed slaves, after the outlawing of the slave trade in 1807. The missionaries went on to play a decisive part in channelling Western values, education and culture into what the Victorians were later to dub the 'Dark Continent'. The Church of England Society for the Propagation of the Gospel sent its first chaplain to Ghana in 1752. Priests from the Church Missionary Society arrived in Freetown in 1806 and set up a second mission in Abeokuta, Nigeria. They were followed by the Basle Mission and the Methodist Missionary Society, which started work in Ghana; the Baptist Missionary Society, Cameroon; the Protestant Episcopal Church of America, Liberia and a veritable army of fellow-Christians.

But it was in the schools that the missionaries exerted their strongest influence, offering Western education to an elite that embraced imported European values as eagerly as their own traditions, sometimes more so. In 1960, Henry Weman, a scholar of Christian music overseas, lamented the rapid intrusion of missionary music into southern Africa: 'Western civilization has marched into Africa like a conqueror in triumph. The missions taught the African to think and speak like a Westerner, and to sing like a Westerner.'[4] Weman details a number of crucial stages in this process: the replacement of African parallel melodies by a single European melody, plus rudimentary harmony; the introduction of four-part harmonies and standard four-bar phrases in place of Africa's freer musical phraseology; the substitution of the basic Western tonalities, major and minor, for the traditional African tones; plus, perhaps most importantly, the introduction of a limited harmonic range, giving African choirs three basic chords, the tonic, dominant and subdominant.

The missionaries' choice of tunes was equally limiting. Weman explains that the nineteenth-century priests brought to Africa a single tune for the Catholic 'Kyrie Eleison'. Musicologist Kazadi Wa Mukuna explains how, in the Belgian Congo, the missionaries welded vernacular lyrics to lullabies and Negro spirituals, including 'Swing Low Sweet Chariot', 'Brahms' Lullaby' and 'My Lord what a Morning'. Sometimes the fusion worked. All too often it did not. Many African languages are tonal, which means that the same syllable carries meanings which differ with its pitch. Sing it high, it means one thing; low, another. A new tune which alters the pitch of the words, thus destroys their sense.[5]

This problem was still unsolved in the fifties. 'The hymns are completely meaningless,' wrote musicologist E.G. Parrinder in 1956. 'All of them. They are quite incomprehensible to an outsider. And if a regular churchgoer is asked about the meaning, he has to think twice about the words, without the tunes, before he can answer.'[6]

For all this, the missionary music, with its African lyrics and Western tunes, sung either unaccompanied or to a portable organ or accordion, lost none of its impact. Church-flavoured harmonies and melodics would go on to play an important part in many of the styles that developed in colonial times, notably highlife and juju music, while the missions' biggest single legacy, the tonic–dominant–subdominant chord pattern, would become as vital to modern African music as it has been to Western pop.

URBANIZATION

The new towns that sprang up during colonization embraced three strands of music: traditional, that remained untouched by Western contact, and continued with the flow of village people to the urban areas; the music of the small, mission-educated elite; and the new fusions of foreign and local forms that appealed to a wider, less exclusive audience. The second group, the wealthy and well-to-do, tended to have European tastes, and their musical leisure activities reflected this, revolving around ragtime, vaudeville and choral music. The performers soon arrived in person. In 1862, the American Harvey Leslie Christy Minstrels toured South Africa. They were followed by the Fisk Jubilee Singers, who specialized in 'Swing Low Sweet Chariot' and other spirituals and cakewalks. In addition, cowboy, music-hall and novelty records poured in from the turn of the century onwards.

A fascinating picture of late-nineteenth-century tastes comes from Alfred Kumalo, a South African building contractor.[7] In 1894 he was given a guitar by his uncle, a South African pastor who had just returned from London. The present wasn't welcome. Up to then, Kumalo had been playing accordion at township dances and making four guineas a night. On the guitar, he learnt some of the popular tunes of the day, adapted to a ragtime pick. Interviewed in 1964 by David Rycroft, a scholar of Zulu music, he agreed to tape one of his favourites, a mixture of Victorian sentimentality and a sugary melody that evoked a London music hall rather than a Johannesburg dancefloor. As did the lyrics:

> There'll come a time one day
> When I'll have passed away
> There'll be no father to guide you
> From day to day

Think well of all I said
Honour the man you wed
This is the end of the story
There'll come a day

Later Kumalo took up the banjo and went on, in 1932, to form a male-voice choir in Durban, singing Christian hymns and Zulu melodies.

Elite groups flourished throughout Africa. Lagos in the 1880s was a cosmopolitan town, served by several newspapers, and preoccupied with debates about whether Nigerians should continue wearing European suits and waistcoats or return to African gowns. High culture predominated, with a flourishing Philharmonic Society, the Lagos Glee Singers and a range of choirs and entertainment societies, from the Academy to the Brazilian Dramatic Society and the Royal, which put on plays and concerts. In 1882 Professor R.A. Coker, the 'Mozart of West Africa', organized the Lagos Handel festival.

This pattern repeated itself in Freetown and the coastal towns of the Gold Coast, now Ghana. By 1914, the Excelsior Orchestra was entertaining the wealthy of Accra, both indigenous and European, with a mixture of waltzes and ballroom standards, played on strings and brass.

In Kenya, where such mixing was virtually forbidden, educated groups listened to 'dansi' music, ballroom favourites played on guitars, accordions and harmonicas.

Elite culture blossomed. Waltzes and foxtrots, choral ensembles and ragtime groups provided its hallmarks. Top performers visited Africa; top African acts travelled abroad. In 1893, a Zulu choir toured Britain, Canada and the United States. In London, several members left to join music halls. In the twenties, jazz hit Africa. A Ghanaian band, the Cape Coast Sugar Babies, toured Nigeria. In Accra, musicians like R.C. Nathaniels recorded parlour and jazz-age novelties with titles like 'Telephone My Baby'.[8]

If the lives and the tastes of the well-to-do seem at first sight puzzlingly remote from those of the large African majority, it would be wrong to suggest that they were indeed totally separated. In its early days, for instance, the Excelsior Orchestra had mixed Western repertoire with versions of local Akan street melodies, and between the wars, other bands appeared, whose experiments with local rhythms would pave the way for the dance-band highlife boom that swept west Africa in the forties and fifties.

South African musicians too were equally aware of what was happening beyond the bow ties and ballrooms. While bands of the thirties like the Merry Blackbirds concentrated on American jazz, the Jazz Maniacs exploited local forms, playing occasional big-band arrangements of the marabi music that was making the windows rattle in shanty-town bars and drink dens.

It was in these bars, on the street corners and in the back yards, rather than in the town halls, salons and official residences, that the scene was set for the emergence of lasting and typically African forms of popular music. Where wing-collar musicians embraced high-society European styles, street and folk musicians reworked local rhythms on imported guitars, banjos and accordions to create a broad musical tradition that persists to this day.

Cape Town gives an early example of the development of musical fusions. As David Coplan points out, African musicians were playing European melodies on the ramkie, or lute, as early as the 1650s.[9] But it was the discovery of diamonds, in Kimberley 200 years later, that created the right social conditions for a mix of musical cultures. Like a southern Klondike, Kimberley (founded in 1871) attracted a diverse population of panhandlers, plus barroom musicians of every sort: African violinists, American ragtime and honky-tonk pianists, concertina and guitar players, and mixed-race musicians whose 'tickey draai' dance music was adapted by African musicians and blended with their own traditional material.

On the fast-growing mining compounds, Sotho miners played music constructed according to traditional idioms on guitars and Czechoslovakian concertinas, the latter being particularly effective in capturing the full, dense flavours and the two- and three-part harmonies of the original vocal music. The three-chord pattern gave the usual structure for the reworked traditional melodies.

SAILORS' INSTRUMENTS

A similar process took place in industrial centres and coastal towns throughout Africa, but nowhere so vigorously as on the western seaboard, where visiting West Indian and American sailors injected sea shanties and folk songs into a flourishing music scene. One of the key groups in the spread of guitar music were the Kru, an itinerant people from Liberia. As migrant workers they moved up and down the coast from Sierra Leone to Fernando Po. They were among the earliest people to work with the

Europeans, as sailors travelling on merchant ships between Liverpool and west Africa, America and the West Indies. They adopted both fanciful nicknames such as Bottle of Beer, Flying Fish and Pipe of Tobacco, and new manners and technologies, among them the guitar and various techniques that had a profound effect on the traditional musicians of the coast. By the 1920s the Kru had introduced three guitar picks, all played in 4/4 time. They were mainline, dagomba and fireman, this last a style which, according to John Collins, takes its name from the coal-fired steamships on which the Kru seamen travelled.

Acoustic music caught on rapidly. In Liberia itself, musicians played folk songs, quadrilles, foxtrots, even the occasional calypso. In Sierra Leone, Collins traces the acoustic guitar back to the 1920s, when the Freetown Kru played in the red-light areas, accompanied by the huge kongoma 'hand bass', a large wooden box set with iron keys. Musicians like Waking Profit made their money playing at funerals and wakes, incorporating a scraped musical saw into the accompaniment.[10]

The guitar styles caught on quickly. They were especially popular among musicians who had been playing traditional instruments, such as the seprewa, or lute, and the kora, a harp-lute which is played by Mandinka people further up the coast. In Ghana, coastal musicians switched from the seprewa to the guitar, creating an early form of guitar band – the rhythm supplied by claves, hand percussion and the large apremprensua, or bass box, while the melodies drew on local music and strident church harmonies. Through the work of Kwame Asare, or 'Sam' as he was better known, the sound spread inland from the coast, and took on different, usually 6/8 rhythms, minor keys and an increasingly African feel.

Nigeria produced its own forms of street music. In the south east, S.S. Peters added acoustic guitar to a small band that included the square itembe drums and a large imported military bass drum. His greatest hit was 'Canaan Canaan Calabar', recorded in the late thirties. Tunde King, the main precursor of modern juju music, introduced the six-stringed guitar-banjo into a small group that included tambourine, shekere (a large gourd covered in rattling cowrie shells) and a second vocalist, who sometimes played triangle.

By 1936, when King made his first records for Parlophone, the acoustic guitar, along with other 'sailors' instruments' such as the banjo and concertina, had become a permanent feature of urban life. Early records prove the point. In the mid-twenties, Zonophone's EZ west African recordings featured a set of full-throated vocal and percussion troupes, accompanied by finger-picked acoustic guitars

One of Africa's most influential guitar sounds comes from Zaire, formerly the Belgian Congo. Here, again, sailors played an important part. According to Franco, the greatest Zairean musician, it was a Congolese sailor, Dondo Daniel, who introduced the acoustic guitar, around 1914, into the port of Matadi.[11] The instrument was adopted by local musicians often in preference to the likembe, the hand-held 'thumb piano', and gave out a sound that bore a close resemblance to the flowing music of the earlier instrument.

STREET MUSIC
AND THE BOX GUITAR

By the late twenties, Leopoldville, later Kinshasa, offered Congolese guitarists a range of materials and influences. African migration, through the travelling administrators known as 'coastmen', had created a diverse population that included Nigerians, Cameroonians and Ghanaians, all of whom brought their own brands of guitar music into the city.

In Lagos, Accra and Freetown the picture was much the same, with a mix of indigenous residents, descendants of freed slaves from Brazil and Cuba and migrant workers from up and down the coast. Chris Waterman explains that in Lagos the old slave communities added to the city's entertainments, introducing carnival masquerades, the square-frame drum known as samba, and the caretta, or 'fancy' dance.[12] As the Sierra Leonean expatriates danced to the waltzes and ballroom music, African and West Indian migrant workers played their own guitar versions of rumba, ragtime and merengue.

While the amount of guitar music continued to grow, other forms of music shook the streets, in most cases quite literally. One of the most celebrated was the konkomba, a Ghanaian street music which developed from the Westernized brass bands. Konkomba drummers and dancers wore uniforms and shuffled down the streets, parade-style. Occasionally guitarists joined the line-up, as palm-wine player Kwaa Mensah recalls:

In 1939, the Silver Stars konkomba group was founded and I left the antwem [adaha] band. The konkomba band has jazz drums, pati [side]

15

drums, bass, alto and tenor tambourines and thirty singers. I was the first to bring the guitar to them. We played adaha, adesim, which is a fast highlife, Ashanti (local blues), rumbas, foxtrots, bumps-a-daisy, sambas, La Congas: Spanish music and Dagomba highlifes. I went on to form my own Akote Special konkomba group and left when the war finished. [13]

Konkomba spread to Nigeria, where it was popularized by Ghanaian dancers in Lagos and the western region. Street-parade music was equally popular in Kinshasa, where the 'fanfares' or brass bands paraded to the sound of a reclaimed Latin rhythm, dubbed locally matindique. In Nigeria, the Calabar Brass Band 'steamed' from one end of Lagos to the other, with a large crowd drawn along, dancing to its syncopated military music.

As time went on, guitar music became increasingly popular. Its leading exponents, from Ebenezer Calendar in Sierra Leone to Jean Bosco Mwenda in Zaire, were the true founders of today's African pop. They took up new instruments and merged foreign and indigenous rhythms; they played not for colonialists or the African elites, but for a wider, urban audience. Where music had traditionally been a community affair, with everyone joining in, the new guitarists were semi-professional, sometimes professional, enjoying (or suffering) a lifestyle that put them on the further fringes of mainstream society. To some people, they were seen as little more than tramps. But to the broader urban communities, the guitarists were important, and for a variety of reasons – not just because they provided entertainment, but because they bridged the gap between old and new. Symbolically, the guitarists belonged to urban Africa, playing an instrument whose appeal, like that of cars, records, radios, films, depended on its modernity. At the same time, the musicians reflected an older way of life. Their songs contained proverbs, inherited wisdom, ancient stories and words of praise. Traditional rhythms and techniques lived on. In many cases, the acoustic guitar music was 'new' only in its choice of instrument. A Cameroonian politician, Ndeh Ntumazah, recalls a popular guitarist from the 1930s:

Awagom started by going to the coast. He came back with a guitar, which he'd play at parties and pubs, when he wasn't working – he repaired bicycles. Like most musicians, Awagom was very jovial and sociable and had a high interest in women. Most of what he played was local music, traditional songs. But the difference wasn't really in the music, but in the instrument. For us the guitar represented a new society, and the transportation of Western values. Musically, it was little different from our own traditional guitars, made of wood, a sound box and strings. They were played exactly like the traditional guitar.[14]

Musicologist Dr Gerhard Kubik continues the analysis, with a study of acoustic guitarists like Zairean Jean Bosco Mwenda, who flourished in Katanga, now Shaba, from the forties. The music may sound Westernized, he explains. But that is only because of the Western instruments and tunings. The guitarists use two-finger styles in the same way as earlier mbira and zither players. This gives the music the same 'motional' pattern. The rhythms, too, show strong evidence of continuity as the guitarists, and their rhythm players, pick up the sixteen-pulse time-line pattern that had been played by earlier musicians. While the Katanga players reworked the old likembe patterns, Kenya's Luo guitarists made similar use of traditional dance rhythms and the techniques employed by the old lute, or nyatiti players. In both cases, the guitar music kept its strong traditional content. It was only in larger cities, notably Kinshasa, that the guitarists turned to readily available outside influences rather than to purer local forms. And when they did, these forms were more often than not Afro-Cuban.[15]

In another study, David Rycroft explores African and outside influences on Bosco's music:

For his song melodies he seems to have drawn little from an African heritage, but rather to have adopted, wholeheartedly, some of our less worthy musical clichés . . . On the other hand, Bosco uses short phrases and a generally descending melodic line which are typically African, and introduces few, if any of the rhythmic tricks and gimmicks common to Western popular music of his time. His vocal rhythmic phrasing is largely regular and even, in sharp contrast to the rhythmic interest created on the guitar. This may stem from tribal practice. In the few examples of tribal music from that area which I have been able to hear, rhythmic regularity in the vocal line, contrasting with rhythmic subtleties in the accompaniment, appears to be common.[16]

Many of the acoustic guitarists travelled. Their love songs and lyrics about city life and the hardships faced by migrant workers offered reassurance and consolation to listeners at a time of rapid social change.

This acoustic era produced a number of celebrated musicians, many of whom, like early juju pioneer Ayinde Bakare, would later go electric. In Ghana, KaKaiKu and E.K. Nyame were among the most famous of the palm-wine musicians. From eastern Nigeria, Israel Mwoba and Harcourt Whyte achieved similar success. Of the Sierra Leoneans, S.E. Rogers brought rural rhythms, and the African twist, into his music, while in Freetown, Ebenezer Calendar produced street music and dashes of merengue over a rousing percussion and sousaphone backing. The Congolese guitarists proved hugely influential, most of all Bosco, who plucked, traditional-style, rather than strummed. In Kenya, rural guitarists and Nairobi musicians created a number of distinctive new forms, most influenced by traditional music, others by Congolese. Almost as influential was George Sibanda, from Bulawayo, in what is now Zimbabwe. Sibanda's driving 'tsaba-tsaba' guitar style – a kind of fast kwela vamp – made a big impact through east and west Africa.

A selection of the guitarists found themselves on record. Working on behalf of the Gallo record company of South Africa, Hugh Tracey recorded throughout east, central and southern Africa for a series that was released under the title 'The Music of Africa'. The artists, ranging from George Sibanda to Bosco, whom Tracey came across playing guitar under the post-office clock in Jadotville, played solo or in small groups, their voices ringing out with unexpected gruffness and force. The modern 'sweetness' of African music would seem to be a product of the electric age.

Acoustic music took different names in different areas. In west Africa, soloists played 'palm-wine' style, so named after the bars where they drank and played. East Africa and the Belgian Congo developed 'dry' or 'box' guitar music. Despite different names and a variety of regional variations, the sound that emerged contained a number of common features, such as the strummed chords and time-lines tapped out on bottles, that became common property as musicians travelled across Africa.

THE MUSIC BUSINESS

The growth of the African recording industry helped spread the acoustic music and the names of the artists in a way that until then had not been possible. To illustrate this point, John Collins and Paul Richards describe how, in Sierra Leone, a Jean Bosco song, recorded on Gallotone, was known not for its title, which was incomprehensible, but by its record number, 'C089'.[17] To others, it became 'Magbosi', the name of a small village east of Freetown where a passenger lorry once broke down. To pass the time, the passengers played Bosco's tune on a wind-up gramophone, and the name of the village stuck. Corroboration is provided by Ambrose Ganda, a solicitor from Sierra Leone, who recalls his neighbours dancing to Bosco, and making up new Mende lyrics to fit the tunes. This is how he describes the social life of his village, outside the town of Bo.

I remember a young boy standing around the gramophone on a moonlit night. It was a tremendous novelty, and was owned by a local teacher or some big businessman. The music was mainly Sierra Leonean – songs by Ebenezer Calendar and others, in Mende, by the accordionist Salliah. We grew up on Salliah, who taught us Mende proverbs to fit almost any situation in our lives. In the absence of a griot we had a gramophone placed in the middle of the courtyard.

Around 1955 we started getting Zulu records. We used to have dances in the main courtyard, to music by Jean Bosco and Jim Lasco. We called it all Zulu, without having any clear idea of where it came from. Later we had the authentic Zulu jives, mainly guitar music with 'Jive' in brackets on the label.

To get the records, we'd make a list and someone would go to the nearest town, Bo, to buy them from an Indian shop. The only problem was the gramophone. It was a wind-up. When the spring went, the whole place came to a standstill.[18]

Radio, which first appeared in Africa in 1924, offered a further means of dissemination. Wole Soyinka, in his autobiography *Ake*, explains the Yoruba name for the new apparatus: 'As'oromagb'esi' or 'one who speaks without expecting a reply'. By 1951, Nigeria's Radio Kaduna offered daily selections that ranged from local agidigbo, or hand-piano bands, to the latest overseas dance music: '. . . vernacular and dance records; the Accordion Band, the Anambra Ibo Band, Fayi Mai Goge and Band, Spanish and vernacular dance records, English dance records'. In the same year, the *Nigerian Citizen* carried advertisements for Nigerian music: 'Enjoy Your Own Songs, Sung by Your Own People in the Way You Love. Masterly Renderings of Traditional African Music is Yours on His Master's Voice Yellow Label Records. Sold by All the Best Stores and Distributed by the United Africa Company.'[19]

THE AFRO-CUBAN IMPACT

The volume of records increased. Some, like the early vaudeville and classical, had little lasting impact. Others were to change the direction of African music. Of all the imports, none proved more crucial than the rumbas, boleros and mambos that sprang from Havana – and New York – from the thirties and went on to create a worldwide Latin boom. In Africa, these records had a special significance. Where earlier imports such as waltzes and swing had sounded distinctly Western, Cuban music had a familiar flavour, particularly in its rhythms, which were still essentially African.

The boom started in earnest after the end of the Second World War when EMI released its celebrated 'GV' series. This consisted of over 200 titles, recorded before the war and reissued in a bid to boost exports in the lean late forties. The series kicked off with 'GV1', a foxtrot, 'The One Sincere Love' by Don Azpiazu and his Orquestra Casino Havana. But it was the flip side that proved the more enduring. 'The Peanut Vendor (Rumba/Foxtrot)' went on to become a staple of dance bands throughout west Africa. The rest of the GVs ranged through sons, boleros and sambas, stretching from 'Sacudiendo Mis Maracas', a son-sonete by Sexteto Habanero to 'Elixir de la Vida', a bolero by Trio Matamoros and 'Madalena', a samba from Banda Rico Creole. Not for nothing were the GVs dubbed 'Spanish' records. Later titles reflected a wider range of styles, from congas by Xavier Cugat and his Orquestra Waldorf Astoria to calypsos and African numbers from such musicians as Shake Keane and the West African Swing Stars, who covered a number of E.T. Mensah songs.

These GV or 'Spanish' records, with their vital African flavour, arrived at a crucial point in the history of the continent. From the Second World War, a new self-assertiveness characterized African affairs. Politically it showed itself in a rising tide of nationalism, accompanied by renewed calls for independence; culturally in a new awareness of the African heritage – art, theatre and music, suppressed during colonial times; and socially with the increasing growth of major cities where appalling poverty rubbed shoulders with new-fangled nightclubs, bars and cinemas.

The Latin boom, with its tropical self-confidence, was symbolic of a new era. European music lost its grip as ballroom and orchestral numbers faded, and musicians at all levels, from street to elite, adapted to the music that was now so readily available on record. From Kenya to Zaire, acoustic guitar bands brought the rumba into their repertoire. Wing-collared dance bands took a leaf from the Latin bands' book and introduced Afro-Cuban instruments and rhythms. 'Spanish' music provided repertoire, rhythms and inspiration as urban dance bands reclaimed the music, from rumba to cha cha and mambo, that had started its life in Africa centuries before, and created new, jazzy arrangements for the indigenous rhythms around them.

The Latin sound was to have its strongest impact in the French and Belgian colonies of Guinea, Mali, Senegal and the French and Belgian Congos. Up to now, there had been little chance for the African and French musicians to mingle, little opportunity for a synthesis to develop. The colonialists assumed the superiority of European culture and, where the British in west Africa had adopted a laissez-faire attitude and helped train local bandsmen, the French and Belgians for the most part had brought in their own musicians. In east Africa, where white settlers held on to the best land, British rule was harsher than it was to the west and a virtual apartheid had prevented the two cultures from meeting. Only in the post-war years did matters begin to change.

In the forties, Latin music was popular with Senegal's elite, as well-heeled audiences danced to jazz, rumba, the paso doble and the bolero, the common sounds of French west Africa. Slowly, though, other musics filtered through: from Afro-Cuban to traditional, purely African rhythms. In his novel *Climbie*, Côte d'Ivoire author Bernard Dadie explores the nightlife of colonial Abidjan:

> There was dancing every Saturday night at the African Club, the Senegalese Club or the Dahomian-owned Rose Pavilion . . . How animated the dances at the Rose Pavilion were! The band forgot none of the popular songs, from 'I Have My Scheme' and 'Under the Bridges of Paris' to 'China Night'. The waltz and the tango were not very popular now . . . As soon as the first notes of a march were sounded, everyone sprang to his feet as if propelled by a piece of elastic . . . But the joy of dancing would not reach its peak until the cornet, with a few quick notes, announced a pathy, a traditional song, or an agbass, a dance of the homeland. People now danced singly, each yielding to the impulses of his heart and spirit as if to stamp out all worries, past and future . . .

In the African quarter of the city, Dadie finds other forms of entertainment: 'The Paris Bar and the France Hotel . . . entertained the Europeans with gala evenings given by performers from France or Dakar. These performers more often than not had a Negro accordionist or violinist accompanying them. The Africans would therefore run to these hotels to see the spectacle of one of their own people playing with a group of Europeans . . .'

Later, the novel's hero, Climbie, travels to Dakar in Senegal, and finds: '. . . a city of taverns and nightclubs with such prestigious names as Oasis, Floreal, Gerbe d'Or, Lido and Tabarin, a city where such famous artists as Tino Rossi and Josephine Baker often performed . . .'[20] Other artists were to prove even more popular than Josephine Baker. Among them were Johnny Pacheco and Ray Barreto, whose records had a huge impact both on the listening and dancing public, and on the musicians too. Having mastered the Latin repertoire, Francophone bands turned, with new energy, to their own indigenous music.

A TRADITION RESTORED

The growth of African nationalism went hand in hand with a new emphasis on the traditional African heritage. In most cases, politicians led the way. Ghana's Kwame Nkrumah explored the concept of the African personality and put his ideas about cultural transformation into practical effect by encouraging musicians to work with traditional instruments and rhythms and to wear national costume. He also took popular artists, including E.K. Nyame and the Uhuru Dance Band, on his trips outside Ghana. His writings struck a chord with other leaders. In Guinea, Sékou Touré turned his back on union with France and encouraged a vigorous cultural revolution. Among his achievements was the foundation in 1953 of the African Ballet of Keita Fodeba, which carried the message of a strong and self-confident traditional culture across west Africa and was influential in the setting up of other, similar national troupes. Musicians hymned the new dawn with songs explaining government plans and policies. State-subsidized bands like Syli Orchestre and later, Bembeya Jazz, modernized a set of folk rhythms that had, until now, been the preserve of griots and local village communities. In the cities, old dance orchestras were abolished, a national record label was set up to promote local bands and local rhythms. The army fell into line, as colonial marching songs were swept aside, and traditional tunes brought back to life. A national music was born.

In Senegal, the President, Leopold Senghor, championed the concept of negritude, whose roots lie in the writings of W.E. DuBois, Aimé Cesaire and Marcus Garvey. In 1939, Senghor and a group of fellow-intellectuals based in France had set up *L'Etudiant Noir*, a journal which carried articles on African culture and history. In 1947, a second, hugely influential journal, *Présence Africaine*, was launched. Senghor's own poetry laid a strong emphasis on the strength of African culture and personality, something which had been actively denied during colonialism.

Some years later, the Tanzanian President, Julius Nyerere, put such ideas into a solidly musical context:

Some of us, particularly those of us who had acquired a European type of education, set ourselves out to prove to our colonial rulers that we had become 'civilized'; and by that we meant that we had abandoned everything connected with our own past and learnt to imitate Western ways. Our young men's ambition was not to become well-educated Africans, but to become black Europeans!

When we were at school we were taught to sing the songs of the Europeans. How many of us were taught the songs of the Wanyamwezi or of the Wahehe? Many of us have learnt to dance the rumba, or the cha cha, to rock and roll and to twist and even to dance the waltz and foxtrot. But how many of us can dance, or have even heard of the gombe sugu, the mangala, nyang'umumi, kiduo, or lele mama? Lots of us can play the guitar . . . how many . . . among the educated can play the African drums? . . . And even though we dance and play the piano, how often does that dancing — even if it is rock and roll or twist — how often does it really give us the sort of thrill we get from dancing the mganda or the gombe sugu?[21]

SOUNDS OF THE FIFTIES

Some countries launched cultural revolutions. Others took a more laissez-faire attitude. When Senghor preached negritude, Wole Soyinka gave the Nigerian reply: 'A tiger does not need to proclaim its tigritude.' Yet across Africa, from socialist Ghana to capitalist Kenya and Zaire, new sounds burst in alongside the old. Highlife spread from Ghana throughout west Africa, from Guinea, which enjoyed close links with Ghana during Nkrumah's presidency, to Nigeria, where E.T. Mensah caused a storm during the early fifties. A Nigerian music scene that previously boasted everything from agidigbo bands, playing acoustic hand-piano music, to Western varieties of jazz and dance music, now shook to a modern, orchestrated highlife.

In his 1954 novel *People of the City* Cyprian Ekwensi had, as his hero, a young crime reporter Amusa Sango, who also leads a dance band specializing in 'calypsos and konkomas'.[22] Sango worships Louis Armstrong, listens to 'Basin Street Blues', plays like Harry James and works alongside other bands who play jazz and 'highlife drumming'. Around the same time that Ekwensi's book appeared, Eddie Edem, a Nigerian trumpeter now based in London, worked as a merchant seaman in the Nigerian town of Port Harcourt, of which he says:

It was the most swinging town in west Africa. Any seaman would bear me out. The French towns, Dakar and Douala, were more beautiful. The French made them clean and suitable. There were no open gutters, no mosquitos. But the only music you'd hear there would be Congolese and GVs. Port Harcourt was big. It had a long quay that could take eight ships at a time. The quay was walking distance from the town. I'd go out all night, get back to the ship at 4.30, start work at 5.30. Every street was full of clubs and hotels, with seamen from all over. You could go into bars and hear palm-wine singers. This Ibo guy, Djamanza, was very popular. He had a song about a woman whose baby died and she left it on a bus, wrapped up in paper. Someone comes and opens the parcel . . . He used to sing in local hotels.

The GV records were popular, especially 'The Peanut Vendor' everyone knew that, and the bands would all play them, along with country and western songs. Jim Reeves was big in Port Harcourt. We'd also jive to boogie-woogie music, stuff like 'Saturday Fish Fry'. The band would play all that stuff plus country and highlife. Some even played waltzes. The musicians copied the records, playing them in their own way, and the people would dance, men with men, women with women, the men wearing either European clothes or long printed cloths tied around their waists and stretching to the floor. When the moon came out, konkoma bands, using frame drums, guitar, maybe accordion, would drift from one place to another. People would bring out palm wine and African gin . . .[23]

In South Africa, jazz and swing prevailed, with vocal groups like the Manhattan Brothers spreading a close-harmony vocal style across southern Africa. To some musicologists, Western music had virtually destroyed the traditional subtleties of the African heritage. When an American visitor,

Professor Willard Rhodes, arrived in Zimbabwe in 1958, he rubbed his eyes, and his ears, in disbelief:

> In the Central beer hall in Bulawayo, a three-piece dance band, of a saxophone, amplified guitar and bass viol, provides jive music for dancing every afternoon between three and five o'clock. In the townships dance plazas have been designated as 'Jive Klubs' and there on Saturday and Sunday afternoon heterogeneous jazz ensembles play for the dancers. By European and American standards the African jazz is but a pallid imitation of American models, copied by ear from phonograph records. The popularity of this 'new music' is beyond estimate . . . Alan Merriam has made the pertinent observation that the process of acculturation of music is most active when there are common elements in the musics of the two impinging cultures. This being so, it is not surprising that the detribalized, urban African neglects his traditional music in favour of the prestige-laden European-American jazz, for the basic techniques of rock and roll have their origin in African music . . . .

Rhodes' next observation is illuminating. 'One wonders what this invasion of American popular music will do for African music. Some Africans believe that it is only a temporary phase of acculturation through which they are passing and that sooner or later the roots of their indigenous culture, after a dormant period, will awaken and send forth new shoots and flowers.'[24]

A prophetic comment. Since those days, African swing survives merely as a footnote to the growth of later, folk-based African forms. The emergence of a popular, rather than an elite culture was speeding up. Ghana's guitar bands, which could trace their origins back to the palm-wine styles of the 1920s, created an expanding audience for themes and rhythms that were once considered crude and unworthy of attention. With the rise of I.K. Dairo, juju music took on a deeper, more traditional flavour, offering a marked contrast to the Afro-Cuban and calypso that still permeated the dance-band scene.

But of all the post-war styles, few proved as influential as the Congolese guitar music that exploded from Kinshasa with the formation of the city's first modern band, African Jazz, in 1953. Developing their sound from the rumba folk guitarists and the small acoustic bands that flourished in city bars during the forties, African Jazz absorbed Afro-Cuban rhythms and arrangements and reinterpreted them in a purely African way. Adroit harmonies and cleverly arranged guitar parts took the stridency out of the Latin originals. The Congolese sound, with its sweet harmonies and increasingly African rhythms, carried across the continent: on records and radio and live, through the work of travelling Congolese bands.

The civil war, which broke out after independence in 1960, drove a number of musicians into exile – to southern Africa, north to Sierra Leone and the Côte d'Ivoire, and east to Kenya and Tanzania. The music attracted a huge following. Local musicians adopted the new styles, providing their own rumba variations. In Kenya, Congo jazz threatened to kill off local music. In Tanzania, it stimulated a new generation of jazz bands who sang Swahili lyrics over Congolese rhythms. Even Ghana, the home of dance-band highlife, fell to the new sound, as horn-led dance bands felt the competition and incorporated Congolese music into their repertoire.

AFRICAN PRIDE

If Latin music was the first step in the post-war re-Africanization of urban music, Congolese music provided the second. Its influence was felt everywhere. Smaller countries, such as the Côte d'Ivoire and Sierra Leone, became virtual rumba satellites. Larger countries, like Kenya, tried to ban it. But Zaire offered more than a dominant musical form. In 1972, President Mobutu launched his 'Authenticity' campaign, which replaced the colonial legacy – of Belgian names, fashions and forms of address – with Zairean. Towns and cities were renamed. The leadership sported African fashions and accessories; the people replaced Christian with authentic names.

The campaign struck a number of chords. In America, the Black Power movement was a growing force. Its leaders visited Africa, where the American concept overlapped with Negritude. Black Americans, searching for their roots, came to Ghana, The Gambia and Senegal to find a link with their African past. Soul music made a huge impact, the 1971 Accra Soul to Soul Festival offering a line-up that included Roberta Flack and Wilson Pickett. When James Brown's records first appeared in Ghana, an astounded audience recognized in number after number the rhythms and vocal inflections of northern Ghana.

'Say it loud, I'm black and I'm proud' became a rallying cry in a number of countries. In some, soul music paved the way for fusions like

Manu Dibango's 'Soul Makossa'. In others, it presented a new music for a new generation. Dance-band highlife virtually disappeared under its influence. But it was the French-speaking countries that benefited most, not so much from the music itself, as from the Black Pride message that lay inside it. In Senegal the open-door cultural policy, which had encouraged a confusion of Western imports, came to a gradual end. African musicians, who had been singing in French and Spanish, took stock of the situation. The movement started in The Gambia, where the best-known band, the Super Eagles, swapped London suits for African clothes and replaced a repertoire that included 'Tobacco Road', 'Hey Jude' and a mass of highlife and rumba for a hard new sound based on traditional Mandinka rhythms and instruments. Senegal musicians followed suit. Bands like Etoile de Dakar gave up the rumba and developed new sounds from traditional sources. In Mali, kora players like Mory Kante threw themselves into the new electric age, while singers like Salif Keita reworked, for city ears, the songs that had been handed down by griots for centuries.

ROOTS REVIVALS

Throughout the seventies, 'modern traditionalists', to use a term coined by Nana Ampadu of the African Brothers, came to the fore. In the Côte d'Ivoire, Ernesto Djedje gave up soul music to produce an electric version of the ziglibithy, a traditional rhythm played during rural celebrations. The roots movement continued in Ghana, with bands like Wulomei and Hedzolleh Soundz exploiting old, traditional forms; and in Zimbabwe, where, in 1976, Thomas Mapfumo, a singer brought up on Sam Cooke and Otis Redding, risked public ridicule, first by singing in Shona, rather than English, and then bringing into his playlist a direct transposition of the country's ancient and spiritual mbira music.

South Africa saw similar developments, although here the picture was clouded by the racism of apartheid. A movement back to traditional forms made little sense when government policies dictated that separate racial groups should live in separate areas, and that urban populations should return to 'tribal homelands'. When tradition and ethnicity became a wing of government policy, and a tool of suppression, they became deeply suspect. As a result, urban culture, based on American models from the cinema to jazz and swing, flourished alongside choral and instrumental forms that were kept alive by migrants from the rural areas. South Africa's first street craze of the fififties, kwela, remodelled swing and boogie-woogie on pennywhistles. In 1964, a roots renaissance gathered force when the Malombo Jazzmen scored a huge success with a lilting new music based on traditional percussion rhythms. For the next two decades, South African urban music saw the growth of a harder dancehall style, mbaqanga, which preserved traditional harmonies and themes inside a driving urban music.

Across Africa, bars and dancehalls rang to new urban music. The cultural revival triggered by independence brought the continent's music into the electric age. The old, pre-electric palm-wine players seemed to have been superseded by this boom. Or had they? A number of the old players continued their trade into the age of the jukebox and the transistor radio. In countries like Zaire, they were heralded as pioneering figures in the growth of authentic modern culture. More important, they wielded a strong influence on many of the new stars. 'The first electric guitarists fell into two groups,' says Sierra Leonean musician Abdul Tee-Jay.

> On the one hand you have Dr Nico and Sekou Diabate of Bembeya Jazz, who introduced fast runs, diminished chords, and jazzy solo patterns while still keeping the polyrhythmic flavour of the music. Diabate still sounds like a traditional player to me. Nico could do the most amazing things, like playing a solo in a completely different rhythm to the accompaniment. These guys were the modernists. On the other hand, you have Franco, who uses his fingers instead of a plectrum, and plays in chords, almost like an old palm-wine player, and Victor Uwaifo, another guitarist whose playing keeps the old palm-wine feeling.[25]

The bass guitar proved equally important in carrying traditional patterns into modern music, by taking over roles previously associated with traditional drum and string players. In benga music, from Kenya, the bass guitar picks up melodies played by the nyatati, a large lute; while in the 'African feeling' music of Super Diamono, from Senegal, the bass guitarist takes on the part played, in traditional percussion ensembles, by the 'mbung-mbung' drum.

Such transpositions happen in many forms of African pop. A recent tendency has been to reintroduce the older instruments into the electric context. Having reworked Zimbabwe's ancient mbira music on to electric guitars, Thomas Mapfumo then introduced a traditional mbira player on to his 1985 album *Congress*. In his classic 'Mandjou', Salif Keita works with a balafon player, a path later pursued by his guitarist Ousmane Kouyate on his album *Haminanko*. One of the finest models for the mixture of electric and folk instruments came from Franklin Boukaka, from the Congo, who in the late 1960s made a classic set of recordings featuring the sanza, or hand piano, alongside electric bass, percussion and saxophone from a member of OK Jazz.

Despite this range of 'modern traditional' forms, Western influence remained strong, and since the seventies, African bands have laced their live sets with soul, funk, reggae and pop. For some, 'copyright' provided a reliable source of income. If the audience wanted Western music, they played it. Nor could copyright be considered totally foreign: most of the imports, above all funk and reggae, were traceable back to Africa in the first place. Other musicians remained sceptical and saw foreign music as a direct threat to local forms, and, like the African Brothers, gave them up completely.

THE EUROPEAN CONNECTION

The seventies, though, will be remembered not so much for copyright or imitation but for the growing power of African urban music. Its high point came in 1977 when FESTAC, the Second World Black and African Festival of Arts and Culture, brought to a massive Lagos complex a group of top artists that stretched from Africa 70 from Tanzania, to Les Amazones from Guinea and Tabu Ley from Zaire. Tabu Ley was an important force in African music in the seventies – not only for his restless powers of innovation, but also for his French television appearances and gigs at the Paris Olympia. His search for a world market, rather than a purely African one, accelerated the flow of African musicians to Paris, where they took advantage of sophisticated recording equipment to pump out a seemingly endless stream of albums. British interest in African music, which had been dormant since the fall of Osibisa in the mid-seventies, reawoke when Island records released an album by Sunny Ade in 1982, following two collections of rumba and soukous, hot from the Paris studios.

Perhaps more important than the mere presence of African musicians in Europe was the mixing that took place among them there. Cameroonians and Zaireans worked alongside each other; labels like EddySon and Safari Ambiance promoted a gradual mix of African and French West Indian music that confirmed the link that had always existed between Africa and its musical heritage in the Caribbean and South America. In 1980, musicians from Kassav, the top zouk band from the French-speaking West Indies, started to work with Paris-based African artists, such as Toto Guillaume and Aladji Toure. The fashion caught on. Over the next seven years, Zaireans, Cameroonians and Ivoirians from M'Pongo Love to Sam Fan Thomas and Daouda joined the zouk revolution. Back in 1980, a group of session men, including Jean-Claude Naimro from Kassav, issued an early statement of intent, with an album called *Roots Relations*. The sleevenotes celebrated the new cross-fertilization that was now taking place between African and Western black music. 'From the beguine to makossa, passing by "soukous souleve" and reggae, the "groove noir" is constantly present. Bringing together some of the best "in" musicians of the moment, this album reflects the new wave . . .' By 1986, the hook-up between zouk, makossa and soukous was firmly established. Kassav toured west and central Africa several times, to massive acclaim.

Expressed through fusion, modern electro, or simply taken neat, the vitality and endless variety of African music continues, filling every corner of modern life. Ghanaian guitar bands play at wakes and funerals; Wolof and Mandinka bands add new layers to a griot tradition that has lasted centuries; while juju bands sing the praises of the wealthy and important, put paid advertisements on their records and receive the traditional gifts – money applied to the forehead – and the less traditional, car keys. The traditions of licensed critic, truth-teller and jester continue in the work of Fela Kuti, best known for his harsh anti-authority broadsides, less so for the humour and clowning that accompanies his live shows; and Luambo Makiadi, better known as Franco, who combines a key role of explainer of government policies with subtle mockery and criticism. Ancient music is played on modern instruments, kora and mbira sliding effortlessly on to the electric guitars of bands from Senegal and Zimbabwe, while the modern synthesized keyboards pick up the trance-like web of the wooden balafon. Musicians from every background push the new music. Some are fresh from university; others, like Youssou N'Dour or Mory Kante, come from a long line of traditional musicians.

The link between the old and the new remains strong and provides the key to an urban culture that grows, paradoxically, more rather than less African with every breath it takes.

STYLES
AND
PROFILES

WEST AFRICA

HIGHLIFE

Highlife is a west African music, popular throughout English-speaking countries, from Nigeria to Ghana and Sierra Leone. It is found in two main forms: dance-band, which makes extensive use of horns and has a Western, at times calypso flavour; and guitar-band, which offers a leaner, rootsier and rural alternative.

In Ghana, guitar-band highlife is the sound of the African Brothers, Eddie Donkor, Onyina, E.K. Nyame; it is the music of the concert party, with its dramatized folk stories and running commentary on wealth, life and love; the sound of younger bands like Canadoes and the City Boys. Where dance bands look West, and the lead guitars fill in with jazzy interludes and improvisations, guitar-band music lays stories and proverbs over traditional rhythms, frequent minor chords and a lead-guitar style that repeats or 'sings' the melody line. As recently as the sixties, guitar music was looked down on as being rural, 'local', crude. Today, the bands load up their painted coaches and take their roots rhythms and play to country and city audiences alike.

The sound goes back to the period around the end of the First World War which saw the growth of major ports along the west African coast. In Ghana, Sekondi, Takoradi, Winneba and Cape Coast attracted a mixture of Akan people and migrants from inside and outside the country. Sailors stopped over, bringing acoustic guitars, concertinas and a repertoire of sea shanties and folk songs. New styles developed as the Akan musicians

33

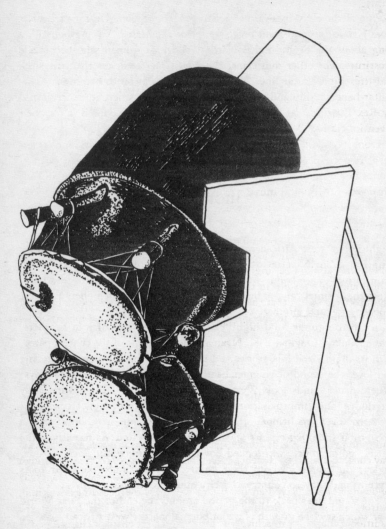

Atumpan, a drum traditionally associated with the Akan people of Ghana

traded lutes for acoustic guitars, adding the new instrument to their existing percussion groups to create osibisaba, and other early highlife forms.

One of the early innovators, Kwame Asare or 'Sam', learnt the guitar from Kru sailors and went on to write the celebrated 'Yaa Amponsah', a song about the bright lights of the city and a woman who becomes a prostitute. For other musicians, the words mattered less than the sleek and irresistible guitar line. 'Yaa Amponsah' went on to become a classic guitar-band rhythm and reached as far as Nigeria, where it was reworked by Rex Lawson; and Guinea, where Bembeya Jazz adapted it for their seventies classic, 'Mammy Watta'.

From its coastal origins, dockside dives and palm-wine bars, and its less than 'respectable' purveyors — sailors, marginal figures playing guitars, banjos and accordions for pin money — palm-wine music spread inland. Musicians fused guitar music with indigenous rhythms to create a deeper, more African sound, with words sung in local languages, and dubbed Ashanti or African blues.

The new style inspired a number of classic Ghanaian musicians. Among them were Sam's nephew, Kwaa Mensah, who played guitar with bands of up to thirty konkomba singers in the late thirties; Onyina, who added jazz chords and progressions in the fifties, and was the leader of a band whose rhythms were so hot that the conga player's thumbs were said to be stuck almost permanently in the 'play' position; the late Moses Oppong, alias KaKaiKu, whose band formed a training ground for many top guitar-band players such as A.K. Yeboah and the celebrated C.K. Mann; and, perhaps the single most important person in the development of the guitar-band highlife, E.K. Nyame.

Nyame revolutionized the music by bringing in modern percussion, jazz drums and bongos, in place of tambourines, and boosted its popularity by incorporating it into one of the country's best-loved entertainment forms, the concert party. This has its origins in the Empire Day concerts staged by Teacher Yalley in Sekondi in 1918. Yalley's shows mixed jokes, singing, dancing and fancy dress and inspired a ready following. Music played an important part in the proceedings: ragtime, foxtrots and waltzes fleshing out dramatized stories that featured the traditional anansi, or mischievous spider, and a set of stock characters: the gentleman, the female impersonator and the joker or Bob, named after Bob Johnson, an early pioneer in the concert-party form.[1]

In the fifties E.K. Nyame, with his E.K.'s Band, took the revolutionary step of replacing the now outmoded ragtime with guitar highlife and went on to introduce Twi, rather than English, as the main language.

After Nyame, guitar-band music increased in popularity and adapted to changing social conditions. The old acoustic sound, with its easy swing, clave percussion and high-pitched singers, gave way to a faster, electric beat, as guitar-band players competed with reggae and soul for public attention.

But today the old underlying feel of the music beats as strongly as ever. Nana Ampadu of the African Brothers has created a host of variations on the old rhythms, creating numerous versions of the 'Yaa Amponsah' lick. In 1972 a national contest took place in Accra to find the two bands, one guitar and one dance-band, that could best interpret the melody. Ampadu's band walked away with the guitar section. The other prize went to Hedzolleh Soundz, best known for their work with Hugh Masekela, but originally formed by manager Faisal Helwani to breathe new life into the agbadza sound.

A number of other roots rhythms have inspired Ghana's guitar bands, stretching from the adowa, a percussion and vocal music associated with the royal palaces of the Ashanti, and recast into modern forms by songs like Yamoah's 'To Wo Botu Wu', and osode, a coastal folk music modernized in the early seventies by C.K. Mann and his Carousel 7. One of Mann's first hits with the new sound was 'Odina Benya'; by the early 1970s, he was one of the kings of highlife – a crown he tarnished slightly in the course of a subsequent switch to dance-band music.

An equally influential figure on the guitar-band scene was Dr K. Gyasi, who ran a hotel and a musical instrument shop in Kumasi. In the mid-sixties, Gyasi's musicians, including the young Eric Agyeman, created a modern version of the traditional sikyi dance rhythm, performed in the Ashanti area. The album *Sikyi Hi-Life* is a classic of modern traditional highlife, replacing the old bass-box rhythms with a solid electric bass and laying saxes and plaintive vocals over the most melancholy of minor chords. Further changes took place with the folk revival of the early seventies, which saw new bands appearing in areas which had, until then, lacked a guitar-playing tradition. The most important of the back-to-the-roots movement was Wulomei, whose percussion and acoustic guitar line-up created a flurry of interest with their public performances and records in the mid-seventies. They were followed by Suku Troup and Ashiedu Keteke, both of whom kept alive the new acoustic sound.

Guitar music, with its street wisdom and street ambience, has only recently begun to find favour with the Ghanaian elite. In so doing it has stepped into the gap left by the old highlife dance bands, of whom a mere handful remain.

Dance-band music captured the optimism of west Africa in the forties and fifties, when all things seemed possible and the dream of a free Africa was at last becoming reality. It attracted a well-to-do urban audience, made up of white-collar workers, its Western flavours reflecting their own Western standards of living. The conventions of a highlife dance – the formal dress, gowns and bow ties, the printed cards noting the order of the tangoes, waltzes and foxtrots, conjure up the spirit of a bygone age. So does the sound of highlife: a gentle and nostalgic blending of jazzy guitars; sweet, occasionally wobbly, horn parts; and subtle, muted rhythms.

The roots of dance-band highlife go back to the arrival of brass instruments, which Ghanaian musicians learnt either in the old European armies of the west coast or at mission schools. Ghanaian musicians were playing in brass bands by 1750. Ninety years later a dance band played at the Cape Coast Castle. The beginning of the twentieth century saw the arrival of large dance orchestras, such as the Excelsior Orchestra, playing Western dance tunes and orchestrated versions of local street tunes.

By the 1920s, large dance orchestras like the Jazz Kings, the Rag-a-Jazzbo Orchestra, Cape Coast Sugar Babies and the Winneba Orchestra played ballroom music alongside local rhythms, such as the timo and the ashiko, which were lumped together as 'highlife'. A graphic description of its origins comes from Yebuah Mensah, brother of the celebrated bandleader E.T. Mensah.

The term highlife was created by people who gathered around the dancing-clubs, such as the Roger Club, to watch and listen to the couples enjoying themselves . . . The people outside called it highlife as they did not reach the class of the couples going inside, who not only had to pay a relatively high entrance fee of about 7/6d, but also had to wear full evening-dress, including top hats if they could afford it. [2]

The passing of the jazz age ushered in new bands, relying less on strings, more on brass instruments, saxes, trumpets and trombones, a process culminating in the new, slimline dance bands of the Second World War. The pioneer of the style that blew out the old cobwebs of the quickstep and foxtrot and replaced them with cha cha, Afro-Cuba and a heavier dose of local rhythms was E.T. Mensah. His Tempos Band included a number of top musicians, none more influential than Guy Warren, a drummer who immersed himself in calypso and Cuban music and went on to play with Duke Ellington and Max Roach in America. Warren is reckoned to be the first musician successfully to integrate African rhythms with jazz.

The dance-band revolution chimed in with Kwame Nkrumah's cultural revolution in Ghana. Highlifers serenaded the CPP Party with songs like 'Padmore', dedicated to the early nationalist hero, and the Broadway's 'Nkae', a song which listed the prominent CPP men who'd died in the struggle for independence. As the new flag was raised, Lord Kitchener's calypso 'Ghana is the Name' echoed throughout the country. Nkrumah took highlife under his wing; bands like the Messengers joined the President on his trips overseas. The Arts Council set up three-month courses to retrain dance-band musicians in traditional instruments and rhythms; the musicians were encouraged to swap their tuxedos for traditional robes; the roots name, osibi, was to replace the Western-sounding highlife. Nkrumah also ruled that any band playing on the radio had to sing at least one traditional song.

In Nigeria, a different, more laissez-faire attitude prevailed. Acoustic music had made an early impact in the coastal areas through the work of men like S.S. Peters, who introduced the guitar into percussion bands featuring square samba drums and large military bass drums. Konkoma, said to have been imported by Ghanaians and Nigerian emigrés returning home, offered a lively street music; by the late forties, it had filtered into the repertoire of the urban dance bands, where it rubbed shoulders with calypsos, jazz and other ballroom styles to which the stigma of 'colonial' had yet to be applied. One of the most famous of the Lagos musicians was Bobby Benson, who formed his Jam Session Orchestra around this time. In 1947 he became the first musician to play electric guitar in Nigeria, expanding his interests a year later to form a variety troupe that put on comic plays, in English, with musical interludes featuring Western dance music. The *Daily Service* of 22 February 1950 records his progress:

When Bobby Benson and his Jam Session Orchestra got their new kit they decided to take a joy ride around the western towns and see how the other half lives. The other half would not let them go, so they gave them good old calypso, then samba, the blues and all the titillating stuff that Lagos dance fans had grown to associate Benson with.

Benson gave up his troupe in 1952 to concentrate on music. The timing was right. Thanks to E.T. Mensah's great tour of 1951, highlife was now enjoying a boom in Nigeria. Inspired by the slick new sound, Benson created his own Lagos style, setting up a band that would attract many of Nigeria's later highlife stars, from Victor Olaiya to Rex Lawson and Eddie Okonta. New talents sprouted: Bill Friday, one of highlife's first beboppers; and Roy Chicago, whose band included talking drums. But Lagos was only one cog in the wheel. After leaving Benson, Rex Lawson, better known as Cardinal, went on to create his own sound based on Kalabari roots rhythms, and added to the growing body of east Nigerian highlife bands. Among them, Chuck's Dance Band, from Onitsha, helped update the old palm-wine sounds that had been popular in the region. 'Highlife music in the forties – it was just palm wine, Israel Mwoba style,' says Chief Stephen Osita Osadebe, the top Nigerian highlife star. 'In the west, you had sakara, apala, the music of Tunde Nightingale. In the east, solo guitarists, like the great Djamanze.'

Osadebe sees the Ghanaians as the inspiration for much of the new music. 'Before the fifties, and Mensah's tour, you had the old brass bands and orchestras playing sentimental music – the waltzes, samba and quickstep. All Western music. It was highly popular. We had private schools where you'd go to learn how to dance rumba and quickstep and all those things.'[3]

Osadebe himself became one of the leaders of modern eastern highlife. Following Lawson's example, he left Lagos, and set up on his own, with the Nigeria Soundmakers.

The big dance bands ran into trouble when the civil war broke out in 1967. Eastern musicians joined the exodus from Lagos. The rise of rock music, followed by Afrobeat, put further dents in the old superstructure. When Rex Lawson was killed in a road accident in 1971, it seemed like the end of an era.

Despite these considerable setbacks, new highlife stars and new sounds soon established themselves. Celestine Ukwu created a new dance, the igbede, and dominated the seventies highlife scene. In Owerri, Ejiogu, a former Rex Lawson guitarist, formed the Peacocks Dance Band, who took their inspiration chiefly from the old, mournful palm-wine sounds. In Bendel state, Victor Uwaifo, a passionate admirer of E.T. Mensah, developed a guitar-band sound that fused traditional-sounding guitars with roots dance rhythms. But it was the eastern market town of Onitsha that was to prove a lasting centre for Nigerian highlife. In the sixties, a studio jointly owned by Philips and Mr C. Onyekwelu produced hits for Rex Lawson, Celestine Ukwu and Stephen Osita Osadebe.

By the late seventies, a new sound had developed, mixing local rhythms with the up-front Zairean guitar style, which reached eastern Nigeria either on record or via the steady trickle of musicians who crossed the border from next-door Cameroon.

One of the biggest stars to emerge on the Onitsha scene was Prince Nico Mbarga, whose panko music, heard at full heat on his 1977 hit 'Sweet Mother', carried Zairean guitars, and a Cameroonian rhythmic feel, inherited from Nico's Cameroonian mother. Other artists, from the Ikengas, a breakaway unit from Stephen Osadebe's band, to Muddy Ibe and Super Negro Bantous, kept up a steady flow of eastern highlife, along with Oliver de Coque, with his ogene sound, and Warrior, the former leader of the Oriental Brothers, who released a string of lusty highlife albums.

The Onitsha studios attracted a range of other musicians, and turned out albums whose covers, sprinkled with vast stack heels, large cars and fancy costumes, gave a good idea of the bustling condition of the local market. Among the beneficiaries was a stream of Ghanaian guitar-band musicians, including Okukuseku and Canadoes, who left the now largely defunct recording scene at home in search of decent production and the chance to broaden their appeal, switching between Ghanaian roots music to the open, jostling guitars and krio, or pidgin English lyrics of the eastern highlife model.

The Ghana they left behind seemed in disarray. After Mensah, new talented bands appeared — some, like the Black Beats, following his style with the horns picking up the vocal melody lines; others, like the Uhuru Dance Band, creating a stronger, jazzier element, with references to Ellington and bebop. The Broadway Dance Band followed the Uhurus, while Jerry Hansen's Ramblers, with two vocalists singing in harmony, had wide success, mixing their highlife numbers with soul and Latin standards.

Despite this renewal of energy, the impetus was slowing. The general reappraisal of all things considered colonial, the mounting economic difficulties of keeping a big band together, plus changing musical fashions, led slowly but inexorably to the disappearance of the old dance bands.

Of the bands to emerge in the seventies, few achieved greater success than the Sweet Talks, who carried some of the sweetness, and the instruments, of dance-band music into street songs, bawdy tales and new sounds based on Ghanaian rhythms like osode and traditional northern sounds lumped together as the kusum beat. As the economy deteriorated, so the church, always a vital pillar of Ghanaian life, became a focal point for struggling musicians, providing both regular gigs during times of curfew and the instruments themselves.

But the gospel boom has other roots. Since the early days, Christian hymns and harmonies have been part of the fabric of highlife. More recently, in the mid-seventies, Kumasi's National Cultural Centre made efforts to promote the music with a major festival. Since then, gospel has blossomed, with groups like the Born Again Gospel Band singing Christian lyrics over highlife rhythms and melodies. Most offer a wide musical choice: Aboa Offei's Noble Mission Band, offering highlife, funk and adowa, is far from atypical.

Few bands have remained uninfluenced by Christian themes and songs. The Sweet Talks and the Sunsum Band both play 'spiritual' highlifes. Pat Thomas used a religious song, 'Yesu San Bra' to open a new chapter in the spread of highlife. A nephew of the guitarist Onyina, Thomas left Ghana for Berlin, where he recorded his epic 1980 album. His smooth blend of Ashanti rhythms and synthesized, electro beats provided the blueprint for much of the later highlife funk of George Darko and Kantata.

The economic problems that held back Ghana's musical growth have had an equal effect in Sierra Leone, where local bands face the choice of travelling overseas or staying inside the country and plugging into the Western-oriented hotel circuit.

Like other west African countries, Sierra Leone has absorbed a considerable amount of imported music, from waltzes and tangos to Latin American records, all of which have had a big impact on the local music. According to Naomi Ware, records by local artists, sung in Mende and Temne languages, were sold widely in the thirties in the capital, Freetown, while live music was provided by the Royal West African Frontier Force band, many of whose members came from the West Indies.

The forties saw the further growth of popular local dance bands such as Scrubbs Banjo Band, which played jitterbug and swing music, the Cuban Swing Band and Cisko Kids, while Sierra Leone's calypso king, Ali Ganda, backed by a Lebanese guitarist, went on to play and record throughout west Africa, at a time when calypso in general, and Lord Kitchener in particular, ruled.

One of the great sources of outside music was the Congo. Radio Brazzaville was listened to avidly in Sierra Leone, a pachanga craze gripping the country from 1959 to 1962. When Congolese band Rico Jazz settled in the country, Sierra Leone went rumba-mad. Of the local bands, the Ticklers stuck largely to Ghanaian-style highlife, while the Heartbeats, with guitarist Doctor Dynamite, shifted their repertoire from pop to Congolese rumbas and cha chas. In the late 1960s, the band produced a new James Brown sound and, under the leadership of Geraldo Pino, set off on a west African tour.

Other Sierra Leonean bands followed, to a greater or lesser degree, the Congolese stimulus. From 1964, Akpata Jazz took up the torch. Later Super Combo and Afro National worked the sound into a typical Sierra Leonean rumba, incorporating Mende and Temne folk songs into their repertoire. Despite the Congolese feel, the bands made full use of the local Sierra Leone rhythm, the maringa, which had been associated up to that point with palm-wine guitarists such as S.E. Rogers and Ebenezer Calendar.

Of the two bands, Combo established themselves as the nation's top youth band, the Zaiko of Sierra Leone. They left for London in 1974. National, a more 'respectable' outfit, moved to America twelve years later.

By this time, the live scene, deprived of the stimulus of a large market or local studios, had dried up, leaving the focus on the burgeoning street music that centred on the capital Freetown. In the early days, the streets had pulsated to a percussion and vocal music called goombay, whose sensuous beat had found its way into the 1970s rumba bands. The modern variation, milo jazz, finds its most vigorous exponent in Dr Orloh and his Milo Jazz, one of whose cassette albums included a song of praise to the new President Momoh, and was voted the album of the year for 1985.

Milo jazz, like goombay, has many variations. With acoustic guitarists, like Calendar, the goombay beat increased its popularity. Today, milo vies with near relatives like 'something butu', which takes its name from the Freetown slack talk: 'something butu' (bends down), 'something timap' (stands up).

In milo jazz, electricity may be absent, but the charge remains.

E.T. MENSAH

For a man frequently hailed as the king of highlife, E.T. Mensah shows a refreshing modesty, bemusement almost, at the extent of his reputation.

'It's the young generation who are trying to explain what I did,' he says. 'I just played highlife, in the same way that I played calypso, Congolese music, even the old conventional stuff like waltzes, slow foxtrots and tangos and quicksteps.' His love of Caribbean music remains undimmed. 'During the time I was playing with the band, Lord Kitchener was very popular. We heard all his records, which sold widely in Ghana. My favourite? "Don't Touch Mi Tomato".'[4] He laughs.

Mensah's career attracted renewed interest in 1986 with the release of a compilation album of his greatest hits and a biography entitled *E.T. Mensah, King of Highlife*.[5] Mensah started his career at school when he joined a fife band formed by a teacher, Joe Lamptey, in 1924. The band specialized in military marches and local sounds, which Mensah has described as 'a music of free expression based on the native tunes picked from the streets'. By 1932, Lamptey had relaunched his school band as the new and highly influential Accra Orchestra, a massive ensemble which boasted clarinets, sousaphones, bassoons, violins, baritone saxes, acoustic guitars, a whistle and a musical saw. Mensah's first job, as a carrier of musical instruments, resulted as much in muscular as in musical development.

Between 1936 and 1944, Mensah continued his apprenticeship with the Accra Rhythmic Orchestra and the Black and White Spots, a band formed by a Scottish sergeant, Jack Leopard, to entertain foreign troops based in Accra. In 1947 he switched to the Tempos Band, which was to inaugurate a new era in Ghanaian highlife music. The change of style happened almost by chance. In the early days, the band worked on a system of rotating leadership, with other members, such as drummer Guy Warren and sax player Joe Kelly, taking their turns. Mensah's turn came in 1948, the year in which Warren left the band for a temporary stay in Britain. The ensuing shake-up introduced a new sound and a new style to the nightclubs that had recently sprung up in downtown Accra.

Mensah explains the shift as follows. 'What happened was this. I could play jazz well, but I wasn't a fanatic like Guy or Joe. I really wanted to promote our own music. The new players I brought in couldn't play jazz at all, and I had to train them. I decided that the best way was to concentrate on what suited them best, which meant playing highlife and seeing that it was properly orchestrated.'[6] To do this, Mensah turned his attention to the rhythm section. 'Any new dance music depends on the beat,' he explains. Afro-Cuban instruments appeared: the clips, maraccas and congas. The Tempos became the first band to use bongos, making a music that relied less on the old Western dance steps, more on the increasingly fashionable Afro-Cuban rumbas and cha chas that were sweeping across east, west and central Africa.

Above all, though, Mensah promoted Ghana's own music, played in a fashionable and up-to-date new way. In a vast repertoire recorded by Decca for their West African series, the Tempos juggled calypsos, merengues and sambas alongside a collection of classic highlifes, including orchestrated konkombas, a dance-band version of the yaa amponsah rhythm and a blistering version of S.S. Peters's old Nigerian acoustic guitar song, 'Canaan Canaan Calabar', rerecorded by the Tempos with an unnamed woman vocalist.

Apart from shifting the musical axis of the band, Mensah revolutionized the look and the stance of highlife music. The pre-war orchestras faded. The bands that followed Mensah were smaller, sleeker. The new Tempos' horn section consisted of no more than one trumpet, one sax and a trombone. It also boasted, for the first time, electric guitars and microphones.

The Tempos also introduced new musical structures into Ghana. 'When we first started,' says Mensah, 'there were no professional bands. But when I trained my musicians, I also started paying them. Around that time, a sousa band would get maybe £4 a month. My musicians, when they toured Nigeria, were paid between £40 and £60. They were the first ones to become professional.' Mensah helped found the Ghana Musicians Union, at a time when royalty payments were conspicuous largely by their absence.

Mensah's reputation spread throughout west Africa. He toured Nigeria several times from 1948 onwards and inspired local bands who, until then, had played largely jazz and Latin music, to rediscover their own roots and express them through highlife. His 'Ghana, Guinea, Mali' calypso celebrated the political union set up by Kwame Nkrumah, while his appearance in Guinea shortly after independence helped to cement the acceptance of highlife music in French-speaking west Africa.

Although dance-band music was to lose its appeal in the 1960s and 1970s, when it was increasingly regarded as outmoded and elitist, Mensah still enjoys an untarnished reputation, among both musicians and members of the public, a reputation bolstered by occasional live performances. He also keeps an eye on the latest developments in highlife music. 'Most musicians have all the benefits of sophisticated modern instruments,' he explains. 'But you only have to listen to their recordings to see that many of them have lost touch with the necessary rhythms . . .'

OSITA OSADEBE

Chief Stephen Osita Osadebe, one of the founding fathers of eastern Nigerian highlife, started as a singer and percussion player, specializing in konkoma and other forms of street music. His real interest lay in dance-band music, typified by the sound of Stephen Amechi and other Lagos-based outfits. When Amechi's band visited his home town, Onitsha, Osadebe contacted them, saying he could 'play congas well and sing better'. 'I was allowed to sing one Negro spiritual and the man was convinced,' he recalls. Before he could join, though, Amechi's band split up, re-forming, with Osadebe on maraccas, in 1958.

Osadebe stayed three months, then joined the Central Dance Band, playing jazz drums, congas, maraccas and alto sax. The same year saw his first recordings, for Philips West Africa: among them 'No Money No Woman' backed by trumpeter Zeal Onyia's band and, under his own name, 'Lagos Life Na So So Enjoyment'.

Osadebe was now established. He gathered his backing musicians into a band, the Nigeria Soundmakers International, and met with wide, but by no means universal acclaim. The real dampener came from his father. 'When he heard my voice, over the Nigerian Broadcasting Service, he had a telegram sent to me saying he was dead,' says Osadebe. 'Finally my uncle persuaded him to let me continue.'

Since then, Osadebe has cut over 200 albums, earning four gold discs and a platinum for his *Osadebe 75* album. Despite the traditional flavour of his music, with its mournful guitars and strong percussion, Osadebe sees himself as very much a dance-band man. 'I can't play guitar music,' he says. 'I need altos.' He looks back to E.T. Mensah as a big influence. 'I jumped over the fence to see him when he toured Nigeria,' he says. 'He started highlife in Nigeria. It then picked up with Victor Olaiya, E.C. Arinze and Charles Iwegbe, all in Lagos.'

The Nigerian scene expanded rapidly. Hotels hired the new, Ghanaian-influenced bands, Osadebe's among them: 'We had four bands sponsored by one hotel in Lagos. The man had two hotels and we played shifts. We played the first set, Rex Lawson the second, Amechi the third and Agu Norris the fourth.'

Today Osadebe remains a pillar of the Nigerian highlife, with firm views about the changes that have taken place since the fifties. The tendency to look outside, to Zaire in particular, for inspiration, clearly rankles. 'Some of our musicians are lazy,' he says. 'They don't have time to sit down and do proper research. They have the materials, so it's not a question of import licences or anything like that. They have the materials on their own doorstep to produce good music, something that reflects our own culture. But instead, they copy outside music.'[7]

AFRICAN BROTHERS

For over twenty years, the African Brothers have been Ghana's best-known guitar band.

They started in Accra in 1963 and formed part of a wave of modern roots musicians, from K. Gyasi's Noble Kings to T.O. Jazz and K. Frimpong and his Cubano Fiestas, later C.K. Mann, that were to take guitar-band highlife to new peaks of popularity.

At the start, the city elites looked down on traditional rural music, scorning it as 'bush' and inferior and turning instead to the Western imports and dance-band highlife. Today, the position is different. 'The dance bands have just about vanished,' says Nana Ampadu, the leader of the African Brothers. 'I'm proud to say that I'm one of the people who helped to change the scene. The upper class in Ghana now recognizes the guitar band.'[8]

In the early days, the band played part-time. Their first single, 'Agyanka Dabere', came out in 1966, and was followed by fifty-six further singles before the band's first album, *Ena Eye A Mane Me*, appeared in 1970, a mix of fleeting rhythms and rapid guitar work with lyrics that emphasized the role of the guitar band in transmitting street wisdom and veiled anti-authority comment.

The most famous song from the album is 'Ebi Te Yie', which describes a democratic meeting at which all the weaker animals complain that they are being squashed, jostled and mistreated. They wish to complain about their plight. The chairman's verdict, 'Some are well seated', reflects the gap that exists between the rich and powerful and the poorer members of society. 'Some are not seated at all,' continues the song.

In later songs, Ampadu would mourn the loss of friends, offer advice and, in the 1984 'Me Poma', descend into chauvinism and compare a woman to a walking-stick: 'When the stick grows too long, the man cuts it back.'

He sees his role as positive, helping people with valued advice: 'We have a proverb in Ghana. If no one advises you, you have to advise yourself. There's no place you can find it. But by coming to the African

Brothers Band, the lyrics will give the key to a careful life, to solve your problems. The guitar-band man is close to the people, much closer than the dance bands.'

Born in the east of Ghana, Ampadu came to the capital, Accra, in the early 1960s, looking for an office job, had no luck, and switched to music. He joined first Yamoah's Band, a popular guitar outfit, and then in 1963 formed the African Brothers which, in the early days, worked on a co-operative basis.

Like other guitar bands, the African Brothers have their own concert party, a group of twenty-four musicians and actors which tours the country for up to twenty-one days a month – more during the dry season. Ampadu's plays delight Ghana's concert-party enthusiasts but it is his music that really sets him apart.

'He's a modern traditionalist,' says his producer Mohammed Malcolm Ben. 'He's done something that the old men should have done, by restoring and modernizing our ancient music . . .'[9]

Ben's remarks are apposite, for in the space of twenty-five years and sixty-odd albums, Ampadu has built up a formidable body of electric music based on various roots forms. These styles begin with 'Yaa Amponsah', heard on the African Brothers' song 'Agatha', recorded in 1979; to odonson, a street rhythm performed by percussionists and singers; and osode, a music sung by the Ghanaian fishermen in the western region. Ampadu reckons to have created ten new rhythms and countless variations, some more traditional than others.

During the early seventies, he experimented with a range of styles, the best example being his album *Odo Paa Nie*, which embraces reggae, rumba, agbadza and a fusion of highlife guitar and a James Brown-inspired percussion beat that Ampadu christened Afro-hili – his attempt to ward off Fela's Afrobeat, which was then swamping west Africa. Its failure turned Ampadu back to more traditional sounds. As early as 1973, he had decided to give up making cover versions of Western songs. 'I made the decision after I had toured Britain,' he explains. 'When I reached home I put an announcement in the press that the African Brothers would no longer play copyright material. It was a bad time. We'd play a dance and the audience would shout out for soul or merengue. I had to try and explain to them. Some would be disappointed. Some understood. But I didn't budge. Before you can come to a dance, you'd know that the African Brothers were not going to play copyright.'

Despite Ampadu's stand against imported music, other bands kept on going. 'It's dangerous, in my country,' he says. 'Why should you throw away your country's culture?'

And if people keep on asking for foreign music?

'Well, it's left to you, the musician. You're a public figure.'

Since those days, Ampadu and his producer and brother-in-law Mohammed Malcolm Ben have moved towards a less purist position and worked out a combined strategy to market highlife in the West. Ben, with his band African Feeling, added horns and English lyrics to his music to attack the overseas market, while Ampadu remained the traditionalist. If Ben's music took off, he would follow.

By 1982, the project was under way. Ampadu had already toyed with horns in his music. Ben recorded the well-received *African Feeling* album on the Sterns label. Ampadu followed with a second Sterns album, *Me Poma*, which brought a heavy funk backbeat into his music, and *Me Maame*, which stretched to synthesizers. Once, the purists would have been aghast at the sullying of pure guitar-band highlife. Ampadu is unapologetic. 'When I first introduced saxes into the music, people objected,' he says. 'But I went on to explain it to them, to tell them that the time had come. You must move ahead.'

KO NIMO

Born in the Ashanti region of Ghana in 1934, Ko Nimo is an acoustic guitarist with a range of styles and one overriding aim: to preserve Ghana's rich heritage of traditional guitar music.

Nimo started his training young. His father was a trumpeter and guitarist, his mother a chorister in the local Methodist church. At high school, Nimo learnt to play the church organ and guitar, joining I.E.'s Band, which had various hits including the 1954 'Go Inside'. The following year, Nimo joned the Antobre Guitar Band, in Kumasi, and decided to switch from the old jazz-flavoured Onyina style of acoustic playing to older traditional styles, based on traditional modes and a single-string rather than chord approach.

In 1962, Nimo left for Britain, where he studied science technology and took guitar lessons from John Williams's father. In 1969 he was in Britain again, studying at the Manchester School of Music and widening his interest in the jazz of Ellington, Monk, Peterson and Charlie Byrd.

Nimo's own style, however, took different directions. Having mastered a range of techniques, he decided to apply them to his music, as a way of preserving the old styles and translating them into living material. His original inspiration came from Kwabena Onyina, the founder of the famous guitar band and a personal friend; E.K. Nyame; and earlier figures such as Sam and Kwaa Mensah. 'By the time I started, they had their own individual styles, so I decided not to double, not to imitate. I decided to go deeper to the very roots, to play indigenous music.'[10]

The roots, for Nimo, begin with the seprewa, the six-stringed lute which was used for playing a folk music known as odonson. Nimo found an 100-year-old man who taught him to play the instrument. Later he created a number of guitar variations.

He also flavoured his music with blues and jazz. 'I play indigenous music for an indigenous audience,' he says. 'And I try to stop those influences coming in. But highlife itself is a hybrid music that developed when new instruments came in. So for colour and aesthetics, I also use diminished chords and model my music to give it colour and taste.'

Nimo's songs mix modern and traditional lyrics. He writes many himself; others he researches from elderly people: 'The old people are my friends. I think of them as libraries on fire. They are passing away. The old lady who sings with me is sixty-seven. I had to ask her to join. She is a fountain of dirge songs and lyrics. She has a real repertoire and this is important. As a musician you must be versed in the history of your people.'

With the massive import of outside music into Ghana, Nimo's crusade to keep the younger generation in touch with their roots has an added urgency. He performs regularly with his percussion and choral group Adadam (meaning Roots) at festivals and concerts featuring younger, electric bands. He also trained the highlife guitarist George Darko, who was brought to his house to learn the traditions of Ghanaian roots music. 'George became a good friend,' says Nimo. 'He was one of the coffin bearers of my late wife. He is very dear to me.'

For his part, Nimo respects the guitar-band musicians who keep the flame of Ghana's culture alive. 'Nana Ampadu is a storyteller,' he says. 'He's recorded a lot of stories in permanent form, which is good. And he has gone up country, entertaining people, keeping up the old traditions.'

On the one hand, Nimo fights to keep the music alive. But his larger musical message is for the rest of the world, and what he describes as its 'musical astigmatism': 'There's been a lot of misinformation. Written histories select what interests them and leave out the subtle things. Things that do not look so important to them are actually very important.

The missionaries could not understand our culture, saw it as either pagan or heathen. But it was our religion.'

To date Ko Nimo has made two albums in Ghana, with *Odonson Nkoaa* on the Philips label offering a fine collection of rich harmonies, percussion and choral music. He has also recorded an electric album at Faisal Helwani's studio in Liberia. The times are changing – and Ko Nimo is changing with them.

S.E. ROGERS AND SUPER COMBO KINGS

In the forties, there was less need for preservation orders. Acoustic music, away from the elite bands playing Western and Latin music, became the authentic sound of urban Africa as countries from Zimbabwe to Kenya, Ghana to Zaire, developed their own distinctive variations.

One of Sierra Leone's best-known guitarists was Ebenezer Calendar, who lived and worked in the capital, Freetown. Calendar's palm-wine band forged a range of influences, from the Caribbean rhythms that had been present in Freetown since the arrival of the first freed slaves in the eighteenth century, to the percussion street rhythms of milo jazz music which was played on a range of frame drums.

The Freetown musicians developed new line-ups. Calendar's back-up, a large kongoma, or hand piano bass, a scraped saw, more percussion and a sousaphone, known locally as 'bombadi' (the biggest) provided a rousing backdrop for comments on local life and politics. Other songs, like 'Abbe Jube Done Bless Mi Toto', established him as a double-entendrist of calypsonian proportions.

Sierra Leone's palm-wine music entered the electric age through the work of S.E. Rogers. The subject of two recent compilation albums, Rogers played up-country rhythms from the Bo area, and outside music, the most notable being the twist, which swept Africa in the early sixties. Emil Ogoo recalls seeing Rogers's newspaper advertisement for a lead guitarist for his new band, the Morning Stars, in 1965. 'I turned up for the audition and there was no one else there,' he says, 'People were in awe of Rogers who, by now, was well-known across Africa. I got the job.'[11] Ogoo played on a number of Rogers's best-known tracks, including his tough-edged, melodic 'Twist with the Morning Stars'.

Twist is perhaps a misnomer. Ogoo recalls hearing palm-wine music played twist-style well before the actual craze hit Africa. In Sierra Leone, the sound was dubbed the jitterbug; it developed largely from South African guitar music which, by now, was popular in large parts of Africa. Ogoo's other interests lay with Sierra Leone's own palm-wine music, which he heard from the well-known Freetown acoustic player, Sam; Zairean music, through the work of African Jazz, which established itself as a standard of reference for many aspiring young guitar players; and the highlife and juju music from further down the coast. I.K. Dairo was a particular favourite. Nearer home, such diverse forces as Ali Ganda, with his songs about cricket, Alec Bedser and the introduction of double-decker buses in Freetown helped boost the popularity of calypso.

The early Morning Stars sessions took place at the African Clubhouse, a small hall with function rooms, in Bo town. Rogers recorded the tracks on his twin-track tape recorder, and they were later released on his Massam label, the name coming from his home town of Massam Kpaka, near Pujehun. Rogers's musical interests covered a wide range. He introduced the electric guitar into palm-wine music and left Ogoo to play freely over solid palm-wine patterns. The vocals have a gruff warmth; the guitar work, mixing acoustic with echoey lead electric lines, marks an important transition point between the old all-acoustic palm-wine days and the pure electric bands that were to follow. Rogers also absorbed, and gave contemporary expression to a number of important rhythms that went on to become mainstays of west African, particularly Sierra Leonean music. 'Please Go Easy with Me' Ogoo describes as a palm-wine rumba; 'She Caught Me Red Hot', a version of the Ghanaian yaa amponsah, a rhythm which was well-known in Sierra Leone before anyone was aware that the Ghanaians played it too; 'Baby Lef Marah' mixes Zairean guitar licks with palm-wine music. The rest of the tracks included 'A Time in My Life', a waltz with a dash of Jim Reeves, an enormously popular singer in Africa; 'Man Stupid Being' where the lead guitarist, not Ogoo this time, played Zairean style; and the rousing and effervescent 'Twist with the Morning Stars'. 'I picked up the guitar part from an east African rhythm,' says Ogoo. 'It was almost a cover version. The song itself is African twist. It had nothing to do with Chubby Checker.'

The most auspicious song, though, turned out to be 'My Lovely Elizabeth', which was later released on EMI and became a best-seller. Rogers left Sierra Leone for America in 1973. By this time, Ogoo had left the twist far behind, and was playing lead guitar for Sierra Leone's top band Super Combo Kings. His first moves had come about through government sponsorship. In 1967, Sierra Leone's Produce Marketing Board had set up a band, with a line-up that included Ogoo, his brother

Dwight, Mamadi Kamara and Sidikie Fofona. The band, Premier Produce, collapsed when the army took over the government. Ogoo joined Afro Combo followed by Super Combo, based at the Splendide club in Bo. 'Congolese music was our big influence at the time,' says Ogoo. 'Nico, Franco, Papa Noel, Rochereau, Lipua Lipua, they were all popular in Sierra Leone. We started playing mainly Zairean style, which was extremely popular at the time . . .'

Combo's success was immediate. When Ogoo left with the Echoes Band for Ghana where he would later work with the Ramblers, his place was taken by the erratic genius, Dr Freddie Green, whose passion for Dr Nico's work was so great, that when the Zairean visited Freetown, Green leapt on the stage, and played note for note alongside his hero. By all accounts, Nico was vastly impressed. He later recorded a slow ballad entitled 'Adieu Freetown', plus songs that warned Sierra Leone women not to follow 'Congo men'.

Combo became youth champions. While other bands, notably Afro National, catered for the more conservative audiences, Combo attracted the youth. Their music covered all bases, from Zairean to copyright. The Sierra Leonean merengue, a fusion of rumba and local palm-wine rhythms, is heard on their greatest hits like 'Memona' and 'Abi Mama', whose rhythms pick up those of Rogers's 'Nyalima Nyapoi'. They also explored deeper cultural rhythms in the secret-society song 'Ngombu'. In fashion as well as musical terms, Combo ruled. When flares were à la mode, Combo sported the widest conceivable 'Elephant-foot', and 'Go Show'. They created mottos and catchphrases that were sprayed on walls and lorries and repeated in songs like 'All Bellars Must Die' (a bellar being an unfashionable bore); 'You Lekam Force' (you like it at first, but that's about it); and 'N'Ya You De, You Go Soba', a local slang directed at people from different parts of the country. In 1974, Combo left for Britain, quit the music scene, but re-emerged with the renewal of interest in the eighties, when they played regularly on the club circuit and recorded radio sessions for Capital Radio. And as interest in the early work of S.E. Rogers grew, a former Combo member King Milo emerged with a London-style new palm-wine band, Mampama Tapper.

SWEET TALKS

The Sweet Talks were more than just a band. They became an institution, a training-ground for Ghanaian highlifers, a community that included many of the country's top musicians. The name has been imitated, taken in vain, stolen. There have been Sweet Beans and Talkative Sweets. But there has been only one – or at the most, two – Sweet Talks.

The band was born officially on 15 December 1973 at the Talk of the Town hotel in Tema. The members included A.B. Crentsil, on vocals; Smart Nkansah, guitar; and Pope Flynn, vocals. In the next few years, other talents were to follow, including vocalist Jewel Ackah and Eric Agyeman, guitarist.

The band's early music had two distinct styles. One was a relic of the old dance-band days in which the Sweet Talks played copyright music: ballroom, funk, even reggae sung by Pope Flynn. The second was Ghanaian cultural music, polished up for the big-band style, and sung by A.B. Crentsil in his uniquely husky, red-blooded voice. Born in the western region, Crentsil spent his early years listening to osode music and absorbing the palm-wine sounds of Kwaa Mensah and Sam. He worked part-time in Takoradi, as a railwayman and a singer in the evenings, before joining the Eldoradoes, a dance band, and the Medican Lantics, a band attached to the Atlantic Hotel – the manager supplying the instruments and the white-collared audience.

It was here that Crentsil teamed up with Smart Nkansah, a guitarist who had played with a church band, and then in Yamoah's Guitar Band. The Sweet Talks made their first hit with 'Adam and Eve' in 1975. The song reflected Crentsil's love of long, biblical narratives, which would later find expression in 'Moses', a track whose E.K. Nyame melody delighted listeners to the same extent that the lyrics, thick with innuendo, shocked them. Crentsil was treated leniently. He had poetic licence and he used it to the full.

In 1976 the band followed with *The Kusum Beat*, an update of northern traditional sounds based around percussion and xylophones; and *Spiritual Ghana*, a testament to the Sweet Talks' love of religious melodies and plaintive osode rhythms.

By 1979, when the band were ready to take off for America, Smart Nkansah left and was replaced by one of Ghana's leading roots guitarists. Eric Agyeman was born in Kumasi and made his name with Dr K. Gyasi's Noble Kings. Growing up in the Ashanti region, he had started his career playing highlife, pop and Beatles in a local band, Afro Boateng's Midnight Movers, in 1963. By 1972 he joined Gyasi as guitarist and arranger and developed an incisive new form of music, 'sikyi highlife'.

Sikyi is a traditional Ashanti dance, accompanied by acoustic guitar, calabash, bells and apremprensuah – a large bass box with metal keys set over a central sound hole. Gyasi's band switched the box to the electric bass, which kept the typical sikyi beat, and retained the typical minor guitar chords, in deference to a tradition that stretched back to the early palm-wine guitarists. 'It is palm-wine music that we polished up to be commercial,' says Agyeman. 'We put in wind instruments, which was unusual for a guitar band, plus keyboards.'[12]

'The idea was to promote typical Ashanti music,' recalls Thomas Frempong, Agyeman's partner in the Noble Kings. 'Accra had the Uhurus and the Ramblers. The western region had Jewel Ackah, C.K. Mann, Osei Tutu and the Sweet Talks. With sikyi, we were saying, "Here it is, here's our music."'[13]

In the Sweet Talks Agyeman switched to the alternative brass-fronted modern form of dance-band highlife. His adaptation can be heard on the classic *Highlife Safari* album, released as a solo in 1978.

The band spent two months in America, recording *Hollywood Highlife Party* and working on an album with the Crusaders. Plagued by bad weather, they returned to Ghana, where they had a dispute with their manager and disbanded. Agyeman and Crentsil formed a band, Super Brain, which lasted only a short time. Agyeman returned to Gyasi and then went solo; Crentsil picked up the pieces with a new band, Super Sweet Talks International, and released the *The Lord's Prayer* album. Nothing illustrates better Crentsil's gift of mixing the fleshly with the spiritual. The title track, 'Lord's Prayer', was blessed with a beautiful riff, floating horn charts and churchy harmonies. The flip resurrected 'Adjoa', a scurrilous soldier's song thick with colloquial sexual references. 'I heard it when I was young,' says Crentsil. 'Soldiers used to sing it waiting for the boat to go to India, or when they'd come back. Later on I'd hear them singing it on marches and parades.'[14]

Crentsil has other classics to his credit. 'Atea Special' from the album follows a government health warning about the dangers of drinking local gin – and suggests the milder pito, palm wine, instead. 'Yewo Adze A Oye' portrays the different areas of Ghana, poking fun at the way people behave, their food and their language: Nzima with its atcheke and pear; the west where the sailors speak Afro-American slang – 'I don't give a damn, my ship is sailing tomorrow morning, take it easy, brother, take it easy . . .'

After *The Lord's Prayer*, Crentsil recorded *Tantie Alaba* in the Côte d'Ivoire, creating a further booze classic, 'Akpetechi Seller', akpetechi being a form of Ghanaian spirit, and then turned his attention to Britain where he fronted a band put together by Osibisa and called Highlife Stars. Their only British album, released by Flying Elephant, brought together a bristling version of Agyeman's 'Matutu Mirika' and an old Teddy Osei number, 'Pete Pete', which had a huge west African hit in the 1950s.

Neither the album, nor the band's two series of gigs, broke highlife in Britain. By 1984, Crentsil was at work with his band Ahenfo, and Agyeman was involved in Kokroko and other solo projects. The name Sweet Talks passed to Jewel Ackah, who wrapped his tonsils round 'The Lord's Prayer' and set off for Abidjan. Whatever the rights and wrongs of Ackah's assumption of the Sweet Talks mantle – some claim that he poached the title to cash in on the band's success with 'The Lord's Prayer' – few would doubt his musical talent.

Born in western Ghana, Jewel Ackah started as a professional footballer, and went on to stretch his powerful soul-tinged voice in a copyright band, the Pick Ups, in 1965; followed by C.K. Mann's Carousel 7; the Eldoradoes and the Medican Lantics – the latter two based at the prominent hotels in Takoradi. In 1973, serious ructions hit the Medican Lantics. They were tempted by the promise of new instruments, left the Atlantic Hotel to set up a new band, were arrested and put into custody.

On their release, the old Lantics band became the Sweet Talks and moved to Tema. Ackah branched out on his own, joined Pat Thomas in the Sweet Beans, and then rejoined C.K. Mann for an American tour. 'We were playing copyright, funk and soul,' he remembers. 'Not much highlife. We went to a school in Dallas. It was a disgrace. There we were, one of Africa's top bands, playing funk. When we started, people laughed, saying we weren't playing the right stuff. C.K. said we weren't going back to funk again. We were going to play highlife. And when we did, it was fantastic.'[15]

Ackah returned home, started a solo career with an album called *Asomdwee Henee*, after which he joined the Great Pilsner's Band, a brewery-sponsored outfit which enjoyed a brief run of popularity. But it was drugs, not lager, that took the sparkle from the Great Pilsners. They were due to tour Côte d'Ivoire, but were searched en route. Marijuana was discovered; the band folded. Ackah headed back to Abidjan in 1979, with a new Sweet Talks, recording the *Haleluyah! Amen!* album with the renamed 'S.T. Express'.

Solo albums followed. In 1980 Ackah joined up with dance-band guitarist Kwame Nkrumah, who had made his name with the Stargazers

Band in the 1950s. Their album, *Yeredi A Wu*, resurrected a number of fifties hits; Ackah had first heard the title track at a beauty contest in Accra – won by his wife.

His other records cover a range of styles. Early in his career he recorded a tribute to the acoustic guitarist Kwaa Mensah, called *Odonson*. 'He was one of the best blues guitarists,' says Ackah; his music had a strong influence on the young singer.

'I mix up guitar-band and dance-band so that you can play it anywhere, go anywhere,' he says. 'The asase, yaa amponsah, ashewa – we have so many traditional sounds. Osode is the guitar-band style. You can't play it with chords; it has to be picked. Kwaa Mensah, Ko Nimo, they know the indigenous guitar-band beats. I can use them in my music, but I also put horns on top. It's still the same beat, though.'

Later albums turned him towards funky highlife, as on the football anthem 'Akaraka-Chi', a song that celebrates his favourite team; on *Super Pawa*, soca and religious rhythms associated with the spiritual sound of Ghana's Christian churches; and *London Connection*, where the bass guitar picks up the old brass-band rhythms.

Despite his success, Ackah remains constantly on the move with new material, new labels, new musicians. This instability reflects the general instability of the Ghanaian music scene. 'In Nigeria if you want a bus, a set of instruments, they give them to you, and subtract them from the record when it comes out, so you have something left to live off. So you stay with that company. But not in Ghana. No, no, no. I have been duped for a long time. I decided that if something came my way, I'd go along with it. If they agreed to pay the musicians a certain amount, and I need a certain amount, what the hell. If you make a million, take it, it's not my business . . .'

The former Sweet Talks members drifted into new bands. A.B. Crentsil formed Ahenfo, or 'Mighty', and recorded in the Côte d'Ivoire. Eric Agyeman set up Kokroko and continued his adventures in dance-band highlife. The most successful ex-Sweet Talk is Smart Nkansah, the leader of Ghana's top highlife act, the Sunsum Band. Sunsum, meaning Spirit, draws on a variety of influences, from guitar- and dance-band highlife. Nkansah's own style has a strong traditional feel, which dates back to his early days with Yamoah's Guitar Band.

Nkansah was born in eastern Ghana and was brought up by his uncle, who regarded music as the lowest possible form of occupation. 'In those days, musicians were supposed to be people who got drunk and misbehaved,' says Nkansah. 'My uncle didn't want me to follow those ruffians. He said if I did, I shouldn't call him again. I decided to snub him.

'I went to the highest level. To drink, to smoke. In those days I didn't know how to drink beer, only minerals. And smoking was out. But I decided to go to the highest level.'[16]

Nkansah's first band employed him to play guitar for the Eden Revival Church in Kumasi. He then moved to the Youngsters before joining Yamoah's Guitar Band as a soul, rather than a highlife, guitarist and singing behind Lee Dodou's James Brown vocals.

He then left and joined Jewel Ackah and Pope Flynn in the Medican Lantics in Takoradi and took part in a number of moonshine or 'shabo shabo' recordings under the pseudonym of the Powerful Believers. In 1973, the nucleus of the band set themselves up as the Sweet Talks. Nkansah stayed with them until 1978, when he formed the Black Hustlers with his former Yamoah's Band roots singer, Agyaaku.

The Black Hustlers mixed copyright songs, sung by Pope Flynn, with roots numbers, sung by Agyaaku. The two strands were woven together in Sunsum, formed in 1980.

Nkansah's own guitar sound shows a number of influences. 'I followed the style of Kwaa Mensah and E.K. Nyame,' he says, 'and with that I'd mix what I'd learnt from the dance bands.' He also received further useful input on the roots side. 'My mother helped a lot. In the old days, when the moon was bright, we used to play in the evenings and sing folk music. Later I tried to remember the songs, and I'd take my tape recorder to my mother. She'd sing it into the tape. I took the rhythm and I'm still using it today. It's called adakamu.'

Since then, Sunsum have had a number of top albums, from *Disco Spiritual*, with its churchy highlife feel, to the brassier dance-band sounds of *Gye Wani*, and the roots guitar music of *Odo* in 1985. Apart from spanning both the roots and dance-band poles of highlife, Sunsum also deal in copyright material. 'If you play three hours of highlife you won't get a crowd,' says Nkansah. 'It's upsetting, yes, to play other music, but we have to — to get our daily bread.'

PRINCE NICO

By the mid-seventies, Nigerian highlife was enjoying a renaissance and making its mark across west Africa. One of the new-wave pioneers, Victor

Uwaifo, had created a brand of guitar-band music which took its inspiration directly from the early palm-wine players, and its rhythms from traditional sources: the most important the ekassa and the gbadagbada, from Benin. 'Joromi', recorded in 1966, sold over 100,000 copies on the strength of its swaggering and up-front guitar style. But Uwaifo was equally keen to exploit Nigeria's traditional instruments: among them the hand piano, which provides a dramatic introduction to 'Akwete', Uwaifo's own guitar rhythm, and the xylophones featured on his later *Festac* album, from 1977.

The intensity of Uwaifo's guitar playing was matched by that of the great highlife artists based in eastern Nigeria. Among them the Oriental Brothers, led by Doctor Sir Warrior, split into new factions sharing the same relentless rhythms; Oliver de Coque developed his own ogene sound system, while the Ikengas, once part of Stephen Osadebe's dance band, joined the new, brash revolution. Perhaps the biggest name to come out of eastern Nigeria, though, was that of Prince Nico Mbarga, leader of Rocafil Jazz.

Nico's success rested on a finely tuned blend of Nigerian and other African musics, with the guitar ringing out as a fully developed lead instrument. Earlier eastern highlife, from Osadebe and Celestine Ukwu, set a strong 'local' feel against a backdrop of dance-band sweetness. Nico, like Sam Mangwana in Zaire, created a sound that blew across regional and national divisions. He described his creation, 'panko', as 'Zairean music in a Nigerian setting'.[17] It was a lesson that Sam Mangwana would take to heart with his later blend of Antillean and Zairean musics. The hallmark of Nico's music was its accessibility. The guitar, one of Zaire's gifts to the world, replaced horns as the preferred highlife instrument. Above all, Nico valued the Zaireans for the variety and flexibility of their approach. 'We play the instrument in a Zairean way,' he explained. 'After playing lead for some time, I leave it for the rhythm guitar, drums and congas. This is the way the Zaireans play. We call it a "demo", the place where the rhythm section "demonstrates".' A further influence came from the Cameroonians who brought their distinctive bass styles into Rocafil Jazz.

Prince Nico was born in 1950 in Anambra State, of mixed Nigerian and Cameroonian parentage. During the Nigerian civil war he left for Cameroon, where he formed the Melody Orchestra, returning home in 1971. Two years later he cut his first hit with Rocafil Jazz, 'I No Go Marry My Papa', followed in 1977 by 'Sweet Mother': 'When I wrote the song, I was thinking of the suffering of my mother. Other women suffer like that too. My father died when we were all very young. My mother tried to bring us up. So when I thought about that, and the way women suffer in general, God gave me inspiration.'

'Sweet Mother' established Nico's reputation in Nigeria — and beyond. From the Côte d'Ivoire to Ghana and Sierra Leone, Rocafil Jazz helped switch public interest away from Zairean music. The formula could hardly fail: 'Sweet Mother' and the hits that followed were sung in krio, which could be understood readily in all English-speaking countries. For the French speakers, the Zairean guitar style made all the right sounds.

'The market danced,' says Nico. Hit albums followed: *Simplicity*, *Happy Birthday* and *Family Movement*. But the dancing stopped when Nico fell out with his record company, Rogers All Stars. According to Nico, 'Rogers gave wrong accounts for "Sweet Mother" and set up a new band, with instruments and a recording contract to cash in on the best-seller.' In 1981, with the case still in progress, Nico left Rogers, started his own label and recorded further albums, including *Tribalism* and *Man Pass Man*. Their differences were finally resolved in 1985.

Despite his international success with 'Sweet Mother', and British appearances at the WOMAD, World of Music, Arts and Dance Festival in 1982, Nico keeps a realistic balance between the Nigerian and the Western markets. In 1978, he recorded a juju album with Rogers, called *Aye Ele*, in which he sang in Yoruba and krio. 'I hired a talking drummer and a Hawaiian guitarist to give the music its proper African background,' says Nico. 'I can't blend my music with European music. It's no use even trying. Nor do I support those African musicians who record pop, reggae and disco. You can never hope to play a music better than the people who originate it. You can't play reggae better than a Jamaican. But juju has the original African background.'

PAT THOMAS

The wave of disco and reggae that swept Africa in the mid-1970s created differing responses: some musicians like Nana Ampadu pulled away from copyright playing; others took on the music and adapted it to their own purposes. One of the latter is Pat Thomas, a highlife singer who made his name with his band, the Sweet Beans.

Thomas was born in Kumasi, where he stayed with his uncle, Onyina, the celebrated guitar-band leader and owner of a record shop. He first came to public attention when he sang in the street, with the young Thomas Frempong. The duo became known as 'Sam and Dave'. In 1969, he went to visit a friend, Moby Dick, who was playing with the Broadway Dance Band. 'They were rehearsing "Mansa", a K. Gyasi song,' says Thomas. 'But no one could pronounce the words, which were in Twi. I'm from Kumasi; it's my language. I wrote the words out. They asked me to sing them. I sang. They opened their mouths in astonishment.'[18]

Thomas joined the band. In 1970, guitarist Ebo Taylor returned from London to set up the New Broadway Dance Band. At first, he turned Thomas down, as being too young. Thomas pleaded; Taylor relented. Later the same year, he joined the Uhuru Dance Band for a tour of Britain; back in Ghana he played with Taylor's Blue Monks, spent a year in the Côte d'Ivoire before forming the Sweet Beans in 1973.

Like many Ghanaian bands, the Sweet Beans received sponsorship from a government body, in this case the Cocoa Marketing Board. They released one album, *False Lover*, then split and were revamped as Marijata, releasing two albums, *Marijata* and *Pat Thomas Introduces Marijata*, after which Thomas released two reggae-influenced solo sets, *Let's Think It Over* and *Asawado*.

The break-up of the Sweet Beans offers an object lesson to any band that relies on sponsorship. The board supplied cars, lodging and instruments. In return the band represented the board at official functions. 'One day,' says Thomas, 'we were supposed to go and play at a state function. We knew the head of state, Acheampong, was going, but he didn't tell me the time. I went late. The head of state's aides were furious. The President called me in. "We're waiting for you," he said. "Aren't you going to play?" Then he dashed me a nice whiskey and a signed copy of his book, saying, "Go and sing for me." That's all.' Some of the Cocoa Marketing Board were furious; they decided to dissolve the group, which at that time included both Thomas and fellow-highlife singer Jewel Ackah. Thomas left for Berlin, where he recorded the classic *1980* album, a mix of reggae and disco-highlife that featured George Darko on lead guitar. For Thomas this represented a peak. The albums that followed his return to Ghana cast aside the hi-tech slickness. *Sweeter than Honey* dug into calypso and dagomba rhythms but was marred by weak arrangements and production.

When Thomas does hit form, though, he is hard to beat. His 1985 output included three hastily put together albums, including the disastrously undermixed *Pat Thomas and Ebo Taylor* and one blustering triumph, the commemorative *Asanteman*, which combined a history of the

Ashanti kingdom, kicked off by a blast of traditional Ashanti horn playing, with solid production.

By now, Thomas had discovered football. In 1984 he had recorded a mini-album *Asante Kotoko*, dedicated to the Ghanaian club which had won the Africa Cup in 1983. The title track was played over the speakers at the club's home pitch and occasionally played live at half-time by a local highlife band. In 1985, Thomas went to work on a further Asante album – to commemorate the club's fiftieth anniversary.

His conversion to the game had been brief and irreversible. 'A friend took me along,' says Thomas, 'I realized football was sweet . . .'

GEORGE DARKO

George Darko, Pat Thomas's lead guitarist on the *1980* album, went on to further acclaim with the release of 'Akoo Te Brofo', an album track later rerecorded as 'Highlife Time'.

Where Thomas had introduced a disco feel into his 'Yesu San Bra', Darko went further, breaking the cross rhythms with a funk backbeat and translating the lyrics into English. Released as a single in the UK, 'Highlife Time' received a reasonable airplay, mainly on local soul stations, but Darko's live London shows suggested an awkward jostling of funk music pulling one way, and highlife pulling the other.

Darko sees the tug as pretty well inevitable. 'We want people to get into African music and that means creating a crossover. Once the music's accepted, we can always come back home, bringing in more African stuff. But first we need to find the customer.'[19]

The thought of straight African music making an impact overseas strikes Darko as impossible. 'If we really wanted to play African music as it is now, no one would listen to it. People at home listen to it at concerts, but not on record. You put indigenous music on at a disco and the DJ will throw it away. It's just not possible.'

At the start of his career, Darko played Western rock and pop, playing Booker T numbers with bands like the Reborn Avengers and the Soul Believers before joining the army band the Fourth Dimension for five years. During this time he played in the Middle East.

On his return he was taken by a commanding officer to study real Ghanaian guitar with Ko Nimo. 'I dedicated "Highlife Time" to him,' says Darko. 'I studied there for eight months and he taught me the pure

61

guitar-band style, the original music of Kwaa Mensah and Sam. Up till then, I had been playing strictly funk. It was the first time I felt really professional as an African musician. Today I always advise young musicians coming up to go into things like that. That's our gold and we've got to dig it.'

In 1977, he left Ghana for Berlin, where he formed his own band, Bus Stop. 'No one had heard of African music at the time,' he says. 'They didn't even know about Osibisa.' He played sessions with Pat Thomas and then released his first album, *Friends*, a mixture of highlife and reggae, in 1981. The stand-out track, 'Akoo Te Brofo', attracted a lot of attention. 'I have some US people who told me, "Listen man, can you do that again? The same melody but sung in English? It's really going to break through. The feeling, the melody, is there." It's true.'

The single, and the album, came out on Oval in 1984, but did little commercially. For purists, it sounded too commercial. For clubgoers, too 'ethnic'. Darko's solution was to withdraw from the scene, take voice-training and produce something new. The resulting album, the 1986 *Moni Palava*, switched from funk to soca-fusion as a way of attracting Caribbean listeners to Darko's deeper highlife sound: the three guitar-band songs on the B-side, one of which, 'Ashewa', uses the traditional, churchy yaa amponsah guitar lick. 'The soca was a decoy,' says Darko. 'Yet it's not pure soca. On *Moni Palava*, the bass, horns and strummed guitar are soca, but the rhythm is highlife. What really makes the difference between the two is the bass. Highlife basslines flow. Soca's don't. In a lot of African music, it's the bass that carries the weight . . .'[20]

On the highlife B-side, Darko applies electronic drums to a traditional guitar-band sound. 'Linn drums are important,' he says. 'We don't get that consistency from a drummer. To enter the disco market, we need the consistency of a drum machine.'

For all that, Darko sees little sense in the criticism that says he's selling out. 'It's only British purists who have that problem,' he explains. 'It's not a problem at home. I'm at heart a guitar-band man playing in the funk style. If you listen to my music, it's distinctive. But you can't miss the Ko Nimo rhythms, above all, the yaa amponsah.'

AFROBEAT AND AFRO-POP

To a very substantial degree, Afrobeat — one of the dominant styles in contemporary Nigerian music since the mid-1970s — is the creation of a single musician/bandleader, Fela Anikulapo-Kuti. This is in considerable contrast to the history of most other contemporary styles, which have tended to evolve as a result of linked experiments by a number of like-minded musicians, usually over two or three generations. Yet the combination of stylistic devices which characterize Afrobeat have all been stirred and stewed by Kuti, who has himself towered head and shoulders over other Afrobeat bandleaders (most of whom learnt their craft as sidemen in Kuti's Afrika 70 and Egypt 80 line-ups). While other Afrobeat bandleaders may not employ all the devices used by Kuti, his central position in the genre is so all-powerful that his own output can be said to define it.

Although Kuti has introduced a number of modifications to Afrobeat during his career, all the essential devices of the style were clearly put together by him during 1971 and 1972, on the albums *Why Black Men Dey Suffer* and *Shakara*. These devices — which are in origin variously African, Western or purely Kuti's own invention — can be itemized as call-and-response vocals, 'broken English' lyrics, an unusually outspoken political stance, a distinctive beat and tempo, and jazz- and R&B-infused horn and keyboard charts.

Afrobeat's use of call-and-response vocals represents the style's most important retention of traditional African musical form. Because traditional African vocal music is predominantly a communal activity, the role of the chorus is as important as the role of the soloist or cantor: the 'lead' voice sings a line, the chorus repeats or embellishes it, and so the pattern is repeated throughout the performance. (Cross-rhythms are often cited, mistakenly, as the single most important defining characteristic of traditional African music, but in fact they are not found throughout the continent. Call-and-response singing, however, shapes much of the music of practically every African tribal/cultural group.)

While the nature of call-and-response vocals and Kuti's applications of them are both wholly traditional, this is not the case with the second of Afrobeat's defining devices, 'broken' English lyrics. Broken English (known to most British people as 'pidgin English') has of course been used in Africa since the earliest years of British colonization, as indigenous peoples attempted to master the new language and in the process turned it into a largely African form (basically, a mixture of English and African words in African grammatical structures). But until Kuti began using broken English in his music, most African musicians had sung in either their own tribal languages or, less frequently, in 'European' hotels and nightclubs, scrupulously correct Queen's English. A rich and virile form of speech, ideally suited for use in song (like Jamaican patois in reggae), broken English as adopted by Kuti was a commercial as well as artistic masterstroke. In Nigeria there are literally hundreds of different languages in everyday use, and singers using their own tribal language automatically deny themselves an audience among many other people in different tribal groups. By using broken English, Kuti immediately made himself understandable to all Nigerians – and, indeed, to all Anglophone west Africans. Broken English also makes commercial sense in international terms: to Westerners Kuti's lyrics are at the same time understandable (in general outline), mysterious (in detail and nuance) and above all African.

If Kuti's embrace of broken English was a major innovation, so too has been the overtly political nature of so much of his lyric output. For while political dissent and social comment is as well established in African culture as it is in the West, the aggression and temperature of Kuti's political songbook is unprecedented. Self-preservation precluded much overt political comment during the colonial era (as it continues to do in those countries still under white minority rule), while since independence a desire to support and encourage the new administrations, rather than berate them for every shortcoming, has acted as a self-censoring process on many musicians (as has self-censoring pragmatism in a number of severely repressive post-independence regimes). Kuti, however, almost alone among the modern musicians of post-independent black Africa in the 1970s, felt restrained by neither the niceties of supportiveness nor the fear of reprisal. Starting with *Why Black Men Dey Suffer* in 1971, he has released a steady stream of violently polemical albums – attacking the errors and absurdities of post-independence black African regimes, and the continuing economic and cultural dominance of the West upon black Africa, and proposing a radical readoption of traditional African culture, science and technology to counter and replace Westernization. As a consequence, Kuti has suffered continual harassment – and, on occasion, terrorist attacks – from successive Nigerian regimes.

The other defining devices of Afrobeat – the trademark rhythm and tempo, and jazz- and R&B-infused horn and keyboard charts – demonstrate Kuti's ability to adopt certain elements of Western music while subtly Africanizing them. Rhythmically, his music has much in common with black American music, on paper at least, but the way those rhythms are played, their accents and loping tempo in the hands of Afrika 70 and Egypt 80, makes them as assuredly African as the call-and-response vocals which are to be heard alongside them. The same is true of Kuti's use of horns and keyboards, which had its origin in his attempts to compete with James Brown in the late 1960s and early 1970s (Brown was then hugely popular in Nigeria), but which by 1972 had taken on a distinctly African flavour. ('Every other band was playing soul music but me,' Kuti has said of the circa-1970 period, 'the attack was heavy, soul music coming in the country left and right. Man, at one point I was playing James Brown tunes among the innovative things because everybody was demanding it and we had to eat.')

Since 1972, with the hurricane impact of Afrobeat on, first, Nigeria and then other parts of west Africa, Kuti has established a massive audience for Afrobeat, and one that has largely stayed loyal to him throughout the coming and going of competing styles; while no amount of state repression – either jail terms or murder attempts – have deflected him from his lyric stance.

FELA ANIKULAPO-KUTI

While popular music, both within Africa and outside it, has thrown up a heartening number of politically-orientated protest artists during the past twenty years, only a tiny proportion of these people have ever had their ideals and commitments tested in the face of determined state repression. For most, a small drug bust, followed by a fine or suspended sentence, is the extent of the reprisal. Nigeria's Fela Anikulapo-Kuti, by contrast, has faced vicious harassment from a succession of Nigerian regimes, both civilian and military, and this aspect of his life has to be considered as important as the creation of his Afrobeat style of music. Indeed, the two are inextricably linked, for Fela's politics and their consequences for him – have informed the lyrics of many of his most powerful and lasting songs and record releases.

Born 15 October 1938 in Abeokuta, a small town in the Yoruba people's traditional region of south-west Nigeria, Fela was the fourth of five children. Although he was later to identify himself wholly with the poorest, most underprivileged sections of Nigerian society, Fela actually grew up in a relatively well-off, middle-class environment. His father, the Reverend Israel Ransome-Kuti, was the headmaster of Abeokuta Grammar School, and Fela remembers that as a child his was the only black family in the area which possessed a car.

His mother, Funmilayo, was the dominant parental influence on the young Fela, whose later political awareness can be traced directly back to her. During Fela's childhood and early teens, Funmilayo was both more politically active than most Nigerian women and further to the left than most Nigerians of either sex. She led the first street demonstrations against the British colonialists in Abeokuta in the late 1940s, and in the early 1950s she was the first Nigerian woman to travel to the USSR, China, Poland, Yugoslavia and East Germany. It was through his mother that Fela was introduced to the revolutionary Ghanaian leader Kwame Nkrumah in 1957, a meeting that made a big impression on his then emergent political consciousness.

In 1958, Fela was sent to London by his parents, who had agreed to support him there while he studied to become a doctor. Once there, however, Fela promptly enrolled himself at Trinity College of Music, where he was to spend the next four years studying piano, composition and theory. His parents weren't pleased – in Nigeria then (and to a degree now) musicians were regarded on much the same level as street beggars – but there was little they could do. At Trinity, Fela wasn't the best of students. It wasn't that he lacked talent, only that he was more interested in leading his Koola Lobitos jazz and highlife band in the evenings than in applying himself to dusty European composers and their disciplines by day.

By 1961 the Koola Lobitos were a regular fixture on London's growing R&B club scene, playing venues like the Marquee and Birdland alongside their staple outlet of black community dances and social functions. In 1961, too, Fela married his first wife, Remi Taylor, a part-Nigerian working in London. In 1962, he managed to graduate from Trinity (a year later than he should have done), and moved back to Nigeria, basing himself in Lagos, where he got a job with Nigerian Broadcasting as a trainee radio producer. But he was fired after a few months, with bad timekeeping being given as the reason for dismissal. Fela's continuing activities with Koola Lobitos, now a new line-up working the Lagos club circuit, were once again cutting into his more mundane daytime commitments.

Once free of Nigerian Broadcasting, Fela devoted himself totally to Koola Lobitos and never again allowed himself to be sidetracked by the temptation of a regular, nine-to-five weekly wage. In 1966 he discovered 'igbo' (Nigerian grass), something that was to make a major change in his lifestyle, ultimately leading him to reject most aspects of Western culture and to focus increasingly on black African traditions. Grass was also the prime mover in Fela's escalating conflict with the Nigerian establishment, particularly its army and police, which was to boil over in the raids on his Kalakuta commune in 1974 and 1977.

In 1968, Fela began calling the music Koola Lobitos played Afrobeat – as a reaction to the slavish relationship many other Nigerian bandleaders then had with black American music. There were any number of James Brown soundalikes in Lagos, something Fela found ridiculous and embarrassing. What was wrong with *African* music? he demanded. Fela was also keen to reverse the tide of musical influence, and in 1969 he took Koola Lobitos to the USA. But at the time interest in African music among American audiences was very much a small-scale, cult affair and after spending the best part of a year unsuccessfully attempting to make an impact on the west-coast club scene, Fela and Koola Lobitos returned home.

One positive aspect of the American visit for Fela, however, was his friendship with a black American woman named Sandra Isidore. A Black Panther activist, Isidore introduced Fela to the ideas of such people as Malcolm X, Angela Davis, the Last Poets, Stokeley Carmichael and Eldridge Cleaver. Fela's understanding of radical politics was profoundly increased during the American trip, and Isidore was largely responsible. (She was later to work briefly with Afrika 70, and was guest vocalist on the 1976 album *Upside Down*.)

Back in Nigeria, Fela changed the name of Koola Lobitos to Afrika 70, and in 1971 enjoyed a big local hit with the single 'Jeun Ko'ku ('Eat and Die'). He also founded the Shrine Club in Lagos, which was to become the focus for his music – and much drug-squad harassment – over the next seven years.

By 1972 Fela was one of the biggest names in Nigeria, and indeed throughout west Africa: because he sang in broken English rather than Yoruba, his records were understandable in all Anglophone countries. Fela was now the figurehead of a loyal and ever-increasing audience among the ranks of west Africa's urban poor, the sufferers living in the shanty towns around the major cities. Fela sang about their problems in their terms and made furious denunciations of the ruling classes and their enforcers of law and order. A typical early swipe at the ruling black elite was the 1973 album *Gentleman* . . .

'I no be gentleman at all,' exclaimed Fela. 'Africa hot, I like am so; I know what to wear but my friend don't know; him put him socks him put him shoes; him put him pants him put him singlet; him put him trouser him put him shirt; him put him tie him put him coat; him come cover all with him hat; him be gentleman; him go sweat all over; him go faint right down; him go smell like shit.'

Not surprisingly, the Nigerian establishment didn't enjoy hearing songs like these. Yet while Fela's high-profiled propagation of grass gave them a heaven-sent opportunity to put the troublesome singer behind bars, the drug squad consistently failed to pin a conviction on Fela (a point Fela delighted in rubbing in on various hilarious releases). Fela's skirmishes with the police and army first boiled over on 23 November 1974, when Kalakuta was attacked and practically razed to the ground. Fela discussed the affair on the *Alagbon Close* album later that year, questioning the right of uniformed public servants to go around breaking heads at will . . .

'Dem no get respect for human beings,' Fela pointed out. 'Dem no say you get blood like dem; dem send dem dog to bite bite you; dem point dem gun for your face; the gun wey dem take your money to buy; dem don buff my head with dem gun; the gun wey dem take my money to buy; dem go torture you and take your statement from you; dem de call am investigation; dem go lock you for months and months and months; (but) nothing special about uniform − is tailor de sew am like your dress.'

The 1974 attack confirmed Fela's revolutionary politics for all time, and also cemented his total embrace of African mores and customs. In 1975 he changed his middle name from Ransome (which he regarded as a slave name) to Anikulapo. His full name, Fela Anikulapo-Kuti, now meant 'He Who Emanates Greatness' (Fela), 'Having Control Over Death' (Anikulapo), 'Death Cannot be Caused by Human Entity' (Kuti). It was a name-of-power, and Fela was going to need all of it on 18 February 1977.

That day, the biggest, most outrageous army and police assault yet was launched on Kalakuta. Some 1,000 soldiers, most of them armed, swooped on the commune. They cordoned off the surrounding area, broke down the wire fence around the commune buildings, and smashed their way into the central structure. Occupants were stripped and beaten; men had their testicles permanently damaged; women had their nipples smashed with stones. Fela himself was beaten close to death, sustaining a fractured skull and several broken bones. His mother, then eighty-two, was thrown from an upstairs window, fracturing a leg and going into deep shock. The army then set fire to the compound and prevented the fire brigade reaching the area. The ensuing blaze gutted the premises, destroying six Afrika 70 vehicles, all Fela's master tapes and musical instruments, a four-track studio, all the commune members' belongings and, for good measure, the free medical clinic run by Fela's brother, Dr Beko Kuti (also severely beaten in the attack). The first journalists to arrive on the scene were assaulted by soldiers (some also had their cameras broken). Inquisitive passers-by were similarly set upon. The army didn't want any witnesses.

Although Fela won the war of words which followed, he sensibly decided to leave Nigeria for a while, and in October 1977 went into voluntary exile in Ghana – to lick his wounds, regroup and keep out of the way of a Nigerian army bullet. Unfortunately, his musical and political message didn't endear itself to the Ghanaian authorities either, and Fela was deported back to Lagos after a few turbulent months. In February 1978, to mark the anniversary of the previous year's pillage, and to reaffirm his embrace of African culture, Fela married twenty-seven women simultaneously in a traditional ceremony.

Neither has Fela dropped his high revolutionary profile in subsequent years. With albums like *Coffin for Head of State* (which blamed President Obasonjo for his mother's death in 1978), *International Thief Thief*, *Vagabonds in Power*, *Authority Stealing* (all three attacking government corruption and abuses of human rights) and other releases, Fela has continued to keep himself and his band (now renamed Egypt 80) aligned with the poor, exploited people of Nigeria – and by extension the poor, exploited people of Africa and the rest of the world.

In 1984, Fela was jailed in Nigeria under what were widely regarded as trumped-up smuggling charges. During his incarceration, Celluloid producer Bill Laswell was brought in to complete the production of the nearly finished *Army Arrangement* album.

Released after serving twenty months of a five-year sentence, Fela put out the Wally Badarou-produced *Teacher Don't Teach Me Nonsense* album in early 1987 – a rich, dense, at times almost orchestral set which showed Fela apparently recharged, rather than weakened, by his latest jailing. The man promises to be a vital force in Nigerian music for many years yet.

TONY ALLEN

Tony Allen is one of Nigeria's finest kit drummers, the man who put the beat into Afrobeat. 'I was playing with the Western Toppers Band in Lagos in 1964 when Fela discovered me,' says Allen. 'I started playing jazz with him. He was playing strictly jazz then and had his own quintet.'

The two men decided to form a highlife jazz group in 1965. It was a revamped Koola Lobitos and produced a music so complex and full of changes that, according to Allen, the audience didn't known what to expect. 'In five minutes we'd use about five different arrangements,' he says. 'It was far too complicated for the audience. They couldn't understand what was happening; except, possibly, the musically inclined ones who knew that the music was different from all the local things they'd been listening to. It was a bit like showing off, so we decided to simplify things, giving each song two hook lines and a straightforward arrangement so that people wanted to dance.'[1]

The result was a new sound, an early form of the hypnotic Afrobeat that was to put Fela at the forefront of Africa's musical talents. But Afrobeat was nothing without Allen's extraordinary bass-drum patterns.

'His style is different from any other,' says one Allen enthusiast. 'If you listen to the bass drum, it's always *b-boom, b-boom*. Where most drummers play a single beat, Tony makes it double, and that gives it the push.'[2]

Allen agrees. 'The bass drum is unique to me. I'd never play one, one. Any drummer can play that straight beat. It's just like putting a metronome in there.'

Allen's apprenticeship began in 1960 when he joined the Cool Cats, a copyright highlife band in Lagos. When the band split, he returned to his job as a radio technician before leaving to join Agu Norris and the Heatwaves, then the Nigerian Messengers. He subsequently played with two others, the Melody Angels and the Western Toppers before joining Kuti.

The Afrobeat connection lasted for fourteen years. Allen played on all of Fela's greatest songs, from 'Jeun Ko'ku' (1971) onwards. By 1978, he had enough – he felt he'd received little recognition or appreciation for his efforts. He recorded solo albums like *No Discrimination* before forming his own band, the Mighty Irokos, playing strictly Afrobeat, which lasted from 1981 to 1983, when Allen left to do session work.

His fortunes since then have been mixed. Although few other Nigerian musicians show an interest in Afrobeat – too difficult, says Allen – the style has had a profound influence on one other prominent sound: juju. By the late seventies, the kit drum had become a regular part of the juju ensemble; Allen's style had carried over along with the nagging 'tenor guitar' rhythm pick, also taken from Afrobeat. Ade was one of the first to translate the rhythmic power of Afrobeat into juju. By 1984, Allen had guested on Ade's own Island album, *Aura*, contributed one of his own songs, 'Oremi', and had himself released an album with a distinctly juju feel to the rhythms.

'NEPA' or 'Never Expect Power Always', was released by the London company Earthworks in 1984. The song is a mocking comment on the erratic Lagos power supply which leaves the city at the mercy of regular power cuts. The body responsible for the supply, or the lack of it, is the Nigerian Electrical Power Authority, hence the finger-pointing acronym.

The music itself has double power. Allen's music replaces the rickety fringes of Afrobeat with a tight mesh of sound that bears some relation to what the young Cameroonians have done with makossa. Electroclaps provide percussion flavouring: the rest is Allen. The flipside, 'One Door Close, Another Door Open', is equally hard. Afrobeat is Fela's creation. But it has taken Tony Allen, and a batch of solo albums recorded with and without Afrika 70, to show how hard and direct the style can become.

Fela's Afrobeat was just one of many styles that pushed Nigerian music to a new prominence in the seventies. For many artists, Western pop and rock provided an early stepping-stone to new forms that incorporated their own roots rhythms.

SONNY OKOSUNS

The work of Sonny Okosuns received its most fitting accolade in 1980 when, after a successful coup by Samuel K. Doe in Liberia, his revolutionary *Fire in Soweto* album was played non-stop over the national radio.

Few other artists could have produced the right soundtrack for such a revolution: after an early flirtation with pop, Okosuns has established himself as a leading social and political commentator on matters stretching from South Africa to pan-Africanism, the need for honest African leadership and the plight of the continent's children. Unlike Fela, though, Okosuns rarely focuses his attention on Nigeria, beyond bland exhortations to his fellow-Nigerians to help put the country back on its feet, as in his 1984 album *Which Way Nigeria?*

Okosuns' music also runs in less turbulent channels, harnessing different Western models and fashions to Nigerian rhythms in a way that underlines his position as a spiritual mentor to the current generation of Nigerian pop singers – from Christy Essien to Emma Dorgu, and, before his conversion to born-again Christianity, Chris Okotie.

Okosuns started his career with the Postmen, an Enugu band whose Western cover versions earned them the name of the Local Beatles. The band maintained their Beatle-like status until the civil war broke out in 1967, when they split. Okonsuns left for Lagos, then Benin, where in 1969 he joined Nigeria's prime palm-wine modernizer, Victor Uwaifo in the Melody Maestros, and immersed himself in his blend of highlife and roots rhythms.

In 1970, Uwaifo toured Japan and Okosuns returned to set up his own band, Paperback Limited, a Lagos 'underground' outfit steeped in what sounded like Jimi Hendrix, Cream and Traffic. To Okosuns, it was slightly different. 'They thought I was playing underground,' he says. 'In fact I was playing traditional music with rock guitars and bass.'[3]

From there, Okosuns decided to follow the Uwaifo path and create his own form of roots music. He returned to his village and worked on a new sound, based on the melodies, dialects and percussion rhythms of the Esan people.

'He had to discover a sound,' says EMI producer Odion Iruoje. 'He wanted to play rock mixed with Victor Uwaifo music. I realized that he was good singing in his own dialect. So we translated his songs, most of which he wrote originally in Esan, into English. *Papa's Land* was originally in Esan. So was *Fire in Soweto* . . .'[4]

Inspired by the work of poet J.P. Clark, Okosuns called his new band Ozzidi, after the river god of the same name; his music became Ozzidizm and he scored an immediate success with his single, 'Help', which sold 100,000 copies; his first three albums, *Ozzidi*, *Living Music* and *Ozzidi for Sale*, turned a former rock musician into a semi-roots hero. Okosuns' voice, one of Africa's warmest and most distinctive, was a major asset. The rock guitar and funk flavours of *Ozzidi* may have dated, but the rootsman hollers and the relaxed cajolings still have the power to astonish and please.

Lacking Kuti's commitment to a single form, Okosuns ranged more widely, and with effortless assurance. One of his most fascinating works remains an album recorded with Trinidadian star Explainer, in which

Okosuns coasts through a series of calypsos bemoaning high prices and the cost of living in Lagos, and the indiscriminate use of skin-whiteners.

Further experiments followed. In 1977 he released 'Papa's Land', mixed by Eddy Grant, followed by two hugely successful albums recorded at EMI's studios in London. The first, *Fire in Soweto*, dealt with the struggle in South Africa, over a backdrop of Afro reggae rhythms. The second, *Holy Wars*, looked to the day when Africa would be ruled by Africans. The reggae sound was important to Okosuns. 'The slow beat allowed me space to talk,' he said, 'unlike rock or funk, where you have no space to say anything.' Okosuns' main aim was to talk about Africa and its problems in a language the world understood. While Fela concentrated on Nigeria's excesses, Okosuns went worldwide.

'When I first made these records,' he says, 'people said I was cashing in. But it was a big risk for me. All my mates were singing love songs. I was trying to talk about what was happening to black people.'

After *Holy Wars*, Okosuns released *3rd World*, followed in 1982 by *Mother and Child*, to celebrate the Year of the Child. By now, his music had changed direction. Reggae had played itself out. He created a replacement, Afro-carnival – a 'universal sound that could be danced by anyone'. Okosuns saw it as a Nigerian answer to the disco which had been sweeping across Africa in the same way that soul and funk, and earlier jazz, had stood in the way of highlife and konkoma music. 'Afro-carnival combines all the beats,' he says. 'If you want to listen to funk, you'll hear it. The horns are funky, the guitar is rock, the rhythms traditional. It's a new African sound.'

Okosuns' struggle to break his music in the West started when *Papa's Land* was released in Britain on the politically-oriented Radic label. Nothing happened. EMI London showed little sign of interest in picking up Okosuns' work for European release. In 1982 *Fire in Soweto* was licensed to Oti, a small Nigerian-run company in south London. Okosuns dismisses it as a backyard deal and says that he wasn't consulted.

In 1985, Okosuns launched a further attack on the world market, touring America, releasing *Which Way Nigeria?* on Jive Afrika in London, plus further albums and singles on Rounder Records in Philadelphia.

Whether the surge has come too late in a career hampered by the indifference of a large multinational company remains to be seen.

ONYEKA

Onyeka is one of a new rising generation of Nigerian woman artists who have come to the fore in the eighties. Like Christy Essien, another top Nigerian performer, she steers a course between middle-of-the-road pop and her own east Nigerian roots. And now she has started to push for international recognition.

She started the ball rolling in 1984, with a television spectacular in front of 11,000 people in Oslo. Early in 1985 she released a puzzling single on the Sterns lable. 'Trina 4', written by her producer Keni St George, was all the things that Onyeka had avoided in her earlier pursuit of easy-listening African funk. It was a bizarre mixture of reggae rhythms and bagpipe melodies with a title from a Scottish roadsign. The B-side, 'Ekwe', showed Onyeka in better form, applying soukous guitars and a brisk dance tempo to an Ibo folk song sung to accompany a masked dancer of the same name.

The album that followed showed further sides to Onyeka's musical direction — with a reworked Nigerian folk song written by palm-wine guitarist Harcourt Whyte, to a new version of the rocksteady classic, 'The Tide is High'. 'I've changed,' says Onyeka. 'I used to be middle-of-the-road. Now I'm writing and performing songs that are more brazen, rockish, outlandish. It's another side that I've been afraid to show up to now. And I feel good singing them.'[5]

Onyeka has various professional interests outside music. She trained as a journalist, taking a master's degree in communications in America and working at the United Nations headquarters before coming home to work in Nigerian television. In 1984 she presented a BBC film, 'The Squandering of the Riches', which took a critical look at the Nigerian economy.

The title could apply equally well to the Nigerian record business, which Onyeka views with characteristic sharpness: 'We don't really have a decent record company in Nigeria. What most of them do is to take a number of artists, many of whom can't sing, make so many records, put them out and make just enough to cover themselves. They don't put nearly enough into promoting or publicizing an artist.'

Her own experience with one of Nigeria's top companies, EMI, left her puzzled and frustrated. In the end she set up her own label. According to Onyeka, the company showed extreme reluctance to release sales figures for her albums. She reckoned on 17,000 after discussing the matter with people at the pressing-plant. The company told her 500. In the end, she decided against court action, putting her faith instead in PMAN, the performing artists' body which ranks Sunny Ade and Sonny Okosuns among its leading officials.

The tussle with the company appalled Onyeka. 'Painters may have done their best work on an empty stomach,' she says. 'But that won't do for us. A lot of talented Nigerians simply aren't getting anywhere as they receive no support from their record companies. It's not a good formula.'

Her third album, *In the Morning Light*, came out on Onyeka's own label, Ayolo, the name of a small bird and a nickname passed from her grandmother. 'Setting up the label was easy,' she says. 'The rest was awful, especially the distribution.' Only the flimsiest of networks exists in Nigeria – but Onyeka had already gained valuable experience while with her previous company. 'I virtually looked after myself. I had to go into the record office and start distributing them myself. Everywhere I went, people complained they couldn't get hold of my records. I had to drive around myself, between the various shops. The company wouldn't do a thing.'

Nor is the situation unique. 'Prince Nico had a big hit but made no money,' she says. 'Sonny Okosuns made *some* money – but he's been aggressive.'

In the end, Onyeka finds herself, like other Nigerian artists, working in a variety of professions. 'Dora Ifadu paints and photographs. Some of us set up businesses. I design clothes and do some journalism. It can be draining. I'd like to devote all my energy to music, to singing and writing, but it's impossible.'

Despite the precarious business side, she remains confident of her own direction. 'In Nigeria we have a range of influences from the West, and Michael Jackson and all those people slip into your music. It's not a totally bad thing. It means that we get a marriage of Western culture and African and I think what comes out is beautiful and unique. You might not understand the language but you can feel the music.'

OSIBISA

Of all the African bands that have made a splash in the West, none went further than Osibisa. In the seventies, albums like *Woyaya* and *Welcome Home* set new standards of orchestration and commercial appeal. They sold in quantities unheard of for African musicians, before or since.

Since then, Osibisa have suffered the fate of many once-celebrated seventies acts: their pioneering blend of rock and African rhythms has either been overlooked or downgraded for its lack of roots appeal. This is understandable. Osibisa's star was too closely hitched to Western rock to survive the passing of that lumbering waggon, and too much of a fusion to survive the scrutiny of Western audiences which, from 1980, were looking for 'real' African music. It is easy, however, to understand the frustration of the artists themselves.

Nor are Osibisa alone. In 1978 Manu Dibango hit out at Western music critics who accused him of betraying African culture with his fusion of Cameroonian and Western music. 'What is Africa? I want these people to tell me. Because I play sax, does that mean I'm not playing African music? I'm proud to be African – but to me being African is not to be in jail with Africa. If you stay only in your own circle you learn nothing.'[6]

Four years earlier, Osibisa's Teddy Osei had argued along the same lines. 'People always find something to accuse us of,' he said. 'First they said our music was not the pure African stuff since we've Westernized it with the addition of Western instruments like the keyboards and guitars, and that musically, we were moving away from our roots by pandering to the British progressive-rock movement. But as I have always said, we live in a new environment different from what we knew and were used to in Africa, so our music must somehow reflect this new influence.'[7]

Osibisa have a long pedigree. Founder member Teddy Osei and drummer Sol Amarfio played in the Star Gazers, a top Ghanaian highlife band, before setting up the Comets, who scored a large west African hit with their 1958 single, 'Pete Pete'. Osei's brother, Mac Tontoh, was also a member of the Comets, before joining the Uhuru Dance Band, which brought elements of jazz and bebop into Ghanaian highlife. The remaining members included Spartacus R, a Grenadian bass player; Robert Bailey, from Trinidad, on keyboards; and Wendel Richardson, the Antiguan lead guitarist.

The band's debut album, in 1971, came at a low point. Rock music, in one of its periodic slumps, demanded passive, sometimes supine audiences, for whom dancing was vastly uncool. Disco was yet to make its mark. Osibisa stepped into the breach with a music whose rock references, in the guitar solos and progressions, combined with sparkling cross rhythms to attract widespread public attention. Osibisa became a household name. Their albums sat next to Cat Stevens's in bedsitters across Britain. But their true power came across only on stage, when

African-village scenarios and a cool mastery of rhythm and melody summoned up an energy and spirit lacking in other branches of Western pop.

The decline set in in the late seventies, when disco music followed Afrorock as the accepted invitation to dance. Teddy Osei saw the writing on the wall in 1974. 'The super soul session men in America have quietly picked up from the band,' he explained to Sylvia Moore, citing the increasingly percussive nature of American dance music. Trumpeter Mac Tontoh developed the theme. 'The Americans took over, turning the music into disco, with whistles, congas and all that. Western music absorbed our style. The African market couldn't compete. We simply didn't have the machinery at home; and for musicians to come over here and compete was very difficult.'⁸

Business problems followed. After an initial signing to MCA, Osibisa changed companies several times, ending with Bronze records. The moves reflected their growing frustration with British business. 'In each case,' says Tontoh, 'the message was the same. It was suggested that we change our style, to move towards American soul, funk and disco. But that would have meant abandoning our African rhythms. We have our heritage. We can't just change. Our music wasn't a fake. It came straight from us. There was no chance of us changing to disco.'⁹

Since then, Osibisa have directed their attention to the state of the music business in Ghana, planning a studio and theatre which came to nothing, and helping in the promotion of younger highlife artists. In 1983, Tontoh formed a London band to back three visiting Ghanaian musicians, A.B. Crentsil, Eric Agyeman and Thomas Frempong. An album, *Highlife Stars*, followed, on Osibisa's Flying Elephant label.

The change of direction was important for the band. 'One day we'll go back to the roots,' says Tontoh. 'And do what people like Ko Nimo are doing. Ko is a seven-foot man, a giant. He's still doing the highlife, the African blues, the slow ones. We did it with "Woyaya". I hope that one day we'll go back fully.'

JUJU

A Nigerian music, the creation of the Yoruba people, juju — which combines elements of the West (electric guitars) with traditional indigenous culture (talking drums, other percussion instruments and lyric subject matter) — has been the single most popular form of contemporary music played in the country since the 1960s. Since the start of the 1980s, juju has additionally built up solid specialist followings in Europe and North America, following the signing of leading bandleaders Sunny Ade and Ebenezer Obey to major Western record labels. Whether or not juju will ever become a force in the mainstream of Western popular music is a matter of some doubt, for the style demonstrates Africa's ability to absorb Western ideas and then rechannel them in a purely African fashion: its electric (even pedal-steel) guitars, for instance, are played in a manner which owes little to the guitar heroes of rock or country musics, but a lot to the centuries-old court and social music of Yoruba culture. To compound the difficulty, juju's lyrics are sung almost exclusively in the Yoruba language.

The name juju itself didn't emerge until the late 1930s, when British colonials, looking for a word to label Yoruba music, adapted the term from the generic description of the tribe's religions. That, at least, is the most widespread belief among juju musicians. Ebenezer Obey, however, has suggested that the name imitates the sound of the leather-covered tambourine that the early bands used, along with the mandolin, talking drum and a small hand drum called akuba. Alternatively, the word could be a corruption of 'jo jo', the Yoruba word for dance.

While the origins of the style and its name are clouded by uncertainty, what *is* known is that a number of the elements characterizing juju — call-and-response vocals, rhythm patterns, the use of religious folklore in the lyrics — have been common to similar styles stretching back over several centuries. Before the colonial era and the (later) advent of electric guitars, a music like juju was played at shrines to the Yoruba gods Ogun and Oshun: the same percussion instruments were used, notably talking drums and gourd shakers (shekeres), and a single-string violin-like instrument called the goje (generically known in west Africa as the 'Hausa violin') was played as accompaniment by the lead singer. Gradually, some of the shrine music became secular and moved into the courts of the

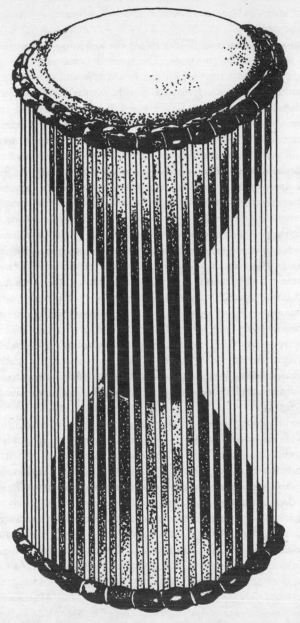

Hourglass talking drum, a staple instrument in fuji, juju and mbalax

Yoruba kings and queens. It was at about this time that British interest, and 'juju', arrived.

The first Nigerian bandleader to use the word juju to describe his own music was Tunde Nightingale. The toast of Lagos nightlife in the late 1930s, Nightingale married guitars to the goje and percussion tradition and, rolling with the colonialists' punch, adopted the juju label. After Nightingale, the next key figure was I.K. Dairo, who led the hugely influential Blue Spots in the late 1950s and 1960s. Aside from his introduction of the accordion, Dairo's most important innovation was rhythmic eclecticism: he broadened the range of beats used in the music in a deliberate attempt to widen the appeal of the music to other tribes than the Yoruba, and so extended juju's following into a larger Nigerian context.

By the mid-1960s, largely thanks to Dairo's groundwork, juju had become the predominant popular music of Nigeria. In Dairo's wake a host of juju bands emerged, and by the late 1960s two rival contenders were jostling for the position on Dairo's throne: first, Ebenezer Obey, leading his International Brothers, then the younger Sunny Ade, with his cheekily named Green Spots. Obey and Ade have spent the subsequent twenty years vying with each other for juju supremacy, Obey with his miliki (enjoyment) style, Ade with his synchro style. As a broad generalization, Obey's approach finds most favour with traditionalists, while Ade's, which on record has included Linn drums, synthesizers and other offshoots of computer technology, has had the bigger overseas impact.

A third contender for juju supremacy has been Dele Abiodun, with his adawa style.

Beyond Obey, Ade and Abiodun, but still broadly within the juju tradition, the early 1980s saw the emergence of two juju-related styles which aimed to satisfy the Nigerian audience's more radically inclined fundamentalists and futurists. The fundamentalists, no longer content with even Obey's close-to-the-roots music, turned increasingly to fuji, while the futurists, who found Ade and even Abiodun too tradition-bound when compared to the innovators of black music in the USA, turned to yopop. Personified by bandleader Segun Adewale, yopop abandoned some of juju's traditional characteristics and replaced them with new devices borrowed from the Caribbean and USA.

SUNNY ADE

Since the early 1980s, Nigeria's Sunny Ade has enjoyed parallel careers: with Ebenezer Obey and Dele Abiodun, he is part of the ruling juju music triumvirate in his own country (a position he has held since the early 1970s); while in Europe and North America he has been responsible for taking juju out of its small cult following and nudging it, slowly but surely, towards the mainstream album market. The process has not been without its problems (in 1984 Island records, who had been releasing Ade's records in the West for two years, dropped him, disappointed by the limited scale of his breakthrough), but substantial progress has been made — with Fela Anikulapo-Kuti, Ade's name is now known widely in the West, even though many of the people who have heard of him may not necessarily have heard his music.

Ade's British breakthrough can be said to have started with a triumphant concert he and his African Beats gave at London's Lyceum Ballroom in January 1983. Raved over without exception by the weekly music press, many of whose critics hailed Ade as one of the emergent dance-music stars of the year, Ade and his band played to a hugely enthusiastic multi-ethnic audience, proving that — in a live context at any rate — juju's use of Yoruba rather than English-language lyrics was no barrier to overseas acceptance. The audience size and composition was in considerable contrast to Ade's previous British visits. In 1975 Ade had made a three-month tour of the country, playing almost exclusively to expatriate Nigerian audiences at specially organized cultural evenings in municipal halls and community centres. When one of the authors of this book caught the show at London's Porchester Hall, he was the only European in an audience of some 600 people.

Since that first British visit, when he was already a big star back home, Ade has gone on to become one of the most successful recording artists Nigeria has ever known, perhaps *the* most successful. Between 1975 and 1984 he released over forty albums domestically, and by the early 1980s the average sale of each was in excess of 200,000 copies (an achievement only slightly minimized by the fact that a substantial proportion of these sales were of bootlegged pressings).

It's unlikely that Ade even fantasized about such a level of success, let alone realistically expected it, when he dropped out of school in 1963 and began to play in semi-professional Lagos juju bands. His parents, from the royal family of Ondo, were horrified by their son's choice of career, but must have been somewhat mollified by his rapid advancement within it.

81

By 1965 Ade was lead guitarist in Moses Olaiya's highly regarded band, and by the end of the following year he had left to form his own Green Spots outfit (the name was a cheeky retort to the grand old man of juju, I.K. Dairo, whose Blue Spots had ruled the roost since the early 1950s). Ade's luck continued when his first release, 'Challenge Cup' (a song about a local football championship) became a national hit in 1967.

The late 1960s and early 1970s saw Ade and his renamed African Beats go from success to success, and in 1975 he felt sufficiently powerful – and financially secure – to set up his own label, Sunny Alade records, now a major independent in Nigeria which continues to release all Ade's domestic albums. The mid-1970s also saw him open up his own juju nightclub in Lagos, the Ariya, the African Beats' home venue when they're not on national or international tours.

Ade's international breakthrough began in 1982, when he signed to Island records in Europe and North America. The previous year the label had launched its African Series of releases with the *Sound d'Afrique* compilation album, with the aim of capitalizing on the then emergent African-music boom in Britain. Ade's first album release under the arrangement was in the summer of 1982. *JuJu Music* was an across-the-board critical success, as was the 1983 follow-up *Synchro System*, which also made encouraging chart entries in Britain and the States.

JuJu Music and *Synchro System* were both produced by a young Frenchman named Martin Meissonnier, who must share much of the credit for Ade's international breakthrough. Meissonnier achieved the difficult balancing act of broadening the appeal of Ade's music – through the introduction of synthesizers and Linn drums – without destroying its root foundation in traditional Yoruba music or endangering Ade's relationship with his domestic audience. Though a minority of Ade's Nigerian fans were disappointed by the internationalization of his music, the vast majority seemed to welcome the new direction. By this time, too, Ade already had a reputation as an innovative stylist, for since 1976, when he'd introduced steel guitar to his line-up, his music had rarely stood still for more than a couple of albums, with new beats and guitar styles regularly being added to the African Beats' repertoire.

For his part, Ade has always been confident that juju can absorb new ingredients and influences without being de-Africanized in any way. In an interview with *Black Music* magazine in 1983 he explained: 'The ancient music we have as the bottom of the sound: the talking drum, the gongs, the shekere. And that foundation is always there. Whatever new textures we might be introducing, Linn drums or synthesizers, are just elaborations. They don't affect the basic substance of the style. We want to appeal to people in Europe *and* Africa, which is why we put the two traditions together, but this way the essential African character isn't lost.'

In 1975, in another interview with *Black Music*, Ade had expressed the same attitude when asked about juju's absorption of the guitar, first the acoustic model (in the 1950s) and later the electric. 'Juju music is traditional Yoruba music,' he said. 'It was only refined with the guitar, not changed. The guitar was there before, only we called it a goje – an instrument with strings made out of horses' tails. The way I play guitar is just the same as when I play goje. It will take more than the introduction of a few Western instruments to change the nature of juju.'

If Western influence has so far failed to colonize juju, Ade believes that it did, as it were, christen it. 'We have many Gods in Nigeria that we have been worshipping since before Christianity came to Africa,' he explains. 'Gods of iron, Gods of thunder, Gods of fire, Gods of water. Juju music is a collective sound which has grown out of what our ancestors used to play at shrines to those Gods. Over the centuries there was interplay between the musicians who played at the shrines, and common characteristics developed. After many years, an overall style emerged, which the musicians then took to play in the courts of our kings and queens. When the colonial masters came, they didn't know what to call this music, but as they called our religion juju, the music which was associated with it became known to them as juju too.'

EBENEZER OBEY

In many African societies, physical size is a direct sign of wealth and importance, so it is perhaps significant that Ebenezer Obey, one of the founders of modern juju music, should carry a hefty load.

Obey was born in Abeokuta, in the west of Nigeria. At mission school, he joined the choir and, on leaving, took up with the Ifelode Mambo band which played a street music on percussion and agidigbo. 'Everyone has a different name for it,' says Obey. 'It's called thumb piano, akuba or gumbay. Mambo music came before juju; it started way back. Take the guitars out of juju and you've got mambo.'[1]

By the early 1960s, Obey had uprooted and left for Lagos where he played with various bands, including Fatayi Rolling Dollar – with whom he played congas – before forming his own band, the International

Brothers, which laid the foundation for a new style of juju music.

Up to now, Obey had followed the percussion and single-guitar style of I.K. Dairo. To this he added further instruments, two front-line guitars and electric bass. He speeded up the tempo and straightened the beat to create the juju sound that ruled through the 1960s and 1970s.

Obey's formula worked straight away. He recorded his first single in 1964, had a hit in 1965, followed by a 1966 breakthrough with 'Olo Mi Gbo Temi'. This is a love song whose words, reflecting a down-to-earth sensibility that would do credit to a country-and-western singer, run: 'My love, listen to me. It takes two to make a home. When we have peace we have everything.'

In 1972, Obey named his music miliki system, the name coming from one of his great hits, 'Esa Ma Miliki' ('Let's Enjoy Ourselves'). The beat itself Obey describes as 'heavier and faster' than the juju of the time. The name also applied to Obey's Lagos nightclub, formerly a pop establishment called Crystal Gardens, then the Miliki Spot, one of the hubs of the Lagos juju scene in the 1970s.

The hits followed. With *Board Members*, Obey took the art of praise singing to new heights. The album singled out a string of prominent businessmen and created one of the best-selling juju records ever.

By the mid-1970s, Obey's lead was increasingly threatened by the younger Sunny Ade. Juju fans split into two camps: those who followed the Master Guitarist Ade, and the 'Jujurist' Obey who appealed with the sweetness of his voice and the philosophical nature of his lyrics.

It was here that the difference between the two made itself plain. Ade started his career as a follower of traditional Yoruba religion. Obey was always the perfect Christian gentleman. His lyrics preached orthodox values – love, the family, peace in the household – and went further to comment on national affairs, offering consolation to those bereaved by floods and rail crashes. Obey also took on the role of government spokesman, explaining the switch to the right-hand side that took place on Nigeria's roads in 1972, and the need to follow more recent campaigns, such as Operation Feed Yourself, or the austerity measures that followed the end of Nigeria's oil-based boom in the early 1980s.

Despite his important role in the modernizing of juju music – taken to its most notable extreme in the rasping, heavyweight *Eyi Yato*, from the late seventies – Obey lost ground to Ade who, by 1982, had signed to Island records, where he went on to make three albums.

By 1983, Obey had belatedly followed suit, and signed a deal with Virgin records. The original plan was to release a greatest-hits package.

Instead, Virgin produced the puzzling *Je Ka Jo*, a woefully under-promoted mixture of juju with funk and highlife. The singalong melodies were catchy enough, but the British audience, unprepared by advance publicity, shunned the new work. A second album followed – greatest hits – but it was left to Sterns to produce an album that – despite its bland support for Nigeria's austerity programme – did better justice to Obey's talents.

Solution, produced, like *Je Ka Jo*, by Joe Mensah, wrested Obey's music away from the gimmickry of the earlier set and replaced it with a brisk juju format, enlivened by irresistible guitar figures, a touch of highlife and the driving blues licks that have remained a hallmark of the Obey style to this day.

DELE ABIODUN

Dele Abiodun's 'adawa' system goes back to 1974. 'It was a matter of identification,' he explains. 'In Nigeria we've got the miliki system and the synchro master. I'm the adawa super king so that I can be identified easily. When I go on the street, everyone says "Adawa! Adawa!" I'm identified easily.'[2]

Much the same can be said of Abiodun's music. True to his trademark, adawa means 'doing your own thing'. Abiodun (known as the Admiral) has created a distinctive juju style whose high level of arrangement and effortless incorporation of pop and funk puts him well above most, if not all of his Nigerian competition.

Obey's *Solution*, with its zesty guitar work, comes close. But little else can touch Abiodun when – and the qualification is important – he hits top form.

The mix of styles reflects his own early training. He was born in western Nigeria but ran off in 1964 with his school fees and studied music at the Young Pioneers College, set up in Accra by the Ghanaian president Kwame Nkrumah. Here Abiodun soaked himself in highlife music, learning above all the importance of the solo guitar and the way that the Ghanaian guitarists could make it 'sing' the vocal melodies. He returned home and formed a highlife band under the name Sweet Abbey and his Top Hitters Band. It was a mistake. While he'd been away, highlife had slipped in popularity and a new electric variety of juju music, associated with Ebenezer Obey, was taking over western Nigeria, even Lagos itself.

Abiodun dropped highlife but kept some of its guitar styles, and dropped Sweet Abbey. From now on it was Dele Abiodun and his Top Hitters Band, the stars of both the Rasco Hotel Lagos and, later, Victor Olaiya's Stadium Hotel.

'When I left Nigeria, it was the time of Tunde Nightingale and the old, deep juju music, called owambe, that was played by I.K. Dairo and others,' he explains. 'There were no strings, nothing. Just a single acoustic guitar and tambourine. When I got back, I decided to follow the trend and blend highlife with funk and owambe to create a new sound.'

Abiodun's first record, *Kino Mo Ko Soke Yi*, came out on Oluomo records in 1971. For the next ten years, he stayed with the company, recording around twenty albums, including one in New York in 1977. By 1981, he split, after a tussle over a record that, he says, appeared in Europe without his knowledge.

For two years, his career foundered. Albums like *E O Fu'ra* set a new low for lacklustre songs and out-of-tune guitars. From there Abiodun climbed slowly back. He patched up the quarrel with Oluomo, recording *Ma Sheka*, before falling into a further dispute. The upshot was Abiodun's own company, Adawa Super records, and a series of brighter new albums, starting with the *The Beginning of a New Era* and continuing with *1,000 Miles*.

By the time his 1984 album, *It's Time for Juju Music*, appeared, Abiodun had widened the scope to introduce electroclaps, heavy congas and a talking drum speaking in English. 'It says, "Good evening, good evening, ladies and gentlemen,"' explains the Admiral. Despite the urgency of the groove, heard at its hardest in the 1985 album *Confrontation*, released in the UK by Earthworks and featuring two 'adawa super dubs', Abiodun could still mix standard juju tricks to good effect: side two of *It's Time for Juju Music* unfolded a slow pattern of guitar interludes, rhythm changes, freewheeling pop passages, and spiky bass riffs. It was a devastating performance. 'The guitars exchange messages non-stop,' says Abiodun. 'You won't be able to understand the language, but it's like two children playing in the playground. One says, "Go forward." The other, "Follow me." The first, "Let's go," the second, "I'll stay behind." It's like a child's game.'

But juju also means big business. Abiodun is sceptical of other artists who produce three albums a year. For him, one a year will do, and he takes exception to the current practice of singing praises on vinyl. 'Praise singing is important in Nigeria,' he says. 'But if I do it, I do it every three albums or so. If someone wants me to advertise their name, it's done on a strict contract basis. I'm not just praising them. Their names come at the end of the record, not in the middle.'

It is ironic that despite his scupulous regard for the way business is carried out, Abiodun's own business arrangements have so far held him back from developing his overseas markets with any degree of success.

SEGUN ADEWALE

Though a developed and precisely defined style, Nigeria's juju music is far from monolithic, including several distinct sub-styles within its mainstream. Sunny Ade has his synchro system, Ebenezer Obey his miliki system, Dele Abiodun his adawa system. While a casual Western listener coming to juju fresh might not notice any differences between the output of these artists, their styles are as instantly identifiable to Nigerian audiences as those of, say, Meatloaf and Bruce Springsteen to the American rock audience.

But while the records of Ade, Obey and Abiodun might well be interchangeable on the average British jukebox, those of Segun Adewale could conceivably make an individual impression. Called yopop – from Yoruba pop – Adewale's music is considerably brasher and more aggressive than that of the three other bandleaders. Younger than they are, Adewale has brought a welcome injection of rude vigour and urgency to juju. He has, however, retained all the defining characteristics of juju within yopop, making him an innovator within the tradition rather than the iconoclastic revolutionary that some of his followers (and record-company personnel) would have us believe.

Born in 1956, into a Yoruba royal family, Adewale resisted early parental pressure to become a doctor or laywer, joining the legendary I.K. Dairo's band immediately on leaving school. After a further spell with Chief S.L. Atolagbe and his Holy Rainbow he then formed his own band – the Superstars – in 1973. The group released one album before breaking up early in 1974. The end of that year found Adewale co-fronting Prince Adekunle's Western Brothers Band with Sir Shina Peters, an outfit he stayed with until, in 1977, he and Peters left (taking six other members with them) to form Shina Adewale and the Superstars International. Shina left this band in 1979, and Adewale put his current Superstars together in 1980. Initially playing a style of juju borrowed from Sunny Ade and Ebenezer Obey, Adewale's Superstars gradually developed an individual

87

identity which was first heard to full effect on 1983's *Endurance* (the group's fifth album). Elements of funk, reggae and highlife were fused into the juju bedrock, while – perhaps most importantly – the group tore into their music with an aggressive abandon unusual among modern juju artists. 'Looking at the music of Sunny Ade and Ebenezer Obey,' Adewale observed in 1984, 'I realized I had to do something different to get ahead. That's yopop, which I call kick-and-start music. Unlike the older juju musicians I don't take time to build my tunes slowly: once I start I am right away in top gear.'[3] Yopop had arrived, and a substantial number of younger juju and fuji fans in Nigeria adopted Adewale as their new hero.

A year later, the *Play for Me* album did for Adewale in Britain what *Endurance* had done for him in Nigeria, and the Superstars made a brief promotional visit to London where they played a critically lauded gig at the Venue.

In press interviews during the 1984 London visit, Adewale seemed confident that yopop was about to take over from the juju of Ade, Obey and Abiodun, particularly with overseas audiences. 'I think yopop had more chance in Europe than juju,' he explained, 'because the energy of kick and start is more in tune with the European pace of life. They rush all the time, while in Africa things go slower.'

Time will tell whether or not Adewale's confidence is justified. Meanwhile it seems prudent to take statements about the coming yopop explosion with large pinch of salt, because for all its individuality, Adewale's yopop nevertheless remains solidly part of the larger juju tradition. What he's presenting is a new model rather than a wholly new product, and juju itself seem to have reached a plateau in its attempted breakthrough in the West – a plateau resulting to some degree from the decision of all the music's key performers to continue singing predominantly in the Yoruba language. So long as Adewale carries on as a signatory to that decision it's hard to see how he can make much impact overseas outside specialist audiences for African music.

APALA/SAKARA

It was an album of apala music that first enthused one of the authors of this book about African music in the mid-1960s, and some twenty years of diligent searching for other British-based enthusiasts has so far failed to turn up more than a handful who follow the style, or its close relative sakara. Few apala or sakara bands have ever played in the West and few records of either style have been exported to specialist shops in either Britain or the USA. Regular monitoring of specialist racks will turn up examples with increasing regularity however, and the search is very well worth the effort.

Apala and sakara are traditional styles which originated in the north of Nigeria among those Yoruba people of the region who had adopted the Muslim faith. As such, both musics display a mixture of Arabic and black African ingredients: traditional drum and percussion instruments and the call-and-response vocal form from black Africa; Arabic melodic and harmonic devices in the vocal lines and arrangements. The combination is unusually powerful, with the vocals, reminiscent of the muezzin's call to prayer from the steeple of a mosque, layered over a peerlessly heavy – and profoundly black – wall of rhythm from the drums and percussion. (Of the two styles, apala is the most percussively dense, with the agidigbo hand piano and six or seven talking drummers weaving in and out of the vocal lines. Sakara has talking 'sakara' drums and a one-string fiddle known as the goje or 'Hausa violin'. Both styles use shekeres, percussion sticks and bass drums.) Yoruba speakers will be aware that ninety per cent of the lyrics are drawn from Yoruba/Muslim culture's rich heritage of proverbs and moral admonishments; while non-Yoruba speakers will simply marvel at the gravelly, rural vocal textures of the cantor and his choir.

Little-known though they may be in the West, both apala and sakara possess huge audiences in Muslim Nigeria, with most popular bandleaders turning out five or six new albums every year. The venerable Haruna Ishola, king (and by his own account, creator) of apala music, released over 300 records during his lifetime (he died in 1983), while sakara's Yusuf Olatunji can boast a similar output.

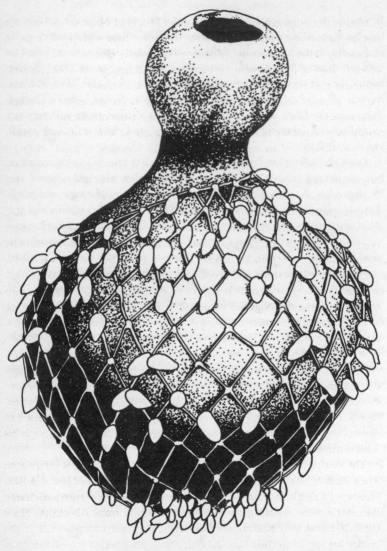

Shekere, or gourd rattle, used in fuji, juju and many other African musical forms

FUJI

A further development among the Yoruba people of Nigeria has been the rise of fuji music, which can now claim to have overtaken juju in popularity. Like apala music, from which it partly descends, fuji uses an acoustic line-up, in this case a mixture of talking drums, bata drums, bells and shekere, and a vocal style that carries a strong Islamic flavour. Fuji is popular for a variety of reasons. One is its reliance on acoustic instruments, which makes economic sense at a time of relative economic stringency. Another is its strong Islamic quality, which offers a deeper African alternative to some of juju's more Western features: churchy harmonies and electric instruments. A third is its appeal to ordinary Nigerians: fuji is predominantly a street music.

Fuji takes its wavering vocal lines from the sound of the ajiwere, an Islamic singer who wakes up the faithful each morning during the annual fast of Ramadan. In the 1960s, public contests to find the best singer revealed a new talent: Alhaji Chief Dr Sikiru Ayinde Barrister. The competitive element continued into fuji history. When he first came into the spotlight, Barrister's main rival was Ayinla Omowura, an apala singer who has been seen as an early influence on fuji. Barrister himself went into the army during the Nigerian civil war, but on his return he put together a new streamlined mixture of were music, apala and sakara which attracted further rivals. The foremost of these was Alhaji Chief Kollington Ayinla, also an army man, who avoided the religious and moral homilies of Barrister's work to concentrate on earthier subjects such as politics and corruption. In musical terms, Kollington's main contribution has been to extend the musical language of fuji, introducing, among other instruments, electric organ and drum kit, a feature that has since been used to devastating effect by a younger fuji star Wasiu Ayinde Barrister, with his Talazo disco.

The rivalry between the two elder statesmen of fuji took a bitter turn when Kollington alleged that Barrister had been responsible for Ayinla Omowura's death in a bar in 1982. A government investigation cleared Barrister's name, putting the blame on a family from Abeokuta. Since then, Barrister and Kollington have made up their differences, but the rivalry has spread to their fans. Kollington is described as the Chairman of Alatika, the name given to his less than respectable and showily dressed followers. Barrister himself is held up as a model of propriety, a fuji star who will advise about birth control, looking after the home and everyday morality, a sure sign of the spiritual importance as well as the entertainment value of this fast-rising form.

HARUNA ISHOLA

Despite his eminence in Nigeria, Alhaji Haruna Ishola Bello remains little known in the West. This was partly because he never toured outside Africa, but to a larger extent it was because the music he created — apala — is so profoundly African that it remains impenetrable to all but the most adventurous non-African listeners. But like the more recent fuji, the wholly traditional apala style commands a huge audience among Nigeria's Yoruba people, both in rural areas and in the towns, where it strikes a deep chord among recently urbanized populations with strong cultural and spiritual connections with traditional village life.

Ishola was born in 1919 into the Muslim Yoruba community, of which he remained part all his life, and to whose members he ultimately became a sort of cross between musical superstar and singing philosopher. The only formal education he ever received was in a Koranic school as a young boy, and as an adult he fathered thirty children by eight different wives. He made the pilgrimage to Mecca, so becoming an Alhaji, as soon as he acquired enough money to allow him to do so.

Ishola began recording in 1935 (aged sixteen), and his early records are stylistically extremely close to those of his maturity and the formal birth of apala in the late 1940s and early 1950s. The call-and-response vocal style, use of traditional proverbs and folklore and drum/percussion instrumentation remains unchanged, but as 78 rpm singles were replaced by albums so Ishola's songs became longer and their lyric ideas more complex. The arrival of guitars, horns and keyboards throughout most popular music in Nigeria in post-war years he regarded at best as an irrelevance, at worst a threat to the Africanness of African music. 'Anything electric is not African, but a ruse,' he once said. 'So I'll never use instruments like the guitar and other such things. The Hausas have their string instruments and they are the only authentic African string instruments available.'[4] Certainly, Ishola had no need of foreign instruments and his twelve-piece band of drummers and percussionists were able to create a staggering range of textural and rhythmic variety.

Ishola was loved and respected not only for his refusal to Westernize his band, but also for his commitment to traditional Yoruba lyric subject matter. Perhaps eighty per cent of his lyrics came from traditional folklore (with the other twenty per cent including praise songs, laments to departed contemporaries and the occasional purely topical commentary). 'I am always going closer to the elders, who are the custodians of our culture,' he explained, 'in search of more facts and ideas for songs. I would always want to say that proverbs are the mainstay of our culture and it's our duty as musicians to pass those ideas on to the oncoming generation.'

Ishola certainly achieved that aim with apala, and much of the credit for the arrival of fuji can also be given to him, for his own success created a climate of confidence about traditional musics and values among younger Nigerian musicians and audiences. Fuji stars Ayinde Barrister and Ayinla Kollington were among the mourners at Ishola's funeral, while leading juju bandleader Dele Abiodun helped carry his coffin.

Though never distributed in the West in any quantity, Ishola's records do turn up fairly regularly in specialist shops. Anyone with a taste for real African root music will find the search for them well worthwhile.

BARRISTER

In 1964, the first of the ajiwere concerts took place in Ibadan, later spreading to Mushin in Lagos. The early stars included Alhaji Dauda Epo-Akara and Monsuru Akande, the first man to record fuji at the TYC record company. Akande has been credited as the man who introduced Barrister to the music.

Lagos Weekend, a Nigerian newspaper, supplies further details.

As far back as 1964 in Ibadan, the regular port of call was Chief Adebisi's court . . . where the first known series of competitions for different ajiwere groups were staged. That was when ajiwere had meaning. People came from all over Ibadan city and they stayed glued to the spot from where they could hear songs of deep philosophy intertwined with religious renditions.[5]

Barrister went on to become the top fuji singer. He describes his music as 'a combination of sakara, as played by Olatunji Yusuf, with Haruna Ishola's apala and a bit of juju flavour. Fuji is a percussion conversation . . .'[6]

Nor is the conversation entirely percussive. Singers work with deep Yoruba proverbs, sing praise songs for wealthy clients, comment on topical events, including elections and economic programmes, and other matters of concern to all. The vitality of the various vocal and percussion forms is illustrated by an Ayinla Omowura song, 'Danfo Osiere', which deals with bad driving by the owners of the Lagos fleets of Danfo minibuses. Having weighed the evidence against Danfo, the singer concludes: 'Don't blame the bus. It's the driver that's mad.'

Salawa Abeni, a star of a women's vocal and percussion music known as waka, has achieved similar reknown for the power and pungency of her lyrics. A long quarrel with fuji star Kollington Ayinla produced attacks and counter-attacks, in which Abeni lampoons Kollington, his parents, his relatives, and other citizens from Kwara State, along with his physical shortcomings: unpleasant lips, eyes like a prawn's, and his tendency to run away with married women. A later album patched up the quarrel, as Abeni paid tribute to the late Haruna Ishola with a series of powerful traditional images: 'The earth eats everyone. Haruna Ishola was too big for the ground to swallow. When you get to heaven, don't eat earthworms or millipedes, eat what the dead people eat . . .'

The fuji revolution, a kind of musical fundamentalism, has produced a range of popular young singers and styles, among them the new Talazo disco. Its founder, Wasiu Ayinde Barrister, had been working as an apprentice for his celebrated namesake, Barrister the elder, for eight years when he decided to branch out on his own. That was in 1978.

'I realized that people needed a change,' he says. 'Kollington and Barrister have rich fans who sit down and listen to the music. They don't take the floor. My fans dance for twenty-four hours non-stop.'[7]

Barrister took his name as a mark of respect for the elder statesman of fuji. Talazo fuji came from a brand of Nigerian laxative. 'Nigerian dance music needs to purge itself,' Barrister explains. And with his own brand of patent dance music, he aims to attract not only weary Kollington fans, but also younger listeners hooked into Western funk, disco and reggae.

Fuji's big selling point is its strong African identity. 'It's a pure Nigerian music,' says Barrister. 'There is no Western influence. It may have started out as an Islamic sound, but now it's for everyone.' Other fuji artists, including the two elder statesmen, have introduced new instruments, including drum kit, even electric organ as a way of broadening the music's commercial appeal. Barrister opted for drum kit, which adds an extra rhythmic flavour to the swirling Talazo sound. But he draws the line at other improvements: 'The guitar would be all wrong. It's too Western. It just won't do.' He feels equal doubts about the electro-drums currently sweeping global dancefloors. 'Fuji artists use nothing but pure African percussion. There's no need for Linn drums. The whole thing can be done manually.'

Drum kit apart, Barrister's biggest innovation has come with his restructuring of the basic fuji line-up. In the older bands, the long talking drum provides the lead voice. For Barrister, this is not enough. It's too slow, he explains, and lacks force: 'Our fathers used those drums for relaxation.' Instead, he has brought the round sakara tension drums to the fore. The difference is primarily one of pace. The sakara drums have round, clay frames. The tone is changed not by squeezing the body of the drum but by pressing the corner of the leather skin with the palm of the hand. The result, says Barrister, is faster, heavier, more urgent. His current band makes full use of the new sound. Five sakara players handle lead, accompaniment and rhythm parts. The rest of the line-up includes a gongon talking drum for the rhythm, a twenty-four-note bell for the time-line, plus drum kit, two congas, four shekere, an agidigbo, or 'African guitar' as Barrister calls it, and small maraccas. The singers include Barrister on lead and five back-up vocalists, ranging from bass to the high-toned 'velvet' voices.

Barrister has released a succession of albums. *Talazo 84* introduced the purge. *Talazo 85* and *Talazo 86* mix injunctions to work hard with calls to come on and dance. The treatment seems to be working. As Barrister explains, 'When I started, fuji was a strictly "local" music. Now it's attracting more and more people.'

GASPER LAWAL

The popularity of fuji in west Africa, and hip hop in the West, have stimulated interest in percussion-based music. One of the leading exponents in this area is Nigerian percussionist Gasper Lawal. A hugely cosmopolitan yet at the same time deeply African stylist, Lawal – London-based since the 1960s – combines a passionate regard for African musical traditions with the firm conviction that those traditions must be encouraged to transmute, change and develop. If positive steps are not taken to encourage this process, Lawal fears that his continent's musical culture will ossify, then disappear altogether. It is a moot point whether this should be regarded as an exercise in damage limitation or as an exercise in progress.

'Traditional music changes and progresses,' says Lawal. 'Younger people take over the traditions and, while the basic formats and structures may stay the same, they introduce new ideas on top. I have respect for what man has done in the past, but at the same time I wasn't born at the time and I couldn't really feel exactly how my grandfather felt in Africa in his own time. He didn't have video, he didn't have all this information about the rest of the world. I think for the younger generation in Africa, they should come up with something a little distinctive, so that you can say, "Well, that was done at that time."'[8] With his albums *Ajomase* (1980) and *Abiosunni* (1985), recorded in London with a Nigerian-orientated yet international pool of musicians, Lawal has put forward, through his 'Afriki' music, a convincing solution to the conundrum of 'How do you update a tradition without destroying it?' Deeply rooted in ancient Nigerian instrumentation and rhythm, 'Afriki' goes on to employ recent Western innovations such as synthesizers – but treats them from a thoroughly African perspective.

Lawal is aware that indiscriminate, gung-ho adoption of non-African ideas and technology threatens Africa's culture rather than preserves it. In his music he is careful to introduce measured doses of stimulation rather than overwhelming onslaughts of gimmickry and faddishness. Black American music's recent wholesale adoption of electronic 'beat box' drum machines, for instance, is not something Lawal would like to see repeated within African music. 'Electronic music and beat boxes are lazy and limited,' he says. 'They're out of touch with the heartbeat rhythms. At the same time, disco and funk have created more awareness of rhythm in the West. What we have to do now is peel it back to the heartbeat, to the drum – which is the root of all music.'

Lawal also stresses that the global aspects of his music have come about naturally, not as part of a prearranged plan on his part. Having lived in Britain for the best part of twenty years – and having played there with a hugely diverse list of musicians, from George Clinton to Barbra Streisand, from the Rolling Stones to Steve Stills – he has participated in most forms of modern popular music. Some of those experiences made lasting impressions on him, to re-emerge later in his own music.

'I'm not just an African musician or just an English rock'n'roll musician. I just wanted to play music – with everybody. I've done sessions with jazz musicians, with folk musicians, for Indian musicians. It's been good for me to play with so many different sorts of musicians. If I hear some group of musicians playing in India I should be able to join in. I can't just tell them, "Look, I'm an African musician,

I just play drums, not tabla." I don't want to restrict myself.'

One feels that with Gasper Lawal, Africa's traditional music will produce new flowers and blossoms, but remain firmly rooted in centuries-old soil. With his the music and culture is safe — but not so safe that it won't experience, and benefit from, cautious change and sensitive experiment.

MAKOSSA

A large west African state bordered in the north by Nigeria, in the south by Gabon and Congo-Brazzaville, Cameroon has produced a strong urban music tradition which has grown up in parallel with other west and central African forms such as juju, highlife and soukous.

From the 1930s, mission schools set up their own marching bands, made up of xylophones and percussion instruments. One of their functions was to usher pupils into assembly. Outside school hours the bands also played dance musics, in a mixture of local and Western styles. Guitars and accordions made their mark around the same time. 'We didn't have any proper bands in those days,' recalls Cameroonian politician Ndeh Ntumazah. 'You'd never see a saxophone or trumpet player. Only guitarists playing a kind of highlife and accompanied by a bottle player.'[1]

Southern Cameroon, with its ports, and resultant early contacts with European traders and missionaries, saw the rise of a number of musical forms which mixed traditional and outside musics. One of the most popular was asiko, a percussion and xylophone music in which the acoustic guitar gradually took a lead role. Guitarists also joined the ambasse bey groups, who played a faster dance rhythm, and would often, like the konkomba bands in Ghana, lead dancers through the streets. Makossa was a third, equally popular, folk dance. The name comes from the verb 'kosa', to remove suddenly and roughly, the dancers' movements simulating a form of striptease. Like asiko and ambasse bey, makossa changed with the times. It became a guitar and percussion music, and absorbed flavours from highlife, rumba and merengue, which became popular with the import of the 'Spanish' records.

The fifties saw the rise of a number of nationally-known musicians who can claim to have pioneered modern Cameroonian music. The best-known were Salle John, an ambasse bey guitarist; Jean-Aladin Bikoko, one of the greatest of the asiko musicians; and guitarist Ebanda Manfred, whose acoustic group, featuring two women singers and a bottle player, laid the foundations for modern makossa. Dance bands saw a similar growth in popularity. In the early sixties, John Gassa, a trumpeter who had lived in Nigeria and worked with Rex Lawson, put together his own dance band in the chief port, Douala, mixing local rhythms with cover versions of Nigerian highlife tunes, rumbas and merengues and other dance steps, including the waltz and quickstep. It was the kind of mixture that would have been heard throughout the west African coastal towns at the time.

Makossa, still the property of Ebanda Manfred and the acoustic musicians playing in local bars, filtered into the dance-band repertoire of such sixties outfits as Black and White Jazz Orchestra, Black Styles and Los Negros. But the interest in outside music continued, as local musicians, including Manu Dibango, left to find work in Europe and nearby African states like Zaire. As Western pop and soul continued to dominate the domestic music scene, the Cameroonian government moved to reduce the amount of imported music played on national radio. This gave a further boost to makossa and other indigenous forms. A national orchestra was formed, to promote new dance musics based on traditional beats. But the biggest single spark came from Cameroonian emigré Manu Dibango who, after years of playing saxophone on some of Kinshasa's best-known rumba singles, returned home, and rode the crest of the new makossa wave with his epic 1973 hit, 'Soul Makossa'. Dibango's success paved the way for further developments: among them the arrival of a strong bass sound that puts makossa alongside mbaqanga as one of Africa's heaviest musics, and the mixture of makossa and Antillean rhythms, which reached a peak in the mid-eighties. The bass style can be traced back to Jean Dikoto Mandenge, who played with Osibisa until 1974, when he returned to Cameroon, Vicky Edimo and Aladji Toure, a pioneering producer and bass guitarist whose funk sensibilities and powers of arrangement played a crucial role in the new-look makossa of Moni Bile and Toto Guillaume. Toure spent a number of years working in the Côte d'Ivoire, where the powerful mixture of Western funk and bass-heavy roots music, from Ernesto Djedje, provided further inspiration. It was here, in 1982, that Cameroonian singer Bebe Manga recorded two songs, 'Amie' by Ebanda Manfred, and Moni Bile's 'Essele Mba', that were to establish her reputation throughout Africa and the French West Indies. Here too, Bile, with producer Aladji Toure, scored massive success with his new-look makossa hit, 'O Si Tapa Lambo Lam'.

For all its current popularity, makossa is just one style of Cameroonian music. A second dance rhythm, the makassi, has inspired crisp new arrangements from Sam Fan Thomas; the peppery rhythms of the bikoutsi feature alongside soukous in the repertoire of Les Veterans, while the mangambeu provides a popular rhythm for Pierre Didi Tchakounte and other top Cameroonian artists.

MANU DIBANGO

In the West, the birthplace of old folks' homes and the idea of voluntary euthanasia for the aged, advancing age brings with it not a greater respect from younger members of society, but their diminished respect and growing impatience. In Africa, by and large, the reverse is true, for the older a person, the wiser he or she is assumed to have become. The sense of this attitude is borne out by the person of Manu Dibango. While hardly geriatric – he was born in 1934 – he is nevertheless one of the oldest African musicians in the contemporary recording and live arenas and at the same time one of the most adventurous and forward-looking. Always catholic and unpredictable, Dibango in 1984 – aged fifty – embraced the electronic-based hiphop music of New York to cut what was for many people the most exciting African-music single of the year, the Martin Meissonnier-produced 'Abele Dance' (Celluloid). The following year he teamed up with Celluloid house producer Bill Laswell to create still more startling collisions of futuristic Western dance music and ancient African traditions, first in the all-star African/American band which made the *Deadline* album, then with his own solo album, *Electric Africa*, for the label. Surely, if anyone proves that advancing years can also bring an increase in risk-taking and experiment, it is Dibango.

Dibango's bent for cross-cultural collision and innovation was almost inevitable, for his life has been nearly equally divided between Europe and Africa, with frequent changes of residence – he is, he says, 'usually en route for somewhere else'. Born in Douala, Cameroon, he was sent to France in 1949 to complete his education, and was resident in Paris until 1956 when, by then a proficient saxophonist and classically trained pianist, he moved to Brussels. There, he played regularly at a jazz-meets-Africa club called At the Black Angels, which was pretty much his home base for the next four years. Then, in 1960, he met and joined the father of modern Zairean music, Joseph Kabasele, returning to Zaire and staying with Kabasele and his band, African Jazz, until 1963, when he returned to Cameroon to lead his own group in Douala. In 1965 Dibango went back to France, just as the soul-music explosion was hitting Europe, and basing himself once more in Paris began to play with leading French and visiting black American artists. He also led the house band on Nino Ferrer's TV chat show 'Pulsations' until 1969, and recorded his first own-name album, *Manu Dibango*, for Philips in 1968. This was followed by *O Boso* in 1971 and *Soma Coba* in 1972.

The beginnings of Dibango's big-time international breakthrough, however, came in 1971, when he returned to Cameroon. President Ahidjo commissioned Dibango to write a patriotic hymn for the Africa Cup football match to be played in Douala – and on the flip side Dibango recorded an almost throwaway instrumental called 'Soul Makossa'. He then forgot all about the song and moved to Zaire again.

It was to take two years for the 'Soul Makossa' seed to sprout, but when it sprouted, it grew fast. In 1973 a New York DJ named Frankie Crocker played the track (on Fiesta import) on station WLIB and unleashed a tidal wave of makossa fever in the city. A total of 30,000 import copies of the record were sold within the week, and twenty-three cover versions recorded within a month. Atlantic records then bought the US rights and shipped an initial 150,000 copies over from France, to tide them over until they could get their own pressings into the shops. Dibango went on to win a Gold Disc for the American sales of the record, and was nominated for the annual Grammy Award (the music business's version of the Oscar) for best R&B Instrumental Performance of the year. Similar success stories occurred all over Europe and Africa.

For the rest of the 1970s, Dibango divided his time between Paris and Douala, travelling all around Africa between times, having further singles successes ('Big Blow', 'Sun Explosion') and making a string of varied albums for various labels – most notably *Super Kumba*, *Waka Juju*, *Ceddo*, *Afrovision*, *Big Blow*, *A l'Olympia* and *Home Made*. He hooked up with the British label Island in 1980, recording two reggae-infused albums for them (*Ambassador*, *Gone Clear*), produced by Geoffrey Chung and featuring the hot-shot Jamaican rhythm team of Sly Dunbar (drums) and Robbie Shakespeare (bass).

In 1983 Dibango made the live album *Deliverance*, the with-strings *Sweet and Soft* and two solo piano albums, *Melodies Africaines* (Volumes 1 and 2), before collaborating with Meissonnier on 'Abele Dance'. The new-funk/African collisions were then further developed on the aforementioned *Deadline* and *Electric Africa* sets produced by Bill Laswell for Celluloid. Late in 1986, Dibango returned to the studio to record a new album, *Afrijazzy*, which included a Bill Laswell-produced remake of 'Soul Makossa' featuring such familiar associates as Bernie Worrell (keyboards) and D. ST (turntables).

Though the precise nature of Dibango's future recording projects has yet to be revealed, it's certain that he will continue to push back the frontiers of what is generally regarded as 'African' music. As he said in a 1984 interview: 'What's important to me about "Abele Dance", maybe more than the record itself, is the way we have tried to get out of the "ethnic music" label, to let people know that there is an electric Africa also; that people there are dealing with electricity and with computers. Our music isn't going to be only in museums any more. A few of us want to go out [of Africa] and deal with all we've got in common in this century. You have to like your roots too, of course, but every country has traditional music, not just Africa. So what! Because Africa is in the Third World, maybe people are thinking that African musicians aren't able to play pianos, synths or saxes. They want to see Africans beating tomtoms and talking drums . . . But things are changing!'

SAM FAN THOMAS AND MONI BILE

Where Manu Dibango led, others followed, with a succession of Cameroonian artists producing their own brands of highly polished, makossa music. The most prominent, code-named the Young Lions of Cameroonian music, were Toto Guillaume and Aladji Toure, both of whom worked regularly with Antillean zouk musicians based in Paris from 1980 onwards, and the two top singers and composers, Moni Bile and Sam Fan Thomas.

Thomas was born Samuel Thomas Ndonfeng in 1952 in Bafoussam in the western province of Cameroon. At the age of thirteen he took up the guitar; by the time he was eighteen, he joined Les Tigres Noires, the band led by the blind tchamassi star Andre Marie Tala. Thomas stayed with the band until 1976, playing on two of their singles, then left for Cotonou where he recorded his first album, *Funky New Bell*, with the Black Santiagos of Cotonou. He returned to Cameroon in 1977 and recorded his second album, *Special Kwongne*, back in Cotonou in 1978, before working as a studio technician on the Temba label. His third album, *Rikiaton*, appeared in 1982 followed by *Makassi*, whose stunning 'African Typic Collection' established his reputation. Although the first flush of its popularity has passed, 'African Typic Collection', with its acoustic guitar framework and medley of African dances, from the tchamassi to kavacha and the makossa, remains a remarkable piece of work; its crisp central melodies leading into a beautiful chanted extract from an OK Jazz song, 'Boma L'Heure'. But it is not typical Sam Fan Thomas. Away from the polished acoustic swing of 'Typic Collection' his more normal approach is to fill all available space with tight guitar patterns and relentless hand-held percussion, reminiscent of the zouk musicians with whom Thomas has worked since the early 1980s.

Bile has taken a different route. Where Thomas introduces the kavacha into his music, Bile goes for biguine. Thomas contracts his sound into a tight, polished, sweep of synthesizers, mixed-down horns and percussion; Bile lets the arrangements flow, expanding into lavish productions that set off his nasal, highly individual voice.

Part of the credit must go to his arranger and producer Aladji Toure, a bass player and pillar of the Cameroonian community in Paris. 'Bile sings about suffering and love,' he says. 'But I don't think that his voice on its own is enough. It needs something to make the sound fuller, more sentimental.'

Bile was born in Douala in Cameroon in 1957, learnt bass guitar and moved to Abidjan in 1979 to make his first record, *Nganda Tumba*, which was released on the Société Ivoirienne de Son. Moving to Paris, he took up with Toure and released a clutch of albums. The first, *Bijou*, appeared in 1982. It was followed by *O Si Tapa Lambo Lam*, and *Chagrin d'Amour. Tout ça c'est la Vie*, his 1985 extravaganza, took his full arrangements to new and lavish heights. Shortly afterwards, Bile parted company with producer Aladji Toure – a schism which took some of the sap and confidence out of his following albums. By the time of *Makossa Ambiance*, Bile sounded best when he kept his arrangements simple.

Bile's new-look makossa has several different elements: the basic makossa rhythm that developed in Douala in the 1960s, mixed with traces of biguine in the congas and bells, and a Zairean rhythm, the kavacha in the kit drums. The result carries a greater, richer percussion sound than does Zairean music, although it lacks the latter's distinctive changes of tempo. 'New look uses one rhythm, it's true,' says Bile, 'but the arrangements have been worked out to give greater variety. The bass lines change within the rhythm. The bass gives punch. It's one of the tricks of new-look makossa. Some of the percussion changes too. It's designed to stimulate the dancers.'[2]

The new-look sound created a boom in central and west Africa in 1984, when Bile and Thomas played at a makossa concert in Abidjan. 'It's a massacre,' said Bile. 'Everywhere it's makossa, in Gabon, central Africa, Zaire. Why not?'

Part of the attraction undoubtedly comes from its novelty – the sudden appearance of a likely contender for the throne currently occupied by Zairean music. The rest comes down to the work that actually goes into the new music. As any makossa musician will confirm, the Cameroonians read music; they are keen to develop their own sounds. 'Soukous is always around,' says Bile, 'but makossa is on a different technical level. We've done a lot of research, adding extra singers, guitar parts and rhythms. Soukous stands still. If you want a music that moves, it's makossa.'

The music has come a long way. 'Twenty years ago there was folklore makossa,' says Bile. 'This developed. Manu contributed. So did Ekambi Brillant. But the father of makossa? I can't say. Makossa has many children. The father is tradition . . .'

MALI AND GUINEA

Mali and Guinea, along with Senegal and The Gambia, were once part of a single, massive Mali empire which reached its peak in the fourteenth century. One of the most vital surviving aspects of this ancient and thriving culture is the music of a caste of musicians such as the Konte, Kouyate and Diabate families, who have passed their skills on down the centuries. In Mandinka, the musicians are known as jalis, in French griots; their original job was to preserve oral history, including stories of famous kings and battles; to sing praises; sometimes to advise the rulers themselves. Many modern musicians, including Mory Kante and Ousmane Kouyate, belong to ancient musical castes. The typical instruments were, and remain, the kora, a large harp; the konting, a small lute; and the balafon, which resembles a wooden xylophone. Until independence, a deep gulf existed between the ancient music of the griots and the new styles and fashions, for the most part Western in origin, that were developing in the cities. The rise of a modern, tradition-based music in Senegal and The Gambia is examined on pp.116–19. The original impetus for the whole region, however, came from Guinea.

The first signs came with the independence of Guinea in 1958. Other Francophone leaders, like Leopold Senghor of Senegal and Houphouet-Boigny of the Côte d'Ivoire, maintained strong links with France; but not Sékou Touré and his colleagues. They preferred 'independence in poverty to riches in slavery' and embarked on a plan that would lead to African unity and 'total decolonization'.

Touré's cultural revolution put a strong emphasis on the rediscovery and rehabilitation of Guinea's music, arts and dance. Before independence, an open-door policy had attracted an influx of music from France and North and Latin America. In the capital, Conakry, Guinean musicians played waltzes, foxtrots and Latin dance music. The names of the bands, La Douce Parisette, L'Africana Swing Band, Le Harlem Jazz Band and Les Joviales Symphonies, speak loudly for themselves. After independence, Guinea cut itself off decisively from the West. According to the Ministry of Culture, 'One of the first things the party had to do was to disband a plethora of dance orchestras and vocal groups in vogue under the colonial regime . . . Musicians and other performers were asked to return to authentic African rhythms and tunes.' The first step was the creation of a national band, the Syli National Orchestre. The second was

Balafon, a wooden xylophone which is found in many forms throughout Africa and offers a continuing inspiration for musicians throughout Mali, Guinea and Senegal to encourage further talent. A traditional choir was set up. The radio was directed to broadcast authentic Guinean music. From 1962, Touré's government sponsored the first of its biennial national festivals, which attracted bands from different parts of the country and became the focus of an emerging, new Guinean music. The first winners were the Syli Orchestre. In 1964 Bembeya Jazz took the prize, and they repeated this feat in 1966, when they became the National Orchestre.

The growth of a new national music depended to an extent on outside influences and for Guinea, indeed Mali, two of these influences were crucial. One came from Ghana, with which Guinea and Mali had created a pan-African union in 1959. The result was a flow of diplomats, white-collar workers and musicians between the three countries; the net musical result was a new interest in Ghanaian highlife. In 1958, E.T. Mensah and his Tempos Band played in Conakry and from around that time, highlife rhythms with lyrics in local languages provided a further inspiration for many of the emerging bands. It is interesting to note that one of Bembeya Jazz's greatest hits, 1973's 'Mammy Watta', used the classic Ghanaian yaa amponsah rhythm.

The second main 'contact' music, traces of which can still be heard in the horn arrangements of Guinean and Malian music, came from Latin America. The door may have closed on Western music in 1958, but as far as Afro-Cuban music went, it was still very much open, so much so that, after Bembeya Jazz won their first gold medal, they were sent to Cuba. In going there, they were following in the footsteps of Les Maravillas de Mali, who had been sent on a musical study trip the previous year. The fruits of their study can be heard on an album of boleros, son montunos and cha chas, where Latin rhythms underpin songs in praise of African freedom and the murdered Congolese leader Patrice Lumumba.

The Guinean government also looked to audiences nearer home, setting up a national ballet under the direction of Keita Fodeba, which toured neighbouring countries and promoted the setting-up of other national dance troupes. By the mid-sixties a number of top Guinean bands were playing authentic music based on different regional folk rhythms. The key modernizers included Keletigui and his Tambourinis and Balla et ses Balladins, both of whom had split from the Syli Orchestre. In line with the government policy of promoting women's rights, the national police force had also set up its all-women Orchestre Feminin de la Gendarmerie Nationale, an acoustic band whose line-up included dry guitar, mandolin, violin and cello. In 1965, Les Amazones, as they had now become, took on electric instruments and started on a series of local tours that would later stretch to Zaire, Senegal and Tanzania.

The new bands shared a number of crucial characteristics, from the falling wavering melody lines and traditional rhythm patterns of the old music to the cascading ripples of the kora and balafon accompaniments which were now duplicated on electric guitars. The link with the traditional music of the jalis lived on, too, in the songs themselves, many of which had been played by the earlier, acoustic musicians.

In Mali, local musicians became the flag bearers of Modibo Keita's socialist revolution. On national radio, traditional kora players and large modern bands playing highlife hybrids praised the revolution, celebrated the departure of the French and the union with Guinea. They also called for hard work. In 1970, two years after Keita's fall from power, the new government started to sponsor local bands, the first being the Rail Band, which played regularly in the buffet of the (Station) Hotel de la Gare in the capital, Bamako. The Rail Band proved vital to the growth of a modern Malian music, drawing together a range of talents from vocalists Mory Kante and Salif Keita to guitarist Kante Manfila, an acoustic musician now a key figure in the development of electric music. For all three, the Rail Band was a vital stepping-stone. Three years later, Keita left, with Manfila, to join Les Ambassadeurs in the Côte d'Ivoire; Kante was later to develop the kora into a modern lead instrument at the front of an all-electric band. The age of the electro-griot was born, bands like Super Biton and Super Djata developing new music from the ancient songs and rhythms of the area.

Traditional players have also adapted to changing times. Singers like the operatic Fanta Damba command enormous respect, her cassettes selling by the thousand. The old concept of praise singing and patronage continues, but now the singers praise businesspeople as much as royalty, and receive Mercedes cars, houses and fabulous jewellery in return. Traditional instrumentation has also changed with the times, not just through electric players like Mory Kante, but a range of musicians who use acoustic, sometimes even electric guitars instead of, or alongside, the old kora and balafon. Nor should one expect centuries-old subject matter. During their 1986 London gigs, the great Malian griots Ousmane Sacko and Yiakare Diabate switched from ancient accounts of war and warriors to songs about modern fashion, and Apollo gowns, created at the time of the American space mission. A sign of the times, and equally a sign of a tradition that is both alive and vibrant.

BEMBEYA JAZZ

The story of modern Guinean music goes back to Sékou Touré and his cultural revolution in the fifties. A ban on imported music and the state sponsorship of local bands created a new flowering of modern folk culture. The blossoms were recorded on Syli-Phone, the state-owned record company which handled record production and sales.

Syli-Phone's roster covered the six national bands and a prodigious range of music from every part of the country. Horoya National Band, formed in 1965, ranged from savanna rumbas, the deep sounds of Haute Guinée, to the tentemba, a further rhythm brought to life with wa-wa pedals. Balla et ses Balladins reworked melodies from acoustic solo guitarists, plus songs like 'Bambo' which had been originated with the National Ballet Company while, on the 1980 *Gon Bia Bia*, Le Nimba de N'Zerekore put into big-band form the rhythms associated with age-old initiation ceremonies. And all the bands, from Horoya to Camayenne Sofa, sung the praises of Guinea and its late president, Sékou Touré.

Such sentiments have been the stock in trade of Guinea's best-known band, the prodigious and flamboyant Bembeya Jazz. Their early work reverberated to the praise of Touré. The flow remained unstinted through the seventies as the band, acting in its role as official state musicians, produced lyrics like 'Ahmed Sékou Touré, you are honest, you are good, you are the person that Guinea needs.' Bembeya came together in Beyla in 1961 and went on to become Guinea's national band in 1966. The title was fitting, not only because of the dazzling musical arrangements and the showmanship that made virtually the whole of west Africa stop in its tracks, but also for its strong roots in local culture. 'Bembeya play folk music,' says journalist Louis Auguste Leroy. 'They represent the authenticity of Guinean culture, the music of the balafon, the kora, the tam tam.'[3]

The band's first hit, 'Ballake', celebrated a Guinean freedom fighter from colonial times. From there, they went on to become one of Africa's great bands. Their reputation rested on musical excellence, their mix of roots percussion, mesmerizing traditional-based guitars, and dazzling big-band arrangements, and partly on their own personalities. Singer Aboubacar Demba Camara established himself as one of the great African singers. In Guinea, he was known as Temtemba Demba, the tentemba rhythm being one of his great specialities. Guitarist Sekou Diabate, a flamboyant person on and off the stage, added further sparks to the band's unique chemistry. From the late sixties, they were known and loved throughout west Africa.

The death of Aboubacar Demba Camara in a car crash in 1973 seemed, to many Bembeya fans, a terminal blow. After a recess, Bembeya took on three new singers, the Trio Ambiance from Tazouka, and carried on with their historic role. 'Before independence the local orchestras just copied other people's music,' says Diabate. 'They did Cuban and Latin American music. Bembeya played all that. Syli Orchestre brought in the true Guinean folklore. And we took it to new levels. Other countries followed our example, abandoning other music in favour of their own folklore. Bembeya opened the door.'

Sekou Diabate is a person who attracts superlatives: the 'Hendrix of Africa' and 'Diamond Fingers', bestowed after the 1977 FESTAC festival, when he was voted top African guitarist. 'My family are traditional musicians,' he says. 'My father plays the balafon, and the dry guitar. I started out playing the balafon but also listened to the guitar. In 1959, Papa Diabate, from Syli Orchestre, taught me the electric guitar. He was the best guitarist in Guinea.'[4]

From there, Diabate developed his own style, based partly on Western chords and progressions, partly on Guinean roots music. 'Our guitarists play two main styles,' he says. 'Balafon style and kora. I mix the two.' Many of Bembeya's greatest songs spring from the Diabate fretboard. ' "Mammy Watta": I wrote that with Aboubacar Camara. It was a well-known traditional song. We added to it, improved on it. "Whisky Soda", it's highlife, yes Ghanaian highlife. "Yekeke" (a song also played by Mory Kante) is a traditional song, from the Malinke people. It's about women who go around à l'ais, to please men. "Solio Wassoulou" is another Malinke song. One of our best known. The BBC chose it as the best African song of 1977.'

Diabate explains further the range and depth of Bembeya's music. 'Mandinka is the best language for music. But we also do forest music, the songs of the Peule, and the Soso. The kora is a Mandinka instrument, so is the balafon. The Peule go for calabashes, flutes and African violins; the Soso, the balafon and the tam tam.' With the instruments come a range of regional rhythms: the yankadi-papou from Basse Guinée, the yole and the kebendo from the forest regions. Bembeya play them all.

For much of Sékou Touré's presidency, Guinea remained closed to the West. Links with the Communist countries were encouraged; those with the West cut off. In the sixties, Bembeya played in Cuba. After Touré's death, in 1984, they turned their attention to Europe, playing an astounding gig at London's Africa Centre and releasing a set of Paris-recorded albums which gave a new crispness to their peppery, big-band arrangements. On 'Telegramme', Bembeya harnessed the electro-drum to the rippling Guinean arrangements. They went on to release *Yekeke* and *Moussokoro*, whose most beautiful track, 'Yelema Yelemaso', sung the praises of a gallery of deceased African stars, from Ernesto Djedje to Dr Nico and, one of the greatest of them all, Bembeya's own Aboubacar Demba Camara.

Other musicians, alongside Bembeya Jazz, have made their mark in Europe. Les Amazones de Guinea, a band made up of policewomen, have recorded a live French album, *A Coeur de Paris*. Super Biton, a harder-hitting Malian band, have trodden a similar path, basing their tough relentless music on traditional Bambara rhythms. Among the other artists to have established a reputation overseas, Super Djata play a particularly relentless form of Malian music, while Ali Farka Toure plays a mesmerizing acoustic music using guitars and percussion.

One of Mali's most astonishing musicians is Salif Keita, the albino singer who made his name with Les Ambassadeurs.

SALIF KEITA

'I come from a noble family. We are not supposed to become singers. If a noble had anything to say, he had to say it through a griot.' Thus, Salif Keita.[5]

'Salif caused a revolution. He was the first Keita to sing in public. Normally when a Keita talks he doesn't address himself directly to the public; he has to do so through a griot who repeats his proposals, adding a little salt. Now we have a Keita standing up and speaking to a thousand people. Salif bypassed the problem. And thanks to him we have all become free.'[6]

Salif Keita was born in Mali in 1949. His family are one of the oldest and most noble families in the region. They can trace their descent directly back to Soundjata Keita, who founded the Mali empire in 1240.

Originally Keita wanted to become a teacher, but unemployment was high, so he decided on music. In other countries, musicians are occasionally thought of as dissolute, irresponsible; in Mali, for the son of a royal family to go into a job that was traditionally the preserve of other, lower castes, was virtually unthinkable.

111

His decision caused a storm. He was dismissed from school, and formed a trio with his brother, playing in Bamako nightclubs. By now, Salif had become a skilled performer of traditional music. 'When I was young, the griots came to my house just to sing and praise me,' he says. The music had got into his blood.

In 1970, Keita was asked to join the Rail Band, playing in the buffet of the Station Hotel in Bamako. Three years later, he switched to Les Ambassadeurs, who were playing what he considered to be a more modern music, with a greater range of outside influences. 'I thought if I mixed traditional folklore with the new stuff the Ambassadeurs were playing, I'd break my sound internationally.' Between 1973 and 1978, Les Ambassadeurs recorded five albums and two singles, representing a marriage of old and new musics. The reception was moderate. The band decided to look outside Mali, with its limited studio facilities, for the brighter lights of Abidjan which soon reverberated to a new name: Les Ambassadeurs International.

Keita's reputation today rests on a selection of classic cuts over a music powered by horns, keyboards and electric guitars which carry the inflections of kora and balafon music. In 1980 Keita took three Ambassadeurs and recorded a modern hi-tech album, *Wassolon-Foli*, in the United States. Local musicians were hired; none could grasp the complexities of the Malian rhythms. The drummer was forced to record each drum separately. The result offered a reasonable collection of deep folklore and electric reggae, but it compared poorly with tracks like 'Prim Prim', an invocation to follow parental advice, or the classic late-1970s 'Mandjou', which praises the late President of Guinea, Sékou Touré, and his ancestors, among them Mandjou himself. In return, Keita became an Officer of the National Order of Guinea. 'Mandjou''s backing includes a rippling guitar from Kante Manfila, a muted trumpet which eases 'Summertime' into the circular and hypnotic rhythms, and balafon from Kaba Kante. By any standards, 'Mandjou' is an epic. From Paris, critic Phil Ekwengi wrote: '"Mandjou" is a Mandinka hymn, the undisputed masterpiece of Les Ambassadeurs du Motel de Bamako, the most perfect synthesis of traditional Malian rhythms and the electric sound. On this album, Salif Keita justifies, almost insolently, the title "Domingo (Lord) of African Song" which the crowds have bestowed upon him.'[7]

Keita's music, with its astonishing vocals and traditional feel, has echoed throughout west Africa — and further afield. In 1984, he set up a base in France. For many listeners, the music is a prime example of modernized traditional forms. For Keita, it is part of a lifelong struggle against the forces that are ranged against him: his responsibilities as a noble and his albino skin.

In Africa, albinos attract varying degrees of abuse. Some societies banished, even sacrificed them; others credited them with supernatural powers. Leaders like Sékou Touré survived with an albino skin, claims Keita, with considerable help from fetish priests.

Today Keita makes little of his skin colour, using his music to speak directly to fellow-albinos, to prove that they can be successful despite the burden of discrimination placed on them. His own feelings have changed. 'I stopped feeling different when I became a musician,' he says. 'The people then realized that I was an artist.'

Art has also helped him to break free from the rigid confines of the caste system, which distributes good and bad according to one's position in society: 'For me, nobility can only be achieved through art. Whether you go to heaven or hell depends on your way of life in society. It doesn't matter whether you come from a poor or a noble family. I happen to be descended from Soundjata. But I also believe that all people are equal.' For Keita, finding a balance has been difficult. One of his uncles explains: 'Salif sings ancient songs. We know that he makes records, that he sings somewhere else, but we would not tolerate that in the village. In his own village, he keeps his noble bearing. For example, he cannot associate with women of other castes, the women of griots, blacksmiths, of jewellers. He cannot fall in love with them.' Salif's father, like all the family, loves what his son does – for Salif infringes only the rule that forbids a noble to sing, respecting all the others.

Keita himself sees the tensions in a different light: 'At home, we are traditionalists. It's an attitude I disapprove of. It's we who make the history, and if we refer only to what has passed, there will be no history. I belong to a century that has little in common with the time of my ancestors. I want society to move, so that a griot can become a noble, or the other way round – that a Keita becomes an artist.'

In 1987, Keita applied similar independence of mind to his own musical history. An astonishing rock-flavoured album, recorded on a forty-eight-track machine in Paris and boasting two keyboard arrangers, *Soro*, delivered a sharp blow to those who still believed that Africa was synonymous with unchanging traditionalism. The following year, Keita was signed to Island records.

MORY KANTE

The buffet of the Station Hotel in Bamako is a local landmark, offering both a resting-place before and after a journey and a place of entertainment where resident bands serenade travellers as they step off the train after the long haul from Dakar in Senegal.

It was in one of Mali's top bands, the Rail Band, that kora player Mory Kante made his first moves in a career that would lead him to create a new synthesis of Western music and the traditional instruments and rhythms of the Mandinka people.

Kante was born in Kissidougou, Guinea, in 1950. His family were well-known musicians: both his parents were griots; his brother Kante Facely played guitar for the ballet of Keita Fodeba, and was one of the first men to transpose traditional material on to the instrument. Kante Manfila of Les Ambassadeurs is his brother; so is the other Kante Manfila, of Balla et ses Balladins.

As with all griots, Mory Kante's training started early: at seven, he was sent to Mali to stay with his aunt, Maman Ba Kamissoko, to study the ancient arts. At fifteen, he left to sing with the Rail Band in Bamako, which fused electric and griot music. During his seven years with the band, Kante recorded the celebrated epic of Mandinka history, *L'Exil de Soundjata, le Fondateur de l'Empire Mandingue*. By 1977, the economic situation had made life difficult for local musicians, and Kante left, with fellow-Rail Band and Ambassadeurs musicians, to find a living in Abidjan.

His approach was radical from the start. Where other modernizers put traditional music into an electric format, Kante created a virtually new language for the kora, creating a sound that would blend with electro-funk, reggae and soul. This took considerable research. Before releasing *Courougnegne* in 1981, an album that he describes as 'kora funk', Kante spent two years working solidly on the project. Since then, he has released further explorations into kora music: among them *Mory Kante à Paris*, an album designed to attract a modern audience and to restore African music to what he considers its rightful place at the forefront of modern culture.

Kante sees African music as the heart of a triangular commerce that started when the slaves were snatched from their birthplace: 'The slaves lost their dignity and their personalities, but they didn't lose their culture. This has spread and developed in different ways. The essential part stayed in Africa; now history has taken its course.

African music, taken from black Africa, is coming to the fore.'

Kante is a griot of the electric age. In the old days, he would have been playing the acoustic kora, singing about families and historical struggles. Today, he has a new message, about African culture and its often overlooked part in the development of Western music, from salsa to breakdance. He uses technological gadgetry to spread the message, but it is also a question of staying abreast of developments. 'We must be able to exchange ideas with the rest of the world,' he says. 'If Africa's to be accepted, it's got to keep up with the rest.'[8]

Kante was as good as his word. By mid 1988, his futuristic album *Akwaba Beach* was lodged in the French album charts, while the single, 'Yé Ké Yé Ké' reached the top ten both in France and Holland.

SENEGAL AND THE GAMBIA

As a result of a quirk of colonialism, The Gambia is almost entirely surrounded by Senegal. Wolof and Mandinka people inhabit both countries, and the modern music that has developed since the 1970s is deeply rooted in the jali tradition associated with both groups. Modern Senegambian music, the sound of Youssou N'Dour, Super Diamono, Ifang Bondi and Orchestre Baobab, owes its existence partly to the ancient music of the kora, balafon and talking drum and partly to the Afro-Cuban sounds that rocked west Africa in the 1940s and 1950s. The bands of that time, such as Sor Jazz and St Louisien Jazz, concentrated on rumbas, marches and waltzes, played for an elite audience who looked to France, rather than Africa, for fashion, music and lifestyle. Perhaps the best-known musician was Grand Diop, who fronted the Orchestre de Grand Diop and had his own nightclub, the Moulin Rouge, in Dakar. But it was a second club, the Miami, which was to take Senegalese music back to its African roots. The owner, Ibra Kasse, attracted a range of talented musicians who had previously played in one of the city's top outfits, the Guinea Band. Among them were Dexter Johnson, a Nigerian horn player whose name suggests the popularity of American jazz and its exponents and, from Liberia, saxman Bob Armstrong. In 1960, Armstrong and Johnson, plus guitarist Jose Ramos, Mady Konate and Mbaye Mabousso, joined Kasse's new Star Band, formed to celebrate the independence of Senegal.

Throughout the 1950s and 1960s, Cuban and American music ruled Senegal's nightspots. The craze spread to neighbourhood choirs, whose repertoire often embraced localized versions of the latest Cuban hits. As a contemporary observer recalled, 'Before a play, we had unaccompanied choirs who'd sing Spanish words to songs like "The Peanut Vendor". Quite often they wouldn't understand the words. By the 1970s they were still singing the songs, although by then they had switched from Spanish to Senegalese languages.'[9]

This wasn't the only change that had taken place. By 1966, the cultural revolution that had taken place in nearby Guinea had sparked a new interest in authentic African music rather than its imported counterpart. In Guinea, government sponsorship, with the rush of new bands and cultural troupes, served as a model for other countries. Among them was Senegal, the scene of a massive black arts festival in 1966.

One of the first Senegalese artists to record was Laba Sose, a member of the Star Band. His 'Sayni' appeared in 1965, but it was hardly a new sound, more a slow pachanga with the words in Spanish. When the Star Band broke up, Sose, Dexter Johnson and singer Papa Sec went to the Côte d'Ivoire to set up Super Star. Sose later formed the Vedettes band, and travelled to Upper Volta and The Gambia.

In 1971 Senegalese music took a further step forward with the formation of Orchestre Baobab. The band's two most prominent musicians were Issi Cissokho, a saxophone pupil of Dexter Johnson, and Laye M'Boup. One of the pioneers of his country's music, M'Boup was a traditional musician who believed that Senegalese music should be Senegalese: as a result, the band introduced Wolof songs, while Cissokho, a Mandinka, introduced a second stream of music into the band. The mixture of Wolof and Mandinka musicians and rhythms made Baobab unique. They started with Western instruments, but it was left to Kasse and his new intake of musicians at the Miami Club to introduce typically African pieces, the most crucial being the tama, the small talking drum. A second popular group, Waatoo Sita, brought acoustic guitar, balafon and kora music, a true Mandinka sound, to well-to-do audiences.

Further impetus came from The Gambia where, in 1973, the celebrated Super Eagles switched from highlife and covers of Western hits like 'Tobacco Road' and 'Hey Jude', took a Mandinka name, Ifang Bondi, and switched their rhythm section from kit drums to a battery of Senegambian instruments including the sabar, a long conga, and the tama. They were also the first band in the region to use electric organ. 'The Ifang Bondi sound started it,' says Senegalese diplomat Abdoulaye Kebe. 'People went mad when they heard it. Before that, bandleaders used to despise griots and players of traditional instruments. Now they would run behind the griots and say, "Please come and join our band." '[10]

After the dissolution of the old Star Band, Kasse formed a new, hotter outfit, Star Band Number One, which included many of the younger generation of Senegalese musicians such as vocalist Pap Sec, Mugatte Niang and one of the creators of modern Senegalese music, Youssou N'Dour. The new band still played Latin rhythms, but as the 1970s progressed, they turned increasingly to local rhythms, powered by dynamic vocals and a rhythm section that used the tama virtually as a lead instrument. By now, Senegalese music was reaching a crucial phase. Folklore was increasingly popular. The musicians, many of whom had been brought up on Hendrix and Santana, were rediscovering their own heritage, and adding traditional players, above all talking drummers, to

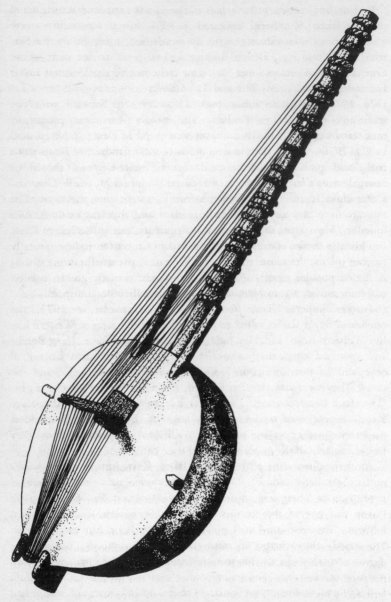

Kora, a harp-lute played traditionally by the jalis or griots, now incorporated into electric music by such artists as Mory Kante

their line-ups. Most, but not all of the bands concentrated on praise songs, celebrating national leaders, local dignatories or figures in history. The first man to introduce new subjects was Ouza, a revolutionary artist, who after fronting Las Hondas, broke away to write songs about Senegalese social issues, neo-colonialism and the fate of Senegal under French rule. One of his best-known numbers celebrates the warrior Lat Dior. Another describes a massacre carried out by the French near Dakar, while a third deplores the random, and, to Ouza's eyes, irresponsible use that was being made of the tama by the new Senegalese bands.

The 1970s saw the rise of a number of such bands, the best-known being Youssou N'Dour's Etoile de Dakar, and Super Diamono, which has boasted such talents as Ismael Lo and current vocalists Moussa N'Gom and Omar Pene. In 1978, N'Dour cemented his reputation as a traditionalist by reworking Senegal's mbalax percussion music into electric form. Like most modern Senegalese bands, N'Dour's rechristened Super Etoile capture the flow and the resonance of traditional music, using guitars to capture the sound of kora or balafon and, in the early days at least, relying on the fuzz box to give the kind of blurred or 'dirty' tone favoured by most players of traditional instruments. Through the efforts of Super Etoile and the more commercial Toure Kunda, Senegalese music has become known outside Africa.

YOUSSOU N'DOUR

The growth of modern Senegalese music developed around a cluster of top bands. In Europe, the best-known are Super Diamono and Super Etoile de Dakar, led by the young and charismatic Youssou N'Dour. Both have made their name with a repertoire of roots rhythms from the different regions of Senegal.

N'Dour has a fascinating history. He was born in the Medina district of Dakar, the son of Ndeye Sokhna Mboup, herself a well-known traditional musician, who gave him his first grounding in traditional Wolof music. The relationship provided him with his early inspiration, but later with a degree of frustration when his detractors, amazed at N'Dour's youthful prowess, insisted that certain of his lyrics were not his own, but had been written by his mother. That, however, was long after N'Dour's reputation had been confirmed.

'It's true, my mother was a great inspiration,' he says. 'In the house

119

where I was brought up, people played tam tams, and traditional guitars. I started music young, singing on holidays and feasts and circumcisions. People encouraged me to continue.'[11]

N'Dour's first public performances came with two local music and theatre troupes, including Sine Dramatic, which he joined in 1972, at the age of twelve. The following year, he made his first public appearance with a modern band, singing with Orchestre Diamono at a concert in St Louis. In 1975, he toured The Gambia with the band, returning after his parents complained; the following year, he took the first steps in a career that would establish him as one of Senegal's greatest musical pioneers, joining the Star Band, a resident band set up by Ibra Kasse, owner of Dakar's Miami Club. 'He was an important influence,' says N'Dour. 'He provided instruments for the musicians. There was really nowhere else to go.'

Before the Star Band, the musicians based at the Miami Club had swung to pachanga, with the lyrics usually sung in Spanish. 'We did a lot of numbers by Aragon, Broadway and Pacheco,' remembers N'Dour. 'Plus other Latin numbers like the "Rumba Ultima". But we also started doing folklore and when we did, I took over as singer.' One of the great innovations of the time was the introduction of the tama or small talking drum into the music. N'Dour says the actual process was gradual, that no one band took the lead. Baobab and Orchestre Le Sahel shared the same mix of Cuban rhythms, with a steady increase in the use of home-based Wolof rhythms. 'The tama was vital as a lead instrument,' he asserts. 'In Nigeria, they use it as an accompaniment. With us, it's like a lead voice, it makes people dance, burst into action.'

By 1979, N'Dour had left the Star Band, and set up Etoile de Dakar, which in 1982 he re-formed as Super Etoile de Dakar. One other musician came with him: Assane Thiam, a traditional tama player who played a vital part in the creation of the Etoile sound. Mbalax in its original state is a percussion rhythm played throughout Wolof-speaking Senegal. Its accompanying dance is called the ndaga. To the tough, rural music, N'Dour added a range of modern instruments: a base of rolling, almost flamenco-like guitars, from which the talking drum explodes, along with fuzz-box guitar solos, inspired perhaps by the excesses of Western rock but offering, more significantly, a distinctively blurred or 'dirty' tone. The use of modern instruments was vital. 'The problem with the old instruments, the kora and the xalam, is that they are limited,' explains N'Dour. 'They can be played in a small number of different keys. On kora, you can play only two, on others, just one. You end up playing the same range of notes. It's interesting, but monotonous, as if you are always playing the same piece. With guitars, we can use different keys and chords, while keeping the traditional flavour of the music.'

The mbalax drum sound carried on as before. Etoile de Dakar used a total of seven traditional drums, from the ndende and the tunguna to gorong, the bougarabu and the mbung-mbung, one of the most common instruments in the non-electric form of mbalax. Each drum continues the traditional role, while N'Dour transferred further drum parts to the guitars and keyboards.

Slowly the sound developed. Ten cassettes, starting with *Tabaski* in 1981, showed an increasing fullness and power of arrangement. The subjects ranged from folk tales to celebrations of life in Dakar, the problems faced by migrants to the cities. *Tabaski* itself celebrates a Muslim festival. According to *Africa Beat*, the band enliven the soundtrack with 'sounds of the innocent sheep bleating to the slaughter'.[12]

In Senegal, N'Dour's reputation as a new-age griot increased. His prowess as a praise singer attracted the wealthy and famous to his concerts, while the presence in the band of Ouzin Ndiaye, who comes from a long line of traditional musicians, added further to the band's mastery of traditional Senegalese music. Outside Senegal, his music achieved wider dispersal with the release of two classic albums, *Immigrés*, on Celluloid, and *Nelson Mandela*, the appearance of which, in 1986, fleshed out the skeletal mbalax of transitional albums like *Mouride* and *Talou Badou Ndiaye* with rich new arrangements and synthesizers.

One of the greatest surprises was Etoile's rerecording of an old seventies soul classic, 'Rubber Band Man' by the Detroit Spinners. At first this seemed a perverse return to the copyright material that Senegalese musicians had so recently renounced. Until, that is, N'Dour broke from the English to Wolof to urge, 'Let's tell the world about mbalax. Europeans love it. But we love it more. If I say mbalax, it's Etoile de Dakar who are playing. If I meet you, you'll forget what I told you. But if we meet again, you'll surely dance for me. You'll never hear a sound like mbalax.' 'I recorded that song because I'd always liked it,' N'Dour says. 'We were rehearsing and I suggested doing "Rubber Band Man". The rest of the band liked it. One day, while we were recording the album, we found we were one number short. So we did "Rubber Band Man", singing partly in English. It was a good way of helping the public discover my music.'[13]

Other songs rooted N'Dour's music deeper into Senegalese society.

'Nelson Mandela' was written to convey the truth about South Africa to rural listeners, many of whom would be unable to read newspaper accounts. 'Sabar', released on cassette in 1986, describes a traditional dance, the wundelow, while a song from the same period discusses the people of Youssou's home, Medina. In colonial times, Medina was designated as a 'native quarter' and still bears something of a stigma. 'Don't believe what you hear about the people of Medina,' sings N'Dour. 'We're the real people of Dakar, you can tell us by the way we walk.' At this point on stage, the band usually walk around with their hands clasped behind their backs.

N'Dour started 1987 in good shape. An American tour with Peter Gabriel had been a resounding success. He'd been described as a Michael Jackson under African skies. And he'd returned with an Akai sampler, with which to record, and further explore the traditional sounds of Senegal. The following year he was signed to Virgin records.

SUPER DIAMONO DE DAKAR

As Youssou N'Dour spreads his name throughout Europe and the States, Super Diamono, his hottest competition at home, have joined the global running with a 1987 album called *People*. The two sounds could hardly be more different. Where N'Dour's mbalax music features frenetic rhythms, loud bursts of talking drum and time signatures of mind-boggling complexity, Super Diamono adopt a leaner, more powerful approach, keyed around heavy bass and murderous kit drums.

Super Diamono were founded in 1975. Like other bands of the time, they played Afro-Cuban music, with songs by Pacheco, Broadway and Aragon, before creating their own brand of Senegalese music. The stimulus came from a two-year expedition through rural Senegal. 'We wanted to reach the deep roots of our civilization, to find our own culture,' says bass guitarist and chef d'orchestre Bob Sene. 'By going to the source, we were able to discover the true sonorities of our music.' In 1977, the band returned to Dakar with the fruits of their work. Among the early albums, *Ndaxona* is remarkable for its wailing vocals from lead singer Omar Pene, rasping guitars and roots-flavoured horn charts. Diamono then introduced traditional percussion instruments into the line-up, not the tama, which became the trademark of other Senegalese bands, but the larger free-standing drum known as the sabar. 'The tama is not important,' says Sene. 'What the tama does, the sabar can do equally well. In Senegalese folklore, we use any number of tam tams, one for the rhythm, others for bass and accompaniment. What Diamono has done is to transpose these parts on to modern instruments.

'For example, we have the large bass sabar, called the lamba. I play the part of the lamba on the bass guitar. There's another large drum called the mbung-mbung, whose role is taken by the kit drum, to re-create the traditional African sound.'

Diamono call the result Afro-feeling music, a sound which draws on rhythms from the whole of Senegal, from the Wolof, to the Mandinka and Jola people. 'The rhythms are many and varied,' he says. 'We've put them together to form a symbiosis.'

Mbalax music has already made an international mark through the work of Youssou N'Dour. For Sene, that is largely by the way. 'Mbalax is just one part of Senegalese music. It's from one, closely defined group. It's a regional sound, whereas ours is from the whole of Senegal.'

Diamono's songs cover a range of national issues, particularly those facing the young. Among them, Sene lists the problem of unemployed graduates, the shortages of accommodation in the cities, the difficulties facing polygamous families who have large numbers of children, plus other, international problems including drought and racism. One of their best-known songs, 'Soweto', was recorded in 1982 but was released outside Senegal only in 1987. The reason, says Sene, lies in lack of promotion.

'Our music industry suffers from poor promotion and presentation. It isn't to denigrate ourselves that we underline the fact that our promoters lack ambition . . . I can name names. Johnny Secka, who died recently. I don't think he was a true promoter. He was the opposite. He took musicians from the outside and brought them to Senegal. He never took a Senegalese band outside the country. There's not a single promoter who has taken a band out. They are happy to take a local group to make cassettes.'

Diamono feel they have suffered from this attitude. '"Soweto" was originally on a cassette,' says Sene. 'It's only now, when we talk about apartheid, that they start playing the song. The producers who have worked with us, I look on as "dioulo-dioulo". They look only for money, by making cassettes to distribute at Sandaga. That's not work. You must promote, sell, present the music properly.'

The band's development, in the eighties, bears out Sene's philosophy. After the rural flavour of the early work, Afro-feeling has become an

123

increasingly hard-edged, funky machine. The extraordinary, parched vocals of Omar Pene, later augmented by those of Moussa N'Gom from The Gambia, and a young singer, Mamadou Maiga, stand out against deep bass drums and Santana-esque guitars. The music draws on a range of Senegalese rhythms: its hardness bolsters the band's own tough, swaggering image. As a British observer, Peter Bradbrook, comments,

> Super Diamono project an altogether more youthful and macho image than their counterparts in Super Etoile . . . Youssou N'Dour can be a distant figure to the youth, increasingly courted by the rich and politically powerful who can buy his praises, surrounded and supported by a sophisticated and bohemian Dakar crowd, his music more to the delight of intellectuals at home and abroad. By contrast, Super Diamono have that prized social commodity, 'street credibility' and the slightly rebellious image appeals to the young male audience who have grown up embracing the militancy of Jamaican reggae in preference to their own culture.[14]

Other Senegalese musicians have followed a route similar to Diamono's. Babar Mal mixes reggae rhythms and electronic drums with rhythms associated with the Fula people. Ismael Lo left Diamono in 1985, and after a stint in Spain, turned to Paris, where he produced a set of albums whose mixture of acoustic guitars, harmonicas, roots rhythms and polished studio sound charted new, middle-of-the-road possibilities. Xalam took a more orthodox line, using a mid-seventies exploration of Senegalese folk rhythms as the basis for an Afro-jazz sound that attracted a large following in Africa and Europe. In 1975, Xalam toured Africa with Hugh Masekela and Miriam Makeba. By 1979, they had shifted their sights to Europe, with appearances at the Berlin Festival and, three years later, the Paris Africa Fête. The appearance of Xalam's rhythm section on the Rolling Stones' 'Under Cover of the Night' had all the hallmarks of the old orthodoxies, presenting African music as an exotic and thoroughly expendable new form of energy.

FODAY MUSA SUSO

At first, it seemed an odd combination. In one corner, Jali Foday Musa Suso, a veteran player of the kora, that most delicate and beautiful of

African instruments. In the other, Bill Laswell, a leading producer of New York avant-funk, known for the stripped-down aggression of his productions and the explosive whiplash of his beat.

Suso comes from a long line of Gambian jalis, or griots. One of his ancestors, Jalimadi Woleng Suso, is said to have discovered the kora. The story goes that Jalimadi was walking along a river bank, one-string harp in hand. A river spirit appeared, and offered to swap it for a larger twenty-one-string version: the kora. Jalimadi agreed to bring it back in a month's time. This he duly did, and played a couple of tunes for the spirit. 'Now give it back,' she said. Jalimadi refused and went home with the kora. From that day, the spirit has been trying to get it back, which is why kora players always cover up their harps before going to sleep.

A keen innovator like Jalimadi would have found little to complain of in his modern descendant's kora manoeuvres. In 1977, Suso decided to leave The Gambia and make his home in America. He settled in Chicago, where he put together a band called Mandingo Griot Society which combined straight kora with a backbone of 1970s funk, and occasionally some reggae. Two albums followed: *Mandingo Griot Society* and, in 1981, *Mighty Rhythm*, both of which recast Suso's folk music in a new, at times rough-sounding fusion.

'On those first two albums I just went into the studio and played typical kora songs,' he explains. 'I didn't know much about recording activities or arranging. I played the kora straight. It was all right, but nothing like what I've done since.'[15]

The early albums are now of mainly historical interest. Since then, Suso has developed a new style of kora playing, one that simplifies the complex rhythm and melody lines of the folk musician's art, streamlining it for a new, harder beat. The new sound reflects a new function. 'Traditionally people don't dance to the kora,' he explains. 'The musician comes to your home, sits down and plays. Everyone sits. He recites the history of the family, praises people, sings their names. They're happy just to sit and listen. But now, if I'm playing in America, people want to dance.'

Suso's move into avant-funk happened by degrees. First, he had been asked to write some of the music for the televised version of *Roots*, the Alex Haley novel set partly in The Gambia. But it did little for Suso's immediate career. By 1984 he was looking for a new deal, away from Flying Fish records, when a business contact put him in touch with Bill Laswell, who was working on an American theme tune for the 1984 Los Angeles Olympics. Laswell had already laid down some of the backing tracks, with pianist Herbie Hancock, and was looking to add an international flavour. Suso fitted the bill. The collaboration resulted in one track, 'Junku', heard on Hancock's *Sound System* album.

Later in 1984, Hancock returned the compliment, guesting on the album that Suso and Laswell had put together. *Watto Sitta* proved to be one of the finest albums in the series of Laswell productions that combined African music with hot electro-funk. There were few compromises. Suso's kora was kept well to the fore, with the electro-backing adding rhythmic underscore rather than a topline distraction. The African elements – the earthy call-and-response vocals, the range of traditional instrumentation – predominated. Occasionally, the beat loosened into shades of highlife. At its best, though, the album proved a model of tautness and concision; it was followed by a 1986 collaboration, on CBS, with Herbie Hancock.

Despite his futuristic moves, Suso remains a guardian of a 400-year-old tradition. The fact that he has chosen Chicago, home of the blues, to live in, gives an added twist to the situation. 'The blues take me back to the kora,' he says. 'The songs, the music is so similar. B.B. King, almost all of Albert King, Junior Wells . . .'

TOURE KUNDA

Paris-based, but Senegal-orientated, Toure Kunda present a bundle of contradictions to the follower of contemporary African music – both culturally and in terms of the varying degrees of breakthrough African bands have so far achieved in the West. Incredible though it may sound to the British African-music enthusiast, numbingly familiar with half-empty 300-capacity club venues in the UK, Toure Kunda enjoy a media and chart profile in France akin to that of a Top Ten pop band in Britain – their albums regularly notch up sales of 50,000 units (while *Sambala* actually came in at 100,000), and they frequently sell out venues the size of London's Earl's Court in Paris and other major French cities.

Even more remarkably for the British African-music fan, Toure Kunda have achieved this success without bowdlerizing their native Senegalese music in search of the lowest pop common denominator. Though their music does embrace Western influence and technology, it is deeply and unmistakably rooted in Senegalese tradition, while its lyrics are as a rule sung in one of the Senegalese languages, rather than French.

Why mainstream French pop fans should be more open to African music than their British counterparts is a subject that will continue to occupy European Afrophiles for some time to come. Ismaila Toure, however, probably hits the nail squarely on the head when he suggests, 'You British are just very conservative.'[16] Certainly, French ears seem currently to be far wider open than British ones, both among pop fans and the broadcast media which cater for them. 'Getting on radio and television is easy in France,' Ismaila continues. 'In Britain you just don't have the openings.'

The other contradiction posed by Toure Kunda concerns the kind of African music they play – it manages to be both ancient and modern at the same time. Instrumentally, the band draw on African and Western sources in roughly equal proportions, at one extreme using traditional Senegalese instruments like the balafon, kora and molo, at the other synthesized representations of those instruments. Melodically and harmonically too, Toure Kunda straddle Europe and Africa.

The synthesis sounds all the more startlingly fresh for being so obviously natural and unforced. Certainly, Toure Kunda themselves find nothing remarkable about it. 'I'm Ismaila,' points out Ismaila. 'Today I'm wearing European clothes. Tomorrow I might wear Senegalese clothes. It doesn't matter. What is important is what is in my heart. I've now accepted European culture – I think Europe should accept ours.'

Toure Kunda (Kunda means 'family' in the Senegalese Soninke language) are led by three brothers who came to Paris round about 1979 – Ismaila, Sixu Tidane and Ousmane Toure. (A fourth brother, Amadou, died of a heart attack in 1983.) For Ismaila, this kinship explains much of the spirit of harmony in the band's music. 'If you are not brothers it takes at least ten years to learn to sing together,' he says. 'Sometimes it is very hard to work together even within the family. But in Africa they teach us to live together and fight together, too.'[17]

At the heart of Toure Kunda's music are rhythms and melodies from a Senegalese coming-of-age ceremony called Djamba Dong or 'Dance of the Leaves'. 'Djamba Dong is a training for young boys and young girls from eight to sixteen,' explains Ismaila. 'During this initiation there is a lot of music – when they want initiates to make some promenades, or go to eat, or have a siesta. That music is where we take our inspiration from. There is percussion, and a chorus and balafon. We also use kora and molo, a small African guitar. When we play with our musicians we ask them to make the same sounds with electric guitars and synthesizers.

'When you hear the different rhythms through the Djamba Dong, you can find many kinds of music. That's why people hear inside our music some reggae, some calypso, some salsa and some highlife and Afrobeat.'[18]

Toure Kunda's taste for experimentation led them, in 1985, to record the *Natalia* album in Paris with Bill Laswell. Featuring sometime George Clinton and Talking Heads keyboard man Bernie Worrell, *Natalia* was a provocative blend of centuries-old Senegalese tradition and state-of-the-art New York electro-funk. International critical response was mixed – though in France it was almost wholly unfavourable, with the majority of observers accusing Laswell of cultural imperialism and the imposition of alien forms on the band's music. For themselves, Toure Kunda enjoyed the experience – though not the relatively low sales the album achieved (at less than 50,000, a failure in their terms). Though the band continue to investigate the shared boundaries of African and Western musical culture, they now prefer to engage on the trek independent of imported producers.

CÔTE D'IVOIRE

The Côte d'Ivoire is one of Africa's more conservative, pro-Western states. Independence, in 1958, meant less a break with the colonial past than a shift of emphasis. The French presence remained as dominant a part of the scene as the tree-lined boulevards, French restaurants and patisseries of the capital, Abidjan.

Culturally, the country kept all doors open, embracing a mixture of outside music from Zaire, Europe, America and the Caribbean. Haitian bands visited Abidjan in the 1960s. So did Cuban outfits – even James Brown. With its high-quality studios, Abidjan became a mecca for African artists, attracting in the 1970s a range of talent from Sam Mangwana and his African All Stars; to Ouza, the radical singer from Senegal; Les Ambassadeurs from Mali; later Moni Bile, whose new-look makossa won its first widespread acclaim in the city.

The Côte d'Ivoire's own music scene reflects some of this diversity. Top names, such as Daouda and Nyanka Bell, sing either soukous or an international disco mixture, heavily flavoured with Antillean rhythms. At the same time, the country has a strong roots scene, typified in the work of Amedee Pierre, the late Ernesto Djedje and Sery Simplice.

The earliest mix of Western and African forms took place along the coast where, in the 1940s, guitarists and accordion players joined the Akan street bands playing a traditional dance rhythm known as akpombo. It was here that the first popular dance bands appeared after independence, through men like Fax Clark, a trumpeter who had played with Manu Dibango in Belgium. Clark's repertoire mixed Akan rhythms with highlife covers and other African material, including songs by the Guinean band, Bembeya Jazz.

The 1960s saw a rapid growth in the number of young bands playing Beatles songs, pop and soul, plus a smaller group who worked with Ivoirian folk rhythms. One of the early pioneers, Amedee Pierre, developed a new style based partly on Western cover versions, partly on the gbegbe, a folk rhythm from the Bete people. Akpombo music retained its popularity, through such bands as Agnebi Jazz, Souers Camoe and Anomar Brou Felix. By the mid-1970s, Ivoirian music took a further step forward with the rise of Ernesto Djedje, who reworked the traditional Bete rhythms to a new level of sophistication. Djedje started his career as a Western-style pop singer and spent a large part of his time singing in

European nightclubs. He returned to the Côte d'Ivoire in 1972 and, under the sponsorship of the Mayor of San Pedro, worked on a new version of a traditional Bete dance, the ziglibithy. His two albums, *Adjissay* and *Zibote*, saw the move from middle-of-the-road soul and pop to a roots music where strong bass lines and multi-layered guitars caught the spark of the frenetic ziglibithy rhythms. By cutting out the Western influences, Djedje won a new African audience for Ivoirian music, and he toured in Guinea, Senegal, Upper Volta and Liberia.

His death, through a mysterious stomach complaint in 1983, put a shadow over Ivoirian music, yet the ziglibithy lived on in the work of Blissi Tebil and Luckson Padaud. Other Ivoirian musicians followed Djedje's example, if not his choice of folklore, and turned their attention to other traditional rhythms. Sery Simplice, a former folk musician, and Bailly Spinto, created their own versions of the gbegbe. Jimmy Yacinthe mixed the goli rhythm into a commercial funk and soukous set, while Gnaza Daniel created his own version of the aloukou dance. By the early 1980s, the renewal of interest in roots music had created further spectacular hybrids. As engineer Rene Kouebi Williams explains, Djedje's music had a strong impact on young Ivoirians, particularly the 'noushi' or 'heavy guys', who had relied on ghetto blasters and break dancing for their chief source of entertainment. 'When I was young, and growing up in Abidjan, we used to mix the ziglibithy and another dance, the zogbo, with break dancing, and hold special contests,' he recalls.[19] The soundtracks varied. Sometimes the dancers would play Zaiko, other times funk, or Djedje himself. The mixture created a new dance: nyama nyama. From there, the dance was quickly absorbed into the mainstream by artists like Kassiry, who gave the old rhythms a polished funk edge.

SERY SIMPLICE

Sery Simplice is one of the Côte d'Ivoire's best-known roots modernizers. He is the chief exponent of gbegbe music, a traditional dance rhythm that has spread far beyond its village confines to the clubs and television studios of Abidjan.

Simplice was born in 1949 and spent his early life moving from village to village, playing traditional songs on a guitar made from a petrol can. At the time, the Ivoirian scene was sharply divided between the city and the countryside. In the former, foreign music ruled. 'To be accepted you had to play Congolese,' says Simplice. 'And before that, merengue. The Cubans had colonized us.'[20]

Simplice left for the city in 1966, joining one of the pioneers of modern Ivoirian music, Amedee Pierre, 'Le Dopé National' who was already singing traditional proverbs and stories over a mix of Ivoirian and Congolese rhythms. As his guitarist, Simplice decided to go further and transpose an entire traditional music into modern form.

The mid-1970s had seen a number of similar ventures. The breakthrough came with Ernesto Djedje, who modernized the ziglibithy rhythm to create a new electric music in 1977. Simplice, who had spent much time working with Djedje in his home, followed suit a year later, when he left Amedee Pierre and set up his own band, Les Frères Djatys. The band's mixture of heavy rhythms and harsh vocals carried the full flavour of the old rural music from the south west of the Côte d'Ivoire. Gbegbe is performed at full moon to the sound of tambour, tam tam, buffalo horns and tubas to celebrate the end of a day's farming or the return of warriors. Simplice added criss-cross guitars, keyboards and saxes, but otherwise made few concessions to the modern world. He was the first Ivoirian artist to bring traditionally dressed dancers on to the modern stage; while his band wear suits and ties, Simplice himself wears traditional cloth, a crown and carries a ceremonial whisk. By 1983 his music had established itself. He received the title of king of gbegbe music and was crowned on television by Ernesto Djedje, ironically a few months before the ziglibithy king died.

Djedje left a strong influence on Simplice. 'He created a music which crossed frontiers,' he says. 'There are several promoters of ziglibithy who can do something traditional. He also showed the world that there is a music here which can give pleasure to all.'

Since 1978, Simplice has made nearly a dozen albums, all promoting gbegbe. The second, *Gbolou*, sums up his attitude to Côte d'Ivoire music. 'The song was written for a boy who lived in the city and who didn't know how to dance the gbegbe,' says Simplice. 'I explain that it is a traditional dance, and that he should go and learn it.' The third album, *Atrikakou*, continues the theme. 'There are lots of musicians in our country,' sings Simplice. 'But they all play reggae and funk. You should stop and listen to Simplice. You should listen to the sound of your own culture.'

Already various musicians have followed the advice. The death of Djedje has started a further jostling to find the true king of roots music. Artists like Luckson Padaud and Blissi Tebil have thrown themselves into ziglibithy; Jimmy Yacinthe has created his own roots version of the goli, and previously Euro-based Bailly Spinto has reworked the women's dance music, the tripo, into a modern form.

For Simplice, the continuation of the scene depends largely on its organization. 'Take Djedje,' he says. 'Everyone's trying to work out who will follow him. That's because he didn't train anyone to take over. With me it's different. When I go, gbegbe will be as strong as ever.'

In 1985, Simplice spread his gbegbe message further afield with a tour of Europe. But one eye remains fixed on the Côte d'Ivoire with its constant parade of new music, from hip hop to makossa, soukous and jazz. 'The young people are happy to follow fashion,' he says. 'But when the fashion has passed, they'll be back. They'll return to the gbegbe. It will always be there.'

An early sceptic was fellow-artist Jimmy Yacinthe. 'He asked me if, as king of gbegbe, I'd be able to keep the music going,' says Simplice. 'He asked me that after my fourth album. Now I've made five more, and all of them gbegbe . . .'

ALPHA BLONDY AND NYANKA BELL

Despite the development of a strong Côte d'Ivoire roots movement, the local scene continues to highlight musicians whose creative instincts point elsewhere. Reggae singer Alpha Blondy has become one of west Africa's most successful artists, his songs prompting cover versions by other reggae bands. Blondy has signalled his international intentions with songs which denounce apartheid and praise the Ivoirian President Houphouet-Boigny over the same pulsating reggae beat. After releasing his searing *Apartheid is Nazism* in 1986, Blondy took the logical next step of flying to Jamaica to record a new album, *Jerusalem*, with the Wailers.

Fellow-Ivoirian singer Nyanka Bell has made similar moves, turning not to Jamaica but to the more sprightly and increasingly fashionable rhythms of the French West Indies. Her 1984 debut, *Amio/Get Up and Dance*, embraced funk, disco and ballads. Two years later, the follow-up, *If You Came to Go*, moved towards the Antilles with one track, 'Emotion', written by Kassav's Jacob Désvarieux, and his own arrangement of the zouk-flavoured 'Chogologo'. Despite a strong international style – she speaks French but sings in English – Bell includes African material in her repertoire. 'Djama' is a Malian song, written by a child at the National Institute for the Blind in Bamoko. The title track pays tribute to her younger brother, who died of epilepsy in 1985. 'He'd suffered for twenty-one years,' she says. 'He was the reason I'd gone into music in the first place, in the hope that I could make enough money to send him to Europe for treatment.'[21]

This is a sad note, but Bell's work generally is full of courage and hope. Both 'If You Came to Go' and 'Djama', express the idea that handicap, blindness and disease are facts of life, not, as traditionalists might believe, punishments for the misdeeds of ancestors. Bell backed up her concern by donating royalties of 'Djama' to the selfsame Malian blind school from where the song first came: musicians using their influence to practical ends in a way that has become similarly commonplace in the West.

CENTRAL, SOUTHERN AND EAST AFRICA

ZAIRE

Zairean music is instantly recognizable through its tight vocal harmonies, interlocking guitars and shuffling, irresistible rhythms. It has a string of names from rumba to Congo jazz and soukous, and boasts a thousand dances. But the root remains the same: the rumba.

The growth of modern Zairean pop started in the early years of the century when an urban dance, the maringa, replaced an earlier favourite, the abgaya. The maringa was danced to an acoustic band whose instruments included the likembe, or hand piano; a bottle, for the rhythm line; and a small drum called the patenge. The rapid development of Zaire's towns and ports attracted a new, heterogeneous population composed of Zaireans, migrant workers from other African countries, and immigrants from the West Indies. The Belgian colonialists' introduction of gramophones and modern dance records gave Zaireans the first taste of the Cuban sounds and rhythms that would later prove crucial to the development of their own music. But even more important were the west African sailors, who brought the guitar and a new rumba style into Zaire. Local musicians took up the new rhythm, playing it alongside guitar versions of their own rhythms, which they dubbed the polka pique and the mazurka.

The rumba proved especially popular with the maringa dancers in Kinshasa, offering similar body movements and a rhythm that sounded at once novel and familiar. Guitarists and accordion players joined the acoustic bands, taking the melody and accompaniment lines once reserved for the likembe. By the early fifties, the new-style rumba bands had stretched their line-ups to include trumpets and saxophones, while some, like the Kasongo group, included both likembe as a lead instrument, and acoustic guitar.

The second wave of Latin American records, featuring post-war stars like Johnny Pacheco, and the orchestras Broadway and Aragon, inspired many of the early bands, among them Kalle's African Jazz, which appeared in 1953. By the late fifties, African Jazz had gone electric, and had swept away many of the old maringa and mazurka memories with a blast of bolero and cha cha, sung in a mixture of French and Lingala. Kalle's classic 'Independence Cha Cha', from 1960, offered a mesmerizing blend of Cuba and Kinshasa. The cha-cha rhythms, fleshed out with maraccas and congas, underlined the debt owed to Latin music. The prominent guitar melodies and the vocal phrasing had the true Zairean feel, while Dr Nico's spidery and ecstatic guitar solo came from somewhere else entirely: possibly divine intervention.

The cha cha, like the bolero, remained popular until 1962. By now, a distinctively Zairean rumba stunned Kinshasa, and Africa too, with faultless harmonies and guitar lines freely adapted from the old Latin horn charts. African Jazz were partly responsible, followed by a younger band, OK Jazz, which went on to champion urban rumba and authentic folk songs and rhythms from rural Zaire. The two rhythm schools – one from the Westernized, progressive 'Tout Grand African Jazz', the other from the rootsier 'Tout Puissant OK Jazz' – went on to define the future shape and sound of Zairean music.

African Jazz had a number of early hits, including 'Para Fifi' and 'Kalle Kato'. They added to their reputation by drawing sax player Essous away from OK Jazz and travelling to Belgium to play, initially for a Zairean wedding, and subsequently for those taking part in the Round Table Conference that was to lead to independence in 1960. Essous then went on to greater heights, forming the top Brazzaville band, Bantous de la Capitale.

The groupings and regroupings continued. African Jazz was joined by a young Cameroonian sax player, Manu Dibango, who left a jazzy imprint on many of their finest singles. Tabu Ley and Dr Nico left Kalle to form their own band, Orchestre African Fiesta. This band itself later split into African Fiesta National, run by Tabu Ley, and African Fiesta Sukisa, run by Dr Nico. New dances came and went. The original rumba, a slow dance, gave birth to a string of newcomers: the kara kara; the boucher, from Les Bantous de la Capitale; Dr Nico's kiri kiri; and, from the mid-sixties, the soukous, which heralded the start of a new generation of youth bands. Orchestre Negro-Succès, with its charismatic guitarist Bavon Marie-Marie, were among the first to shake the old regime, creating a new sound for fashion-conscious Kinshasa youth. Thu-Zaina followed suit. By 1970, Zaiko Langa Langa had thrown the scene into further disarray, blowing away the order and harmony of the old music in a flurry of loud guitars, ragged vocals and a mixture of Zairean sweetness and neurotic strength inspired partly by harder-hitting rock bands like the Rolling Stones. At the same time, Zaiko turned back to tradition with a snare drum that picked up folk rhythms from various parts of the country.

By now, the Zairean guitar style had become one of the wonders of Africa. The chief impetus came from the songs themselves which, with the rise of the youth bands, split increasingly into two distinct parts: a slow rumba introduction, and a faster second section, or seben, where the rhythms changed to folklore, or something from the band's own invention, and the guitarists found space to improvise, over the web of rhythm lines that had, by now, become the hallmark of Zairean music.

African Jazz is usually credited as the first band to introduce a third guitar, or 'mi-solo' between the lead and rhythm parts. OK Jazz used the multiple-guitar line-up to introduce the criss-cross flow of notes associated with the old likembe players. As the sixties progressed, a new form of half-solo appeared, developed by Dr Nico's brother, Dechaud. The 'mi-compose' introduced flowing melody lines and a strange, mournful tone produced by swapping the strings around. The thin, top-E string took the place of the fatter, steel-wound A or D, to give a slack, quavering, almost trampoline-like effect. The mi-compose style became the hallmark of Michelino, a guitarist first with African Fiesta, then Les Grands Maquisards and, later, influenced such seventies bands as Bella Bella and Orchestre Kiam, whose guitarist produced long, intricate and spine-tingling rhythm breaks.

By the early seventies, the scene had divided sharply between the older, well established musicians, who had made their names in the sixties, and the new bands like Shama Shama and Zaiko, which slowly split into a mass of other top youth bands. Among the earliest to leave was Papa Wemba, whose Viva La Musica remains one of Kinshasa's top bands; followed by Manuaku Waku, founder of Grand Zaiko Wa Wa; and Evoloko, who set up Langa Langa Stars. Flamboyant new outfits appeared, among them Trio Madjesi, a favourite with Madame Mobuto for their combination of James Brown licks, outrageous costumes and topical songs: their '8ième Round' celebrated the Ali–Foreman fight of 1974.

The new youth bands owed much to the sponsorship of a young businessman, musician and former member of OK Jazz called Kiamuangana Verckys. His protégés included Orchestre Kiam, as in Kiamuangana, and a string of double-barrelled bands, from Bella Bella to Lipua Lipua, who trod a middle ground between the old music and the increasing roughness of the Zaiko clan. The 'mi-compose' sound had a large impact on east African bands, but across west Africa, Zaire's influence dropped until Sam Mangwana's African All Stars restored the balance with a late-seventies mixture of soukous and biguine. His 1977 'Georgette Eckins', with its singalong melodies and a rock-hard bass line, introduced a new chapter in Zairean music. By the end of the seventies, after a rigorous set of pan-African tours, Mangwana flew to Paris and became one of the first and best-known African artists to live and record in the city. Among those that followed were Kanda Bongo Man and Les Quatre Etoiles, made up of singer Nyboma, and other members of Mangwana's African All Stars.

A second great development has been the rise of women singers, led by the classic rumba artist Abeti Masekini who, by the mid-eighties, was performing and recording with the late Dr Nico. M'Pongo Love has some of Abeti's polish, and has played a spectacular role in incorporating Antillean rhythms into modern soukous and in promoting the concept of the woman singer in Zaire. Abeti and M'Pongo Love are joined by a third, prolific artist, M'Bilia Bel, whose concerns stretch beyond conventional romantic relationships to wider issues, such as the problems of the polygamous marriage, which concern people living in Zaire today.

The interest in Zairean music continues both with women singers and a new generation of bands, such as Choc Stars, Victoria Eleison and Empire Bakuba, all of whom specialize in the modern, echoey and rough-edged sound of Kinshasa. Because for thirty years Zaire's capital, formerly known as Leopoldville, has been the source of Africa's most vibrant popular music, it is essential to examine its contemporary musical life in some detail.

A VISIT TO KINSHASA

Zaire, formerly the Belgian Congo, is the second largest country in

Africa, a vast mass of land that stretches from the western seaboard, the mouth of the river Zaire, to the Tanzanian border in the east, with Zambia at its southernmost tip. Geographically it stands at the crossroads of the continent, poised between the Sahara to the north and the southern African states to the south. Musically, it is less of a crossroads, more the heart of Africa, with a sound and a style that has left its impact over the entire continent.

The old kingdom of the Kongo, which covered a large part of the area now occupied by Zaire, has always been noted for artistic prowess. In the early 1500s, a wealthy and powerful court supported sculptors, sanza players and guitarists. The sweetness of the music won praise from later commentators, at times when it was fashionable to dismiss Africa and its arts as pagan and brutish. 'I have already mentioned the ability these people display in artistic decoration,' wrote H.H. Johnston in 1895. He went on:

> Their love of music is also worthy of notice. Beside the drum, they use the horns of *Tragelaphus gratus*, and other tragelaphine antelopes as trumpets, from which a fine resonant sound is produced. The Ba-teke children make trumpets from rolled banana leaves. For the discoursing of melody, they have a form of 'marimba', an instrument of widespread range which in principle is so many thin strips or keys of metal arranged along a sounding board. When twanged by a practised touch, they yield very sweet sounds. For real beauty of tone, however, the five-stringed lyre of the Congo is remarkable, and the native musicians produce from this stringed instrument melodies both quaint and touching.[1]

By the time Johnston visited the Congo, the path towards colonial rule had already been charted. From the 1850s, European merchants, who had grown fat on the export of slaves from central Africa, switched their attention to ivory, tobacco, palm oil and peanuts. The main trading centre, Stanley Pool, took its name from H. Morton Stanley, who had used that stretch of the Congo as a base for his explorations of central Africa. A number of trading settlements appeared, including Matadi, a depot near the mouth of the river, and two small towns which would later grow into Leopoldville (Kinshasa) and Brazzaville.

The turn of the century was a time of violence and dislocation. King Leopold of Belgium created the Congo Free State, a name which became synonymous with forced labour, torture and arbitrary execution. So voracious was his appetite and so great the international scandal that, by 1908, Leopold was forced to hand over to the Belgian government. The Congo was born. Social changes accelerated, not only with the building of a railway linking Leopoldville and Matadi, but also with the creation of mining centres drawing on a mixed population of African and West Indian labourers. This mixture of people in a new, unfamiliar environment, had a crucial effect on the development of Zairean music. Kazadi Wa Mukuna describes how the abgaya, a dance of the 'detribalized' urban areas, gave way to the maringa, an early forerunner of the rumba, which was danced to the sound of the likembe or sanza, a bell or bottle, and a patenge drum.[2] The music spread, to the distaste of local religious groups and Belgian missionaries alike. 'Maringa dancehalls were generally found only in the urban centres of the Lower Congo,' writes historian David Birmingham. 'But towards the end of World War One, the "bad dances" spread over the whole area.'[3] It is interesting to note that the Congolese religious leader Kimabangu ordered his followers to abstain both from alcohol and the maringa dance.

The plane that dips out of the clouds down to Ndjilly Airport in Kinshasa takes its passengers abruptly from the bland control of international airliner-dom to the sudden rush and exuberance of central Africa. In the arrival hall a portrait of President Mobutu looks down over groups of men in fashionable blue suits, women in expensive full-length dresses, bright printed cloth and large headdresses, greeting each other and chatting. The heat, even at one in the morning, is tremendous. Humidity buffets the crowds as suitcases splutter slowly on to the conveyor belt: a crate with a dog in it, a box full of hi-fi equipment broken at the corner with a selection of knobs and dials poking out.

The taxi ride that follows reveals the sprawling outskirts of the city: low tin-roofed houses, the occasional bar with wall paintings advertising beer and food, numerous large paintings of Franco, Zaire's foremost bandleader; the inner city, with its spacious boulevards and rows of trees, high-rise buildings and hotels, like the Memeling and the Intercontinental ('National Cheese Week' says a large banner); and finally, what was in colonial times part of the African quarter, Matonge, a mass of streets – some surfaced with tarmac, some not – verandahs dotted with furniture, back yards with palm trees.

The hub of the activity is the Rond Point: a crossroads with a central patch of grass; a large record shop, Xadis, pumping out music; the hotels

Luv Zaire and Hotel La Creche, which pump out more music; and two or three bars with coloured lights hanging out of trees and people sitting drinking large bottles of chilled Primus beer. Down the road is an area known as Jakarta (for its constant activity) and the Marche de la Dernière Chance, an all-night market whose fringes are alive with candle-lit stalls selling fried chicken, shoe polish, bread and margarine, oil, fish, soup and soap, boxes of matches and piles of fruit.

Cars, lorries and taxis roll through the night. A pack of gendarmes appears at one corner of the square, a group of youths scatter at the other. Small groups stand huddled outside the white gates of the Vis-à-Vis club, listening and dancing. Others lie flat-out asleep on the grass, or rolled up, foetally, in shop doorways.

And everywhere, there is music. At Hotel Luv Zaire, OK Jazz's mournful 'Mamou' pounds out of the red-lit hotel bar. Outside, smaller bars create a confusion of noise; down the road, red lights and hot music leap from the open-air nightclub of the Veve Centre like sparks from a furnace. Go to sleep at four in the morning, they're playing Tabu Ley's 'Sarah'; wake up at seven, it's the same song, the same bar – probably the same people. The one thing they don't seem to do in Matonge (and they do an awful lot) is sleep.

It is tempting to attempt to locate a cut-off point between the latest electric soukous and the fashion-conscious bands that create it, and the older, acoustic bands' musicians who dominated the Kinshasa scene in the forties. But no such division exists. Men like Antoine Wendo and Jean Bosco Mwenda are still seen as pioneers, the fathers of the new sound. Bosco in particular has been active on the modern scene, recording tributes to President Mobutu's wife, and recording with youth stars like Papa Wemba. Bosco, though, lives a few hundred miles from Kinshasa. When it comes to the true sound of the city, Antoine Wendo is more the godfather.

Wendo lives in a small, concrete bungalow in a quiet suburb some miles from the throb of Matonge. The sitting-room has a sofa and two chairs and a coffee table, plus a display cabinet filled with glasses, religious paintings and photographs of Wendo in a bright sequinned jacket being presented to Madame Mobutu. Such presentations are entirely appropriate, for Wendo is something of a Zairean legend. Although Zonophone Congo had earlier brought out a record by Davis Doaquel, entitled 'Baba Ya Ngo Congo', Wendo is generally credited as the first Zairean to make a record in Zaire. In 1948, Wendo went into a small, blanket-lined studio in Kinshasa and recorded 'Mbeya', a tribute to his dead mother. It came out the same year on the Greek-owned Ngoma label. The following year, his second single, 'Marie Louise', took Kinshasa by storm. 'Look at any woman in her twenties,' says a Zairean journalist. 'Her mother would have worshipped Wendo.'⁴

Like many African musicians, Wendo received his vocation to his chosen career in a dream. His original wish was to become a mechanic. In 1925 he joined a shipping line and spent the next fourteen years travelling the Zairean waterways between Kinshasa, Matadi, Bowende and the equator. In 1939, he returned home, on the death of his mother, who appeared shortly afterwards in the dream. 'She told me to carry on her job as a singer,' says Wendo. 'In the morning I got up and found a guitar in the house. I had no idea of where it had come from.' His first song declared that 'from death there is no protection', over a rumba guitar vamp.

Shortly afterwards, Wendo returned to the ship, playing his guitar after work, in the company of other Congolese sailors. The pilot, he remembers, was an American, a Mr Williams, but there were no radios, gramophones or other Western technological baggage on board. 'We had no contact with outside music,' says Wendo. There was, however, one exception: the rumba, which he first heard in Kinshasa. 'The rumba originally came from Sierra Leone,' he explains. 'The Sierra Leoneans came to Kinshasa as clerks. Many of them were musicians and they played and danced the rumba. I got it from them.'⁵

Wendo settled in Kinshasa in 1941. The city had expanded and developed a distinctive cultural life. Some of this culture was due to the Sierre Leoneans and other west African clerks and office workers who had settled originally in an area known as Citas. The Europeans occupied a quarter known as Sedec, from which all Africans were excluded. Citas, the breeding-ground for the early, eclectic Zairean pop music, developed in a lively sprawl around the city prison. In 1923, a new African quarter, Kintambo, added further variety to Kinshasa life. A theatre troupe, founded by the Moke brothers, flourished and toured Brazzaville. Football and cycling became popular, as did music. In addition to bands playing maringa and other folk dances, Kintambo had its own brass band: founded in 1935 by Sergeant Major Bileko, the Saint Cecilia fanfare, or brass band, took regularly to the streets.

The old fanfares still evoke fond memories among Kinshasa residents. 'They were the first bands in the city,' says Citoyen Basunga, founder of Kinshasa's Chem Chem Yetu dance troupe. 'They had their own, distinctive music: a slow dance that was popular long before the rumba. It came from Martinique, and we called it matindike, the grandmother of the rumba. But when the guitar came along, no one wanted to listen to the fanfares. In effect, they were totally European, full of instruments brought in by the missionaries. Everyone went over to the guitar.'[6]

Wendo's subsequent career illustrates Basunga's assertion. He arrived in Kinshasa at the start of a new age, coinciding with the opening of the city's first African bars. From now on, they would dominate the music scene. The best-known, including Chez Amazoun, Siluvangi, the Kongo Bar, Air France and Macauley, attracted a multitude of solo guitarists and accordion players who dealt the death blow to brass-band music. The new bar musicians included a number of Zaire's best-known names: Wendo; fellow-guitarists Adou Elenga, Leon Bukasa and Bowane; plus the accordion player Feruzi, who helped create the first rumba craze in the forties, with a band including a guitarist and a clarinettist from Guadeloupe.

'I played in bars, pubs and clubs for Africans and Europeans alike,' says Wendo. 'At that time, a black man would never play in front of Europeans. I was the first one, and the only one.' Wendo's home bars, the Siluvangi and the Kongo, soon rang with the sound of small groups, which mixed guitars with mandolins, accordions, the patenge (a small, goat-skin drum) and milk tins filled with pebbles. Wendo's band was called Victoria. 'We played mostly rumba,' he explains. 'Also cha cha. These were outside rhythms. Our own folk rhythms didn't really work so well because the people most interested in what we were doing were the coastmen. So we gave them what they wanted: the rumba.'

His career developed apace: by 1950 Wendo had opened his own bar, providing a showplace for young musicians like Joseph Kabasele, later founder of African Jazz; George Edouard, Feruzi and a group of other musicians who later went on to form the nucleus of OK Jazz. Wendo then took Victoria over the river to Brazzaville, setting up a second version, Vastoria, which proved equally popular. 'It was I who renewed and rejuvenated the music,' he says. 'The music of fanfares was exhausted and attracted no one. The main reason for their downfall was that they lacked singers.' The new acoustic bands, such as Excelsior, made up for the deficiency with vocal harmonies, guitars, trumpets, accordions — sometimes violins. Before long they attracted record-company attention. By 1953, Ngoma had signed Paul Kamba, an early rival of Wendo and Feruzi. Jhimmy, known for his Hawaiian guitar style, was working for Opika, Lando and Rossignol for Loningisa.

While the barroom sound invaded Kinshasa, new guitarists were also coming up in the provinces. The best-known is Jean Bosco Mwenda, whose work survives on early recordings of African guitar music made by Hugh Tracey. 'I met Bosco in the fifties in Lubumbashi,' says Wendo. 'He was very important there, but he played in his own language, Swahili. The rhythm was different. He played the folklore of the Shaba region, not the true rumba which came from the coastmen. My rhythm was played all over Zaire. But not Bosco's.'

Recent work by musicologists like Gerhard Kubik supports his view.[7] By the 1960s, the Kinshasa sound had become the national music of Zaire, using rumba rhythms and lyrics in the inter-ethnic language, Lingala. The rhythms of Shaba were largely overshadowed. For all that, Bosco's influence remains strong. For modern guitarists, he is seen as a crucial link with the past: by developing an intricate finger-picking style, Bosco kept alive the sound and the melodies of the old likembe, while his use of the guitar to play unaccompanied solo lines, instead of the strummed chords favoured by many of his contemporaries, marks him out as the precursor of the modern, plucked electric-guitar patterns favoured by Franco and other Kinshasa guitarists.

A further rhythm that reached Kinshasa through the coastmen was highlife. According to Wendo, it found little favour. 'It was difficult to catch,' he says. 'When we did work it out, we developed it in our own way.' Other changes had also taken place, the most crucial being the arrival of the electric guitar. Wendo first played one in the Ngoma studio in 1949. Over the next decade, it would alter for ever the sound of Kinshasa music. 'Music develops according to its period,' says Wendo. 'So we can't say that any of it is bad. In the old days we were singing out of love for the music. Today everyone is going after money, and that's why the rhythm is fast, fast, fast, because the young are going fast, fast, fast after money.'

At a short distance from Wendo's house stands the Institut National des Arts, a modern complex of buildings with a theatre next door and a constant sound of trumpets, guitars, saxes and pianos. The institute has set up its own dance band, whose repertoire is based not on the ubiquitous rumba but on various folk rhythms associated with weddings, burials and initiation ceremonies. The music has a rich, jazzy flavour. Next door, a second blast of music, sweeter and more familiar, suggests a second form of rediscovery. The guitarists, horn players and singers are all in their sixties and have come together as members of the Orchestre National de Bankolo Miziki or 'old-time music' to protect Zaire's early rumba heritage. Two of the older members, Honore Liengo and Citoyen Mwena, stop work to describe how they first took up music in the mid-forties. They made their guitars from wood, the original models having been brought in by sailors, and were strongly influenced by the Latin music which was released in Zaire on the Olympia label. By now, the reaction against the brass bands was in full swing. 'At the start, the only groups you'd see were the fanfares,' says Mwena, 'the military bands like Odeon and the Americain. There were no guitarists with them, only brass instruments and accordions. For the most part, the musicians were students, who were learning the instruments at school . . .'

The guitarists, according to Mwena, were important in that they changed the music from 'tribal to modern'. The likembe was the grandfather of the guitar, he explains. And the person to change from the old to the new instrument was Dondo Daniel, at Matadi. Adou Elenga followed his example. He was part Zairean, part Senegalese, and having already had contact with people from further up the coast, could play like the true professionals. 'He rivalled even the Ghanaians,' says Mwena.

It was Adou Elenga who wrote one of Zaire's great early rumbas, 'Maria Tebbo', later rerecorded by Sam Mangwana. Like Wendo, Mwena and Liengo see the rumba as a rhythm brought in from outside. Their own dances – the polka pique, the bolero and the mazurka – were purely Congolese in origin, with new, glamorous names added. 'The names were European,' says Liengo. 'We used them to give the music something advanced, something civilized; to bring it up to the standard of the music the Europeans listened to.'

In the early fifties, Liengo and Mwena joined the barroom bands that were to develop into the first electric bands. Liengo joined Bowane, an early influence on OK Jazz, and in 1956 travelled to Angola, returning to help set up Roc-a-Mambo.

The spirit of the times shines out from a series of articles in the magazine, *Belgian Congo Today*.[8] 'Native bars' proliferated: by the mid-fifties, there were over 150 in Kinshasa. The national radio proved equally popular. First developed as Congolia, a private wartime station broadcasting home news and messages for Congolese troops stationed in Nigeria, the system was transformed, in 1956, to Radio Congo Belge, which broadcast around four hours a day and was heard across Africa. In 1953, the magazine reported:

Congolese listeners are not interested in Negro spirituals or for that matter Harlem or New Orleans jazz. The preference goes to sugary French chansons played by Congolese bands. They also appreciate

South American dance music, especially numbers in which the guitar takes an important place. You can hear these for hours on end in any native bar or dancehall.

Around this time, the first of the modern bands appeared, African Jazz their standard bearer. This band was created by Joseph Kabasele, and had a repertoire which included rumbas, boleros and cha chas. Some of the numbers were sung in French. The band had two guitarists, who kept up a flow of precise and interweaving melody, shuffling rhythms and perfectly harmonized vocals, usually in parallel thirds. In the early days, Kabasele had been a chorister in Kinshasa Cathedral. He then played as a soloist in Wendo's bar. Now he was to win acclaim as the father of modern Zairean music with a band whose line-up included Dr Nico and Dechaud, two of Zaire's most famed guitarists and, by 1960, the honey-voiced Tabu Ley. Other bands followed Kabasele, among them OK Jazz, who made the Kongo Bar, later Palace Rouge, into a place of pilgrimage. Open-air clubs, like the Vis à Vis, further stoked the fire. By the end of the decade, Kinshasa had become Africa's most musical city.

Today, its status remains undimmed. The Hotel Luv Zaire stands at the heart of Matonge's clubland. In front is the Vis à Vis, to the right the Veve Centre. The main road, Avenue President Kasavubu, has further attractions: Village Molokai – the small 'kingdom' ruled by top youth star Papa Wemba – and a club bearing the legend, first propagated by Franco, 'On entre OK, on sort KO', the home of the legendary Zaiko Langa Langa. And every two or three yards down Kasavubu, there are record shops. In the space of 100 yards, there are nineteen small one-storey buildings with speakers outside and blackboards chalked with the names of the latest singles. And everywhere, the sound of rumba: from the rumba rude boys of the Zaiko clan and Papa Wemba, the tough tones of Empompo and Tiers Monde, the sweet Paris productions of Nyboma. And above all, the voices of two men, Franco and Tabu Ley, who have dominated the Kinshasa scene for over twenty years.

Franco's band, Tout Puissant OK Jazz, is no misnomer. The man casts a shadow over the entire music scene. In the sixties, musicians got a job and instruments from Franco, or maybe from Tabu Ley, or they didn't get a job at all. Young bands faced stiff opposition from a man who could buy out their best musicians at a moment's notice. Franco sees his power differently. 'A lot of the bands were unstable,' he explains. 'Mine was stable. So where the bands couldn't cope financially, we selected the best musicians. They wouldn't have been able to find anywhere else, so they turned to Franco.'[9]

By the seventies, Franco had consolidated his position in other areas. He became a leading champion of President Mobutu, and played a leading part in his campaign to free Zaire of its colonial mentality, touring the country, explaining the new 'Authenticité', and taking his own, authentic name: L'Okanga La Ndju Pene Luambo Makiadi. He also owns several houses and a lavish club, the Un Deux Trois, which plays OK Jazz on the ground floor, Franco records on the next and international pop on top.

Today Franco's lifestyle and surroundings reflect his vast wealth. He lives in a palatial two-storey white house in a leafy and prosperous part of Kinshasa called Limite. The house is surrounded by a green steel fence; its garden has tables and umbrellas with plastic fringes. Inside the house, there is a huge reception room with a secretary and rows of chairs; upstairs, there are shining marble floors, videos, television sets and large house plants. The visitor waits and waits and is finally ushered to the top floor to find Franco sitting on a large swinging chair, reading a French novel through gold-rimmed glasses. He breaks off to discuss one of his favourite themes, the relationship between the sexes. Although Franco has made his name as a commentator on general social themes, applying a sharply satirical eye to the way people behave and misbehave, he now spends an increasing amount of time writing about the role of women in society, a question keenly debated in Zaire generally. At first sight, Franco would seem to have thrown his weight on to the less progressive side: 'Why do I attack women?' he asks. 'Because they have problems. They deceive men. A wife will say that she'll cook at midday. When the man arrives, she hasn't done it. She's out driving around. That sort of thing makes me angry, so I sing about it.'

The song that puts over Franco's point of view at its most reasoned is his hit '12,600 Lettres', from the 1984 album *Chez Rythmes et Musiques à Paris*, which catalogues the dramas of the Zairean household, in particular the problems between men and women. In the song, Franco singles out a few of the letters in which women talk about their anguish at not producing children and their desperation when the husband takes a second or third, younger wife. But the commonest complaint seems to be the jealousy and bad feeling that flows from the man's sister to his wife. Franco's advice, after a twelve-minute song and a lengthy studio discussion, also on the album, is that the wives should avoid confronting their sisters-in-law and talk to the husband instead. In between, he uses the letters to paint a far from flattering picture of quarrelsome and divided womanhood. It is a picture mitigated slightly by his recent works like 'Mario', which shift the focus to feckless and irresponsible men. But the common view of Franco, as a singer who exposes one, but rarely both of the sexes to ridicule, still obtains. What was the reaction to the song? 'Some women said "Oh, Franco's come to insult us again",' he says. 'Others: "Franco's doing all right. He sings the truth."'

Franco's opinions used to go unchallenged, but the rise of M'Bilia Bel, Zaire's best-known woman singer, has changed that. When Franco insults, M'Bilia Bel and her musical collaborator, Tabu Ley, hit back. On 'Ba Gerants, Ya Mabala' she describes how she married a man to be happy, but finds herself pestered by brothers-in-law. In 'Cadence Mundanda' a dialogue between herself and Tabu Ley, she castigates men for their laziness and dependence on their women, who do the farming and cut the wood. Ley's reply, that the men catch the food in the first place, sounds less than convincing.

Finding Ley is a problem. Franco's life seems regal, well ordered. Ley's is the opposite. He moves around constantly in a variety of cars, turning up in the least expected of places. Drive to his house, and he's away, with the President. The following day, he was there briefly, then went out again. The third time, he's sitting in a Datsun at a nearby crossroads, reading *Salongo*, the daily paper. 'Before M'Bilia Bel it was usual for men to attack women,' he says. 'Now the women are attacking back. The men are curious, the women proud.' Ley then explains that he writes eighty per cent of M'Bilia Bel's material. Does this make him a feminist? 'No, not really, but I do have a weakness for women. I was brought up by my mother. I married straight after my studies; seven of my nine children have been girls. I'm surrounded by sisters and nieces, and have created women dance troupes . . .'

For all the statistics, Ley is sure about where to draw the line. 'According to our traditions, it's the women who look after the children, prepare the food and work in the fields. Today, that has changed. Women go to university, work in offices. But the men still see women in the same old way. This is perhaps understandable. But what I can't tolerate is when a woman simply becomes an instrument of pleasure for men, a prostitute.'

At the end of the interview, Ley, who is famous throughout Zaire as a 'lady's man', walks on to the patio and watches as two gardeners plunge his Flymo into a tangle of long grass. Ley shouts 'Ho' and whistles, but the noise drowns him. Finally the gardener looks up. The machine falls silent. There remains one last question. Would it be possible to talk to M'Bilia Bel? 'C'est pas possible,' he says. With that Tabu Ley hauls himself into a van whose back is loaded with large cardboard boxes and disappears through his palatial gates.

Ley's house, a few hundred yards over the road from Franco's, looks out over a small, tarmac-covered road which runs past the *Salongo* newspaper office and up to a large dual carriageway fringed with trees. In their shade, groups of people stand at kiosks, buying food and tins of Coca-Cola, reading papers, waiting for buses and taxis. In one direction, the vehicles plunge down to the city centre, in the other, back to the dustier hubbub of Matonge.

The street life here is undiminished, a non-stop movement of people, lorries and cars. Gossip circulates like a breeze, as fast and emphatic as the lorries crammed with passengers which roar around the dusty fringes of the Matonge roundabout. Everything is discussed, analysed, from the foibles of sportsmen and politicians to the private lives of Kinshasa's musicians. In 1970, the death of Bavon Marie-Marie caused endless speculation about sorcery. More recently, the talk has focused on Franco's songs, the politicians being lambasted in 'Kimpa Kisangamene', the identity of the older woman in 'Mario', to the name of a well-known singer supposedly suffering from AIDS, and the sideline businesses of well-known record producers – selling drugs and blood plasma, or anything you care to name. 'Producers, they're all the same,' says one man. 'All flour from the same sack.' Kinshasa's street life is buoyed up with gossip, talk, rumour and innuendo, far outstripping the immediacy and relevance of much of the news channelled through the official print and broadcast media. To hear what is really happening, people turn not to the television or the newspapers, but to Kinshasa's grapevine, known as 'pavement radio', or Radio Trottoir.

Nevertheless, newspapers have their appeal. Small boys and adolescents crowd round papers spread out on the pavement and held open at pages filled with sport, music and fashion news; around television sets in bars and shops showing football and wrestling – the latter, mixing sport and fetishism, is huge in Kinshasa. Top wrestlers sport leather masks and Mr T haircuts, freeze their opponents on the spot with a single glance, spark them into uncontrollable dancing, or sprinkle holy water to break a supposed spell. The top wrestler, Endingue, enters the ring to the sound of a lusty brass band. Music is everywhere.

Near Hotel Luv Zaire, a photographer's board stuck with photographs shows Kinshasa's top stars in action: Papa Wemba in black leather and silk shirts; Choc Stars doing their latest dance; Emeneya, leader of Victoria Eleison, opening his shirt and holding it up to reveal the expensive designer label; Bipoli dressed in black brogues and black leather, doing his Honda-inspired dance, the onomatopoeiac mbrototo. 'Take away the beer and the music,' says a well-known Kinshasa journalist, 'and the city falls apart.'[10] He's right. From the wealthy bourgeoisie who come here for kicks and cold beer; to visit the nightclubs or the discotheques, like the Sexi Pop, with their endless funk and soul; or to sit and eat expensive hamburgers on the Rond Point, while a security man stands at the gate and a saxophonist tours the tables, to the sound of 'Strangers in the Night' – down to the small boys who sleep rough and hustle drugs, beer and women for the local stars, Matonge is less a zone, more a microcosm of city life. The activity is constant, sometimes baffling. One night, during a Papa Wemba gig at the Vis à Vis, the guitarist leans over towards a small boy wearing ragged shorts. The boy disappears and returns with a lit cigarette which he places in the guitarist's mouth.

The same club, the Vis à Vis, has its own place in history. In 1959, in the volatile days running up to independence, Franco started a riot with a song about colonialism. Feelings boiled over, and the crowd ran outside, attacking houses and shops belonging to Greek and Belgian traders. Since then, politics and music have lived in relative harmony. Kalle's 'Independence Cha Cha' listed the politicians like Lumumba and Kasavubu who took part in the Round Table independence talks with the Belgians in Brussels. Independence and the need for national unity became a favourite theme with Zairean bands. When Mobutu emerged as the strongest politician in Zaire after the murder of the first Prime Minister, Lumumba, Franco urgently solicited his listeners' support. 'After Lumumba, God has been merciful,' he sang. 'We have found another prophet. The face of Mobutu like the face of Lumumba.' Tabu Ley joined Franco in supporting the new regime. By the end of the late sixties, the two top Zairean singers were acting as unofficial government spokesmen, explaining its actions and singing in praise of Mobutu. In return they received official sponsorship, along with instruments and equipment denied to lesser bands.

After the 1970 election, which unleashed a small flood of pro-Mobutu songs, the 1973 cultural revolution further deepened the relationship between head of state and Zaire's musicians, who turned further back to traditional sources for their inspiration. Annual contests to find the best pro-Mobutu song attracted praise songs from M'Pongo Love, Afrisa and other top bands. Orchestre Veve's contribution has been particularly interesting. The founder of the group, Kiamuangana Verckys, lined himself up solidly with the President through songs like 'Afrique Aux Africains' and his 1980 'Autocritique', which denounced businessmen for preferring commerce to revolution. An earlier Verckys song, 'Ngoubi Na Mobutu' has sealed a rift between Kinshasa and Brazzaville. Occasionally, though, the politics have become controversial. One of Verckys' most famous songs, the 1973 'Nakomitunaka', attacking churches thronged with statues of a white Jesus, virgin and saints, aroused strong feelings, while Franco and Tabu Ley have both run into trouble through what their songs have (or were supposed to have) said. The references to witchcraft in Franco's 1984 'Kimpa Kisangamene' were widely seen as an indirect attack on the Zairean Prime Minister. But for all this, the authorities found it better to have singers for them than against them. Franco himself, despite a couple of jail sentences and a period of self-imposed exile in the eighties, has been awarded Zaire's top honour, the National Order of the Leopard, and his support for Mobutu remains, on the surface at least, absolute. During the presidential elections in 1984, his *Candidat na Biso Mobutu* portrayed a peaceful country whose students, workers, journalists, even prisoners, united in praise of the President and his Mouvement Populaire de la Révolution. 'Afrisa, OK Jazz and Zaiko,' says Franco, 'our candidate is Mobutu.'

A second form of revolution, musical this time, rocked Kinshasa in the late 1960s. From the early days, the rumba was Zaire's single most popular rhythm. It had its own dance, which achieved the greatest popularity at independence in 1960. From there, the musicians catered for changing tastes with a flow of rhythmic variations – and dances to match – which were unleashed during the second, faster sections of the typical Zairean two-part song. This became known as the seben, and its early-sixties dance styles included the kara, meaning 'to avoid'; the twist, which enjoyed a burst of success through the efforts of French singer Johnny Halliday; the yeye, a fast rhythm played by OK Jazz and, around 1965, the boucher, a traditional Congolese dance involving vigorous torso movements, imported from Brazzaville. Other dance crazes ranged from the mambetta, pioneered by OK Jazz and Jean Bokelo; the mobilette; and the kiri kiri, introduced by Dr Nico in the mid-1960s. By 1965, the boucher had developed into a new dance, the soukous (from the French secouer, to shake) and was associated primarily with Tabu Ley and the younger bands that were beginning to storm the clubs.

The first stirrings of the youth movement came with bands like Jazz Baron and Orchestre Negro Succès, with guitarists Bavon Marie-Marie, whose younger image and harder rhythms put them at the front of a wider

Kinshasa youth movement. According to Zairean historian Kolonga Molei, the earliest stirrings of a marginal, semi-delinquent youth movement came in the 1920s with a small group of unemployed youths, often policemen's children, who would find it easier to avoid arrest.[11] Cowboy films provided a new source of identity for a group whose typical representatives sported jeans, carried guitars and smoked marijuana. Instead of horses, the Bills, named after Buffalo Bill, rode bicycles or motorcycles. 'To stop,' writes Molei, 'he jams his heel against the back tyre, just above the chain. The "velo-horse" stops suddenly and, at the same moment, its rider pulls the front tyre up to its full height and shouts, "Bill Oy-Ay". The passers-by reply "Serumba".' The Bills came into their own at the end of the 1950s, when many of Kinshasa's zones sported graffiti featuring new names, from Texas to Dallas. The Bills renamed themselves too, choosing fanciful nicknames like Billy, Neron and Khrushchev, and spoke 'Hindubill', a mixture of French, English, Lingala and other local languages. They were reckoned to have twenty different words for money.

The importance of the Bills, and their later replacements, lay in the value they attached to music. From the youth movement came the new bands that were to change the face of Zairean music. One of the earliest of the Bills' songs was 'Wele Kingo', composed by Neron of Ngiri Ngiri, which according to Molei gave the Bills their first anthem. New bands started up, along with vocal groups and an orchestra of reformed delinquents founded by a priest, Père Biffalo, which became known initially as Minzoto, later Minzoto Wela Wela.

Of the new musicians, none was more charismatic than Bavon Marie-Marie, the self-proclaimed most handsome man in Kinshasa. Despite being the guitarist, rather than leader of Orchestre Negro Succès, he commanded widespread attention, wearing layers of skin-whitening cream and breaking the old tradition of singing rumba in Lingala by recording the first Kikongo rumba, 'Beto Lulendu'. Marie-Marie was Franco's cousin, and it was said that he'd sold his soul to a fetish priest in exchange for musical success. The guitarist seemed to be saying the same, and wrote songs that pointed to imminent tragedy. Lines like 'I'm playing my music peacefully, but people want to kill me. Do whatever you want. I won't die' took on a prophetic ring. The denouement came in 1970, when Bavon Marie-Marie was driving through the suburb of Bandal with his girlfriend Lucy. He pulled out from behind a lorry and smashed into an oncoming car. Bavon was killed; Lucy had both legs amputated, and works today as a market trader.

By 1970, the youth movement was in full swing. Older bands like Afrisa fought back with new styles and gimmicks: dance troupes onstage, new rhythms like the soum-djoum. But it was the young bands that took over, with a rougher form of soukous and frontline singers who bellowed instructions to the crowd, moved away from the microphones and danced in unison. The band that led the breakthrough was Zaiko Langa Langa, still revered today as leaders of the youth cult. Zaiko started as ex-students, bourgeois tearaways who came together at the Bar Hawaii in Avenue Bolongo. They were remarkable, then and now, for their energy, the wildness of their dancing, and singing which blew away the old neat harmonies with a sweet-edged free-for-all, best described as a 'beau désordre' (beautiful disorder). The early rhythms, the yeye national and kuepe puepe, the rhythm that makes cobras dance, gave way to a new sound in 1973, the cavacha, with three variations – the cavacha primer, tambour and mondiale – and enough new-wave energy to spark off a fresh musical boom.

Above all, it was the guitar that distinguished Zaiko. Up to that point, the guitar had provided rhythm and embellishment, most bands using a mix of horns and guitars to stoke up the dance. Zaiko discarded the old, neat horn arrangements and transformed the guitar into a blustering lead instrument. Their original guitarist, Manuaku Waku, is said to have the hardest left hand in Zaire, and is capable of holding an unbroken stream of soukous for forty minutes non-stop. The seben, the wilder, second section, became a Zaiko showpiece, providing the testing-ground for new rhythms, like the zekete zekete, based directly on Zairean folklore. And no one took the seben further than Manuaku.

The young bands took the idea of authenticity to new levels. Oscar Diabanza, of the National Theatre in Kinshasa, explains the changes that took place. 'In the old days, bands like African Jazz played virtually white music. Kalle sang in French, which was very chic. In those days, people were judged by their clothes, which had to be European, and by their ability to speak French. Today, however, we've rediscovered our own traditions. And that goes for music, as well as our attitude to life generally. What Kalle did was to impose an Afro-Cuban structure on the music. But the true songs of Zaire didn't have this structure. Traditional songs are extremely narrative in content, and very free in structure. Someone like Papa Wemba understands this. He explores our traditional material, and the young bands have followed him, playing the traditional rhythms to the sound of the tam tam. It's a reclamation of traditional forms and rhythms, which people now dance to in the seben.'[12]

It would take a team of genealogists to trace the whole Zaiko family tree. Like OK Jazz, the band nurtured a collection of talents that stretch from Papa Wemba to Manuaku, now leaders of Viva La Musica and Grand Zaiko Wa Wa respectively; and Evoloko, the founder of Langa Langa Stars. From these second-generation bands have come a further crop of new-generation stars, such as Emeneya, leader of Victoria Eleison; and Bozy Boziana, founder of Choc Stars. Zaiko's influence was, and still is, huge.

Midnight at the Cosmo Club. An evening with Grand Zaiko Wa Wa starts slowly – at eleven, the open-air club, with tiled floor, tin-roofed stage and backdrop of towering palm trees, had been all but deserted. At the back of the club, a small clutch of people gather round, sitting at metal tables and drinking cold Primus beer as Grand Zaiko warm up with 'Guantanamera'. The singer's voice, a good octave below the trebly Kinshasa norm, booms around the empty floor. The arrival of the Grand Zaiko singers, however, puts an end both to the Latin sound and the empty spaces. Four singers gather in front of a row of mikes, all wet-look hair and gold chains and leather trousers, baggy at the top and riding up from tasselled brogue shoes. Their faces, anointed with whitener, gleam under the coloured lights. In the West, these creams have been condemned for their high mercury content, which can lead to skin cancer. In Zaire, they have been stylish and fashionable for many years.

Grand Zaiko start in traditional style, launching each song with a slow rumba. The audience keep their seats while the harmonies ring their sweet and ragged message into the night, but they hit the floor when the beat quickens, and Manuaku, a tall and moustachioed gent rather than a rumba rude boy, swings into action. Long solos, plucked from the high end of the fretboard, stream out over an insistent rhythm pick. The snare drum beats out a galloping rhythm as singers wheel and dip and the animateur (shouter) bawls instructions and catchphrases into the microphone. The audience responds gleefully with a dance step that involves a fractional raising of the knee and a quick freeze. It's called 'Bayaka Ba Ye Mabe', a traditional step brought up to date for the Cosmo crowd.

The gig finishes around five in the morning, but Manuaku, who walks freely on and off stage, to lean against the back wall or chat with friends, has already gone. His house is virtually next door to the club. He settles back in an armchair and describes how Zaiko took much of their early power from the folklore of the Mongo people. The cavacha, though, was a modern dance, and it astonished the Kinshasa listeners rather more than it astonished Zaiko. 'We were young,' says Manuaku. 'We didn't realize the greatness of what we were doing.'

Others did. In 1972, President Mobutu had visited Peking and, impressed by the vibrancy of China's post-colonial revolution, started his programme to re-Africanize his own country. Authenticity, as it was known, changed the name of the country from the Congo, with its Belgian connotations, to Zaire. Leopoldville became Kinshasa. Zaireans, now addressed as Citoyen or Citoyenne, swapped their former Christian names for new authentic names, while African rather than European suits and clothes became the norm. Large festivals promoted traditional music, fashions and hairstyles, worked or 'planted' into hundreds of intricate shapes. The cultural movement gave added muscle to a re-Africanization that had already been taking place in the music. Mobutu's directive was clear. In a broadcast on the state of the nation in December 1972, he explained:

> We must at all costs revitalize our music . . . what shocks us is that many of us know the exact details – and it's not a bad point, quite the contrary – of the lives of great musicians like Mozart, Beethoven and Wagner, up to the point that they'll overlook nothing in the chronicle of their love lives, nor the names of their mistresses. At the same time, they know nothing about our own artists. It is a little as if our own musicians, the singers of our own authenticity, had neither the talent, nor the love life worthy of being remembered by posterity.[13]

To make up the deficiency, the Department of Culture and Arts put together an anthology of rerecorded masterpieces by many of the early musicians, from Wendo to Adou Elenga, Feruzi and Leon Bukasa. The new generation of younger musicians was already working along the same lines, with authentic instruments, rhythms and even names. Zaiko, for example, took their name from the Zaire of their ancestors, Zaire ba Ko Ko. (Langa Langa was chosen for its pleasant sound, but turned out later to be the name of a curative plant that grows on the banks of the River Zaire.)

Authenticity encouraged other Zairean stars, none more flamboyant than Papa Wemba. Eccentric on the grand scale, Wemba sports the flashiest of imported clothes, straight from the couturières of Paris and Rome, plus straightened hair and unorthodox behaviour. He lives in his own imaginary chiefdom, Village Molokai, and uses his own language, street argot based on Lingala, French and American expressions. Asked to appear on Zairean television, Wemba turns up wearing a pith helmet, baggy shorts, ivory-tipped cane and white socks. And so do the ten small children with him. Onstage he is master of 'la griffe' (from 'griffer', to stamp with a signature), a perverse display of his latest clothes – trousers from France and Italian shoes sometimes balanced on his head for greater visibility. Designer labels are held up, prices quoted, often more for a jacket than a monthly Kinshasa pay cheque. Everybody loves a cheeky chappie, and Zaireans are no exception. But Wemba's talent goes beyond the ability to patronize high-class fashion houses. After splitting from Zaiko in 1974, he formed his own band, Isife Lokole, which introduced a traditional log drum, the lokole, into the line-up. Bypassing the accepted styles, he'd appear on stage dressed in traditional clothes, sporting raffia skirt, cowrie shells and pointed, shell-covered hat. For his young followers, this was a shock exposure to a way of life that had been dismissed in colonial times as crude and shameful.

Today, Wemba is back with flamboyant import labels and designer clothes. 'Papa Wemba plays Brazzaville,' says a newspaper hoarding, 'four dead.' The crowd had turned up not to hear him, but to see his latest clothes. A similar fever has hit Kinshasa where, as if to rebut President Mobutu's criticism, the lives and loves of Zairean musicians are held up for constant examination, while the appearance of a musician in the street guarantees far more excitement, today, than if the ghost of Mozart were suddenly to appear.

A sudden commotion marks the arrival of Emeneya, the charismatic leader of Victoria Eleison, at the Xadis record shop. Two vast speakers, flanking the door, pump out one of his great songs, 'Sans Préavis'. A car purrs up to the store, with Emeneya standing in the open back. Of all Kinshasa's youth stars, Emeneya is the most charismatic. He has the hauteur of the true star, along with the looks. His hair, cropped Carl Lewis-style at the sides, stands up straight, wet-look on top. A short, scrubby beard and staring eyes have earned him the name Jesus. At home, Emeneya sits in front of videos of Madonna and Stevie Wonder, but his real inspiration comes from above. 'My songs are mostly about God,' he says. 'God, the Bible and morals. I can't compose something without first looking in the Bible, especially the Apocalypse in Revelations. For any problem you can think of, the Bible has the answer.' The next night, however, the Bible proves itself less than omnipotent. Emeneya is due to play at the Veve Centre. By midnight, nothing has happened. The rest of the band are hanging around outside. The difficulty: instruments, which for reasons best known to himself, the owner won't let the band use.

The man on whom Victoria Eleison depend for their instruments, and much more besides, is Kiamuangana Verckys, a musician turned businessman who, thanks to his wealth and hard work, virtually controls the music scene. Finding him is easy. Flag down a taxi, say 'Verckys' and sit back as the taxi bumps its way to the tallest, most castle-like tower in Matonge. This is the five-floor Veve Centre, which has offices, rehearsal rooms and stores, all built around a high-walled, tiled courtyard which houses the Veve Centre nightclub. Down one side of the building, a huge whisky advertisement shines down, like the spirit of Bacchanal, over Matonge. On the dusty pavement a huddle of businessmen are standing, gesticulating, around a blue Mercedes. One man is sucking petrol from the pump and directing it into a can. A row of women selling fried food in the shade of the building, plus a couple of beggars, look on nonchalantly. In the middle of the huddle stands a man with a blue suit, a stony expression and an air of absolute authority. While still a sax player with OK Jazz, Kiamuangana Verckys started sponsoring a new generation of youth bands by providing instruments and recording facilities. In the early 1970s, his own band, Orchestre Veve, continued the OK Jazz style, producing a string of melodic singles, such as 'Nakomitunaka', whose radical, pro-Mobutist sentiments put him at the forefront of Mobutu's cultural revolution.

In the business world, Verckys has been equally clear-sighted. His reputation springs from a mixture of acumen, wealth and opportunism. As few instrument are made in Zaire, the music scene depends entirely on imports; so he who holds the import licence holds the key. Using his power of patronage, Verckys has built up a stable of top bands, from Victoria Eleison to Grand Zaiko Wa Wa and Empire Bakuba. All receive their instruments from Verckys. They record in his studio, creating a garage-band soukous whose wildness and echo define the new sound of Kinshasa.

Verckys' office is a large, imposingly gloomy room with brown felt-covered walls, one of which is filled with a blown-up poster showing palm trees, blue sea and endless golden sand and a desk the size of an aircraft carrier. A woman, baby on her back, stands in the doorway remonstrating with Verckys. A business aide guides her back along the corridor, still shouting as the head of the Veve empire looks up briefly and replies, 'Madame, you are impolite.' Verckys provokes strong feelings. To some young musicians, he is seen, publicly at least, as a saviour. To others, he is an exploiter. And to Tabu Ley and Franco he is an arch enemy, a businessman rather than a musician, an upstart who has usurped their once impregnable position by snapping up much of the city's younger talent. The situation became worse when Verckys took extra power and kudos as head of the Musicians' Union. He has been set upon, attacked in the press. Pure jealousy, says Verckys. He produces a letter signed by Franco and Tabu Ley asking him to a meeting. 'Why should I stand down?' he asks. 'If I leave, it will be by the front door, not round the back.' Three days later, Radio Trottoir was buzzing with rumours that Verckys had finally resigned. The quarrel with Franco continued as the OK Jazz leader accused Verckys of stealing his top singer, Dalienst.

In a first-floor room Verckys' old band, Orchestre Veve, is rehearsing for a comeback and a possible European tour. The line-up includes Abbé Imana, a Catholic priest, on vocals; and Dizzy Mandjeku, one of the founding members of Sam Mangwana's African All Stars, from the late 1970s. After Franco and Tabu Ley, Sam Mangwana is one of Zaire's great innovators, restoring African interest in a music that had fallen well behind the Nigerian highlife of Prince Nico and Oliver de Coque. Mandjeku, his right-hand man, now Verckys' musical director, plays a couple of quick riffs and the introduction to Mangwana's classic soukous-biguine 'Nsimba Eli'. He then leads the way to a nearby roadside bar which, like most of Matonge drinking-places, offers a small dancefloor, open-air drinking under a tree strung with coloured lightbulbs, and booming music. For the man who helped define a new African crossover, Mandjeku had the right credentials. He started playing jazz guitar in 1964 with small, largely European bands. Before the African All Stars, he'd worked as an arranger with Tabu Ley. He joined Mangwana in Festival du Maquisards, before working on Mangwana's new, accessible mixture of soukous and Antillean rhythms. The heavy bass drum and four-square beat made a lasting impression on other top bands. 'Everyone followed,' explains Mandjeku. 'Tabu Ley's "Sarah" has the African All Stars sound. So does much of what OK Jazz is now doing.'

Mangwana's interest in Afro-Cuban music continued unabated. When Johnny Pacheco visited Kinshasa in the early 1970s, he was photographed conferring a mock blessing on the kneeling Zairean star. A new generation of Kinshasa musicians has now followed Mangwana's example, embracing the new form of Antillean music known as zouk. Two of the best-known are Nyboma, of Les Quatre Etoiles, and Pepe Kalle, whose joint 1986 album featured an Antillean-flavoured track called 'Zouké Zouké'.

Nyboma's collaborator lives in the quiet suburb of Bandal, whose back streets are lined with palm trees and, at night, people sitting and talking in pools of candlelight, playing guitars, table tennis or reading. An air of deep tranquillity fills the neighbourhood. The leader of Empire Bakuba, Kalle is a flamboyant figure, towering well over six feet with a girth that has earned him the name the Elephant of Zaire. Everything around him seems smaller than life – the red Volkswagen that he drives and Emauro, the Pygmy who dances with the band. Kalle's recreations include football and karate; onstage he displays new, agile dances, among them the sousmarine, with its chorus line: 'Oh nagez, oh nagez.'

Kalle's house is full of wonder. In a white courtyard sit a row of women and children wearing white, holding candles and chanting from prayer books. Inside, the lounge is heaped with furniture, tourist items, spears, raffia mats and a large refrigerator, from which Kalle dispenses regular bottles of Primus. A large plastic chicken sits on the television set, from which President Mobutu is making one of his regular broadcasts. Kalle sits back and talks about his career. Like Nigerian juju star Ebenezer Obey, he started singing as a chorister in a mission school, and he shares the same breathy vocal style. He then lived and worked in Joseph Kabasele's house for two years, and dates his own African Jazz influence, the sweet vocals and sharp melodies, to that early experience. Today, Empire Bakuba is one of Zaire's foremost youth bands, mixing rumba with a range of folk rhythms from the Luba and Kongo people, his 1984 *Amour Propre* incorporating the traditional rhythms from lower Zaire. Lyrically, though, Kalle has his limitations. 'If you want to eat in Zaire, you have to sing about love,' he explains. 'That's the one subject that interests people. It is also something of a problem. Johnny Halliday, for example, can sing stuff like "If I were a Carpenter" and "I was Born in the Night". Nana Mouskouri sings about flowers, roses and beautiful evenings. Zaireans are too amorous. It's hard to sing about rivers, roads or fridges. To eat, you have to sing about love.'

Few bands in Kinshasa seem willing to break the mould. Songs about politics are left largely to Franco. To step outside rumba and soukous, it is necessary to turn to the rootsier likembe bands and traditional outfits like Kintoene National, or to try Kinshasa's non-soukous band, Bobongo Stars. Nearly everything about the band is different. They have their own nightclub, with shining mirrors and air conditioning, a European manager and a musical policy that goes beyond what sells in Kinshasa to embrace jazz, funk and soul. Bobongo Stars are unpacking their equipment in an upstairs studio. Santana plays over the loudspeakers, followed by silence, then 'Take Five', then Frank Sinatra. 'Most of the bands here, like Zaiko, play the music of Kinshasa,' says Bobongo's leader, Bastia. 'When I think of Zairean music, though, it's something different. I think of folklore, music from the villages. As for soukous, I don't find anything extraordinary in it. I'm inspired by other people — Earth Wind & Fire, Manu Dibango, classical music. We're looking for a world audience, not just success in Kinshasa.'[14]

Bobongo Stars call their music Zairo, a sound based on Zairean roots rhythms, with the keyboards picking up the traditional flavours of the likembe. They have produced three albums, *Zairo* appearing on RCA in 1980. The band have played in France and counter their lack of acceptance at home by writing advertising jingles for Zairean television. 'It's only now that young musicians are beginning to follow us,' says Bastia. 'They are slowly beginning to copy our way of playing solos, the Bobongo look, which has its own choreography and fashions . . .'

Launching new fashions in a city that houses the irrepressible Papa Wemba and his numerous acolytes sounds an uphill task. Of Wemba's young musicians, few have gone further than Bipoli, a former Viva La Musica dancer and singer who left to join Emeneya in Victoria Eleison and then form his own band, Victoria Principal — 'Dallas' is big in Zaire. Late in 1985, Bipoli rejoined Papa Wemba. He cuts a slightly menacing figure, wearing black leather trousers and shirt and carrying a spiky steel walking-stick, but he still attracts the punters by creating new dances, like the mbrototo, with the necessary regularity. His name has appropriately new-wave overtones. Bipoli Na Foun means something rotten, something from a bin. For Western audiences, Rotten has inevitably links with the Sex Pistols, but this is of little interest to Zaireans. The name came from a group of Kinshasa journalists who were amazed at Bipoli's high-speed dancing on stage. Bipoli confirms this. 'It's true. I dance so fast that I can't see what's in front of me,' he explains.

Bipoli talks endlessly about the changing Kinshasa fashions, the vogue for American brogues and French trousers, about the range of hairstyles, the curly, or wet look, trademarked by Grand Zaiko in 1984, and the Wife, whose short sides and spiky top are seen to advantage in Victoria Eleison. The 1985 look, he explains, was drôle de choses, a mixture of wool and leather clothes, while most singers follow either the rasta look, which is seen as distinctly uncool, or the Julio Iglesias style, with all its modern, European chic. The one thing that seems to unite Kinshasa's fashion-conscious musical community, however, is the use of skin whiteners. 'It's normal here,' he says. 'Singers are like flowers. We put on the cosmetics for the women. Without them, there is no ambience. And when the women turn up, they attract a larger clientele.'

Back at Ndjilly Airport, the Air Zaire plane waits on the blistering tarmac. In the departure lounge sits Emeneya with sundry Veve personnel. He explains that he's off to Paris, possibly to buy new instruments, new clothes, too. In Kinshasa, both are essential . . .

JOSEPH KALLE

The father of modern Zairean music, Joseph Kabasele, aka Le Grand Kalle, was born in Matadi in 1930, subsequently moving to Kinshasa where, in 1950, he made his debut. This was with OTC, Orchestre de Tendence Congolaise, a band which specialized in acoustic polka pique and mazurka rhythms. With his own band, African Jazz, launched in 1953, Kalle turned towards the Afro-Cuban sound, in particular the rumba, samba and cha cha, all played in a distinctively Congolese style by a line-up that included, later, electric guitars.

Kalle made further marks on the scene. In 1960 he created his own label, Surboum African Jazz, sending musicians like Franco and OK Jazz to Belgium to record. He also composed a hymn to the new independent Congo, 'Independence Cha Cha'. Seven years later, at the Organization of African Unity summit in Kinshasa, he presented each of the thirty heads of state with a single hymning their own countries in the appropriate local melody and rhythm. It was, said Kalle, a mark of his craftsmanship. Kalle's days in Kinshasa, however, were numbered. In 1969, feeling himself to be under surveillance and his freedom of movement limited, he left for Paris, where he formed the Afro-Latin fusion band African Team with Manu Dibango, Jean-Serge Essous and Don Gonzalo. From then on Paris was his base. He returned to Zaire in the late 1970s, but worked and recorded in Europe. He died in the French capital on 11 February 1983.

Kalle was important not just for the wealth of songs he recorded, but also for the development of the Latin tendency in Zairean music, creating a style whose sweetness and melodic strength is still in evidence in Zaire today. He also provided a training-ground for a new generation of musicians. Among them, Dr Nico joined African Jazz in the late 1950s and contributed a stunning, swaggering solo to the 'Independence' single which still rings true today. Nico, who went on to join Tabu Ley in African Fiesta before forming his own band African Fiesta Sukisa, was known as the God of the Guitar. He developed a sweet single-note style, plus a dance rhythm, the kiri kiri, occasionally playing Hawaiian style in

161

the manner of his early mentor, the slide guitarist Jhimmy.

Nico's career faded in the late 1970s when his record company collapsed, taking his health with it. By 1983, though, he had started recording in Lome, and working live with the top Zairean singer Abeti. Nico cut four albums before falling fatally ill in 1985.

Kalle's African Jazz stimulated other great artists; some followed, others developed in opposition, producing a rootsier, more Zairean music. The father of the opposition is Luambo Makiadi, known either as Luambo or Franco.

FRANCO

'When I was small, all the world was astounded at how I played the guitar. I was tiny. The guitar was bigger than I was. People asked how such a small person could play such a big guitar.'[15]

Times have changed and so has Franco. After a quarter of a century in the music business, he has the size and the status of a colossus. He has recorded over 150 albums, created a rhythm that has become a permanent part of Zairean music and, through his band OK Jazz, showcased many of Zaire's top musicians, from Sam Mangwana to Dalienst, Youlou Mabiala and Michelino. His organization is equally vast: with three labels — Edipop, Visa 80 and Choc — and, in the mid-1980s, three separate bands — one OK Jazz in Belgium, two in Zaire.

Franco was born in 1939 in a small village called Sona Bata, seventy-eight kilometres from Kinshasa. His father wanted him to be a doctor. Franco had other ideas. Armed with a home-made tin-can guitar and folk-song repertoire, he played around the markets in Kinshasa before joining an acoustic group called Bikunda. In 1950, Bikunda became Watam. It had two guitarists, Franco and Paul Ebongo Dewayon, and a rhythm section playing frame drums. Loningisa, a local record company owned by a Greek businessman, Papadimitriou, moved in. Three years later, Watam recorded its first single, 'Bolingo Na Ngai Na Beatrice'. Three more hits followed.

In 1956, OK Jazz was born. OK meant two things: Orchestre Kinois, Kinois being a citizen of Kinshasa; OK were also the initials of an early sponsor, Omar Kashama, who ran a bar called Chez Cassien OK Bar. And Jazz: 'In 1956 we were still a colony,' says Franco. 'There were many Europeans in Kinshasa. We had to play everything and, as the Europeans danced to jazz, we played a little jazz.'

But not for long. While Kalle's African Jazz developed a sweet, progressive style based as much on the cha cha as the evolving Kinshasa rumba, Franco led his band off on a different path. The first references came from Latin music. 'When we started, everyone wanted the bolero and the cha cha,' he explained. 'Then they switched to rumba. For us, it was better. If you play the cha cha, people only dance in twos. With rumba, everyone joins in.'

Further transformations took place. In 1960, Franco's love affair with a woman called Majos inspired a set of classic songs and a rumba style that would form the basis for his later, sprawling satirical pieces. Kalle and his young singer Tabu Ley developed new dances and styles. Franco stuck with the rumba and his own, faster variant, which he christened rumba odemba. Later he incorporated new dance rhythms. But, he says, the rumba ruled: 'It's like jazz. You've got reggae, rock and twist. But jazz is the mother. It's always there. It's the same with Zaire. You've got the boucher, the cavacha and the yeki yeki. But the rumba is the root.'

Culturally, Franco was a key figure. His earthy vocals and love of street wisdom and gossip created memorable songs and defined a new style, that looked, not to Belgium or Latin America, but back to Zaire itself. Franco's rumba was primarily a city creation. As the 1960s progressed, he developed a second string, bringing Zairean folklore into his music. For Franco, the two strands remain separate: 'The rumba is rumba, folklore is folklore.' His interest is undimmed. In 1984, 'Kimpa Kisangamene' took authentic rhythms from bas-Zaire into the bars and hotels of Kinshasa.

Like all true artists, Franco has moved with the times. In the early days, a Franco rumba sounded for the most part impossibly fast, clean and well ordered, all pit-a-pat congas and racing harmonies. The modern music has slowed down. It has bulk and self-importance: the bass is heavier, bass drums giving a pronounced thwack to the rustic ticking of the rhythm guitars. These are no longer songs. They are vehicles. And Franco has room to talk.

As a singer, Franco has few equals. His voice is large, gruff and conversational. He sings about everyday issues in tones that seem to boom from the back of a Kinshasa taxi rather than the tonsils of a love-sick rumba star. As if to point up the contrast, he surrounds himself with back-up singers whose fruity tones conjure up the energy and gusto of an Edwardian barber's-shop quintet. Like Fela and Mahlathini, Franco dominates his material. The melody is less important than the total sound. The backing fades into a well-oiled gently ticking piece of machinery.

His guitar playing is no less individual. Where Kinshasa's virtuoso players, like Dr Nico, took flight on elaborate volleys and clusters of single notes, Franco prefers a fatter souud, plucking the melody on two strings, holding a single chord while the band chop and change around him. His finger style is important: a form of playing whose technique and sound put Franco closer to the old likembe players than the great single-note men of the 1960s.

When he first started, though, Franco was considered a modernizer. One of his great influences was a Belgian guitarist, Bill Alexandre, the Django Reinhardt of Kinshasa, who, says Franco, introduced solo guitar playing into the city. Up to that point the Kinshasa guitar players had played folk-style. Alexandre introduced single notes, at the top as well as the bottom of the fretboard. 'Our elders told us not to follow the new music,' says Franco. 'But we said no. And we were right. We're still playing. The old style has gone.'

Franco's output has been prodigious. He himself has lost count, but most estimates of it settle at around 150 albums. His themes are many and varied. He sings about love – usually when it goes wrong; relates street gossip, current events and political issues. When President Mobutu decided to change the name of the country to Zaire, in 1973, and to rename all the country's main towns and provinces, Franco toured the country explaining the changes. During general elections, he has thrown his weight behind Mobutu. And when things go bad, he picks up on what people are saying – complaints about the economy perhaps – and works them into songs.

His position is unique. He is a man of the people – a folk musician but also a confidant of the President. He can sing openly on subjects that are usually merely whispered about: 'I have my freedom,' says Franco. 'I can sing about things that people think, but don't like to say out loud.' As an example, he cites 'Lettre à Monsieur le Directeur Général' on his *Choc Choc Choc* album of 1983. European listeners have interpreted this as an attack on Mobutu. Franco denies this. 'It's an attack on company managers who don't listen to what their employees are saying,' he explains. 'The manager directs thousands of people, but only relies on what one or two people close to him are saying. He is completely out of touch.' The director general is any director, anywhere. 'It's for all of them,' says Franco. 'In London, France, America. All over the world.' He struck a similarly universal note in 1987 with an album warning against AIDS.

As with most important figures, rumour often takes the place of truth. Franco has been arrested and imprisoned twice for sure – once for a motoring offence, once for cutting an indecent song, back in the 1960s. His legend puts the figure far higher, with Franco paying the price for his frequent attacks on minor officials who later rise to high office and take their revenge. Among these, none proved more oblique, more devastating than the robust 'Kimpa Kisangamene', a song directed against a sorcerer, and propelled by a swaggering bass line that captures the whooping vibrations of the traditional nkuiti drum from bas-Zaire.

The song features on Franco's 1984 album *Chez Rythmes et Musiques à Paris*, alongside the extraordinary '12,600 Lettres à Franco' in which he takes on the role of agony aunt to wade through a string of letters dealing with marriage Zaire-style. In Britain, the in-laws traditionally pose problems. In Zaire, sparks fly between the man's wife and his sisters – or so the letters say. Franco sings his way through a handful, calling out the women's names and their problems. 'This one's from Citoyenne Mosapi,' he says. 'Her sister-in-law doesn't want her to cook for her husband any more. She's doing it instead . . . Madame Dikuma, from the Republic of the Congo, says she can't conceive. Her sister-in-law insults her, saying that the only thing she can do properly is to run around in cars, wearing expensive jewellery.' The list continues: Madame Obibia, whose sister-in-law insults her in front of her own children; Madame Afia, whose husband gave her money to set up a stall selling material in the market, and whose sister-in-law now comes to help herself to cloth without paying.

Franco chews the problem over and decides, chauvinistically, that 'women will never build a city: they're always quarrelling among themselves'. To the sister, he says: 'If your brother is married and you realize there's something wrong, never talk to the wife. Go straight to the brother.'

In his 1985 epic, 'Mario', Franco takes the real-life situation of a young Zairean gigolo living with the older widow of a prominent politician. For once, Franco attacks the man, blaming him for taking the woman's money, deliberately smashing up her furniture and her Mercedes, storing up other women's addresses. The woman complains about his new-fangled tastes, his preference for rice and ground cassava plantain to the old cassava bread; his insistence on new, white stainless razor blades in place of the old blue ones. The last straw comes when Mario insists that the woman buy him a big necklace with a cross attached. 'It's on show at Jacques et Mère,' he says. 'If I don't get it, that's it.' Franco advises him to return to his family house, sleep in his old bed, and get a job that will repay all the money that has been spent on his studies.

Franco's work contains frequent references to other singers. During his time he has quarrelled with a number of artists, including Tabu Ley and one of his early musicians, Kwamy. All were attacked in song. When Kwamy left, he dedicated a song to Franco called 'Faux Millionaire'. Franco replied with 'Cours au Pouvoir' in which he sings: 'You are running me down everywhere, but I take it as a joke. You suffer when you get news about everything Franco is doing. You wish Franco's name would disappear for ever . . .'

At other times, Franco lends his name to commercial products: 'Azda' from 1973 advertised Volkswagen cars; 'Fabrice', in 1984, a Zairean tailor living in Brussels; while in 1985 he recorded a long, lilting song in praise of the Gabon's national football team, FC 105 De Libreville.

Although he offers a broadsheet view of Kinshasa life, Franco is also keen to spread his wings. In 1983 he toured America and played a stunning London concert. For Franco the visit was long overdue, a recognition that Africa had something to teach the West, just as the West had something to teach Africa. The tragedy is that, up till now, the trade has been strictly one-way. 'When I'm abroad, I'm an ambassador, passing on a message from Zaire, that the rest of the world can learn from us. When Western music comes to Zaire, we listen to it, even though we may not understand the words. We make the effort. When our music goes to the West, though, it's different. Very often people don't understand it. My message is that music is universal. It can be enjoyed by everyone. The instruments are the same. A saxophone is a saxophone. The notes are the same. What is played here can be played by Africans, and what is played in Africa can be played by Europeans. Thats why we're here – to increase understanding.'[16]

ROCHEREAU/TABU LEY

For thirty years, Pascal Tabu, better known as Seigneur Rochereau or Tabu Ley, has been one of the top voices in Zairean, not to say African, music. The heir to the progressive African Jazz style, Ley has kept the flame burning with new dances and rhythms, poetic and romantic lyrics, plus new fashions and forms of stage presentation.

His output – over 100 albums, around 1,000 songs – puts him in the same heavyweight bracket as Franco. But there the similarity ends. Where Franco plays a rootsier version of Zairean rumba, Ley has made his mark with a melodic, sweet-voiced ballad sound that has inspired a new generation of Zairean artists, from Empire Bakuba, Kanda Bongo Man to Langa Langa Stars and Victoria Eleison.

Ley was born in 1940 in Bandoundou, and attended one of Kinshasa's most prestigious schools which spawned a host of politicians and public figures. His first great musical influence was Le Grand Kalle, whose songs Ley would sing at school. His first public appearance on stage at the vast Stadium du 20 Mai in 1955, made Ley an overnight success at the age of fourteen. He met Kalle the following year and started writing songs for him — all of which appeared under the bandleader's name. Three years later, 'Kelia' gave Ley his first writing credit.

By 1959, Tabu Ley had joined African Jazz as a full-time member, plus artistic director, alongside Dr Nico and Manu Dibango. Three years later, ructions split the band. The entire membership left, leaving Kalle on his own. Rochereau found himself with Roger Izeidi, guitarist Dr Nico and Dechaud at the head of a new African Jazz. This band subsequently fell apart, and Ley left with Dr Nico and his brother Dechaud to form African Fiesta. Two years later, a further split took place. Nico and Dechaud left to form African Fiesta Sukisa: Ley's own band took the suffix 'National', later changing to Afrisa, the band that would spread his reputation across Africa and Europe.

A tour across the continent, in 1968, took Ley to Brazzaville, Douala, Contonou, Lome, Niamey, Bobo-Dioulasso and Abidjan, where he stayed for three months. Two years later, he set the seal on his success with an epic appearance at the Paris Olympia, crossing later to London.

Ley's desire for international recognition was apparent from the start. In the early days he sang in Spanish and French as well as Lingala; and immersed himself in the Afro-Cuban music that was available both on records and the occasional tours — Ley, along with Nico and Kabasele, visited Cuba in the late fifties.

He made further innovations. The first was to do with the drum kit, which was initially dismissed as a 'white instrument'. As journalist Francis Laloupo explains, the kit was later to find full acceptance — but only when it was clear that 'the bass drum would not replace the bass guitar which has influenced the listening habits of most Africans'. It is used 'like a percussion instrument itself, a tumba'.[17]

Ley's second great novelty was the spectacular stage show. His first west African tour in front of seated, indifferent audiences, he describes as 'the worst experience of my life'. Up to that point, Zairean bands would remain rooted to the spot, moving imperceptibly, in what Ley describes as a 'rigid posture, tainted with pride and indifference'.[18] To give his shows the necessary physical interest, Ley introduced choreography, a variety of rhythms and his own troupe, the Leyrettes. In Laloupo's words, the 'most timid singer of the two banks' (Zaire and the Congo) became the 'Mohammed Ali of spectacle'. Although his choice of material has been equally wide, stretching from masterpieces of soukous to Zairean versions of Beatles songs like 'Let It Be', it would be wrong to paint Ley as a progressive, looking only to the West for inspiration. He has a strong pan-African streak, and has been known to introduce juju and Afrobeat into his stage shows: playing live with Fela in Dakar in the early 1970s, recording Afrobeat on his live FESTAC album in 1977 and, some years earlier, a Miriam Makeba song called 'Pole M'Ze'. His 'Kaful Mayay', from 1972, dug back into percussive Zairean roots music to become a classic of Authenticité.

It is usual to point to Franco as the main spokesman on life and politics in Zaire, but Ley has also made his mark. Songs like 'Congo Nouveau, Afrique Nouvelle', 'Salongo' and a host of later pro-Mobutu numbers made him into a leading government praise singer. And, like Franco, Ley has also run into problems. In 1969, the government interpreted 'Kashama Nkoi' as a defence of an anti-Mobutu rebel who was later executed. A second earlier song supposedly took the side of three other government opponents who had just faced the firing-squad.

'Makolo Nakokufa' is one of Ley's most plaintive and beautiful songs. The title, which raised official eyebrows, translates as 'The Day I Die'. Ley summons four representatives of Zairean society – a poor man, a rich man, a prostitute and a drunkard – and asks them what they will most miss. The poor man lists his wife, children, and 'all the joy that is in the world'; the rich man his mother, his money, his land, cars and his children, whom he proposes to send to Europe. The drinker will regret leaving his glass of wine, and not being able to get drunk any more; the prostitute her wig, her blouses and 'the sound of African Fiesta'.

A sublime guitar performance, starting with a melodic rhythm line and an economical but devastating solo pattern, complements the power, sorrow and sadness of Ley's lyrics. The words hardly seem revolutionary, yet the song itself is a landmark. For Kazadi Wa Mukuna, it represents a return to the accompaniment and rhythm style of the old masters of the 1950s, Paul Kamba and Wendo.

But Ley looked forward, too. By 1969, he had become a leading exponent of the soukous rhythm that was sweeping Kinshasa. Today the name describes a whole genre of fast Zairean rhythms. In Kinshasa it started life as a single sound: an attempt to accelerate the rumba and to mix it with a peppier disco feel put Ley among the fast-emerging youth bands, who were later to revolutionize the scene with their own rhythms.

A second rhythm, the soumdjoum, owed its genesis to a trip to Senegal in 1972. 'I was inspired by a local dance, the soumbey djoum,' says Ley. 'The Senegalese women seemed to be doing the rumba in an odd kind of way. I asked my dancers to follow the steps and to make something attractive out of it.'[19] The new sound gave Ley a series of numbers like 'Cherie Samba', 'Lolede' and 'Silikane'. Their author describes them as great successes — although the soumdjoum is often seen as a low point in his career.

With the rhythm came a new guitar sound called the soum. Most guitarists in Zaire, says Ley, start by learning soum, which involves the use of chords and arpeggios, rather than the finger-picking characteristic of the standard Zairean playing.

Since then, Ley has continued to mix old and new forms, harnessing technology to re-create the traditional rhythms of his birthplace in Bandoundou. His song 'Cadence Mudanda', recorded in 1984 with his co-singer and lover M'Bilia Bel, uses chattering guitars to pick out the jangling and repetitive sound of the old likembe. The original rhythm, says Ley, came from Bandoundou and was played on traditional instruments: likembe, xylophone, tam tam and bells.

The one area which Ley avoids is the creation of new dances, a task that he leaves firmly, and disdainfully, in the hands of the youth bands. 'The younger musicians have, if you'll pardon the expression, prostituted themselves,' he says. 'One year it's the zekete zekete, next it's the choc. Every time you dance the rumba badly you've got a new dance. I could take my dancers and say — follow that man over there, he dances really badly. They develop it and you have a new dance. For me, the new dances are all deformations of the rumba.'

In 1982 Ley's career, which had been sagging slightly over the years, received a new impetus when he teamed up with M'Bilia Bel and produced a succession of songs that defended Zairean women against the musical onslaughts from Franco and his right-hand man, Lutumba Simarro. A pattern appeared with Franco attacking, Bel and Ley defending, as in 'Eswi Yo Wapi', which throws its weight behind divorced women, and other songs which describe the plight of the older wives in a polygamous triangle.

Ley's relations with Franco have also had their ups and downs. Both started out as the poets laureate of independence, praising the politicians and giving full support to Mobutu when he took office. But their alternative musical strategies also led to strong rivalries. Today, Franco denies this existed, and puts it down to factionalism among the fans. Ley, on the other hand, agrees that there were differences, and says that they would attack each other regularly in song: 'It was all done in a very civilized manner.' Such arguments have been left far behind. The new era of co-operation between the two giants culminated with their working together on a series of joint albums, sharing musicians, contributing their own songs and creating a new, beefy, disco-flavoured sound that is notable for its polished production and hefty bass drum.

The impetus for the reunion may have been the meteoric rise of Verckys as a musical (and business) threat. It may also have had something to do with the death of the father of Zairean music Ley's great mentor Joseph Kabasele, in 1983. 'Kalle was the grand master,' says Ley. 'He initiated me into music and made me what I am today, both in life and in art. When I had a problem, Kalle would help me to the maximum.'

A fuller, musical tribute to Le Grand Kalle coincided with Ley's reunion with his old rival, Franco, on the 1983 Choc Choc Choc album *Incroyable! mais Vrai! Rochereau et Franco à Paris*. A host of references to sorcerers and fetish priests underlined the significance of the meeting. The elders, the magicians of Zairean music, were at work. To Kalle, Ley wrote the emotion-charged 'Kabasele in Memoriam', which asks: 'Where is the doctor who can bring life back to Kabasele, our friend, the father of modern Zairean music . . .'

SAM MANGWANA

A protégé of both Tabu Ley and Franco, Sam Mangwana is one of Zaire's least conventional stars. He is known as Le Pigeon Voyageur, the travelling pigeon, an artist who constantly travels, sidestepping the usual stereotypes. Big stars have regular bands – Mangwana has none. They buy houses, hotels, clubs – Mangwana values his art above his bank balance or strings of luxury villas. His career has provoked controversy, rumour and violence – plus a new Zairean style which mixes the rumba with biguine to give a distinctive Afro-Antillean mixture.

Mangwana was born in 1945 and started his career in 1963 when he joined Tabu Ley in African Fiesta. Over the next nine years, he worked on and off with Ley, quitting for brief spells with Negros Band, Tembo

Orchestre and Vox Afrique, and, in 1968, a successful stint with Orchestre Maquisards, which had a number of hits including 'Zelangaina Sala'. In 1972, Mangwana, restless to the last, changed camps and moved to Franco's TPOK Jazz. Such a change caused unheard-of controversy. Rochereau and Franco were considered to be poles apart: they had their own styles – and their own fans in opposing camps. The change was simply unthinkable. Mangwana even received threatening letters; he was forced to hide in a hotel guarded by gendarmes. Finally the dispute grew too much for him; Mangwana decided it was time for a change.

In 1976, he embarked on a tour of Africa that took him from Zaire to Accra, Ghana, Nigeria, Cameroon, Togo, Lome and finally the Côte d'Ivoire. In the capital Abidjan, Mangwana, with guitarist Dizzy Mandjeku and singer Theo Blaise Kounkou, formed a band called Amida, to modernize Zairean folklore. The plan failed. Next, the trio created African All Stars, with guitarist Syran Mbenza and a large, fluctuating membership that included, at various times, Nyboma, Lokassa Ya Mbongo, Syran Mbenza and Bopol, and with it, a new hugely influential style of soukous. Rather than stick to the old Zairean-style rumba, African All Stars blended it with highlife, Afrobeat and above all, biguine to create a solid Afro-Antilles crossover.

Guitarist Mandjeku explains the switch: 'Our music wasn't well-known here on the west coast. For them it sounded too light. It had to become heavier. In Abidjan I started experimenting with jazz-funk sounds, adopting the flanger, the wah wah, the shifter. I developed a finger-picking, rather than the thumb-picking bass-guitar style, which I learnt from the makossa bands. The rhythms were Zairean while the drummer played in Antilles biguine style with a pronounced bass drum.'[20] The structure of the music also changed. In place of the old two-part songs, with a slow rumba leading into a hectic seben, Mangwana pioneered a 'non-stop' style, inspired partly by a James Brown epic, 'There was a Time' and offering a single dance rhythm.

The African All Stars, however, ran into problems. According to Mandjeku himself, Mangwana was unsure. His first reaction to the finished tapes was: 'Is this good or not?' When the band performed at a reception for the Zairean Ambassador in Abidjan, they were accused of forgetting their own music and asked to play Zaiko numbers. At home the suspicion was equally pronounced. Only when OK Jazz played a version of his massive hit 'Georgette Eckins' did the mistrust die down. The style took over. 'Everyone followed our bass-drum sound,' says

Mandjeku. 'Before, the drum set was of little importance. They'd never think of pushing the kit into the foreground. Now it became fashionable.'[21] Mangwana himself has few qualms. 'To be modern and interesting to people, you must create music that people can understand, you must speak to them in their own language. If you meet someone dancing to Afrobeat, you must move towards them, make something that will get through to them. That's my philosophy. My music has no name, it's just African music.'

Out of the new music came a string of hits, each mixing Zairean guitars with a solid beat and a singing style – from the sweetest of tenors to the most swaggering of middle registers – that has become Mangwana's hallmark. The first hit, created in Abidjan, was 'Georgette Eckins'. Others followed, with Mangwana mixing not only musical idioms but also languages, from Lingala to Spanish and French, a linguistic gift that goes back to the early days when, as a member of Rochereau's band, he was made to learn the whole repertoire of Orchestre Aragon.

Throughout the late 1970s, Mangwana remained a force on the African scene, influencing such musicians as Bopol, Nyboma and Souzy Kasseya. His music swept the continent, and so did the piracy in its wake. Mangwana was astonished. 'I've been exploited savagely,' he says. 'My records have been reproduced on cassette, and pirated up and down Africa. Economically we are sinking and the main problem is that the artists have no control over their means of production. There are great names in Africa, people who have sold millions of records, but they've made nothing. They've been exploited.'[22]

In 1979, Mangwana arrived in Paris with a slimmer line-up of Syran, Bopol and Pablo. He rerecorded 'Georgette Eckins' and cut the *Maria Tebbo* album, which mixed the tenderness of the title track with the political exultation of 'Chimurenga Zimbabwe' – a celebration of that country's new-found freedom. Three years later, Mangwana was himself to fly to southern Africa and throw himself further into the great political struggles of the region.

But first, he returned to Zaire and a particularly bizarre welcome. The public hadn't forgotten Mangwana's 'desertion' four years earlier. The press appeared to be stung by his lifestyle, his apparent rootlessness. During his absence, rumours had been put around that Mangwana had been killed in Paris: 'The work of the mafia, the producers whom I had previously refused to work with,' says Mangwana. Further criticisms stung Mangwana – that he was unstable, that he had chosen to work solo, while other artists kept with their bands. Finally, he appeared on television, explaining how his work had spread the fame of Zaire.

The seal was finally set on Mangwana's return when he released an album with Franco in 1982, entitled *Co Operation*, and joined him onstage at a concert in Kinshasa. Afterwards, Franco was so delighted that he presented Mangwana with a new car.

Politically, Mangwana has shown himself as a strong champion of African liberation, through albums like the 1983 *Canta Moçambique*, which he recorded as a tribute and an encouragement to the revolution that had ousted the Portuguese in favour of a new independent Mozambique. Mangwana arrived in the country to find the people demoralized by the continuing struggle with South Africa, brought to their knees by drought and, finally, forced into a humiliating treaty with the architects of apartheid.

The treaty saddened Mangwana, but he refuses to dismiss it as a defeat. 'The people have made enormous sacrifices and it was time to change tactics,' he explains. 'The rivers were dry. There was no food, nothing left to fight the war with.'[23] Nor will he issue a blanket condemnation of South Africa. 'I can't judge a racist, because I don't know why he does it. I'm against racism, but not the person who practises it. Maybe it's the way they see things. It's not a disease. It's a way of life, a human response . . .'

For Mangwana, music remains one of the few sources of hope in the world. 'With music, one can communicate with anyone, even a wild animal. It's a way of getting through, reaching people who can't read or write. That's why a musician must never sing nonsense. He must remain cool and think about what he's saying.

'With music, the essence is to satisfy yourself morally, rather than make money. If you have peace of mind, you'll have a long life.'

CLAN LANGA LANGA

They were wild. It was like the Sex Pistols coming on to the scene. They twisted everything around . . . Zaiko were uncompromising. They challenged the old established musical norms of Zaire, and the youth followed . . . (Mwana Musa, in an interview with CS, London 1987).

They'd make you feel like you were flying. The sound was totally new.

Before Zaiko came to Ghana, all we'd hear was stuff like Franco doing 'Azda' . . . 'Zaiko Wa Wa Wa' went to number one. All the small kids were singing it all over Ghana; Zaiko used to play it every night at the Hotel Caprice. All the bands, except Ampadu, would play it, along with Orchestre Cavacha's 'Shama Shama'. It was a surprise to hear this hot and fast guitar . . . (Kofi Gray, in an interview with CS, London 1987).

Zaire's greatest youth band, Zaiko Langa Langa, formed in 1970, its founding members including Papa Wemba, N'Yoka-Longo, Manuaku Waku on guitar, and Evoloko 'Jocker' on vocals. Their style, background and musical range were considerable changes in a scene dominated, up to then, by an older generation of rumba stars.

Zaiko was made up of students, sons of the bourgeoisie. In Kinshasa they are compared to the hippies, for their well-to-do background, their attitude of revolt; specifically to the Rolling Stones for introducing a hard swaggering guitar sound into their music.

If earlier Zairean bands adopted sweet melodies and neatly clipped arrangements, Zaiko blew a rude, rough-house blast of folk rhythms, hard snare drums, wild guitars and rough vocals through the whole neatly ordered system. They were not the first, but they were the wildest. The youth sound took off with Jazz Baron, Bavon Marie-Marie, Thu-Zaina and Los Nickelos, but where some of the earlier bands kept their neat ambience, Zaiko took off into uncharted realms.

The band captivated Kinshasa's youth, while rhythms like the cavacha, from the early 70s, later the zekete zekete, based on Bateke folk rhythms, put them at the front of Zaire's roots movement. In 1986, Zaiko joined forces with a group of Bateke traditional musicians on the *Papa Omar* album. Their creativity continued: and so did their influence, diffused through a network of former Zaiko members.

The first to leave the band was Shungu Wembiado, or Papa Wemba, who founded Isifi Lokole in 1970, then Yoka Lokole and, in 1974, Viva La Musica.

Wemba's music kept up the ragged, streetwise sound, the 'beau désordre' associated with Zaiko, his voice adding a high wailing tone that cut through two decades of sweet Kinshasa harmonies. Wemba is known as the Jeun Premier, and is looked on as the youth star of Zaire – for his extravagant fashions, his music and his outlandish way of life.

Radio Trottoir first fastened on Wemba during his Isifi Lokole days when he was accused of an illicit affair with a young girl and spent a few days in jail. With Viva La Musica, he became a talking-point for his elaborate clothes fresh from Dior and Cardin, and for his new styles – the 'Ungaru' look, a kind of 1930s revisited with baggy pleated trousers and tapered trouser bottoms riding above immaculate brogues. A tweed hat, bought in Europe, was dubbed 'moniere', with hair, clipped at the sides and riding up into a formidable box. At other times he has sported blousons and large baggy shorts in extravagant check.

His language is equally well-known. Wemba splices his Lingala with English phrases, 'goway', 'Black and Proud' and 'Mistah'. Village Molokai, his 'empire', takes its name from an acrostic of the seven Kinshasa streets that border his house.

His rhythms extend the concept. The jamosket of the later 1970s was developed as a complement to his 'Gentleman' style, while later rhythms, such as rumba rock and la Firenze, found equal favour with Zaire's fashion-conscious fans. In Zaire, Brussels and Paris, Wemba's followers, and those of other great fashion leaders, are known as Sapeurs, members of the 'Société des Ambianceurs et des Personnes Elégantes'. The hallmarks are the same: expensive clothes, bearing the most prestigious of designer labels from Giorgio Armani to Cardin and Jimmy Weston. One particular song, 'Matebu', has become the Sapeurs' hymn. During the course of such songs, Wemba has been known to balance his shoes, doubtless Westons, on his head and turn round his vest to show off the labels.

Wemba's position as a leader of taste and fashion has not gone unremarked by students of the scene. Yoka Lye Mudaba, from the National Institute of Arts, describes the vitality and some of the contradictions of Wemba's posturing: 'When, for example, the most popular youth singer Shungu Wembiado, or Papa Wemba, declares, without laughing, that he is the "hereditary chief of village Molokai" . . . and at the same time declares himself the "Jeun Premier", the promoter of the "Made in Miguel" fashions [Miguel = Europe] so that all the youth copy his every detail, walking his own "dégingandé [gangling] walk, in the Western style, speaking Hindubill, a mix of French and Kinois languages, and wearing the Retro style, in contempt, sometimes, of official orders, one comes to understand the spread of the fashion group both as a kind of collective idolatry and as a deep generation gap which sets up and tears apart all utopias . . .'[24]

'It's enough,' comments the Kinshasa paper *Elima*, 'for Papa Wemba to appear on the small screen in Retro-style trousers known as "Ungaru". The next day, the clothes sellers make their killing. All the fans of Kuru Yaku [Wemba] and the other Kinois snobs will move heaven and earth to procure, at no matter what price, Ungaru trousers . . .'[25]

But Wemba also finds support higher up. Since the authenticity campaign, he has been held up as a leading purveyor and modernizer of traditional folk rhythms, and he speaks glowingly of an incident in which President Mobutu, the 'Guide Fondateur', danced to a Wemba song.

Overseas, Wemba has also made an impact — with 'La Firenze', which praises Florence, Paris, Tokyo and other style centres, introducing electro handclaps and a beat-box sound into a straight, sharper soukous style. For the true, exuberant Papa Wemba, though, it is necessary to turn to albums like the 1984 La Vie Comme Elle Va Bola, with its electric-saw vocals rising above echoing guitars and a wall of ragged harmonies that seem to have come straight from a hard night at the Vis à Vis club.

Kester Emeneya is one of Wemba's best-known protégés, the leader of a second generation that keeps the Zaiko sound pulsing through Kinshasa. He has the same fashion-consciousness as Wemba, but his origins are respectable: he started as a student, singing in the style of Tabu Ley – and remains rooted in Ley's progressive, melodic sound, incorporating snatches of the older man's hits into his own music. Shama Shama, one of the popular 1970s bands, provided Emeneya with his first taste of success. From there he joined Wemba in Isifi Lokole and then Viva La Musica. His decision to go into music was easily taken. Emeneya was studying at university, but saw that a successful musician could earn four times the salary of a successful professional.

Musically, he follows the Wemba route, working old rhythms and songs into hits like the 1984 'Sans Préavis' with its long loose structure and exuberant call-and-response sections. 'It's the villages that inspire us,' says Emeneya, although he does also look to the Bible and haute couture for further inspiration. 'David Bowie,' says Emeneya, 'is le premier sapeur du monde entier [in the whole world]. He makes himself look good all the time.'

Zaiko's original guitarist, Manuaku Waku, is less bothered about Bowie, more interested in music, and Zaiko's past. He left the band in 1975 to form Grand Zaiko Wa Wa. They were voted best orchestra in 1984. He looks back with affection to the old days: 'We were all students,' he says. 'What we did was originally just for our friends. Before, we had Franco and OK Jazz, and we had African Jazz. Zaiko introduced a new current, with the guitar playing something boiling. We didn't need brass. It was the guitar that brought the music to life.'

A second prominent figure in the line-up was Evoloko, the singer, who is credited with creating the band's cavacha rhythm. 'Music has no frontiers,' he says. 'In Zaire, we had the charanga, European stuff, the jerk and disco music. I had the idea of creating a Zairean rhythm with a Zairean name. That was it: cavacha; it was hot.'

Zaiko sent a shock through the city's musicians. 'After cavacha, everyone changed their percussion, the way they created animation. Everyone. Even Franco and Tabu Ley. Before that, it was the rumba. With Zaiko came new rhythms, and everyone followed.'[26]

Evoloko saw Zaiko less as a career than a sudden flash of inspiration. In 1974 he left to continue his studies — his family disliked the idea of a musician in the family — and went to Europe. Here he teamed up with fellow-musicians Mavuela and Bozi Boziana, now leader of Choc Stars. On his return Evoloko joined Papa Wemba briefly, before forming Langa Langa Stars in 1981, and recording a series of albums, *Requiem*, *Kalolo* and *Soleil*, which provided further explorations of the rumba-cavacha style and threw up new dances, such as the sansaku. 'My style follows African Jazz,' says Evoloko: 'melodic but hot.'

As with other Kinshasa youth stars, Evoloko sets great store by fashion, sporting necklaces and bracelets. 'Ça fait l'homme,' he explains, and draws a sharp distinction between the various styles on offer. 'We follow the European styles without exaggerating them. We go for something sharp. There are two looks. One is Iglesias, the other Bob Marley: a dope smoker, a punk. They are very different. For me, it has to be Julio Iglesias. Punk is no good.'

If Zaiko, and its splinter groups, represent the vanguard of the youth movement in Zaire, the business brains belong to musician, composer and entrepreneur Kiamuangana Verckys. Verckys made his name as sax player with OK Jazz, and was among the first to introduce the trumpet into the OK Jazz style. While still with Franco, he set up his own label, Editions Veve, which was to prove crucial in the promoting of his own band, Orchestre Veve, and other Kinshasa new-wave outfits. The first to receive the Veve touch were Grand Maquisards, led by Dalienst; the later bands included Orchestre Bella Bella, with Les Frères Soki, Le Trio Madjesi, with Orchestre Sosoliso, Orchestre Les Kamale and Orchestre Kiam, Empire Bakuba and various Zaiko splinters including Yoka Lokole and Viva La Musica. He also promoted other youth bands, including Zaiko, Thu-Zaina and Lita Bembo's band, Stukas.

Verckys' own work includes much that is patriotic, nationalistic, fulsome in its praise of the President. On tracks like 'Mobutu Dix Ans' he salutes the Guide Fondateur for his first ten years in office. Other songs criticize the reactionary elements in Zairean society — like 'Autocritique', lambasting party members for not carrying out the President's decisions.

Verckys remains equally strong and self-assured in his own business dealings. Little love has been lost between himself and the older generation leaders, Franco and Tabu Ley. 'Whenever I started a band, they'd take the musicians,' he says. 'There were always problems. They've had help from high places. I've done it all myself. As a result, people get jealous.'[27]

QUATRE ETOILES

The flow of Zairean artists to Belgium and France began with Kalle in 1960, Rochereau's triumphant Olympia gigs in 1970 and built from there into a steady flow during the late 1970s.

Paris had a significant effect on the music; its studios offered multiple tracking and electronic effects that remain the property of few African studios even today, while also providing a useful meeting-place for Cameroonians, Zaireans, Congolese and West Indian session artists. The 'Antilles effect' influenced many of the newcomers into bringing biguine, later zouk influences into their music. For some, though, it was already part of their style.

Les Quatre Etoiles (Four Stars) is a Paris-based supergroup that embraces four top Zairean musicians: Nyboma and Wuta May on vocals, Bopol and Syran Mbenza, guitars. Apart from Wuta May, they all worked with African All Stars in the late 1970s, Bopol and Syran working in the original band, Nyboma taking over in 1979.

The quartet came together as a studio band in Paris in 1982. 'An artist's life is all about records,' says Nyboma. 'In Zaire, we play in clubs. That's the difference. We left so that we could continue to make a living. It wasn't for pleasure. The bad thing about Zaire is that although you play the clubs, you're not considered a musician. That's why we came to France.'

Their first Afro Rythmes album, *Mayi*, announced the arrival of 'Quatre Grandes Vedettes de la musique Africaine', and contained one song from each musician. Nyboma's contribution, 'Mama Iye Ye', rerecorded a song that he had written in the 1970s when he was singing with Orchestre Bella Bella in Zaire. The new version, replacing the sweetness of the original with a solid beat and faint reggae inflection in the guitar rhythms, showed the Etoiles' willingness to change their music for Western ears.

The name of the band is no idle boast. In Zaire, the individual members of the Quatre Etoiles had made their names with many of the country's best musicians. Wuta May started his career in 1967 and played with Jamel National, Bambala and Rock-A-Mambo before joining Orchestre Continentale, one of the bands who brought in the new youth music in the later sixties. In 1974, he joined Franco in TPOK Jazz.

Wuta May's vocal brilliance is matched only by that of Nyboma, who has one of the classic voices of Zaire — high, pure and unbreaking even on the top of the range. Nyboma cut his teeth with Baby National in 1969 and moved to Negro Succès before joining two of Zaire's biggest bands, Orchestre Bella Bella, and then Orchestre Lipua Lipua. By the late 1970s he had split, to join African All Stars, later forming Orchestre Les Kamale du Zaire.

Syran worked as a guitarist with Orchestres Abanite and Lovy du Zaire while Bopol, who released a series of his own albums in the early 1980s under the title *Innovations*, has worked as a bass guitarist with Dr Nico's African Fiesta and Afrisa before creating his distinctive, needle-sharp rhythm lines for Sam Mangwana.

Together, Les Quatre Etoiles produce an infectious brand of rumba saccade, a fast dance music which blows fresh heat on to the rumba of Zaire. Their second album, *Enfant Bamileke*, released in 1984, offered further tracks from each of the musicians. Their 1985 outing *Dance* introduced electronic drums into the mix to underscore their new dance, the kinsensengoma, or 'cricket'. The rhythm remained the same: the Four Stars' own blend of pure vocal melody over a hot rumba saccade base. In the meantime, the Etoiles had also released a succession of solo albums, Nyboma's 1981 *Doublé Doublé* proving an early classic, while later ones, including Bopol's *Helena*, drew on the service of Jean-Claude Naimro and Jacob Désvarieux, from Kassav, to create a strong Afro-zouk fusion. Nyboma followed suit in 1986 with an album co-recorded with Pepe Kalle, from Empire Bakuba, which used zouk rhythms and guitar patterns, but little of the technology; the following year, Syran Mbenza formed his own zouk-flavoured outfit, Kass Kass, and joined the Four Stars for their epic of hi-tech and elaborate arrangement, *6 Tubes*.

The move to Paris has given Quatre Etoiles room to develop. In Zaire, competition and infighting threatened even the most successful of bands. New names would appear, but their members were quickly drawn into the older, well-established outfits. Lack of equipment compounded their difficulties. Established musicians, like Franco and Rochereau, were heavily sponsored by the government. None of this happened for the

younger bands, who either had to hire kit at great cost or make do with
inferior equipment or none at all.

Many other African musicians have taken the route north, including a
sizeable number of Cameroonians, who some people are claiming have
knocked the Zaireans from their pedestal, with their sophisticated
productions and willingness to improve on their music.

The Quatre Etoiles beg to differ. 'It all comes down to producers,' says
Nyboma. 'Fashions change all the time. They launched Kenyan music,
and that was meant to be the strongest. Then Nigerian, now
Cameroonian. But many of the rhythms are the same as ours. At one
point, we were all one people.

'Where you do get a difference is in the production. They have good
studios and make good-quality records. At home we've only got poor
studio facilities. That gives Cameroonian makossa an advantage. But, as
regards rhythms, Zaire is still on top.'

RAY LEMA

'There is a great gap between African traditional and modern music. I'd
like to help traditional become modern without losing its roots quality.'[28]

Ray Lema is based in Paris and working towards a single goal: the
recasting of traditional music on purely electronic instruments. The
project sounds revolutionary, in that it bypasses the normal rules of
musical evolution, where musics mix and resolve themselves into a
hybrid. According to the Lema method, the music jumps unscathed into a
modern format, with little or no compromise along the way.

On 'Koteja', released in 1985, Lema worked with Stewart Copeland of
the Police on a folk song from the Baluba people of Zaire. The lyric
centred on a purification ceremony by which the participants had to
cleanse themselves ritually before entering the dance. The music, a
marriage of electronic keyboards with a heavy funk drum and synthesized
percussion, created a sound that goes far beyond what is normally thought
of as standard Zairean music.

Lema has always been an innovator and outsider. He started adult life
by training as a priest in Kinshasa, entering a seminary at the age of
eleven. For five years he played the organ every day in church. At his first
proper concert, in 1962, he played the 'Moonlight Sonata' to an audience
of 1,000 white people. There were only two Africans in the audience – his
brothers.

When he left the seminary and became a professional musician, with a series of musicians from Abeti to M'Pongo Love, the stigma followed him. Lema was a classical musician, a piano player – the piano was virtually unknown in Zairean music – and a 'white black'. 'I tried so hard,' he says. 'It became a trip in my head to get accepted by my own people. That's why I went to the villages to find traditional music.'

As musical director for the Zairean national ballet, Lema made far-reaching studies of the country's massive, largely uncharted traditional music and discovered a new sense of direction. As a keyboard player, he had already made connections between the piano and the traditional balafon or xylophone played in the villages. A visit from a group of traditional players made his mind up.

'I had a Fender Rhodes at home. I heard a very brilliant balafon player who came to my house. He saw the piano, I plugged it in for him to check the sound. He played it and said, "This sound is deep but it's too clean. The sound goes upwards. If I were you I'd put a resonator on the notes so that they'd go down. There is no equilibrium. I don't see any symmetry. How do you find your balance?" I said there wasn't any balance. The thing was there. You had to cope with it.'

The balafon player attacked the Fender with two fingers. Lema was transfixed. He started work on a way of reproducing the traditional sounds – which mix melody and percussion – on the piano, using different, traditional modes.

In 1981, Lema went to the United States as a music student with the Rockefeller Foundation, but his hopes to take the music further were defeated: 'I had so many arguments with black American musicians. They felt they had to teach me about African music. It was too much. I tried funk and jazz players. They were all the same.'

Finally Lema turned to new technology. Rather than create a programme, with its stiff, repetitive cycle, he played each percussion and keyboard part through – no sequencers or repeaters – to reproduce the original music: initially as a model for the Americans to learn; later as a music in its own right.

In Paris, Lema has recorded a handful of albums, including *Kinshasa–Washington D.C.–Paris* which mixes a range of music, from funk to salsa and updates of traditional Pygmy and Sahara songs. After 'Koteja', which he made with producer Martin Meissonnier, he produced a second single, 'Marabout (Iyolela)' and an album *Medicine* which continued the electro innovations.

The sound may be electric but it has done nothing to take away the richness of African traditional music. 'I don't like to talk about African rhythm as something special. It's the approach to it that is special. In Africa, we have to start with, say, a 6/8. Someone puts a 4/4 against it, another brings in a 12/8. We don't have fast or slow rhythms. We have all the speeds in one rhythm. This means that you have to arrange the tune differently. For the Westerner, it becomes a huge vibration, a mess. For the African, it's like a huge game. When you play with Africans you always hear those beats that say, "Get off my toes." If you're playing one beat, and the guitarist comes in with another, the drummer is going to say, "What are you doing in my place; find your own place. Not my beat." This is against all the concepts of modern arrangement in the West.'

SOUZY KASSEYA

One of the leading Zairean lights on the current Paris scene is writer, guitarist and producer Souzy Kasseya.

An early colleague of Sam Mangwana in Vox Afrique, Kasseya started his solo career in 1973 as a session player in M'Pongo Love's band. After four years, he left for Paris where he produced his *Princesse Gyonne* album and its equally celebrated opening track, 'Le Téléphone Sonne'.

The single attracted widespread interest. In Paris it was picked up by Philips and became one of the few African records to have penetrated the French hit parade. In Britain, Earthworks stepped in and were able to gain considerable airplay for it, above all on Charlie Gillett's Capital Radio programme, 'City Beats'.

'Le Téléphone Sonne' became a test case for the success, or otherwise, of African music in Britain. But after healthy French sales, it sold badly across the Channel. Kasseya himself visited London in 1984, as part of Sam Mangwana's backing band. In 1985 he returned, to promote the single. Problems with visas robbed him of half his band and what should have been a triumph turned sour. At the same time, Philips' inability to supply Earthworks with the seven-inch pressings necessary for daytime radio play further damaged Kasseya's chances.

In 1985, Kasseya put out his first British album, the long-awaited *The Phenomenal*. From the simplicities of his earlier single, he moved to a new, electro-charged sound, built around a series of complex, finely shaded arrangements.

Fela Anikulapo-Kuti, bandleader, politician and pan-African nationalist
(JAK KILBY)

Left: Foday Musa Suso, Gambian kora player, master of traditional forms and American collisions

(JAK KILBY)

Above: Miriam Makeba, Empress of African song

(JAK KILBY)

Left: Mahlathini, the
South African 'groaner',
on stage with the
Makgona Tsohle Band
(DAVID BROWNE)

Above: Franco, Zaire's
most illustrious
musician, commentator
on current affairs and
conveyor of slyly
ambiguous lyrics
(JAK KILBY)

Left: Salif Keita, the
Malian singer, on stage
in London, 1987
(DAVID BROWNE)

Above: Thomas
Mapfumo, who created a
new form of
Zimbabwean pop from
ancient Shona music
(DAVID BROWNE)

Right: Sam Mangwana
(right) with Ringo Star
on guitar—Mangwana
has been a great
innovator in Zairean
music since the
mid-seventies
(JAK KILBY)

Left: Kanda Bongo Man (left) with Diblo on guitar—the Zairean singer is now a leading light of the Paris scene (JAK KILBY)

eft: Tabu Ley
Rochereau) and M'Bilia
el, a partnership that
uts the woman's point
f view into Zairean
usic
(AK KILBY)

Above: Manu Dibango,
Cameroonian
saxophonist and master
of modern makossa
(DAVID BROWNE)

Left: The Bhundu
Boys—they took
Zimbabwean music up
and down the UK and to
the top of the
independent charts in
1987
(JAK KILBY)

Above (left to right):
Kwabena Oduro-
Kwarteng, Sunny Ade,
Julian Bahula and (in
cap) Tsepo Tshola at the
reception to mark Ade's
signing for Island
(JAK KILBY)

Right: Shirati Jazz
popularized benga
music, Kenya's answer
to Zairean rumba
(JAK KILBY)

Right: Youssou N'Dour, chief instigator of the mid-seventies revolution which carried Senegalese music away from Afro-Cuba covers and back to its roots (JAK KILBY)

Left: E. T. Mensah, the celebrated highlife bandleader and trumpeter, here playing saxophone
(JAK KILBY)

Right: Fan Fan (here with Kenyan bassist Bonny Wanda), a former guitarist with OK Jazz, led an attack on the UK market in the mid-eighties with his band Somo Somo
(JAK KILBY)

Left: Hugh Masekela–
he carried South African
music overseas
(DAVID BROWNE)

Left: Real Sounds, one of Zimbabwe's
better-known bands specializing in
Zairean rumba
(DAVID BROWNE)

Above: Mory Kante enjoyed
phenomenal European chart success
in 1988 with his single 'Yé Ké Yé Ké'
(DAVID BROWNE)

Eric Agyeman, Ghanaian highlife guitarist
known for his work with K. Gyasi's Noble
Kings and the Sweet Talks

(JAK KILBY)

Kasseya sees himself, above all, as an originator. In a scene dominated by people who have made their names in clubs rather than studios, he has taken the opposite course. After Vox Afrique, he moved into session work, joining Asi Kapela, Bopol and Empompo as part of M'Pongo Love's session band. He wrote several tunes for the Zairean singer before working with Tshala Muana, later Bebe Manga, and Ivoirian François Lougha.

From this varied experience, Kasseya has created a style that draws on both the great Zairean rhythm schools of Franco and African Jazz. 'It was the first time anyone had mixed the two,' he explains. The result is a shift away from the old orthodoxies. 'In the beginning you just had the two styles. Today, though, it is no longer possible to say that Zaiko plays like Franco or like Tabu Ley. Following one style is a sign of weakness. You still get artists who look back to see what Franco has done and then follow that. To me that shows a lack of originality.'[29]

One of Kasseya's aims with *The Phenomenal* was to broaden his base still further – widening the scope of the music to create a new fuller percussion sound. 'We've never really had our own percussion,' he says. 'So it's necessary to go elsewhere: to the Antilles, to Nigeria. And why not? They've been getting stuff from us all the time. They've borrowed our rhythms, our guitar sounds, our melodies. They may not have much to offer us in the way of melody, but they've certainly got percussion.'

KANDA BONGO MAN

Kanda Bongo Man's story has a familiar ring. Frustrated by the lack of opportunity at home in Zaire, he packed his bags and headed for Paris, where he spent his first two years working in a factory.

In 1981, Bongo Man signed to Afro Rythmes, a Paris-based record company, and went on to release two albums, *Iyole* and *Djessy*, that mix a hot soukous with crisp pop melodies. On the second, he broadened his scope, bringing biguine into the rhythms.

'The difference between the two rhythms is small,' he explains. 'In Zaire, it's common to mix the two, biguine being the softer, soukous slightly harder.'[30]

Kanda Bongo Man was born in 1958 and heard his first music from his uncle, the celebrated Jean Bokelo. His greatest inspirations proved to be Rochereau, with his soft-edged ballad style, inherited from the great Kalle, and a smattering of Western singers including Jimmy Cliff.

In 1973, Bongo Man met two brothers, Soki and Dianzenza Vangu, who had formed a band, Orchestre Bella Mambo, and were later to make their names with Orchestre Bella Bella. After touring Uganda with the brothers, Bongo Man split and left for Paris.

If he expected instant success, he was soon disillusioned. 'The Africans in Paris go for Zairean music,' he says, 'but with the French themselves, it's another matter. Until the music is properly exposed it will continue to have little impact. But the media aren't bothered.'

To date, the only artist to have received any kind of sustained attention has been Souzy Kasseya. Other African and Antillean artists based in Paris, Toure Kunda and Kassav, went on to achieve a wider acclaim, but for the Zaireans, the going seemed relatively tough. 'Souzy has now been discovered,' says Bongo Man. 'He played Zairean music and now the French public has seen how good it is. He was the first one to really attract the attention of the media and through being played on national radio, a lot of French people listened to it and liked it.'

For Bongo Man, lack of media attention is compounded by poor management and lack of organization among the record houses, both in France and Zaire. The main blame falls on the powerful producers who claim complete artistic and business control.

'They're not serious,' says Bongo Man. 'Either you don't get paid at all, or there are a lot of other problems, legal problems, because they simply don't want to pay. If they owe you F20,000 they'll give you F2,000, saying come back tomorrow, come next month. It's difficult. I've got to the stage where one has actually pulled out a revolver on me. There are good ones, of course, Martin Meissonnier, for example, who pays his artists well and keeps them happy. But on the whole, the scene is disorganized. Artists are selling records but nothing comes back to them.'

Zaire has its own problems: 'It's difficult for young musicians to develop. They need better studios and more promotion. The older musicians have a virtual monopoly – they have the instruments; the younger ones simply can't afford them. They also have their own clubs to play in. Life is difficult for the younger generation.'

After his two albums with Afro Rythmes, Bongo Man decided to take matters into his own hands. His third album *Amour Fou* marked the inauguration of Bongo Man records, a response to the meanness of the other houses when it came to putting any realistic money up front.

'A lot of companies contacted me,' says Bongo Man. 'But their terms were the problem – the percentages were all wrong. Now I'm producing myself – and the house still want sixty per cent for distribution. Forty per cent is all right – but sixty? Far too much.'

In 1986, Bongo Man released his second album on his own label, *Malinga*, and made his British debut with a GlobeStyle compilation, before moving firmly into the zouk camp, early in 1987, with an album, *Lela Lela*, which set zouk rhythms and 'international' melodies against a series of sebens where the guitars and snare drums beat as vigorously as ever. The presence of his guitarists, Ringo Star and Diblo, on a number of zouk albums, doubtless pushed Bongo Man further towards the hit sound of the mid-eighties, a direction he confirmed with a guest appearance, alongside the Kassav rhythm machine, on one of the top Paris albums of 1987, the irresistible *Zouk Time*. The follow-up, *Sai Liza*, struck a less frenetic note carrying strong memories of the old Bella Bella sound.

TOWNSHIP POP

'Khulu, Monty and I drank at Shirley Scott's shebeen, so called because she only played jazz. It was one way of keeping out the township riff-raff, who preferred mbaqanga and considered jazz as music for "situations", meaning those who liked to situate themselves above ordinary township folk.'[1]

Mbaqanga, one of Africa's hardest, most upbeat sounds, is the poor relative of South African pop: frowned on by the more discerning listeners, who turn to jazz and classical music; looked down on by jazz artists, who see it as a few simple chords and quick money; recently, absorbed into funk and soul to form the basis of township pop; and largely beyond the understanding of the whites who still think of kwela and street kids – if they think about African music at all.

The characteristics of mbaqanga – heavy-duty bass, clipped guitars played at the top end of the fretboard, and choral vocals – solidified in the work of the Dark City Sisters, Mahlathini, the Mahotella Queens and other 1960s stars, but to identify the roots of what is essentially a proletarian music, it is necessary to go back a good deal further into history.

In a region short on percussion, choral music was always the prime means of expression for rural people. When the mining towns sprang up at the end of the last century, the migrant workers brought their music with them. Compounds echoed to the sound of traditional dancers, the ingoma ebusuku choral groups and solo musicians, many of whom had made the switch from traditional stringed instruments to the guitar, violin and accordion. The townships bred new hybrids. In the shebeens, keyboard players created a lowlife blend of ragtime and traditional music known as marabi. Taking its name, possibly, from Marabastad, a part of Pretoria, the new music blossomed from around 1930, and went on to utilize banjos, guitars, brass instruments – anything that came to hand. By 1939, it had died away, replaced by swing, leaving a few records and the odd written testament to its raw power. For writer Todd Matshikiza, marabi consisted of 'hot, highly rhythmic, repetitious, single-themed dance tunes of the late twenties'.[2] The music may have gone, but its power remains, inspiring a generation of jazz artists, among them Abdullah Ibrahim, whose 'Mannenberg' feeds the repetitious power of marabi through a refined, classical filter.

Away from the shebeens, the better off looked to polished dance bands like the Merry Blackbirds for their entertainment. Dale Quaker, a former musician, recalls:

They were a class band, and they were employed to do all the white jobs. In 1936, they were resident band for the British Empire Exhibition, to the displeasure of many white musicians. The trumpeter, Sterling Monkoe, used to play in the Salvation Army; he modelled himself on Louis Armstrong, even down to the handkerchief. He was the greatest black musician and trumpeter in South Africa.[3]

At the other extreme, the Jazz Maniacs, under Zulu Boy Cele, and Wilson 'King Force' Silgee picked up on the local marabi music and worked it into their repertoire. 'The rivalry between the two bands was intense,' says Quaker. 'Of the two, the Maniacs were the more flexible. They'd play marabi, even busking the old standards like "Tomatie Saus". The Blackbirds wouldn't go near marabi.'

South Africa's racial policies hardened during the 1940s as white politicians called for tougher measures to perpetuate the privileged position of the whites. In 1948, the Nationalist government formalized years of oppression and discrimination in the new, rigid code of apartheid, an official structure carrying white supremacy into jobs, education, housing, every area of life. One of the harshest blows came with the Group Areas Act of 1950, which drove different racial groups into separate urban areas.

By this time, Dale Quaker was organizing music festivals for a township social centre. 'We had coloureds, Africans, Indians, all taking part,' he says. 'There were no problems at all until they closed the centre because of the Group Areas Act. People had to have their functions in their respective racial areas. Permits were needed to take part in functions in other areas. It discouraged the whole thing.'[4] Old, well-established townships disappeared when it was discovered that the land could be redeveloped for white housing. One of the major losses was Sophiatown, the home of countless shebeens and a flourishing music scene. Further pressures piled up in the aftermath of the Sharpeville massacre of 1960, when gatherings of more than ten people were prohibited.

Apartheid damaged black music in other ways. Forced into segregated townships, the musicians had little hope of joining all-white unions, of playing on the radio or moving into the comfortable theatre circuit. The pass laws made it illegal to move between townships at night. As a result,

187

the initiative fell into white hands. Variety shows like 'African Jazz and Variety', from 1951, and 'Township Jazz' brought American-influenced African music, from choirs to swing bands and tap dancers, the Manhattan Brothers to Miriam Makeba, to white audiences. But it left the country's progressive, urban jazz players facing a blank future.

The selective white absorption of black township music can also be seen with kwela, a style that dates back to 1950, when a film called *The Magic Garden*, featuring a small boy playing boogie on a pennywhistle, was shown in South Africa. The film received a rapturous reception. Boys took to the streets, playing their own American swing on whistles, guitars and tea-chest bass. Among the new stars, Spokes Mashiyane (whistle) and Lemmy Special Mabaso (pennywhistle and later sax), were snapped up by record companies, along with a host of other street-corner virtuosi. 'Tom Hark', by Aaron Lerole, was a huge hit overseas in 1954. According to David Coplan, it netted Columbia a quarter of a million rand. (Lerole was said to have received thirty.) Kwela also spread throughout east and southern Africa. Among its leading exponents were George Sibanda, who created his own kwela-influenced guitar vamp, and the Malawian Donald Kachamba.[5]

The vigour of township music also powered an epoch-making South African musical, *King Kong*, the story of a heavyweight boxer set to a score that, in writer Harry Bloom's words, reflected 'all the shades and moods and contrasts of life in Johannesburg's shanty towns. Modern "hit"-type tunes alternated with pennywhistle blues or a road-gang chant, liturgical music drawn from the mission schools, hot barbaric jive from the shebeens, choral harmonies from tribal life, patter numbers, operatic solos . . .'[6] Lionel Rogosin's anti-apartheid film *Come Back Africa* offered further insight into street music 1950s-style: groups of acapella singers doing Everly Brothers numbers, kwela bands attracting large crowds and gumboot dancers on street corners.

The success of kwela signalled a new direction in South African music. It proved that black music could sell records. But this made little impression on the authorities. In 1960, the government, acting on behalf of white musicians, used an amendment to the Group Areas Act to bar black jazz bands from inner-city clubs. Faced by a non-existent township scene, and a gradual drying up of venues, musicians went destitute or left the country. From now on, the studios, offering quick money for commercial records, carried the swing. In 1965, Gallo, in Johannesburg, echoed to a township sound inspired partly by the Western 'beat' boom, partly by the arrival of new, electric instruments. After the light skiffle of kwela, the new sound, dubbed first simanje-manje, then mbaqanga, offered a harder, electric alternative. The easy swing of the pennywhistle music gave way to a faster beat, insistent bass lines and vocals that gradually absorbed the tones and textures of South African choral music. Mbaqanga literally means dough, a substance as heavy as the beat that developed in Robert Bopape's studio. It also, less aptly, means easy money — few musicians made any money at all.

Bopape's studio brought together a range of talent, from Simon Nkabinde, or Mahlathini, the famous bass groaner, to the Dark City Sisters and the Mahotella Queens, who took their name from the large number of hotels they stayed in while on tour. Early mbaqanga records still carried a slight, acoustic, kwela swing, but there was no mistaking the powerful bass sound developed by Joseph Makwela, or Marks Mankwane's tight guitar work. On stage, Bopape's posse would run through hymns, mbaqanga songs and finish with further hymns, Marks Mankwane using his wa-wa pedal to spell the titles out to the rest of the band.

Mahlathini, the king of the groaners, gave the studio recordings an added edge. Inspired by groaners like Aaron Lerole, Mahlathini started his career singing traditional choral music, joining Lerole's Alexandra Black Mambazo in 1952. He went on to make his name with the Mahotella Queens, having been signed by Bopape in 1958. Mahlathini reflects various mythical qualities. To musicologist David Coplan, he represents an ideal of rural, traditional virility, which has been kept alive in the confusion of the townships. His early names, including "Indoda" Mahlathini or "Mahlathini The Man", confirm this. The legend spread. Mahlathini evoked fearsome images as a person who could cast spells, do voodoo. He was given the name Mahlathini, 'Jungle on His Head', after the sangomas, or African herbal doctors, who sported similar dreadlocks. The magic spread. By 1988, Mahlathini and the Queens were playing to ecstatic audiences across Europe.

Mbaqanga spelt quick money for the studios, who produced new bands at a phenomenal rate. The Soweto Brothers, on Satbel records, provided the backing for a succession of Zulu traditional artists, many of them virtually hauled in off the streets. After the success of the Mahotella Queens, Gallo formed further top-selling acts, including Amaswazi Emvelo, who leapt to the top in 1980 and remained there until they split in 1986.

Instrumental music prompts equally high sales — particularly sax and accordion jive — new tags and rhythm variations such as the Mahotella Queens' zomgqashiyo giving new flavours to the basic mbaqanga beat.

Dances appeared in great numbers, among them the 1973 phenomenon mabone. 'It was pure exploitation,' says Joe Ditsebe Legwabe, who played in Bopape's studio. 'There'd be hundreds of groups churning the stuff out. The studios would do eighteen groups in eight hours. Bopape would say, "Guys, I've booked a studio from the fifteenth." He'd turn up with a couple of lyrics, go, come back four hours later and give you something else to do.'[7]

Larger studios also put a toe in the market. CBS's main signing was the Soul Brothers, who took mbaqanga to a new level of polish and, by the early 1980s, were selling 200,000 copies of each new album. The band started as the Intuthuko Brothers, playing as freelancers at CBS, where they recorded mabazo or moonshine records while signed to another company. They created a distinctive sound based around a slower beat, florid organ lines and the use of township slang, spoken by tsotsis or gangsters. Up to that point, most had used the 'pure' Zulu and other South African languages.

South African music casts a wide net, from the highly polished sounds of Nelcy Sidebe, the Soul Brothers and the Super Tens, to the earthy rural sounds of the great Zulu and Sotho jive artists. Of these, Moses Mchunu, Philemon Zulu and Aaron Mbambo specialize in an acoustic-guitar sound with thunderous bass lines and raucous violin or guitar top lines. Sotho musicians raise the energy level with hollering vocals and accordions while the Shangaan stars like Obed Ngobeni and the Kurhula Sisters wipe out audiences with their deep vocals and solid guitars.

For some studios, country jive, which thrusts street musicians in front of seasoned studio players, is the last word in fast money; for the artists it provides the chance to continue a traditional sound that sells by the lorryload to homesick migrants from the rural areas.

In addition, South Africa has a range of other sounds and styles. Zulu gospel, from bands like the Holy Brothers, is popular, while the young listeners turn to home-grown fusions of township music and American soul and funk, the fastest-selling music in the country today. Artists like Brenda and the Big Dudes offer a heavily Western sound, while Sipho Mabuse and Margaret Singana work traditional elements – township sax solos and rhythms – into new varieties of Soweto pop and soul.

And always there are the dances. In the 1950s, pata pata ruled. By the mid-1970s, mbaqanga had created its own dance crazes. In a magnificent mbaqanga album, *2 Mabone 6 Mabone*, from 1973, Robert Bopape and West Nkosi assembled a string of guitarists and violinists to launch a new dance craze: mabone, or headlights. 'Ladies and gentlemen, the AGB label presents something wonderful. The light . . . The light . . . The light . . . Two lights. Mabubuto Ikanda . . . one, two . . . two mabone . . .'

A second massively popular township music is ingoma ebusuku, the sound of the unaccompanied choir. Its origins go back to the early towns, where the migrant workers developed a distinctive urban sound based on traditional rural music. Ingoma ebusuku transplanted the music into an urban setting of mining compounds and city halls where, by the late 1930s, all-night contests would attract eager audiences and vibrant working men's choirs. By the 1940s, ingoma ebusuku had appeared under a new guise: 'bombing' or mbube music. Bombing is said to come from the explosive nature of the singing, which imitated the noise made by wartime aircraft shown on local film shows. As Priscilla A. Clark explains, the choral sound kept strong links with the rural past. The power and volume of the singing, the prominent bass and the adaptation of age-old melodies, kept the traditional feeling alive. The harmonic structure, with its open fourths and fifths, followed traditional patterns, as did the use of 'explosive yells' and accompanying dance steps and gestures. New features included the introduction of township slang into the lyrics.[8]

The best account of male-voice choirs in action comes from David Rycroft, who describes the singers, back in the 1950s, dressed in 'zoot suit jackets with odd-coloured pockets, specially tailored to knee-length and worn with stove-pipe trousers or a college-length blazer with an ornate meaningless badge. Accessories such as lionskin capes, watch chain worn at the droop and two-tone black leather shoes are fashionable.'[9] The choirs took elaborate names, from Hamlets Male Voice Choir to the Zululand Home Defenders and the Cycle Lost Brothers. Bombing sessions lasted until five or six in the morning, when the judge, usually a white passer-by attracted by a two-pound fee, would deliver the verdict.

Since the 1950s, male-voice choirs have retained their popularity, few surpassing Ladysmith Black Mambazo, one of South Africa's top-selling acts. Choral music has also traditionally carried the full weight of protest against apartheid. Outside South Africa, the choir of the banned African National Congress keeps alive a tradition of freedom song that goes back to the early days of racial segregation. The great African hymn, 'Nkosi Sikelel' iAfrika', has now become an emotional national anthem for the black people of South Africa, while a host of companies and trade-union choirs voice the hopes and frustrations of the black population. And wherever public gatherings take place, and feelings run high, people turn to song. In his *Children of Soweto*, Mbulelo Vizikhungo Mzamane shows the closeness of the two:

As we were leaving, some started to sing 'Thina Sizwe', a popular freedom song. Other voices joined in. The mournful strains of the song rose, timidly at first, and filled the air. The women in the kitchen picked up the song and hummed it under their breath.

Thina Sizwe: thina sizwe esinsundu
    We the nation: we the black nation
Sikhalel: sikhalela izwelethu
    We mourn: we mourn for our land
Elathathwa: slathathwa ngabamhlophe
    Stolen from us: stolen from us by the white man
Mabayeke: mabayek'umhl aba wethu
    Let them leave: let them leave our land

. . . All over Soweto the flames had now gathered strength, as if the whole place was one huge bonfire . . .[10]

MANHATTAN BROTHERS

The history of urban black South African music is strongly linked to the history of black American music, above all jazz. A number of reasons have been put forward for this. As David Coplan suggests, in *Labour, Townships and Protest*, South African blacks had 'tribally heterogeneous ethnic origins and downgraded these as emphatically as the Afro-Americans did their "slave" society of the past'. Both cultures were subject to massive discrimination from a white Christian establishment, and shared the need to find a unifying culture, a model to which they could aspire. For South Africans, the black America provided a unique model; and from the early days, American music, entertainment and fashion were of immense importance to the black town populations.

The rise of top-class bands, such as the Merry Blackbirds led by Peter Rezant, and the swing-based Jazz Maniacs, led by Zulu Boy Cele, predated the arrival of South Africa's greatest vocal group, the Manhattan Brothers. The group was formed by Joseph Mogotsi, Nathan Mdedle, Ronnie Majola and Rufus Khoza in the early forties at a crucial period in the history of South African music. For the first time, all-black companies dealing in black music were coming to the fore. By the time Gallo, one of the main companies, had taken on a black talent scout — Griffiths Motsieloa, newly returned from London — the Manhattan Brothers had already been signed up and had made the first of the recordings that were to alter the whole shape of the recording scene. The large jazz bands were rarely recorded, possibly because American jazz was so readily available. The Manhattan Brothers, who could equal and surpass many of the American vocal imports, were recorded non-stop. From then on, the industry fed off black South African talent.

The band's origins go back to the thirties. Joe Mogotsi remembers the Pixley Follies, who played Jack Hylton-style English dance music at his home town of Pimville. Reuben Caluza, with his choir and orchestra, had provided entertainment of a kind that Mogotsi describes as 'school and eisteddfod-based'. 'Our times were jazzy times,' he says.[11] His first musical experiences came from his father's choir which held singing contests against other choirs in the area — one of them run by the father of Kippie Moeketsi, South Africa's greatest alto-sax player. At school, Mogotsi joined small groups tap dancing and singing 'Pennies from Heaven' in the streets. They were frequently arrested. Musically, at any rate, it seemed a fitting start for a band that would go on to become South Africa's answer to the Mills Brothers and the Ink Spots.

'When we were introduced to Gallo's, there were a lot of groups before us,' says Mogotsi. 'But they were not internationally known. They concentrated on authentic stuff, music sung by miners, that sort of thing. No one else recognized the importance of vocal music until Gallo came along and started recording. Solomon Linda was with us at Gallo. We were already there. We'd sing "Mbube" with him in the studio.'

Apart from radio broadcasts and recording, the Manhattan Brothers put together elaborate variety shows, and created their own back-up band, the Jazz Dazzlers, which was led by Mackay Davashe and went on to feature Hugh Masekela, Dollar Brand (now Abdullah Ibrahim) and Jonas Gwangwa. They also took on Miriam Makeba as a young singer, launching her career and, in the process, encouraging her to become one of the first women to perform the traditionally male gumboot dance. The affluent, white-collar scene flourished. Large shows, often held at the Bantu Men's Social Centre, brought together top acts, from the Brothers and the Jazz Maniacs to the African Ink Spots, the Synco-Fans and the Harlem Swingsters, and tap dancers like Mad Joe and School Boy. It was a time of blossoming talent, when the well-to-do professional audiences were seduced by a range of artists who drew their inspiration from American greats such as Basie and Ellington and the great jazz and blues singers. 'The Maniacs and the Swingsters could have done well overseas,' says Mogotsi. 'So could their vocalists, Emily Kwenane, the singer with the Maniacs; Dolly Rathebe, with the Swingsters; the Merry Blackbirds' Marjorie Pretorius. Great artists who have never featured in the history of black music.'

The interest in American music, Mogotsi attributes largely to commerce; the Manhattan Brothers' audiences were fully acquainted with the American way of life and the band had to produce something that lived up to their expectations. Sometimes, these would be Mills Brothers and Ink Spots songs, rewritten in Zulu, Sotho or Xhosa. At others, traditional African songs. 'We'd take maybe two bars and polish them to suit,' says Mogotsi. 'We'd write new passages, put in new lyrics, and add middle phrases. We were doing something that other people had never thought of: taking the authentic music and putting a bit of jazz and pop stuff behind.' The early Manhattan Brothers recordings were accompanied by a single, acoustic guitar vamp. Later, drums, a clarinet or alto or tenor lead lines were added; to give a sprightly rhythmic feel, the kind of vigour and bounce that pre-empted the kwela boom by a decade. Among their hits were 'Kilimanjaro', which was popular in America in the fifties, and 'Mbube', a close-harmony reading of the Solomon Linda original.

By the fifties, the South African scene had changed irrevocably, a reflection of the arrival of the National Party government in 1948, and the changing tempo of urban life in South Africa. Mogotsi sees the forties as 'interesting times', a period of calm and relative prosperity. 'During the time of the Smuts government, there were segregated audiences, but people like ourselves and the Merry Blackbirds would play the nightclubs in the centre of town. Apartheid was never talked about. We could see we weren't needed, it's true, but we penetrated anyway, because of what the people wanted from us: our talent, our music. It was pure business; the Afrikaans musicians really had nothing to offer.'

The change of government started a new era of enforced segregation, pass laws and the forced removal of black populations from urban areas into the modern-day townships. 'The laws came in,' says Mogotsi. 'We were stopped from performing in town at certain hours unless we'd got a permit. If we hadn't, we'd get arrested for vagrancy. But people can get used to certain things. You learn how to handle them. We'd put aside a certain amount of money for emergencies, so that when people got arrested, we could pay the fine. This was more usual, than for people to go go to prison. The whole system was ridiculous and unnecessary. But I think that it was the government just making money from people. I can't see why else it was done.

'It was worse for our audiences. Most of them were black. They'd come from all over the townships to hear good music. But when they went back home, after midnight, they'd be harassed. Other people simply didn't risk coming to see us.'

Around this time, further changes took place in the music scene. White entrepreneurs began to take an interest in black music, bringing together large revues, like 'African Jazz and Variety', which brought jazz, tap dancing and vocal groups to major urban venues. The idea, says Mogotsi, came from a group called Zonk, who entertained the troops with a mixture of minstrelsy and variety, during the war years. But it also reflected the wealth of the white establishment. At that time, he explains, black artists could find little or no financial support – the Manhattan Brothers being one of the few bands who did not need this kind of patronage.

Another factor was the rise of violence in the established black clubs and social centres. 'At the start, we had no problems at all,' says Mogotsi. 'Our shows were filled with homely people. Families would come with their children, to sit and listen. When the gangsters started coming, we'd announce the last number and they'd come up and say, "Hey look, brother, the Real Thing has just arrived. How come you want to close the show?" We had to deal with that, or face a shoot out. At the same time, gangsters would come and harass Miriam, and our other vocalists, so we'd have to stand in their way. That's when things started to get a little too Americanized . . .'

Faced by violence and lack of money, the big bands faded away. The musicians formed smaller groups, some of them took to playing mbaqanga, 'a sort of African stuff', says Mogotsi. 'They also called it going for the fast buck.'

The Manhattan Brothers, with Makeba, took part in *King Kong*, a musical which, as Mogotsi explains, had politics at its heart. 'The story concerns a black fighter who has defeated all his black and coloured opponents, but is forbidden, by apartheid, to meet his chief white challenger. The frustration and bitterness lead to his downfall, as the boxer turns gangster and finally commits suicide.' The Brothers came to Britain with the musical; Makeba went to America. Their subsequent history is one of frustration. While delighted by Makeba's success in America, the Manhattan Brothers feel saddened and disappointed that there has been no recognition or acknowledgement of their contribution to her repertoire of traditional songs, recorded by the Brothers in the fifties.

The going in Britain became increasingly difficult. The Brothers recorded a live album at the Cecil Sharp House in 1964. A second, picked up by EMI in the following year, featured many of their best-known songs, including 'Kilimanjaro', 'Mbube' — credited, wrongly, to Peter Campbell — and 'Thimlela'. The pettiness and racism that plagued the cabaret circuit came into the open when the Manhattan Brothers, at the top of the bill, discovered that people lower down the bill were receiving larger fees.

Since then, the band have largely retired from performing, a sad conclusion to a career that has made them into the giants of the South African entertainment industry.

MIRIAM MAKEBA

Miriam Makeba won early acclaim for her work with the Manhattan Brothers. Her first records, including 'Pata Pata', a dance craze that rocked South Africa, further established a reputation for a singer who felt equally at ease with jazz and traditional songs.

Over the years, Makeba has become one of South Africa's best-known artists in exile. She took the first steps towards world acclaim by joining the cast of *King Kong*, in 1958, followed by a part in Lionel Rogosin's anti-apartheid film *Come Back Africa*. When Makeba left South Africa, to attend the première at the Venice Film Festival, and later flew to New York, the government revoked her citizenship.

Since then, Makeba has travelled widely, spoken against apartheid at the United Nations, and emerged as the Queen of African song. Her early hits, like 'Mbube', 'The Click Song', and a collection of jazz and folk standards and semi-standards, she recorded under the direction of Harry Belafonte, in America. She has also shown a strong interest in the music of other African countries, drawing material from Zaire, Tanzania, Guinea — where she lived for nine years with her husband at the time, Stokeley Carmichael — and Kenya, which added the lilting 'Malaika' to her repertoire.

As South Africa's foremost musical ambassador, Makeba has walked at the front of a line of artists in exile that stretches from Abdullah Ibrahim, to the Manhattan Brothers and Jonas Gwangwa. But the person with whom she has shared the strongest links is her former husband Hugh Masekela, who followed Makeba's route to the West in 1960. Since then, the two musicians have shared the stage at an historic reunion concert in Botswana in 1982, which drew large crowds over the border from South Africa and, more recently, joined Paul Simon for his controversial Graceland tour.

HUGH MASEKELA

Hugh Masekela was born in Johannesburg in 1939. 'When kids in Europe were going to nursery school, I was winding up the gramophone for my mother and father and uncles,' he says. 'They listened to Glenn Miller, Tommy Dorsey, Duke Ellington, Count Basie and the Andrews Sisters.'

With the encouragement of his school chaplain, Father Trevor Huddlestone, he took up the trumpet. The first one was presented by a member of the Johannesburg Native Municipal Band. The second was a gift, arranged by Fr Huddlestone, from Louis Armstrong, whom the priest met in New York in 1955. Masekela's first tune was 'I'm in the Mood for Love'. He joined the school band and, at fifteen, under the tutorship of fellow-musicians like Zakes Nkosi and Kippie Moeketsi became a 'bebopper on the side', before setting off to join them as a part-time member of the Merry Makers Band. Being the youngest, Masekela was chosen to drive the car, with instruments, to the township weddings and dances. 'We'd concentrate mainly on bebop and swing,' he remembers. 'Then they'd move the chairs back and we'd play mbaqanga, to get the people dancing. We had to play mbaqanga to eat.'[12]

But Masekela's time in South Africa was running out. In 1948 the South African government's creation of the apartheid state had bewildered him. 'The government came and took away the apple, the orange, the vegetable soup, the piece of brown bread, the strawberry jam that we had every day at school. I said, "What's happening?" They said, "The government says that because you're black you can't have it any more." I said, "Fuck them, I am going somewhere else."

'When I was fourteen or thirteen, they brought in the pass laws. They came and carried us in buses to go to the mines. They were giving us all identity numbers. I felt it was like going to Nazi concentration camps. And I made up my mind. I said, "I'm getting out of this fucking place. I don't know how, but I'm leaving."'

197

In 1959, Masekela joined the orchestra for the South African musical *King Kong*, followed by the Jazz Epistles with Dollar Brand (Abdullah Ibrahim). This was the first black jazz group to record an album in South Africa, all the recordings up to then having been on 78s.

In 1960, Masekela arrived in London, to study at the Guildhall School of Music. Later the same year, he took up studies in New York: 'When I got to New York, people there didn't know shit about South Africa. Anyone from Africa, as far as they were concerned, was a communist. This was the year after McCarthy; Kennedy was campaigning against Nixon. They were still lynching people of African origin in the States. When I came, it was the time of civil rights, of Malcolm X, of Khrushchev, Nkrumah, Castro. Nkrumah was just flabbergasting everybody with his rhetoric and sensibility. The week I arrived, Lumumba went to ask people for help against the Belgians. They said, "Fuck it, you're a communist." It wasn't a very welcoming time. In London, there was Bertrand Russell at Trafalgar Square; the anti-nuclear thing had started. There were big rallies against South Africa. It was a violent time just after Sharpeville . . .'

In America, Masekela teamed up with producer Stewart Levine, a colleague from music school in New York. His first record, *Trumpet Africa*, came out on Mercury in 1962. Two years later, he recorded a live album, *The Americanisation of Ooga Booga*, which became a hit two years later, after making its way on to the Californian radio playlists.

Masekela and Levine's own company, Chisa, released eleven albums between 1966 and 1976; their greatest success came with the single 'Grazing in the Grass', which topped the American charts, above the Rolling Stones' 'Jumping Jack Flash' and Herb Alpert's 'This Guy's in Love with You', for two weeks in July 1968. Prior to that, Masekela had reached number seventy-one with an instrumental version of 'Up, Up and Away'; his follow-up, 'Puffin' on down the Track', also reached seventy-one, a far cry from a chart-topper selling over four million copies. Masekela followed up with 'Riot' and 'Fuzz', using a West Coast jazz sound and titles which reflected the radical mood of the times.

By the 1970s, the trumpeter was looking for a change of direction. He wanted a more African feel. His first venture, the Union of South Africa, with trombonist Jonas Gwangwa, drummer Makhaya Mtshoko and singer Caiphus Semenya, fell flat. In 1972, Masekela visited London, where he recorded an album, *Home is where the Music is*, with fellow-South African sax player Dudu Pukwana. He then left on an extended six-year spiritual pilgrimage to Africa.

The trip took him from Senegal — where he worked with Xalam — to Guinea, Liberia and Zaire, where he sat in with OK Jazz. In Lagos, he hit a peak of activity: 'I stayed at the Mainland Hotel and joined up with Fela every day. I found a certain vitality in Afrobeat. Playing with the band was like being on a big fat cloud. You couldn't fall off.' The song 'Lady' remained stamped on his memory: Masekela joined Fela up on his roof as the Afrobeat star directed his women for the cover shot of the *Africa 70* album.

The two men then travelled to Ghana, where Fela introduced him to Faisal Helwani, the producer of Hedzolleh Soundz. Masekela took up with the band, playing straight melody lines over their complex cross-rhythms, and finally set off with the band for America. The agbadza–highlife–Afrobeat partnership produced six albums, which are reckoned to be the finest of Masekela's career.

The Hedzolleh experiment collapsed in 1978, taking Chisa with it. Masekela then recorded two albums with Herb Alpert. All the time, he was looking in vain for a new direction; he found it once again in Africa. In 1982, Masekela, with Miriam Makeba, played a concert in Lesotho, close to the South African border. 'They had to send army trucks to South Africa to get supplies,' says Masekela. 'The audience knew every song we'd ever recorded. They sang along, and came back afterwards to complain if we'd changed the arrangements.'

Masekela stayed three months in Lesotho, then left for Botswana, where he hooked up with a band in what, fifteen years earlier, had been an old colonial club. The following weekend, the band and Masekela did a three-hour concert. 'Those guys played it like it was supposed to be played,' he says. 'We were doing something that would have taken nine months in the States. Here it took one week. I decided that I was going to go back.'

The chance came in 1984. Masekela signed with Jive records. A mobile studio was shipped to Botswana for a series of albums, with artists such as the Soul Brothers and Caiphus Semenya. Masekela's *Techno-Bush*, featuring the Soul Brothers, Gasper Lawal and his own band, Kalahari, was conceived as a collection of South Africa's greatest hits, including, alongside new, mbaqanga-flavoured songs, a reworking of three classics: 'The Lion Never Sleeps', first recorded as 'Mbube', a choral song by Solomon Linda from the late 1930s, later popularized as 'Wimoweh' in the 1950s; 'Skokiaan', a drinking-song from Bulawayo which had been rerecorded several times in America and southern Africa; and an update of Masekela's earlier hit, 'Grazing in the Grass'.

Despite the success in the clubs of the single, 'Don't Go Lose It Baby', the album sold poorly. Masekela had seen it as a 'feeler', to gauge public reactions to the township sound, but nothing seemed to be happening. His follow-up, *Waiting for the Rain*, proved more cautious, offering an international sound composed of equal doses of funk and jazz, with an electro-flavoured reading of Fela's 'Lady'.

By now, Masekela had tired of presenting a typically African sound and was seeking world approval as a musician – full stop. 'I don't want people to listen to an African record and say, "That's an African record,"' he says. 'That's like being in a zoo. We don't want to limit ourselves. We want to be seen as good musicians, who can play mbaqanga, jazz, Afrobeat . . .' The concept is one that summarizes Masekela's approach to making records. After leaving Jive records in 1986, Masekela signed to Warner Brothers and, in 1987, released *Tomorrow*, a sharply produced collection which mixed tough, township-flavoured songs like the Mandela tribute 'Bring Him Back Home' with the softer ballad approach of 'London Fog'. By now, Masekela was receiving considerable publicity, alongside Miriam Makeba and Ladysmith Black Mambazo, for joining the world tour organized by Paul Simon to promote his South African-based *Graceland* album. Critics castigated the tour; accused Simon of breaking the UN cultural boycott of South Africa. Masekela was unimpressed.

'Today, the spectator sport overseas is observing the South Africa situation, which is important, but sometimes it is not from the right direction . . . As far as a cultural boycott is concerned, I am completely in favour of it when it stops people playing in South Africa. But Paul Simon has brought the music of South Africa to ten million ears – that's never been managed before.'[13]

While the boycott argument rages, the effect of apartheid continues to fill him with horror. When Masekela's former sax player Barney Rachebane played in New York, musicians like Weather Report and Archie Shepp were, in Masekela's words, 'blown away'.

'But there are hundreds of musicians in South Africa like that,' he says. 'Because of the apartheid system, people with international capabilities never get the opportunity to be heard. If it was just talent and there was no racism involved, all the genius would be out here . . .

'I've seen people destroyed by the system of discrimination all over the world. I've seen it in Jamaica. I've seen it in America. When I arrived just about everyone in bebop was a junky. Most blues singers were boozers. It seems like any music comes with its drug, its destructive element. Then you add to that racial discrimination . . .

'Apartheid destroys the whole nation, black and white. It destroys black people; the European population are deprived of a rich cultural experience by being separated from them.'

The tension between Europe and Africa is one that informs the whole of Masekela's career. Unable to return to a South Africa in chains, he has spent most of his working life seeking and enjoying worldwide success. But the urge to build a musical heartland in the southern hemisphere, reflected in his trips to Africa, his work with Herb Alpert, and his recent Graceland operations with South Africa's finest resident musicians, remains a strong motive force. During the Graceland tour, in April 1987, he explained: 'We're in a very unnatural environment. Our careers are started, but we're only now getting attention overseas. It's a colonial attitude. We shouldn't have to be subjected to Western approval to be successful artists. The real secret of the development of our talent lies in the removal of the South African government, because from there we'll be able to assess what we really have, our capabilities. We'll be able to be self-sufficient and not have to come and sit in this rain and fog all the time . . .'[14]

MALOMBO JAZZ

For all the popularity of Western music – soul, reggae and jazz – South African traditional forms still hold an enormous appeal. Records by Ladysmith Black Mambazo, capturing the full richness of Zulu choral music, feature strongly in the national charts, while the small record labels sell rural Zulu, Shangaan, Sotho and Xhosa material accompanied by assembly-line studio bands. In a country like South Africa, though, tradition is a two-edged weapon: the promotion of simplistic rural values can all too easily reinforce the basic apartheid contention that the cities and modern life are for the whites; homelands and tradition for the blacks. The resulting conflict lends a particular intensity to many forms of South African music, including township jazz which, through the work of expatriate artists like Abdullah Ibrahim and Dudu Pukwana, keeps folk memories alive in the most modern and hard-edged of musics.

One of the early attractions of jazz, though, was that it rose above government-imposed divisions of tribe and ethnicity. The point was well made in the 1950s by a townsman talking to journalist Anthony Sampson. 'Tribal music! Tribal history! Chiefs! We don't care about chiefs! Give us jazz and film stars, man! We want Duke Ellington,

Satchmo and hot dames! Yes, brother, anything American. You can cut out all this junk about kraals and folk tales and Basutos in blankets — forget it! You're just trying to keep us backward, that's what!'[15]

Such attitudes gradually lost currency as the sixties brought new forms of black consciousness into play. Jazz musicians took stock of traditional forms, incorporated them into their music. Among the best-known of the new bands was the Malombo Jazzmen, made up of Julian Bahula (drums), Philip Tabane (guitar), and Abe Cindi, flute. Basing their music on the healing rhythms of the Venda people, Malombo pushed rootswards with a vengeance. In 1964 they won first prize at the Castle Jazz Festival in Orlando Stadium. For writer Mbulelo Vizikhungho Mzamane, the Pretoria trio signalled 'a cultural reawakening, an end to the period of mourning after the ravages of Sharpeville'.[16]

Malombo owes at least some of its existence to chance. Julian Bahula describes how he came across a set of 'traditional Zulu drums for sale in a Pretoria market . . . The next day I sold my kit drums and since then I've always used my people's traditional drums.'[17]

Tabane, a guitarist whose style defies definition or imitation, recalls that the organizers of the festival were unable to decide in which category to place the band. Twenty years later, the South African *Star* echoed Tabane's words.

All the clevers and 'moggos' from Pimville, Sophiatown, western Native Township and Alexandria, who prided themselves as heavy cats in mainstream jazz, found themselves reeling from music with a natural rhythm. The debut of Malombo had a devastating effect, and was the forerunner of a musical awakening among black musicians. It was in a sense the predecessor to the black-consciousness philosophy.[18]

Malombo applied lyrical, at times lilting, guitar and flute melodies to a percussion sound steeped in rural Venda culture. The main instrument, the Malombo drums, carved from the roots of the baobab tree and draped with cowhide, are used to communicate with ancestral spirits, as a way of healing the sick. Tabane, who learned the guitar from a folk musician, Mashabe, adds a further traditional gloss, mixing jazz and traditional music in a way that captures some of the fire and spirit of the old marabi players.

Malombo's line-up underwent a number of changes. Bahula and Abe Cindi left to form their own Malombo Jazzmen. Tabane and percussionist Gabriel Thobejane carried on as Malombo. Bahula later left South Africa for London, where his work as a promoter, and the founder of Jabula, Jazz Afrika and Electric Dream, put him at the forefront of the British African scene. By 1981, Cindi had rejoined Tabane briefly, but was later replaced by new musicians.

For all the changes, Tabane's musical policy has remained constant. Malombo is a healing, contemplative music, designed for listening, not dancing. It draws on jazz, but as Tabane explains, remains rooted in traditional culture: 'Why imitate the Americans? All they're doing is trying to find their own roots . . . and those roots are right here in Africa. There is enough talent in us to play our own rhythm without polluting it with foreign material.'[19]

Tabane has also expressed interest in forming a 'Homeland Symphony Orchestra', composed of 'raw musicians, playing marimbas, flutes, jaws harp, horns, even baritone sax, and perhaps two guitars'. Such a plan will doubtless open a new chapter for Malombo music. In the meantime, it is interesting to note that the band preserves its life-enhancing rhythms. 'Malombo still heals,' says Tabane. 'One time, when I was still playing with Julian and Abe, a brother came up to me before the show and said he was intending to marry a particular woman, but she refused to go out. We were playing later that evening at a community hall, when the guy came over with the girl. I saw him three weeks later and he told me what had happened. While we were playing, the girl had started to jump up and down and cry. "I had to catch her and take her home," he said. "The music was too much for her." She then agreed to get married, and the couple are still together now . . .'

SIPHO MABUSE

One of the giants of township pop, Sipho Mabuse started his career as a drummer with the Beaters in the late sixties. 'When we started, our main influences were the Beatles, the Rolling Stones, plus South African bands like the Manhattan Brothers and Skylarks,' he explains. 'We were caught up with pop music. Mbaqanga was popular, but we considered it inferior. As members of the so-called elite, we listened mostly to foreign music.'[20] The seventies saw further developments in the township music, with the arrival of Soweto soul, a sound based partly on the music of Booker T and other leading American acts. But the outside influence faded by degrees, as the growth of black consciousness that took place throughout the decade left its mark on South African pop and soul bands. 'We needed an African identity,' says Mabuse. 'The only way we could find it was to change our style of music. The Beaters suddenly became like an English monster.'

A three-month tour of Zimbabwe provided the necessary inspiration. Deeply influenced by the lifestyle of the capital, Harare, and by the local rumba, played by bands like OK Success, the Beaters wrote a rumba-influenced song, 'Harari', which became a huge hit in 1974 and provided a new African sound and a new name for the band, as the tide of black consciousness rose around them. Mabuse recalls the mid-seventies as a time of change: an era when established 'roots' bands, like Malombo, came increasingly to the fore, and when newer outfits, like Dashiki and Batsumi, followed their lead. 'So many of the musicians had assumed the pan-African ideology,' he says. 'They were all going back to their roots. But none of them played mbaqanga. It was more jazz, with drums, whistles, alongside horns and guitars.' Harari led the pop wing of the new black consciousness. 'Osibisa was a big influence,' says Mabuse. 'They created a wide interest, among the companies, in the new sound. I valued the authenticity of their music. It was as if you were actually in the bush. It was so fresh on the ear.'

Harari enjoyed widespread success, plus a number of personal problems, not least the deaths of two prominent members. Their sound changed, away from the rumba feel towards South Africa's own township music. 'We became more rootsy, more township-based as we went along,' says Mabuse. In 1984, the band split, leaving Mabuse to press ahead as a solo singer and instrumentalist. His first release, 'Rise', became a huge commercial hit in the same year. The album, *Burn Out*, sold 230,000 copies in South Africa and was later released in America by CBS. In Britain, the release of the irresistible 'Jive Soweto' established Mabuse's reputation among African-music fans. The overseas moves hotted up when he signed a deal with Virgin in 1987, brought out 'Shikisha', a single taken from his *Afrodizzia* album, followed by an album entitled simply *Sipho Mabuse*.

Mabuse claims a number of inspirations, from Hugh Masekela, who recorded three township classics on his *Techno-Bush* album, to Marks Mankwane, a veteran mbaqanga guitarist and producer. A trip to Britain, and the sight of a British band playing mbaqanga, turned him further towards using authentic South African music: a ploy that was shortly afterwards adopted by Malcolm McLaren with his South African *Duck Rock* recordings.

On *Burn Out*, Mabuse charted a new path, concentrating less on guitar, the great staple of African pop, more on keyboards. Piano was still a comparative rarity: Mabuse was inspired by Abdullah Ibrahim, and what he terms Ibrahim's 'classical' feel. 'Jive Soweto' keyed itself further into the township rhythms of Soweto. 'The bass line determined the sound,' says Mabuse. 'It's round and woolly. If music hasn't got a strong bass, it doesn't hit us. Even when people sing, in choral groups, it's always the bass that comes out strongest.' The township sound was further deepened by the use of rim-shot drum patterns, common to many mbaqanga records, and the meeting between Mabuse, and one of the great giants of sax jive and township music generally, West Nkosi. 'I just asked him to come and play,' remembers Mabuse. 'He said, "What do you want me to play?" I said, "You'll see when you get here." He turned up in jeans and slip-ons carrying a case. His sax had been put away for years, but when he took it out, it was brand-new. He started polishing it. I played the melody line from "Jive Soweto" and said, "Now you play it, but with the real West Nkosi feel."'

Mabuse's plan was to find the original artists, because only they knew the secrets of how the township sound was made. 'If you listen to an African sax player, as opposed to David Sanborn, say, he plays with a completely different feeling. The African sax has a wailing tone; every note bends. Musicians trained to play jazz find it hard to bend those notes.' 'Jive Soweto', for Mabuse, was a test case, to find public reaction to a new, commercial form of mbaqanga-influenced township pop. The reaction inspired him to continue the experiment, with an album that included Lemmy Special Mabaso, the sax player and former king of kwela, and Hansford Ntemu, 'an unbelievable guitarist and mbaqanga player'. The music includes Shangaan rhythms, on a track called 'Ti Nyanga' and 'Shikisha', which features a range of South African dances. 'When I was young, I was always fascinated by the traditional dancers,' says Mabuse. 'I'd go into the township hostels, where you'd see the Shangaan performers, with their own drums, and dancing — it was far more aggressive than the Zulus.'

Such early contacts have provided Mabuse with much of his later political and cultural inspiration. In 1986, he became a leading figure in SA Musicians Against Apartheid, a body which calls for the end of the state of emergency and for fundamental changes in the system, both political and musical.

'Basically we can do almost anything we like. There are certain places we can't play, because of the Group Areas Act or because of certain

Afrikaner councillors who don't want to be associated with what they call "Bantus". At one time, the police would raid studios; musicians who didn't have passes would be arrested and put in prison. We haven't seen pass raids lately. But nothing has really changed. Black musicians never get a fair deal except when they stand up and say, "This is what I want. This is what I'm worth."

'The whites never buy local stuff. The record industry really survives on black sales. But that doesn't stop the companies from paying as little on royalties, promotion as they can . . .'

MALOPOETS

The back-to-the-roots movement spoken of by Sipho Mabuse and Johnny Clegg (see Savuka) is central to another celebrated South African band, Malopoets who, from their formation in 1978 to their demise in exile, in 1986, proved to be one of South Africa's best-known exponents of pop-flavoured mbaqanga.

Like many of the roots bands of the seventies, Malopoets came to mbaqanga out of a conscious wish to rediscover township music, after years spent playing music that was felt to be more prestigious; not only by the members themselves, who had played in such bands as Malombo and the rock-oriented Purple Haze, but also by their audience, who considered mbaqanga to be rough, unfashionable and lacking sophistication. 'Before we formed Malopoets, we were playing disco and American soul,' lead singer Pat Sefolosha told *Blues and Soul* in June 1985. 'It was what the promoters wanted. It was very hard to play our own music. But it was getting us nowhere. In the end we asked ourselves why we were neglecting our own music. We lived in the townships . . . we should be playing township music . . .'

Apart from the rigidly defined public attitudes to mbaqanga, a further obstacle stood in the band's way: the notorious difficulties of running a band in South Africa. Since the sixties, when Robert Bopape set up his studio and scouted for local talent, session players, rather than bands, ruled the music scene. The Malopoets stuck it longer than most. 'It's hard to find groups in South Africa who really stick together,' says Patrick. 'The economic situation is impossible. A group gets together for six months. Three members leave. Some go solo. If a mbaqanga band stays together for two years, it's strong.'

Lead guitarist Kenny Mathaba explains further difficulties. 'Musicians are handled badly. The studios have the best equipment, then they go and get people in from the streets to operate it.

'But the greatest difficulty is apartheid. Musicians have no security. A company can get a musician, pay him nothing, make him pay for his transport . . . the internationals treat black artists the same as local companies, like cheap labour. The contracts are so long and complicated. People don't understand them. After signing, you find a publishing deal has been stuck into it.

'If I work in a studio, I know I'll be paid half of a white fee, even though the conditions are the same. If you don't go along with it, you starve. Those that have resisted, they can't go on. Some die young, become paupers. They come to nothing. Some become alcoholics. One of my friends died without a cent. Kippie Moeketsi wouldn't take such jobs. He died penniless. Apartheid kills so much talent: people pass away unnoticed.'

In 1983, Patrick Sefolosha left South Africa, and teamed up with producer Martin Meissonnier in Paris. The others joined him: their EMI debut album, *Malopoets*, kept the hard bass lines, but chipped the rough power from the township mbaqanga sound. 'Mbaqanga talks about the daily life of people in South Africa,' says Kenny Mathaba. 'When musicians start to improve they always overlook what's around them, they want to play like Coltrane, to deny their own. But now more and more are going back to the roots. Before, you could hardly mention the word mbaqanga. It was really Hugh Masekela who started this rediscovery of the music. What we're doing is now beginning to be accepted overseas, which is one of the reasons why more people are now playing mbaqanga.'

RAY PHIRI

Ray Phiri's career shows the further extent to which township pop draws on, and transforms, other, more traditional forms and styles. His father, 'Just Now' Phiri, was a swimming-pool cleaner and an acoustic guitarist who played highlife music, from his Malawi homeland, at 'stokvels', or fund-raising neighbourhood parties. Phiri started his career dancing to his father's music, switching to guitar when a faulty machine took off three of his father's fingers.

He joined his first band, Jabuvu Queens, in 1967. It was a mbaqanga outfit, with five singers, and Phiri was the groaner. The following year, the band had a sizeable hit with a song called 'Sponono', which remained popular, and on catalogue, for ten years, long after Jabuvu Queens had broken up. In the early seventies, Phiri joined the Cannibals, one of the bands which rode the crest of the Soweto soul boom. The electric organ became the dominant sound as township bands created repertoires of four-chord songs, their inspiration beamed in from Memphis.

For the next eight years, Phiri, with the Cannibals' outstanding soul singer Jacob Mparanyana Radebe, who can be heard on the *Rhythm of Resistance* album, enjoyed a fruitful collaboration, producing twenty-nine gold singles and three gold albums. Radebe's death, in 1978, led to the band's demise and ultimately the formation of Stimela who, after a period of heavy session work, produced a commercial pop sound grounded in jazz, mbaqanga and jive. Phiri assumed effortlessly the role of social commentator and teacher, asking people to look inside, rather than outside, for the answer to life's problems; to fight back after failure, to avoid self-pity. In a country where inflamed sensitivities and paranoid authoritarianism can read new meanings into innocently straightforward lyrics, it is hardly surprising that Phiri has run into trouble. His epic 'Highland Drift', recorded at the height of Zimbabwe's struggle for independence, was banned by the South African Broadcasting Corporation, while the 1986 'Whisper in the Deep' faced the not-unrelated phenomena of a radio ban and large sales: 157,000 copies in five months. 'I wasn't saying that black should turn against white, or that white should turn against black,' says Phiri. 'We're all trapped in a great river of pain. We don't have to whisper in the deep . . .'[21]

Phiri's philosophical approach to songwriting sets Stimela apart from other pop bands. 'We're seen as the People's band,' he says. 'The songs are not just "Squeeze me, love me tonight". They set out to show what should be done, what we can do for ourselves. There's a better world out there . . .'

In 1986, Phiri worked with Paul Simon on the *Graceland* album, joining the controversial tour, along with a group of other top African musicians, in early 1987. 'I've learnt a lot, mixing with different people, hearing different types of music,' he says. 'But I've realized that to be creative, the only way really is to go back to the roots, to see if I can find the missing chord.'

One of his great inspirations, both as a singer, in the early days, and now at the front of a township pop band, has been his father. Phiri commemorates his brand of Malawian music on a song called 'Crazy Love'. Another is the renowned groaner Mahlathini. 'He's played a vital role in our musical life,' says Phiri. 'He's one guy who decided not to sell out, not to do bubblegum music. He retained the culture for us. And if you've got no culture, you're like a soul wandering till dawn . . .'

SAVUKA

Township pop, with its increasingly 'cultural' flavour, finds further exponents in Savuka, a group which released a single and album on EMI in 1987 and played a series of successful London gigs.

Savuka's guitarist and singer Johnny Clegg was born in Rochdale, in the UK, and arrived in South Africa in 1959 at the age of six. His first experience of Zulu music came from a street performer, Mntonanazo Mzila, followed, more crucially, by Sipho Mchunu, a migrant worker with whom Clegg set up a strong musical and personal rapport. The duo worked together from 1970, first as Johnny and Sipho and, by 1976, with a full band, as Juluka, the Zulu for sweat. The name speaks volumes: until the band started finding it relatively easy to find gigs, they suffered from racist abuse, threats of violence and then an extreme shortage of venues in a country where mixed, multi-racial gatherings were, to all intents and purposes, forbidden.

Journalist Hamilton Malaza described the significance of Juluka's early work. 'Juluka reflect at the level of music a critical period in the development of South Africa and its peoples. It is an exciting blend of new music, a blend of traditional and new music, which isolates and distils hitherto unexplored facets of the South African experience in a way that has already been hailed as a landmark in the history of recording in this country.'[22] Seven albums, including *Universal Men*, a musical journey into the life of a Zulu migrant worker, followed the band's first hit record, 'Woza Friday'. By 1987, though, Mchunu had left the band and Johannesburg for his family home, to run his cattle business. Clegg, deprived of his former teacher and cultural mentor, set up a new band, Savuka.

'Juluka appeared at a time when black people were buying up records by the O'Jays in their hundreds and thousands,' he recalls. 'We went back to our roots. A cult fashion began, with people playing roots music. You had something similar in 1970, and again in 1976 with the black-consciousness movement, an attempt to recapture and to stress African roots and origins.'[23]

In musical terms, Clegg followed Mchunu's lead towards the guitar styles of the Zulu street musicians: a sound which incorporates minor chords, largely unknown in mbaqanga, and a drone effect, created by the bass doubling the guitar parts, and by the guitarists playing every pulse of the beat on the bass string. The appeal of the rural-based music has not been lost on other township musicians, who are working street music into some of the glossiest and most commercial of modern pop sounds. 'Township pop is a new genre,' says Clegg. 'It's a genre where reggae and mbaqanga meet, where soul and mbaqanga meet, where funk and mbaqanga meet.' The resulting techno-mbaqanga can all too easily be dismissed as lacking the true African feel, the rootsiness of the great mbaqanga bands of the sixties and seventies. For Clegg, such talk verges on the nonsensical.

'The process of technologizing the sound started in the seventies, when the DX7 and the Linn drum caused a revolution in South African music,' he explains. 'It's also caused problems. Guys could play and record songs on their own. Bands would split up, and five new singers and writers would emerge. Everyone became a star, giving the record companies a massive amount of product to deal with. The attitudes overseas are puzzling. People are looking for a nostalgic sound, what they would *like* to see played. But it doesn't happen any more. Today it's people like Condry Ziqubu, Brenda Fassie and Sipho Mabuse who are playing the real sound of Soweto. It's monster stuff, shifting massive amounts of albums.

'Paul Simon picked up on a music that was five, ten, fifteen years out of date. South African musicians are saying, "Christ, is this the way our music is going to be broken overseas? All this old stuff? We've left that behind." Mbaqanga used to be a black working-class music. But the working class itself has changed.'

The crucial difference between African and Western sensibilities centres on the question of 'roots', a valuable and highly prized commodity with some music lovers in the West, but a meaningless concept to someone living in a township like Soweto where, says Clegg, 'Apartheid has generated a negative feeling towards ethnicity. One doesn't want to stress the fact that one is a Zulu or a Xhosa. One wants to stress the fact that one is a citizen of the world, in the music you listen to, the food you eat, your clothes, the furniture in your home . . .'

As an extension of such a basic misunderstanding, Clegg feels that there is now a growing anger among African musicians who feel that the roots argument has been turned against them in the form of cultural imperialism. 'The musicians see the Western roots attitude as a form of slavery. African musicians want to experiment with Western music and Western culture. And, if not experiment, then to be able to use the techniques and the technology available to them. But when they start to use drum boxes, they get branded as cultural sell-outs. There's a feeling among roots people that African music has to be frozen into a timewarp . . . .

'Our approach is that there should be a democracy of music: the new forms should get as much support as the old. There should be a balance. There is a growing resistance to people saying, "This isn't groaners; this isn't mbaqanga." This isn't South Africa in 1950, this is 1987, going on 1990 and many African musicians have spent a lot of time and energy trying to find a place for themselves in the new musical world.'

LADYSMITH BLACK MAMBAZO

One of the tangible effects of *Graceland* has been the rise to prominence in the West of the choral group, Ladysmith Black Mambazo. By April 1987, their WEA debut album, *Shaka Zulu*, had reached twenty-seven in the British album charts, creating further success for one of South Africa's top acts.

Ladysmith have been going since 1960, professionally since 1971, with a version of ingoma ebusuku (or night music) that the band call cothoza mfana — literally to walk proudly, as if on tiptoe. Their founder, Joseph Shabalala, explains that the band members came from rural South Africa; their sound is a deep Zulu music which they have polished and modernized, while keeping many of the essential features of the old choral sound: the loud booming tones, the choreographed movements, the distinctive harmonies.

'The people that went before us were going about things in the wrong way,' he explains. 'The music was in the wrong key and lacked melody. We had to sit down, practise, to get the right harmonies.'[24]

His own inspiration came from a dream in which he heard children singing in a strange language. It was impossible to catch the words; but the harmonies, melodies and gestures made a lasting impact and live on in Ladysmith's music.

Until the arrival of the band, choral music had suffered severe commercial neglect in South Africa. Only Solomon Linda, the composer of 'Mbube', had achieved any marked degree of recognition. Like Shabalala, Solomon Linda came from the area around the town of Ladysmith. But the new band came with a keen commercial and competitive edge. Explaining how Mambazo means axe, Shabalala goes on, 'When we did competitions with other choral groups, we defeated them, we always chopped them down.'

Since they started, Ladysmith have released over twenty-four albums, changing course, in 1975, to take on religious subjects. The concept came from Shabalala who had joined the Church of God of Prophecy in Southern Africa. 'A voice came to me saying, "Abstain from food for four days. If you do that, you'll defeat your enemy." Two brothers of mine were sick. The man came, laid hands on them and they were healed. I then joined the church.'

Ladysmith's music attracts young and old audiences in South Africa. 'It's amazing,' says the leader. 'At first no one cared for our style of music. Then they started to support it. We're leading the field. Even young people, who normally like to dance, will come and sit down quietly.'

CHIMURENGA

The protest song has a long, honourable tradition in southern Africa. In 1897 Enoch Sontoga wrote his classic 'Nkosi Sikelel' iAfrika' (God Bless Africa), which was later translated into Shona and Ndebele and carried the full weight of pan-African pride during the years of colonial oppression. Zimbabwe's own period of colonial rule, which began in 1890, ran through the Shona and Ndebele uprisings of 1896–8, the two world wars, and ended after a prolonged struggle in 1980, saw the creation of similar protest songs which fused traditional call-and-response patterns with harmonies and melodies derived from Christian missions.

As Zimbabwean academic G.P. Kahari points out, the songs covered a catalogue of injustices suffered under colonial rule, from the evils of forced labour to the harshness of the police, 'the white men's underdog', and the torture and humiliation inflicted by the Europeans. As the words were in Shona, Ndebele or other Zimbabwean languages, they were incomprehensible to the majority of whites. They could therefore be sung openly, often in front of district commissioners and other agents of colonial rule. [1]

The protest movement reached new peaks during the war of liberation, when electric bands led by Thomas Mapfumo, Oliver Mtukudzi and other Zimbabwean artists, spoke out against white minority rule and the hated security forces. With the songs came a new music, a hard Shona sound derived from the country's ancient mbira music and transposed, by Thomas Mapfumo and his guitarists Jonah Sithole and Pickett, on to electric instruments. Chimurenga music, the authentic sound of modern Zimbabwe, has various precedents, among them the work of acoustic musicians, including Saferio Madzikatere, who sang Shona folk music to an acoustic-guitar backing. Chimurenga music differs, though, in its wide distribution, the impact it has had on a scene dominated largely by overseas music, and its emergence as part of a national revolution. Before Mapfumo, it was a free-for-all. 'When I started, everyone was into simanje-manje,' he says. 'A lot of South African groups were coming to Rhodesia at that time. The Mahotella Queens invaded our country. Some groups from the Congo got contracts to come and work here. There were bands from all over. It was confusion.'[2]

The same conditions applied long before Mapfumo's time. Lack of local recordings made Zimbabwe a target for imported music, while the crude insensitivities of the missionaries and settlers left most

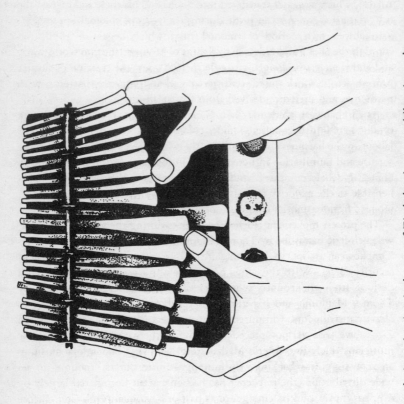

The mbira, a form of hand piano, has inspired some of Zimbabwe's most exhilarating urban pop music

Zimbabweans with a feeling that their own culture was of little value.

In the 1940s, Zimbabwe's townships swam in a sea of imported South African music, much of it based on black American sounds: the Swingsters, the Woody Woodpeckers and the Manhattan Brothers stimulated a host of local bands who sang in harmony over a swing background of jazz guitars, sax and drums. Jive and jitterbug boomed. In Bulawayo, the annual eisteddfod drew ballroom dancers, massed choirs and classical musicians, but shunned the 'disreputable' street and folk artists.

In the 1950s, kwela made a huge impact, with Lemmy Special and Spokes Mashiyane records attracting attention. Local records followed: George Sibanda from Bulawayo created a kwela-influenced guitar sound known as tsaba-tsaba, and two other guitarists, Mataga and Jordan Chataika, played a harder street sound known as mahobo – a catch-all phrase that embraces most of the music played on street corners by solo musicians wielding imported or home-made tin-can guitars. In the rural areas, the guitar had long been an indispensable part of local entertainment.

Zimbabwean journalist Fred Zindi describes the early days of rural mahobo in the 1940s.

Each village would have some kind of party, a blues or a jazz party. Each week there'd be someone different; each family would hold it every six months, like a timetable. There'd be musicians, a banjo or a guitar player, who'd come along with a dancer who played hosho – or people just dance and drink this home-made beer, opaque beer called Seven Days because it took that long to brew. They'd start Friday and finish when all the beer had been sold, usually two or three forty-four-gallon cans. Then they'd go on to the next village. Selling booze was one way of earning cash.[3]

In the 1960s, Zimbabwe saw further imports of foreign music, including pop and rock, simanje-manje and the music of the Belgian Congo (Zaire) which was now freely available in record stores. Congolese musicians formed the backbone of bands like OK Success, Limpopo Jazz and later the Real Sounds, and went on to influence local bands like the Harare Mambos, Great Sounds and MD Rhythm Success. A new Zimbabwean sound developed as musicians took the rumba, speeded it up, adding trebly guitars – pointing to South Africa rather than to the more languid Congo – and lyrics in local languages. The name, sungura, came from the labels of the imported records, while the bands themselves, including Nyami Nyami Sounds, the Four Brothers and the Sounds of Muddy Face, built up large followings. The country's top-selling act, since their formation in 1979, has been Devera Ngwena, a guitar band whose records, reflecting the popularity of the rumba as a pan-African music, sell widely inside and outside Zimbabwe.

The creation of a modern pop repertoire based on traditional Zimbabwean music, and the adaptation of traditional instruments, has come from elsewhere: the chimurenga music of Thomas Mapfumo, Oliver Mtukudzi and other artists working in the mbira, or hand-piano tradition, while the increasingly popular Lovemore Majaivana is adding his distinctively Bulawayan voice to the sound of modern Zimbabwe.

THOMAS MAPFUMO

I left this country [Zimbabwe] in September 1972 for further studies in the United Kingdom . . . I came back home in January 1978 to be confronted with an earth-shaking revival of ethnic music. Where local artists had made their names by emulating the Beatles, Elvis Presley etc, I found Thomas Mapfumo, Oliver Mtukudzi and others holding sway and quite confidently and resignedly hugging the ground of African culture in their music. This amounted to a re-entry shock for me.[4]

'Thomas's music! Whew! If you knew what the words were like before . . . we had to change some of the words to a certain extent, and let the meaning be understood through innuendo.'[5]

Thomas Mapfumo has been given numerous accolades. He is seen as the modernizer of traditional Shona music, as the 'Lion of Zimbabwe', the figurehead of the Zimbabwean musical revolution that took place in tandem with the independence struggle in the mid-1970s.

None of this could have been predicted from his early career. He was born in 1945 in Marondera, moved to what was then Salisbury, now Harare, left school in 1964 and travelled briefly to Zambia. On his return a year later, Mapfumo started singing with local bands, including the Cosmic Dots and the Springfields, who were working at nightclubs in the capital. This music, like the name, had strong Western influences and Mapfumo cemented his early reputation with Elvis Presley, Otis Redding and Sam Cooke numbers – 'A Change is Gonna Come' being a particular favourite. His first tentative step towards the musical upheavals that he would effect in the 1970s took place when he started translating the words into his own language. 'They were singing Shona stuff,' says Fred Zindi. 'It was jazzy but sung in Shona. They also did twelve-bar blues. Thomas just used to make up the words. One popular song was a blues called "The Heel of My Shoe is Gone".'[6]

Thomas Mapfumo's habit of using his own language left the audience bemused. 'It was a mockery. Everyone was laughing. They'd never heard anyone singing in Shona, and they thought I was going mad. But I kept on and began getting a few supporters . . .'[7]

By 1973 Mapfumo had outgrown the Springfields. He joined the Hallelujah Chicken Run Band, which in 1974 signed to the Teal record company, and started his research into traditional Zimbabwean music.

The key instrument was the mbira, a small hand piano which consists of a large calabash resonator and a set of iron keys which produce a melodic, buzzing and rattling sound. Mbira is part of Zimbabwe's ancient musical traditions, and was first described, in written form, by a Portuguese missionary priest in 1589.

In modern Zimbabwe, mbira players are important figures, providing social music and, more importantly, the music for religious ceremonies at which spirit mediums become entranced and pass on messages, advice and warnings from the ancestors.

Mapfumo, with his guitarist Jonah Sithole, translated the intricate patterns of the mbira on to electric guitars, working in both the repeated kutsinhira, or rhythm pattern, and the kushaura, or lead melody line. The guitar strings were dampened to capture the exact tone of the mbira keys, while the hi-hat and bass drum echoed the traditional hosho or gourd-rattle rhythms and the stamping of the dancers' feet.

'The man who keeps the whole thing going is the drummer,' says Mapfumo. 'He keeps the people together. Each guitarist plays something similar to what the other is doing. The bass is a little off beat; he stops for maybe two bars while the others carry on. The timing is very complicated.'[8]

The difficulty of the sound, coupled with the rustic connotations of the mbira, did little to popularize the sound with urban audiences hooked on Western rock and soul, rumba from Zaire and simanje-manje from South Africa. 'People thought the mbira was an old-fashioned music for people who lived in the communal areas,' says Mapfumo.

Slowly the attitudes changed. Mapfumo's first song, 'Morento', with its warning that war was on its way and that people must fight, set the pattern for what was to follow. In 1975 Mapfumo cut a traditional song, 'Ngoma Yarira', which had hidden political connotations. After working as a part-time singer with the Pied Pipers Mapfumo joined the Acid Band. His first album, the 1977 *Hokoyo!*, meaning 'watch out', established Mapfumo as an important new voice, a man who could bring together a youthful urban audience and rural listeners who would recognize songs like 'Ja Ja Go Moja', which Mapfumo first heard from his uncle in his village.

Some, though, remained sceptical. So accurate was Mapfumo's reworking of the old music that he was accused of being a medium — a charge which he denied, although members of his audience would go into trances when the Acid Band struck up.

Equally ambiguous was the response of white Rhodesians. The authorities were alarmed by Mapfumo's subversive messages and asked Teal to prevent Mapfumo's music from being released. The records were, accordingly, denied airplay. In 1977 Mapfumo was locked up for ninety days, then set about recording further singles and albums that offered encouragement both to the ZANU freedom fighters and the citizens of war-torn Zimbabwe.

Mapfumo's 'Chimurenga' or 'struggle' singles contain some of his finest work. They were recorded on poor equipment between 1976 and 1980, the earlier cuts carrying warnings and encouragement in a form sufficiently clouded to escape the notice of the authorities. Although they were denied airplay at home, the singles became well-known — played either at discos and in public places, or blown into Zimbabwe from the Voice of Mozambique radio station, which also carried traditional music, choirs and speeches from the ZANU leaders. The late 1970s saw further developments. In 1978, Mapfumo formed his current band Blacks Unlimited; as the struggle reached its peak, and Bishop Abel Muzorewa emerged as a white-backed last hope, Mapfumo found his music hijacked by the government. A series of 'sky-shouts' took place. Helicopters flew over the countryside, blasting Mapfumo's music from horn speakers. The music was followed by messages telling the people that Mapfumo had deserted ZANU and that he was now backing Muzorewa, and calling on everyone to stop fighting and support the government. The propaganda failed. As Mapfumo explained, the people already knew who their liberators were, who their leaders were.

After 1980, and the birth of independent Zimbabwe, Mapfumo remained a strong figurehead and spokesman. In albums like *Mabasa* he sang about work, and encouraged people to start rebuilding the country. His *Congress* album called people to attend the ZANU convention in Harare and looked forward to freedom in South Africa.

His music remained rooted in the traditional Shona sound: the British release *Mr Music* bringing an mbira player into the line-up. On each album, Mapfumo explores different rhythms: *Ndangariro*, from the early 1980s, mixes mbira beats with Shangaan traditional sounds on 'Mari', and the upbeat 'Temerina', which reworks a percussion rhythm played by young people in the rural areas. *Mabasa* adopts various Shona rhythms while *Mr Music* includes what Mapfumo describes as a Zimbabwean calypso in the form of 'Juanita'; the Shangaan sound of 'Maria' and the mbira rhythms of 'Kufa Kwangu'. 'Congress', Mapfumo describes as a 'sarenga', a Zimbabwean mixture of the highlife and rumba from further north.

Mapfumo's tours of 1984 and 1985 brought European audiences into startled contact with a musician who sported dreadlocks and seemed to embody many of the moves and mannerisms of the late Bob Marley. His music, too, showed a reggae influence, although Mapfumo describes this as a typically Zimbabwean beat, the shangara. It is interesting to note, however, that the Blacks Unlimited started their 1985 British tour with a strongly reggae-influenced set which was cast aside only after protests from the Zimbabwean community in London.

'We've got so many different musics in Zimbabwe,' says Mapfumo. 'So far we've only scratched the surface. We have rhythms that sound like rock and like reggae, things like shangara and mbakumba. Some of them we're playing at the moment. Some of it sounds like Afro-rock — that's not our fault. That's the way the music is.'

In Harare, Mapfumo keeps his idealism alive, promoting the message of Zimbabwe's cultural and political revolution and in setting up a co-operative to help other artists escape the exploitation of the local record companies. His long-term aim is to set up what the country needs most — a new recording studio.

Western reaction to Mapfumo tends to concentrate on his role as a political figure, the voice of the liberation war. Less attention has been paid to his work on updating Zimbabwe's traditional music, a transformation that hit a polished commercial peak on his 1986 album *Chimurenga for Justice*. After the starkness of the earlier mbira transpositions, Mapfumo opted for a more relaxed sound, that relied as much on keyboards as guitars for its central thrust. But the power remained. A fitting accolade came from the British magazine *Folk Roots*, which cites

Mapfumo and the Blacks Unlimited as 'possibly the best folk-rock band on the planet'.[9]

OLIVER MTUKUDZI

A second musician credited with modernizing Zimbabwe's traditional music is Oliver Mtukudzi who, with his Black Spirits, mixes modern soul with tracks based on mbira music and other traditional Zimbabwean beats.

Mtukudzi recorded his first single, 'Pezuna', for the Teal company in 1976, after which he joined the Wagon Wheels Band, and recorded his first hit, 'Dzandimometera'. The band was steeped in Zairean rumba, but Oliver had already planned a new direction, as he explained to Zimbabwean journalist Tinos Guvi. 'Before joining the Wagon Wheels, I shared the stage one day with Thomas Mapfumo. You see, it was Thomas who started it all. He decided to do his own thing rather than the copyright like most other bands were doing. I admired him and still do for the stand he took, so I said to myself, "Look man, you can do the same thing too."'[10] As good as his word, Mtukudzi recorded a second hit, 'Mutavara', and changed the Wagon Wheels into the Black Spirits. The renamed band released its first album, *Ndipeyiozano*, on the heels of Mapfumo's ground-breaking *Hokoyo!*, in 1978.

The albums that followed offered an uneasy mixture of international-sounding reggae, soul and deeper Zimbabwe sounds like the mbakumba and katekwe, which helped maintain Mtukudzi's position as one of Zimbabwe's great innovators.

BHUNDU BOYS

Once little-known in Britain, Zimbabwean music has recently made inroads with regular visits from Thomas Mapfumo and a second, younger band, the Bhundu Boys. From a Scottish base established by manager Gordon Muir the band built a sizeable British following, attracting pop fans and critics alike. 'The most flowing, natural music I can remember hearing,' wrote BBC disc jockey John Peel.[11] The band's British debut, *Shabini*, received considerable airplay on Peel's late-night show, his enthusiasm matched by his BBC colleague, Andy Kershaw, and Capital

Radio's Charlie Gillett. By April 1987, the album had sold around 10,000 copies and reached number one in the *Melody Maker* independent charts.

The Bhundu Boys have a style and an approach all their own. While many visiting African bands have been presented as 'cultural ambassadors', performing a small number of gigs before flying back to Africa, the Bhundu Boys came and stayed: for six months in 1986, longer in 1987. There is nothing solemn about them. Skirting the larger venues, they gigged endlessly in small clubs and pubs throughout Britain. Instead of taking the stage with vast collections of musicians, back-up singers and dancers, the band gave British clubgoers what they knew already: the small beat group, who pay hard and fast, with no distractions. By 1987, the Bhundu Boys had combined frenetic roots rhythms with an energy and pace reminiscent of the punk explosion, to become one of Britain's most dazzling live acts.

Some of the same qualities have cemented the band's reputation in Zimbabwe. The Bhundu Boys' raw energy centres round a speedy, young people's music known as jit. 'It originates in the rural areas,' explains the Bhundus' guitarist and singer Biggie Tembo. 'A young person's music played out in the open when the moon's full. It's like rock almost, all percussion and singing.'[12] Jit-jive, as the Bhundus describe it, puts the band at some distance from the elders of modern Zimbabwe pop, among them Thomas Mapfumo, who base their repertoire around the ancient mbira tradition. For the Bhundu Boys, mbira is virtually a classical music, played by elders at religious and ceremonial occasions. Jit-jive has no spiritual connotations. It connects less with deep ancestral voices, more with the young people's need for fast dance music. But it still nods towards tradition. The mbira guitar style, pioneered by Mapfumo, is a strong influence, and so is Zimbabwe's store of traditional music, such as 'Manhenga', an old mbira song which features on the *Shabini* album.

The band itself is a product of Zimbabwe's war of liberation, the name Bhundu or 'bush' being chosen to commemorate the freedom fighters who carried on the struggle in the rural areas. The original members came together as the Wild Dragons, a back-up band for Zimbabwean roots singer Son Takura. In 1980 they became part of the cultural renaissance that followed independence. 'Under white rule, everything had to be presented in a Rhodesian way,' says Tembo. 'Our own traditional music was considered primitive and was kept down. During the war, though, people started to experiment. By 1980, musicians were taking a whole new direction.'

Some bands followed the Congolese example, playing rumba music. For the Bhundu Boys this wasn't enough. Their live act has included versions of Les Wanyika's 'Sina Makossa' and 'Pamela', the evergreen 'Shauri Yako' plus mbaqanga tracks from the South African band the Super Tens. But to subsist on copyright material seemed wrong. 'By the time we started, Zimbabwean rumba was already well established,' says Tembo. 'People were looking for something new, so we charted a different path.'

Jit-jive won rapid acceptance. Between 1981 and 1984, the band had four number-one singles in Zimbabwe, including 'Baba Munini Francis', the story of an unfaithful wife; 'Wenhamo Haaneti' and 'Hatisitose', which deals with a ruined love affair. Other songs celebrate the birth of independence and examine current social problems, among them a lack of urban housing, the subject of 'Kuroja Chete'. Three albums, *The Bhundu Boys* (1981), *Hupenyu Hwenasi* (1984) and *Shabini* proved equally successful, the latter helping to establish the band in Europe. Early in 1987, the Bhundu Boys signed with WEA, released a second DiscAfrique album *Tsvimbodzemoto*, and appeared with Madonna at Wembley.

THE REAL SOUNDS

Despite the attractions of jit-jive, chimurenga and other roots sounds, imported music — especially Zairean rumba — is still big in Zimbabwe. Its popularity stems partly from the imported records, partly from local bands such as Devera Ngwena, whose fast tempo and relentless guitar and vocal sound has as much in common with modern South African or Tanzanian pop as with the mellower Zairean original.

The full flavour of seventies Kinshasa music, particularly the sound of OK Jazz, lives on in a second top Zimbabwean band, the Real Sounds. This is hardly surprising as the eleven-piece band is made up of Zimbabwean musicians and a group of Zaireans resident in Harare. The founder member, Ghaby Mumba, was born in Kinshasa and played with a number of local bands before joining the government-sponsored Orchestre Diables Noirs, which played a mixture of jazz, rock and roll and rumba in the OK Jazz mould. In 1967, two years after the end of the civil war, he left for Zambia, capitalizing on local interest in Congolese music with a soukous-boucher band called OC Jazz. His second outfit, Les Elite Bantous, with its less-than-subtle reference to the influential Congolese band Bantous de la Capitale, took the name game further. 'Life in Zambia was good,' he recalls. 'It was less expensive than Zaire, and it was a lot easier to buy instruments.'[13] The band's fortunes changed when their second patron, a Zimbabwean, invited them over the border to take up a residency in a hotel in Umtali. As the war hotted up, Mumba and his fellow-musicians left Umtali and headed for Harare.

By now, Zairean music was already an established part of the local music scene. In the sixties, bands like OK Success, Limpopo Jazz and Vedette Jazz had all fuelled local interest in Congolese rumba. The Real Sounds found an eager audience for their own brand of soukous which resulted in two hit albums, *Harare* and *Funky Lady*, and a set of singles. Of these, 'Dynamos Versus Caps', on the battle between two top national football teams, followed by 'Dynamos Versus Tornados' on their 1987 album *Wende Zako*, showed the extent to which the band, with its dual-nationality line-up, had sunk their teeth into local issues. The rhythms changed too. In the late seventies, the Real Sounds experimented with sungura, but soon changed back to the mellower, Zairean rumba sound. 'It gave people the chance to dance easily, without tearing themselves up,' says Mumba.

By 1986, the band had moved one step forward, one back. A single commemorating the meeting in Harare of delegates from the non-aligned nations extolled the Mugabe government over a smooth rumba beat. The flipside dug into a mixture of rumba with Zimbabwe's mbira sound, which by now the band had christened rhumbira. The same year, the band took another surprise step by rerecording the 1973 OK Jazz hit 'Azda'. Proof, if it were needed, of the continuing appeal of the Kinshasa sound.

DEVERA NGWENA

The growth of an identifiable Zimbabwean rumba began in the late seventies when bands like Devera Ngwena moved from playing copies of Zairean songs to create a music of their own.

After the Zairean sound, the new version sounded altogether leaner and sprightlier. Guitar predominated, with a vocal style which recalled the plainer melodies of Kenyan benga, and a rhythm which drew some of its power from the bass-heavy sounds of South Africa.

Devera Ngwena came together in 1979 as a four-piece who spent their mornings working at the Mashaba asbestos mine, and three evenings a week, on overtime, playing for the miners. Their popularity soared: the name itself, which translates as 'follow the crocodile', refers to the columns of fans who would follow them from gig to gig.

They were attracted by the band's innovative sound, which blended Zairean rumba with traditional Zimbabwean beats. 'I started that beat,' says the leader Jonah Moyo. 'People couldn't believe that it came from a band working at a mine. How could we make such good music?'[14]

At the time, he explains, many bands subsisted on Zairean rumba, often singing in Lingala. Some musicians, like Thomas Mapfumo, Oliver Mtukudzi and Zexie Manatsa, played a deeper traditional music. Devera Ngwena attracted a wider market beyond any one particular region or language group – they sing both in Shona and Ndebele – using a rumba style which, in one shading or another, has become common currency through large parts of Africa.

The band's own chart success reflects this inter-ethnic appeal. Between 1981 and 1987 they recorded eleven albums and fifty singles, with songs like 'Solo Na Mutsai' selling over 100,000 copies, and 'Lekani Kuula' – sung in Chewa, a language from Malawi – becoming one of the biggest-ever sellers in central and southern Africa. But they also keep one eye on the local scene and local issues: one of their 1987 hits, 'Chiredzi', took its name from a town well-known for its sugar-cane industry while 'Masvingo ne Carpet' describes how a person driving on the new road from Harare to the band's home town, Masvingo, travels 'not on tarmac, but on a carpet'.

Moyo's own influences are diverse. His favourite artists include Sam Mangwana, whose Zairean rumba sells across the continent, and the Soul Brothers, South Africa's top mbaqanga band. On some of their numbers, Moyo blends the two sounds: 'People want something they can dance to. And what we've found is that traditional music is less danceable than rumba.'

Devera Ngwena's skill lies in a judicious blend of tempos and textures. Moyo claims that Zimbabwean rumba is simpler than the Zairean version, but it has its own subtle shifts and changes, peeling away the main instruments and keeping the dancefloor filled, and the tension high, with the slimmest of rhythm-guitar workouts. The rhythm break was a technique favoured by many of the new-wave Zairean bands of the seventies, Orchestre Kiam being the most audacious, while Sam Mangwana's Paris recordings with Bopol kept the tradition alive. As British audiences discovered in summer 1987, Devera Ngwena could keep people dancing by doing virtually nothing.

Occasionally the pace slows right down — but not for long. Devera Ngwena operate in two modes: the faster, being sungura; the slower, the cha cha, which gave them one of their greatest hits: 'Ruva Re Moyo Wangu', from 1983. 'The title means "My Sweetheart",' says Moyo. 'We like to sing about love, everyday things . . .' In the year the record came out, the band left the mining company — who seemed reluctant to over-invest in new instruments or European tours — and set up on their own. It was a risk, admits Moyo, but a risk that has paid off: the number of people following the crocodile continues to grow.

KENYA AND TANZANIA

Kenyan pop music owes much of its character to the mixture of outside –
particularly Zairean – music, and indigenous, regional sounds. The flow
of music from Zaire began in the 1950s, with the acoustic guitarists, and
continued throughout the 1960s and 1970s, when emigré bands took the
Kenyan club scene and record business by storm. One of the first to make
an impact was the OS Africa Band, led by the flamboyant Pascal Onema.
According to one Kenyan musician, 'No one in Nairobi wanted anything
else.'[1]

Other musicians followed suit. Over the next twenty years, artists like
Franco, Sam Mangwana and Tabu Ley built up huge followings in east
Africa generally, setting a precedent for musicians like Mzee Makassy and
Samba Mapangala, who settled permanently in the area. But for all the
foreign influence, east African pop has a number of its own distinctive and
highly exuberant forms. One of the most popular is taarab, a Muslim
orchestral music which developed along the coast and soon became an
indispensable part of official functions and ceremonies. With its wavering
vocal lines and elaborately orchestrated banks of guitars, accordions and
violins, taarab sounds like an exercise in Indian–Arabic crossover. But its
use of local rhythms, occasionally rumbas, coupled with what critic John
Storm Roberts calls a 'kind of openness and muscularity', stake out its
African origins.[2] Its recent spread has been remarkable: a music once
restricted to Zanzibar and the east African coastal towns, it is now heard
in eastern parts of Zaire, and there is a top taarab band in Burundi.

Taarab, along with beni, a marching music which took its inspiration,
and some of its instruments, from the brass bands introduced during
colonial times, stretches back to the early years of the century. But the
real beginnings of modern Kenyan pop date from the end of the Second
World War, when Kenyan soldiers, returning from the front, brought
back disposable cash, guitars and accordions. 'Up to that point, our own
music had been actively suppressed,' says Washington Omondi of the
Nairobi International Institute of Music. 'It was associated with the devil.
Any music, apart from hymns and brass-band music, was looked
on as a sin.'[3] After the war, gramophones became popular, and
so did GV records, which had a strong influence on east African
musicians. The chief promoters of the new music were the army and
police bands, the best-known being that of the King's African Rifles,

all of whom included rumbas and cha chas in their dance repertoires.

As in west and central Africa, it was the street musicians, rather than the more 'tasteful' dance bands, that helped create a new, distinctively African urban music. The figure of the solo acoustic, or dry, guitarist, accompanied by a bottle-tapping percussionist, became as common a sight in Kenya as in Zaire, which provided much of the inspiration. Records and radio stations helped spread the new guitar music, while top Zairean players like Jean Bosco Mwenda and Edouard Masengo played the Nairobi clubs and went on tour promoting products like Aspro and Coca-Cola.

New guitar styles developed. On the coast, Omondi recalls guitar players accompanying Christian hymns. Others experimented with Hawaiian styles, using a knife blade and open tunings, or the popular 'Key C', where the bottom string was tuned up a semitone from E to F. In the towns, Bosco's finger-picked melodies and bottle accompaniment attracted imitations by the score, while George Sibanda's vamped chord style, an offspring of kwela, provided further inspiration.

The acoustic guitar had a similar impact in the rural areas, particularly those which already had a strong tradition of stringed-instrument playing. Some of the most prolific guitarists sprang from the Luo and Luhya areas of western Kenya, where the musicians were celebrated for their skill with harps and lyres. Traditional patterns directly influenced the new music: most of the early Kenyan folk and pop stuck to the accepted two-part vocal lines, while well-known rhythms, like the sukuma and umotibi, a Luhya beat with a distinctive compound cross-rhythm, fed into the guitar music.

The 1950s produced a range of influential guitarists, among them John Mwale, Jim Lasco, David Amunga and George Mukabi, whose vibrant finger-picked sukuti music drew heavily on Luhya rhythms and progressions associated with the sukuti percussion music. After the first-generation guitar and bottle players, urban bands appeared, using acoustic instruments, occasionally brass and accordions, and playing a mixture of rumba rhythms and two-part harmonies. The earliest included the Jambo Boys and the Kiko Kids, while the Kenya Broadcasting Service brought together a range of talents from Funde Kondi to Esther John and John Mwale in a line-up which included guitar, double bass, sax and trumpet.

Throughout this period, interest in Latin and Congolese rhythms remained high, particularly among the guitar duos and small bands. At times, the new music threatened to swamp Kenyan guitar styles, but the

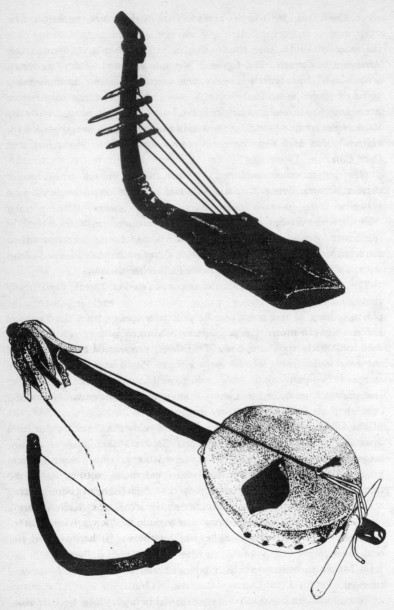

Lutes and harps are played in many parts of Africa in a variety of forms ranging from arched to single-stringed

sukuti musicians, with their vibrant traditional sounds, withstood the attack.

The early 1960s saw the arrival of electric bands, some playing imitations of Zairean rumba, others Western pop, and a form of African twist which leant heavily on the new electrified kwela guitar sounds starting to travel north from South Africa. The man usually credited with introducing twist and kwela was Peter Tsotsi, a South African guitarist based in Nairobi. Among the greatest local exponents was John Mwale who, with his AGS Boys Band, created a string of hits with 'Angelica Twist', 'Amina Twist' and 'Veronica Twist'. Fadhili William created a further Kenyan classic with his 'Malaika', which was later covered by Miriam Makeba, Boney M and others, and led to interminable copyright wrangles.

Despite its outside influences, Kenyan music in the 1950s and early 1960s had a feeling of its own. Guitarist Aziz Salim explains that most of the bands at the time believed in slowing the music down. 'Everything had a slightly foreign feel,' he explains. 'Like a bolero or a rumba. Malaika itself was like a slow rumba. The fastest stuff you'd hear in those days was the cha cha . . .'[4]

The coming of independence injected new confidence and optimism into the Kenyan music scene. Songs in the lingua franca Swahili, rather than less widely spoken regional languages, proclaimed a new spirit of unity and nationhood. But the situation was not to last. Electric Zairean rumba, from OK Jazz and African Fiesta, took east Africa by storm. The first records were brought in by Kenyan students studying at Makerere University in Uganda. As the Congolese civil war raged, musicians followed the records, among them Latina Mawa's Hi-Fives, Pascal Onema's OS Africa and many others. Zairean music found a ready audience: the music enjoyed a high prestige and the bands, being outsiders and, more often than not, underpaid and open to exploitation, found work as easily, if not more easily than their Kenyan counterparts.

Zairean music had a strong influence on the local scene. Kenyan bands sang cover versions, often in Lingala, alongside the new arrivals. Later, the music would attract official censure for the way it had usurped the local music scene.

In Tanzania, however, a different situation developed: a route was followed whereby a strong national music was built up, with lyrics not in regional languages but Swahili, which could be understood by everyone, and rhythms which drew heavily on traditional music. One of the first great modernizers, Salim Abdullah, created his band, Cuban Marimba, in the late 1940s, developing a sound that shared the multiple-guitar parts of Zairean music, with rhythms from the Morogoro area. After Abdullah's untimely death in 1964, Cuban Marimba, under its new leader, Juma Kilaza, continued to dominate the scene, while a second band from the same area, Morogoro Jazz, developed the local likembe rhythm. Other towns and cities moved to the Tanzanian sound. In Dar-es-Salaam, Dar Jazz and Western Jazz pulled in the crowds. Tanga produced the celebrated Atomic Jazz Band.

The growth of the music scene owed much to official encouragement. The government set up new bodies to save and promote Tanzanian arts, to create a 'national' culture and, in 1967, to develop Swahili as the common language. Major companies, like Textile Mills, government bodies and the police force set up their own jazz bands. The trade-union movement set up Juwata Jazz, the National Youth Service, Vijana Orchestre. Most of the earlier bands followed Zairean music, writing Swahili lyrics over imported rumba rhythms; visiting Zaireans and imported records fuelled the craze, but the official Swahili policy stemmed a complete takeover while a national radio ban on imported music in 1973, and the regular broadcast of Tanzanian pop, helped in the growth of a strong local jazz-band scene.

The government policy, however, helped not only local musicians but also migrants from Zaire. In the early 1970s, a wave of Zairean singers and instrumentalists settled in Tanzania. One of the first, Nova Succès, arrived in 1970. They were followed by Marquis du Zaire, Orchestre Fauvette, Mzee Makassy and Baba Gaston, now Baba Ilunga. Rather than stick to their own Lingala styles, the new arrivals adapted to Tanzanian ways, switching languages and adopting local rhythms. The results, a mix of tough rhythms underscored by emphatic hi-hat patterns and harsher-sounding Swahili vocals, bear an unmistakably Tanzanian stamp. The one thing missing was a decent recording industry. Most bands would record tapes at the Film Corporation or National Radio, then take them to Kenya or Malawi for pressing. Sometimes taped radio broadcasts were used, or the bands would travel to Nairobi, which made up for a lack of a cultural policy with decent studio facilities.

In Kenya, the marketplace continued to fragment as small studios turned out a mass of material in local languages and vied with those producing Swahili records. Foreign music remained popular. For a long time it seems as if the country would remain locked in the Zairean embrace, Lingala lyrics and all. But in the mid-1970s, a hard-edged, Kenyan competitor emerged in the shape of benga. Its roots go back to the 1950s, when an acoustic musician, Olima Anditi, pushed Luo dance rhythms into the acoustic guitar. A number of other western-region guitarists followed his example. By the late 1960s, musicians like George Ramogi and D.O. Misiani, leader of Shirati Jazz, made benga into a national craze that stretched beyond Kenya across the heart of Africa. Historically, benga was important for bringing Luo music into the electric age, and for bringing an all-Kenyan music style to the fore. Benga became virtually a national music. It also helped polish off many of the earlier acoustic-guitar and bottle styles, such as the omutibo music made popular by George Mukabi and Herbert Misango. Characterized by plain, trebly harmonies, spirited guitar licks and a swooping and plunging bass line, benga was primarily a music for the man and woman in the street. By the end of the 1970s, however, it had lost its appeal, worn out by production-line recording practices and a lack of new ideas.

Other forms of benga, though, proved popular. While the Luos followed roots rhythms, Kikuyu musicians like Joseph Kamaru, with his City Sounds, and Francis Rugwiti developed their own vernacular sound that took much of its sweetness and bounce from American country and western, Jimmy Rogers being particularly influential, while the Kamba band, the Kilimambogo Boys, created their own mesmerizing benga sound, keyed around instrumental patterns and frequent rhythm-guitar breaks.

The rest of the scene continued to be dominated by rumba. The early Congolese bands were joined by a number of newcomers such as Samba Mapangala from Kinshasa who, with his band Orchestre Virunga, had a huge hit with 'Malako', and Mzee Makassy, a fellow-Zairean who left for Kenya during the civil war. Like the early acoustic men before him, Makassy lent his name to commercial products, his face appearing on Bat cigarette packets. After travelling to Uganda, he settled in Tanzania, where he formed Orchestre Makassy. The band released its first British album, *Agwaya*, on Virgin in 1982, along with a twelve-inch single, 'Mambo Bado'.

The presence of Zairean musicians proved both a boon to music lovers and a thorn in the side of authorities anxious to foster a distinctive national music. In 1980, a presidential commission tried to institute a Swahili-only music policy on the Voice of Kenya radio station. But demand for Zairean and other imported music proved unstoppable and the policy foundered.

The effects of Zairean music can be traced through a range of bands that have enjoyed vast support in Tanzania and Kenya. They include Les

Mangelepa, a mixture of Kenyan and Zairean bands based in Nairobi; Super Matimila, led by the Zairean Remmy Ongala; solo singer Baba Ilunga, who had a huge east African hit with a song called 'Viva Christmas', plus a string of other Zairean or Zairean-influenced bands from Orchestre Virunga to Makassy and Super Mazembe. A number of bands have moved between Tanzania and Kenya, among them Simba Wanyika, a Tanzanian band which built up a large Kenyan following before splitting into X Wanyika and Les Les Wanyika. Orchestre Maquis du Zaire arrived in Tanzania in 1972 as the thirty-six-strong Super Gabby but despite economic stringencies and the lack of studios, stayed put. A number of great east African hits shared a strong Zairean feel, among them Makassy's 'Mosese 2000', written by guitarist Fan Fan, and the ever-popular 'Shauri Yako', which was recorded first by Nguashi N'Timbo with Orchestre Festival du Zaire, later Super Mazembe.

Alongside the rumba, and Tanzanian jazz, other east African forms have kept their popularity. The most significant, chakacha, the dance form of taarab, has found its way into the repertoire of a number of electric pop bands, and has stimulated popular disco versions, such as the 1984 'Cha-ka-cha', a Swahili wedding-song brought up to date by the Kenyan band Mombasa Roots.

SHIRATI JAZZ

'Misiani is the real roots, the only one my mother can dance to. A couple of years ago there was a big marathon competition and Misiani won. People went crazy. It was like the Beatles, I couldn't believe it.'[5]

Kenya may lack a single, national music, but with benga, an electric dance music that appeared in the mid-sixties, it came close to having one. The rhythm spread across Africa. It was danced to from Sierra Leone to Nigeria and Zimbabwe, and found its way into the music of OK Jazz, Afrisa and African All Stars. In Kenya, different versions developed around different language groups. The top Luhya bands, such as Abango Success, created their own style. Manori Jazz led the Kisii musicians, while the Kikuyus found a benga star in Joseph 'DK' Kamaru. The true homes of benga, though, are the Luo-speaking areas of western Kenya, where bands like Victoria Kings Jazz and Shirati Jazz have developed traditional rhythms into a hard, relentless modern dance music.

Shirati Jazz have been around since 1965. Their leader is Daniel Owino

Misiani, also known as D.O. Misiani, occasionally DO7 after the number of letters in his surname. Misiani went into music in 1961 as a maraccas player for two acoustic guitarists, Obonyo Waru and Odira Jombo Ngareya, before taking up the guitar himself.

In Kenya, as in other parts of Africa, musicians are traditionally viewed as vagabonds, drunkards and reprobates. Misiani's father, a highly religious man, was not one to challenge the orthodox view. He broke Misiani's first guitar, confiscated a second and went as far as begging the village authorities to arrest his errant son. For his part, Misiani did his best to live up to the stereotype, travelling with extremely young women singers and, on one occasion, being thrown into jail after the intervention of irate parents. It was only when he started to become successful, and gave his father lavish presents, that peace was re-established.

Benga is a Luo word meaning soft and beautiful. Its origins span two distinct musical cultures: the rhythms and vocals from bodi, a ceremonial music sung by Luo women, and Jean Bosco Mwenda's acoustic-guitar style which was massively popular in Kenya in the late forties and fifties. George Ramogi is often seen as a pioneering figure in the growth of benga. But, according to Shirati Jazz, its roots go back further, to an acoustic guitarist from the fifties, Olima Anditi, the first man to fuse bodi and guitar music. A number of others followed his example, among them Ojwang Jakambare, Oyugi Kembo, Otima Elly and Lango Oguyo.

Shirati Jazz quickly rose to the top, and Misiani had little trouble attracting new musicians. One of them was guitarist Charles Juma. 'I had been playing benga with other bands at the time,' he recalls, 'but I was happy to join Misiani. He was already starting to get famous and was making records, so everyone wanted that opportunity.'[6] When Juma joined, Shirati's line-up hung halfway between modern and folk. There was no drum kit and only two guitars. The rhythm section centred around three tumba drums which created the authentic sound of the traditional bodi music. Bosco, recalls Juma, was a strong influence. 'He plucked the guitar, rather than strummed it. This was a new way of playing the guitar, and it resembled the way we pluck our own traditional instruments. It's an emphatic style: everyone went for it:'

The link between traditional and modern orchestration gave benga much of its earthy power. Although Juma stresses that the acoustic guitar followed the bodi rhythms; the later electric instruments absorbed the fleeting melody lines of the earlier stringed instruments as surely as the Zairean guitarists picked up on the sounds of the likembe. Two instruments are of particular importance: the nyatiti, an eight-stringed harp, which has been seen as one of the inspirations for the benga bass line, which, as Juma points out, 'controls the dancers'; and the orutu, a violin, which carries over to the lead-guitar lines.

Benga moved ahead with the introduction of electric guitars, which Juma credits to Ojira Jomo with his Kisero Jazz Band around 1958. But the old finger-picking style continues. 'The plectrum is all right for slow music,' says Juma. 'But for fast music, like benga, we use finger picks. It was exactly the same when we played acoustic guitars.'

With its vibrant Kenyan feel, benga has attracted imitators from other parts of Africa. Singer Fabian Okoyo singles out a number of recent Zairean benga tracks, including 'Mario' by OK Jazz, and Sam Mangwana's 'Isabella'. With their 1987 European tour, Shirati took steps towards spreading the message further still.

GLORIA AFRICANA

If benga represented a pure, almost national style, a number of Kenyan musicians were still left to pick their way through a maze of other, imported music. Bass guitarist Bonny Wanda started playing with a group of cousins in the Mombasa area, on the Kenyan coast, in the late sixties. 'We played Kenyan music, things like "Malaika", and traditional music,' he recalls. Because Mombasa was a port, people had a strong interest in imported music, most notably American soul records, brought in by visiting sailors; plus Swahili music, which flourished in the coastal areas of Kenya and Tanzania. One of the greatest stars was Salim Abdullah, the Tanzanian singer, who enjoyed massive acclaim wherever Swahili was sung.

In Mombasa, Zairean music had little impact. Nairobi was a different matter. By 1971, Wanda had joined lead guitarist Aziz Salim in a band called Gloria Africana, which played a mix of soukous, soul and Swahili music. 'The thing about Nairobi,' says Wanda, 'is that a band wasn't considered any good unless it could play everything that was available. We had to play everything we heard on the radio and that included Latin and jazz.'[7]

The jazz connection goes back to the fifties when, Wanda recalls, Nairobi had a number of Kenyan jazz musicians whose main source of livelihood came from playing in private clubs. 'If you wanted to work, you had no choice,' he says.

Salim's career reflects a similar range of styles. In the early sixties as a young acoustic guitarist, he played traditional music, and songs by the great Kenyan guitarists like John Mwale and the Zairean Edouard Masengo, whose songs bore a strong similarity to Kenya's own traditional string music. At this time, he was playing in rural Kenya, entertaining audiences or playing at funerals with maraccas and bottle players offering the usual accompaniment. When Salim arrived in Nairobi, fashions were different, with popular tastes demanding jazz, mostly Louis Armstrong, and by the mid-sixties, with the arrival of Pascal Onema and the OS Africa band, Zairean rumba. 'The whole of Nairobi was transformed,' he recalled. 'Everyone went over to Zairean music.'[8]

Salim himself joined OS Africa, touring Tanzania, Zambia and southern Zaire before returning to Nairobi to play 'grill' music on the hotel circuit, the normal practice being to seduce diners with ballads, then move to jazz and pop, 'to make them drink more'. Gloria Africana, his next regular band, was based at the Arcadia Club, and enjoyed a mixed career, splitting, regrouping and being denied the chance to record by a far from atypical manager and club owner, who owned all the instruments, down to amps and guitar strings, and was afraid that a recording contract would wrench the band from his control. By 1979, Salim had left to join Air Fiesta, and travelled to London; Wanda joined the Cavaliers, and worked briefly with Fadhili William before coming to Britain in the early eighties. From there, he joined British benga and mbaqanga band OK Jive, who released an album and a string of singles for CBS, before rejoining Salim with British bass player Chopper in an Afro-pop band called Shokolokobangoshay.

In twenty-five years, Kenyan music has seen a number of changes. Looking back, Wanda sees the rise of benga as a crucial point. 'Before benga, we played a lot of foreign stuff. Then, suddenly, we realized that we had our own music. I think this made us look back at our roots, to the traditional sounds from western and central Kenya. A lot of other musicians, from the Kikuyu and Kikamba areas, were doing the same thing, using benga as their main music. The thing about benga was that it was not taken seriously by the media. The musicians, too, seemed little bothered about the conditions they were working in. When they came to the city, economic factors became very important and most of them had to start playing foreign music.'

Despite benga's rise in the seventies, Wanda sees it as an enduring part of the Kenyan scene, and cites George Mukabi as a particularly influential musician. 'He made a lasting mark,' he says. 'I haven't seen anyone else coming close. His lyrics reflected the time. Before benga came up, and before the big Zairean influence, Mukabi seemed to be doing something similar. His music was fast, it had bursts of bass coming in and out, and a mix of 6/8 and other time-signatures. When I listen to Mukabi, I can see where benga comes from.'

Salim also looks back fondly to the old pre-Zairean days. 'When I was at school, what I listened to seemed far greater than all this stuff,' he says. 'Those were the John Mwale days, the days of Daudi Kabaka and Fundi Konde. The whole country used to listen to those acoustic guys, particularly John Mwale. We had a traditional acoustic Kenyan music, and it lasted until people like Fadhili William came along with all this jazzy Jambo Boys stuff. That's when the whole thing started diverting.'

AFRICAN HERITAGE

After the vivid flowering of Kenyan acoustic and semi-acoustic music in the sixties, the current scene fills many observers with gloom. It is commonly said that the popularity of foreign music in Kenya has led to the down-grading of the country's own artists. In Zaire, musicians like Franco and Tabu Ley own large properties and consort with top politicians. In other countries, from Nigeria to Guinea and Senegal, leading musicians are similarly valued. In Kenya, according to Job Seda, percussionist and founder of African Heritage, 'The musician is nobody. He has no real assets in the Kenyan sense, meaning a house, cars, land. Most just have their own instruments and a job which is usually temporary, lasting a year or six months.'[9]

The problem, he feels, lies with Kenya's colonial legacy. 'We lost a lot of our traditions in colonial times. With the missionaries, it was: "Either take Jesus Christ or be damned for ever. You can't come close to us." It wasn't much of a choice.

'After the British left, people still thought West was best. Kenyan musicians tried to write like Western superstars, going mainly into country and western, and soul. Then, when Zairean music came along, with a strong African-based rhythm, people grabbed it with both hands. As soon as that happened, our musicians lost out. They had no jobs – most of them had gone to the Zairean musicians – no equipment, no music. One answer to the problem lay in following the Zaireans – practically everyone in Kenya was buying Zairean music.'

The structure of the music scene underlined the difficulties. Zaireans, explains Seda, played in the prestigious nightclubs, while Kenyan musicians were hired to play Western music for the hotels. Any chance of playing tradition-based Kenyan music to a largely foreign crowd was doomed. 'Tourists didn't want that stuff,' he says. 'They wanted waltzes, top hits. So we'd spend most of our time sitting down with records, getting them note-perfect. There was no time to work out our own music.'

The benga craze, which took place well away from the hotel circuit, brought a true Kenyan sound into sudden and vivid prominence, and it was a sound that had a strong commercial appeal. Seda moved from his first band, Awengele, which he joined in 1975, to Makonde, which offered a combination of disco and benga. 'It wasn't so difficult,' he explains. 'Basically it's the same kind of beat, which disco emphasizes with the bass drum. It's a matter of what you lay on top of it. Our bass guitar was benga, so were the other guitars. But we had Western-style keyboards and vocals.'

The bass guitar is one of the wonders of benga. Seda explains that in Luo benga, the driving, melodic, and at times seemingly independent patterns, reflect traditional drum rhythms. The bass virtually takes the part of the drum. 'When the music first came up, there were no drum sets,' he says, 'just congas or traditional drums. So you'd have acoustic guitars, with the bass playing virtually a small set of drums, a stream of different melodies.

'The drumming is light in benga, mostly just a hi-hat and snares. The bass is vital and has a close, almost symbiotic relationship with the drums. At home, we say the drum "calls" the bass. If I heard a bass line, I'd know exactly where to put the snare. The bass can also "call" the drums, to get him to do a certain rhythm.'

The interplay of the instruments has a strongly traditional flavour. Seda explains that the Luo guitarists reproduce the sound of the nyatiti or lute which is usually accompanied by bells, worn on the lutist's ankles; a horn; and a lizard-skinned drum which the lute player strikes with a metal toe-ring. The lead guitar picks up the melodies of the nyatiti; the bass part derives partly from the drum, which is called the ohangala, while the bells are reproduced on the snare drums of the modern kit. The music soon developed a life of its own. 'The guitarists, above all, have come on,' says Seda. 'Just listen to Shirati Jazz. The speed and the precision of the guitar work is incredible. It's like in one bar, you get up to three different guitar melodies, and this happens throughout each song.'

Benga spread quickly, as the Kikuyu and Kamba musicians, from Joseph Kamaru to the Kilimambogo Boys, developed their own variations, often with musical backing from Luo guitarists.

Seda left Makonde in 1979, after playing gigs in Britain, and being asked by the promoters to appear in full warpaint, for an 'authentically African effect'. His own search for authenticity led him to create African Heritage in the same year, with the aim of going beyond benga and exploring areas of traditional Kenyan music that had been neglected. The line-up stretched from guitars and keyboards to marimbas, lutes, kalimbas and other traditional instruments. 'We wanted to get an equal mix,' he explains. 'But it wasn't easy, people just didn't want to see traditional music developed. But as musicians, we wanted to see where we could go, using traditional music, and all the equipment, all the electronics and sound effects that the world could provide.'

'The strange thing was that African instruments had stayed the same since they were "discovered". No one wanted them changed: they had a kind of novelty value and were considered quaint. Traditional music had been put into a box and, with African Heritage, we were trying to take it out.'

After two years of playing at their own venue, Nairobi's African Heritage Cafe, the band finally broke into the club and hotel circuit, where they released live cassettes and attracted an audience eager for their own brand of cultural rediscovery. 'They wanted to hear the old instruments. They'd come in traditional clothes. It was more like a jazz-club atmosphere,' says Seda. In general, though, people still looked down on their own traditions: 'They valued them as far as controlling the home, or man's rights, what a woman could or couldn't do, or how a business should be run. But with arts and culture, it was almost completely avoided.'

African Heritage had dissolved before Seda came to Britain in 1986, leaving the question of how further to exploit Kenya's cultural heritage largely unanswered. Seda draws a parallel with neighbouring Tanzania, where the people are 'far more together, and culture and art receive official promotion. In Kenya, we have around forty-five different languages, which makes it hard to get an overall music, an overall cultural understanding. The Luos sing for the Luos, the Kikuyus for the Kikuyus. There's little mixing.'

The national consciousness may be changing: Seda notes the increasing number of university students writing in Kenyan languages and changing Christian for authentic names. There have also been attempts to ban foreign music on national radio: ill-fated moves which fell flat when listeners could simply tune in elsewhere. Despite that, musicians who could be developing a new national sound are still drawn to play reggae and funk at coastal hotels, and the music business remains largely ineffective – or worse. 'There's no concept of investment,' says Seda. 'The companies want quick money. You come across stuff like: "Here's 500 shillings. Thanks for the record. We'll see you next year and talk about royalties." They fiddle them, sending the records and tapes to Zimbabwe or Britain. They sell like mad but the company tells the musician, "Oh well, we've sold around 5,000 copies, so here's your 500 shillings." It's all about the companies making money. Pure piracy.'

Tanzania may lack recording facilities but it has a vigorous urban scene that goes back to the Thirties, when the Dar es Salaam Jazz Band played a mix of brass-band and vocal and percussion music. Today, guitar-led dance bands proliferate, each having a style based on local dance rhythms like sikinde or msondo.

A number of the musicians come from Zaire, the best-known being Remmy Ongala, leader of Orchestre Super Matimila. Ongala came to Tanzania in 1978 and took up with Orchestre Makassy before setting up his own band, playing a mix of rumba and rhythms from the Mdundiko folklore. Ongala used the original name, talakaka, before dubbing his sound Bongo Beat.

Matimila's reputation stems largely from Ongala's personality and poetry. He is known as The Doctor – the question 'Doctor of what?' draws the answer 'Doctor of everything' – and writes songs whose pungent and heartfelt lyrics – sung mostly in Dar-es-Salaam Swahili – have won him a following with poorer Tanzanians – unemployed youth, gin drinkers, petty traders.

Many of his songs are about death. 'Kifo' laments deceased musicians from Orchestre Safari Sounds to Makassy and Marquis plus Ongala's two dead children; 'Siko Ya Kufa' reflecting that 'We come from dust, we go back to dust. We are meat for the earth'. Others deal with the poverty, suffering and high prices faced by Tanzanian city dwellers.

'My words can make the hardest criminal cry', Ongala told Paul Montgomery in the November 1988 issue of *Tradewind*. 'Priests ask how I have these songs. They think I must be very old . . .'

ZOUK'S GRAND PLAN FOR
GLOBAL DISCO DOMINATION

While New York is home for the recording of much of the latest Caribbean music – salsa, merengue, soca, Haitian pop and reggae – it is Paris which makes the running as far as the music styles of the French Antilles and the Francophone African countries are concerned.

In Paris in recent years a musical revolution has been under way. The pop music of Guadeloupe and Martinique – cadence – has been transformed through state-of-the-art recording technology into a new and highly eclectic style: zouk. Le zouk has in turn heavily influenced the new wave of Cameroonian and Côte d'Ivoire makossa artists; even Zairean soukous has not escaped. It has also made inroads closer to its home in the salsa of Puerto Rico and the compas in Venezuela.

Though the cosmopolitan, Paris-based Kassav stand head and shoulders in importance above anyone else in bringing about this revolution, the roots of zouk lie deep in the hills of Guadeloupe and Martinique and in the festivals and carnivals on other Caribbean islands. Zouk, arguably, would still have come about even if its progenitors, Pierre Eduard, George Decimus and Jacob Désvarieux hadn't met in Paris, formed Kassav and set the 'zoukship' on course.

Nine years after Kassav's inception in 1978 they are zouk's flagship, exporting the style's multi-faceted rhythms across the globe. But there is a new-wave, post-Kassav zouk – variants on the original theme – even more in demand in the style's three homes: the discos of Paris and the zouks in Basse-Terre and Fort-de-France, the capitals of Guadeloupe and Martinique.

Zouk is, however, more than a hi-tech, fully matured cadence: it is a peculiarly Parisian version of Caribbean rhythms with, at least in the early banner-waving zouk of 1978–82, a nod towards the golden age of funk, mid-seventies George Clinton and James Brown.

Now Paris is swamped by the Antillean beat. Up around the African quarter, Anvers, zouk competes persuasively with Islamic Malian melodies and the soukous of Africa's music queen M'Bilia Bel for top rhythm on the streets. And in the city's leading specialist record store, Afric Music, it is the chic-zouk of new stars Lazair and Gilles Floro as well as new releases from number-two zouk band Gazoline and Jocelyn Beroard

— the Antilles' M'Bilia Bel — which outsells even the new Zaiko Langa Langa, Bopol, Moni Bile and Sam Fan Thomas.

The story is the same in the city's nightclubs. The most exclusive (in 1986), Timmys, rocks until dawn at the weekends. Paris's love affair with salsa and, of course, the latest soul, is apparently on the wane. Zouk dominates the DJs' playlists, as well as the soukous-zouk of new star Kimoko's Buffalo and the mako-zouk of Georges Dickson. Les Chapelles des Lombards on Bastille's rue de Lappe is Paris's premier live-music club for the new sounds. Over the years this has been *the* spot where Paris-based zouk bands like Simon Jurad and Gazoline can capitalize on their records' success.

Les Chapelles is a snug, cosy, informal (but pricey) haunt where the punters have the proud authority of a self-appointed elite. The club, unlike the flashier Copacabana or Locomotive, has no glass dancefloor with garish lighting. The dancing likewise is not 'show-off' but characterized by graceful couples, part-waltzing, part-winding around the busy but never overcrowded area.

So immersed are they in the mid-tempo zouk groove of Jean Mourillon's 'Getty Getty', Lazair's 'Yche Man Man' (the summer of 1986's number one in the Antilles) and the new-wave soukous of Syran's Kass Kass, that the dancers fail to notice that they have strayed yards from their original spot. This dizzy meandering is an infallible sign of the rapt absorption generated by zouk: for Parisians, black and white, the beat of the moment, the dance they know is theirs, is le zouk.

In London zouk is a well-kept but soon-to-be-exposed secret. Kassav's debut concert in the UK, in March 1987, brought the music to the media and the public's attention for the first time. World-music DJs John Armstrong, Jumbo Vanrenen and Dave Hucker have, however, been aware of the craze for years. What, in their view, has made zouk the way it is?

John Armstrong points to the importance of Haitian band Tabou Combo, most notably their horn arranger Adolpho. During the sixties and early seventies Antilleans listened to very little of their own music; instead they danced to the full brassy swing of Haitian bands like Tabou.

It was the particular way the horns would break up passages, take the lead and pick up melodies, Armstrong explains, which was utilized in the cadence of, say, the Vikings or Georges Plonquitte. This style of horn arrangement is an integral part of zouk, though in the hands of Kassav it has been stylized and abbreviated. This Haitian pop was coined 'cadence-lypso', though it came before Antillean cadence and hadn't depended significantly on calypso for inspiration and patterning. In fact the calypsonian from Montserrat, Arrow, who has credited himself with the making of the modern calypso – soca – sound, has acknowledged the roles Haitian cadence-lypso and Martiniquan biguine played in the building of soca.

Also, Armstrong points out, the highly developed, idiosyncratic guitar styles of Haitian band Coupé Cloué have been translated into cadence and zouk. However, soukous guitaring, largely because of a visit to the Antilles by the Zairean band Orchestre Rico Jazz in the early seventies and the subsequent mixing of ex-colonized Franco-Africans in Paris, is ever-present, bubbling beneath the surface on much cadence and zouk. Additionally, the lead singer of the Haitian guitar band, Coupé Cloué himself, has strongly influenced playback zouk singer Sartana by way of his propensity to rap. Similar to the 'slack' calypsonian, Coupé and Sartana's lyrics are often lewd or melodramatically romantic.

Jumbo Vanrenen is quick to emphasize the Latin stresses in zouk. The chant style of vocal delivery and characteristic tempo breaks have their parallels in Dominican Republic merengue, Puerto Rican salsa and the compas on the mainland. But Vanrenen hears, before all these specific elements, a Latin American/Caribbean swing in zouk, a fusing together of a variety of rhythms from that broad belt of Amerindian, west African and European-descended peoples. Zouk's core, its hidden blue note, he feels sure is Yoruban drum and vocal accenting. This age-old heartbeat is made anew in zouk's chant vocals, call-and-response refrains and gwo ka drum patterns.

Another perspective is offered by Dave Hucker. He cites the 1987 soca hits, like Stalin's 'Burn Dem' as the most significant inroad zouk has yet made into the cross-Caribbean companion genre, soca. The crisp, staccato Linn drum programming, the rhythmic anchor of state-of-the-art zouk, has a more palpable presence in this year's crop of soca than ever before. It provides a radical departure from soca's customary lush, percussive devices.

Like Jumbo Vanrenen, Hucker thinks the latest Latin-Caribbean trend to refer openly in lyrics to zouk is ground-breaking. He sees this phenomenon as the means by which avant-garde Latin artists like Willie Colon are crossing one rhythm with another, breaking out of the confines of a rumba or a mambo. Zouk's forward march is accelerating. Plainly it has made major inroads into the explosive musical vocabularies of soca and salsa.

Rene Williams, an Ivoirian and an authority on eighties Franco-

African/Antillean music, points to zouk's more specific antecedents. 'The Dominican band Exile One strongly influenced the Antillean music, the early cadence, in the mid-seventies, though the strongest single influence was the Haitian cadence-lypso, which dominated the airwaves and dancefloors at the time.

'Exile One fused all sorts of styles inventively, if rather clumsily. They picked up on funk, mixed it in with island rhythms in a way that set a precedent Kassav later exploited. The conditions were there for a new indigenous music to develop. The process Exile One started was continued by the Guadeloupian band the Vikings.'

The Vikings included Exile One singer Gordon Henderson and the multi-instrumentalist and Kassav founder Pierre Eduard Decimus. A succession of ground-breaking records in the mid-seventies put cadence on course. And, with their original balance of funk, Haitian and reinterpreted colonial styles such as the biguine (adapted from the slow French beguine) and quadrilles, plus a dash of neo-African, Rico Jazz input, the zouk potpourri was in its early, mixing stage.

Rene Williams is also quick to emphasize the importance of Paris in the growth of zouk. It was where Kassav, after a meeting between ex-Viking P.E. Decimus and Guadeloupian rock guitarist Jacob Désvarieux, was born. 'More and more bridges between styles are being built in the music mecca Paris. Antilleans like Kassav's Jean-Claude Naimro and Claude Vamur are constantly cropping up on the latest makossa, and leading Cameroonians like the bassist Michel Alibo are frequently on zouk records. Also, Sam Fan Thomas's "African Typic Collection" was a massive hit in the Antilles in 1985, as it was, of course, all over Africa. Clearly since then zouk musicians have experimented more with makossa ideas — most noticeably the forceful bass lines and rhythm guitar picking.'

THE ROOTS OF ZOUK

It is clear, then, that zouk is a Caribbean mélange filtered through Parisian culture. But its roots lie deep beneath this hi-tech mirage: they are from the same source, west African polyrhythms and harmony, as are salsa, calypso, reggae and blues. But in zouk's case the African retentions are twice removed — first to the Caribbean, then to Paris. And zouk's basket of Caribbean influences show a fascinating marriage of colonially imported styles, like European beguines, quadrilles and mazurkas and African drum-ensemble practices.

Of the African styles which survived the diaspora and lived on in Guadeloupe and Martinique to resurface in zouk, one, the Saint Jean rhythm, a fast sambaish carnival beat from Guadeloupe, has its origins in Bantu religious ceremonies. Guadeloupe, due to the historic neglect of the French, has been able to hold on to African percussive skills and religion-focused music more easily than Martinique, which has been, historically, more favoured by the French, as the Parisian bourgeoisie's Caribbean playground. The Saint Jean rhythm was popularized by Kassav when using the pseudonym Soukou Ko Ou on their monster 1984 disc 'Vacances'. The exhilarating, circular dance beat is ingeniously modernized by P.E. Decimus and the band; it even includes Shadows-sounding guitar.

More important African retentions in zouk are, however, the tambour drum triumvirate – the two gwo ka and the one ti bwa drums. Here is the African strand in Antillean Creole life standing proudest and loudest: ka drums are the most African of all things Antillean.

Tambour music, called waka waka, has been recorded only since the mid-seventies, when the cadence of the Vikings triggered the unearthing of indigenous styles previously heard only at carnival and festival time, when across Guadeloupe's hills, from village to village, the messages and anecdotes – a direct line from slavery days – of the ka drums would ring out. Since the mid-seventies, however, record stores stock tambour music and the records are played on some of the islands' fifteen radio stations.

The most renowned waka waka bandleader is Marcel, with his Groupe Toumpak. Their percussive workouts, which often include string bass and flute as well, are uncannily close to Yoruba drumming. Marcel's vocal style is also pure African, by way, not surprisingly, of Haitian voudoun ceremonial styles.

Gwo ka was brought in by P.E. Decimus to the Vikings and from then on was the rhythmic centre of cadence and its cosmopolitan child zouk. Top zouk singers Sartana and Pier Rosier never perform or record without the requisite ka section and the hottest new-wave zouk of '87, for example Servais Liso and Ramon Pyrme's *Zouk Time*, displays a new, more minimal use of ka within an uncluttered synthesizer-sculpted framework. But it was P.E. Decimus who first took the ka unit to Paris and Kassav who first set such a pure African retention alongside elements which could not be further removed from African tribal origins.

The first Kassav LP *Love and Ka Dance* (a play on words which also goes some way towards indicating the origins of the term cadence) was a veiled tribute to ka and, by inference, to the Antillean people's African history. This LP made Decimus and Désvarieux, who had met in Paris, musicians and arrangers for African musicians to hunt out once there. It also set into motion an Antillean pride: a recognition of their African roots, which had almost been quashed by European domination. To emphasize the significance of ka, Kassav even dedicated the title track to the uncontested master, and one-time sole practitioner of gwo ka, the late Velo.

There is much more in zouk, however, besides African drumming patterns. Inter-island communication enabled the merengue and compas beats, as well as the aforementioned Haitian rhythms, to be soaked up by Antilleans. Also the way the Martiniquans adapted the slow, decorative and rather stodgy beguine into a vibrant mid-tempo dance, was highly significant, first for cadence, then for zouk. For it was the jumpy, tight tension of biguine's bass lines which gave the pop styles their peculiar rhythmic anchor. Strait-laced European dances, such as the quadrille and the bolero, can also be detected in zouk (Kassav's song 'Bolero', like the aforementioned 'Vacances', uses traditional moods and structures as a springboard for a fresh, radical, rereading).

Musicians over the two islands are adept in these once-colonial styles. Later on in an evening's entertainment, the older ones are likely to launch into an emphatic biguine, a speedy mazurka or an accordion-led quadrille. Zouk's chanting instructions undoubtedly came from quadrille caliers.

Eddy Gustave modernized the biguine in the mid-seventies, with 'Begin the Biguine', while P.E. Decimus and Willy Salzedo modernized the quadrille, using synthesizer to replicate the accordion over a fast, lush gwo ka beat on the record *Rhythms of the Antilles*. As for recent biguine adaptations: the clarinettist Michael Godzom makes beautiful biguine-soaked cadence; the aforementioned *Zouk Time* has the requisite biguine number, Ramon Pyrme's 'Biguinement Votre', and the early Kassav albums contained many biguine-soaked songs. It is, however, the mid-tempo bass lines of biguine which are its most long-lasting feature in zouk. The space such a rhythm allows for other instrumentation to rise and fall alongside it is essential, given zouk's building-block, eclectic method of arranging.

With such a variety of styles in the island's recent musical history it is not surprising that groups like Georges Plonquitte's GB Orchestra are very popular. They are, in effect, a flexible, chameleon-like Euro-Caribbean swing band adept at coasting through all thee colonial-derived styles as well as more direct Afro-Latin elements, such as salsa piano. They represent the development of Martiniquan jazz, stoked in the thirties and forties when Antillean horn players were much in demand with New Orleans bandleaders like Sidney Bechet.

It is interesting that before the great swing period died out and Martiniquan jazz all but disappeared in the fifties (and the colonial dances, followed by the Haitian groups, ruled the roost) ka drumming was being tentatively used on the few jazz recordings made. Clearly, the foundations for cadence and zouk's appropriation of these disparate elements were lain initially by these tropical swing bands.

KASSAV AND THE MANUFACTURING OF ZOUK

The term zouk is a Creole word, initially a slang term for an action-packed party. The word came into common use when the 'grand bals', live music concerts, died out and were replaced by dance parties, zouks, featuring a sound system, rather like Trinidad carnival fêtes. We learn from this to be wary lest we try to pin down zouk too precisely. It is more a mood, an ambience: its magic is ultimately indescribable but can be witnessed on the Parisian or Fort-de-France dancefloors. The term first came to refer to a specific non-cadence style when the Kassav mission was well under way. Zouks became events where the people danced to Kassav; thus Kassav's music came to be known as zouk. The Kassav machine was born when ex-Vikings arranger Pierre Eduard Decimus met Jacob Désvarieux in Paris around 1977 and Decimus asked Désvarieux if he'd like to help him with a project to make Antillean music which, for the first time, would have the technical standards of American disco. The aim was to make Antillean dance music which could be danced to in Paris discos as well as Antillean zouks. Once the zoukball got rolling in Paris, the busy studios of Henri Debsso in Guadeloupe followed suit and switched from cadence, biguine and mazurka record production to zouk.

Désvarieux was Guadeloupian by birth and had spent many years in Senegal. But he was a rock guitarist and heavy-metal producer by trade. This, however, didn't prove disadvantageous. P.E. Decimus's brief – to make a new, mature disco music out of Antillean and African elements – needed an outside perspective. Désvarieux provided that.

An eleven-piece ka unit appeared on their debut, landmark LP, *Love and Ka Dance* but the first few Kassav albums saw them feeling around for the right balance of elements to gel. These albums, despite the African ka-driven beat, the edgy biguine bass and the complex melodies of the Haitian horns, had an overall funk feel.

During the early 1980s the Kassav 'family' consolidated and their sound found the groove they were searching for. They played no live concerts until 1982, concentrating on building a rock-hard rhythm team around bassist George Decimus, guitarist Désvarieux, keyboardist Jean-Claude Naimro and percussionist Claude Vamur; P.E. Decimus and Désvarieux handled all the arrangements in these early days. Solo projects started around 1983. Oddly, it is with George Decimus's first 'Nwel', and Désvarieux's 'Banzawa', as well as the fourth Kassav album, with its great cadence-zouk song 'Eva' and bolero-zouk 'Bolero', that full-throttle Kassav let rip. The derivative, but at the time obligatory marriage with funk, had all but snapped and the Antillean sources, albeit transmogrified, were paramount.

The greatest single development from the experiments on the early LPs were the strength, complexity and range of effects of the vocal arrangements. The French word 'choeurs', when translated as 'choir' best describes the force of the six-member vocal team Kassav employ. Led by the frontline trio Jocelyn Beroard, Jean-Philippe Marthély and Patrick Saint Eloi, the vocals give the disparate though skin-tight rhythms cohesion and direction. Great cadence singers Philogene Astasie, Willy Salzedo and J.P. Albin are credited by the Decimus brothers as chief influences.

Kassav's massive hit worldwide came in 1983. 'Zouk la Se Sel Medikamen Nou Ni' was the first Antillean record to sell in excess of 100,000 copies. It was a massive hit all over Africa as well as Latin America and the Caribbean. (Recent reports from Senegal indicate that Kassav are the most listened-to non-Senegalese band there.) Also the record raised their profile in France enormously, where they are now on a par with Toure Kunda. In late 1986 they sold out five successive nights at Paris's Zenith.

The song's title translates as 'Zouk is the only medicine we have'. The record has stimulated immense political debate across the islands, for it has gone some way towards reconciling the historic antipathy between them, an antipathy caused by French favouritism for Martinique and the development on Martinique of a neo-Franco anti-African Creole bourgeoisie.

The Kassav song, like the use of ka drums, was a symbol of an Antillean identity separate from the French, a unity across the islands and the building of a national consciousness. Clearly, many Antilleans suffer trauma when arriving in Paris. Their education has told them that they are French first, black and Caribbean second. They are as a result understandably shocked and confused when they have doors slammed in their faces. The French, it seems, reject them. In *their* eyes Antilleans are black, not French. Kassav have, more than any politician (the nationalist movement is small though not non-existent), sowed the seeds of a separatist outlook in their people.

The song, which appeared on the first Decimus/Désvarieux LP *Yelele*, is one of the most dramatically excellent they have ever written and arranged. A fast acoustic-guitar intro leads into a racy vocal from Patrick Saint Eloi echoed at the close of each line by a languorous refrain. Jean-Claude Naimro's haunting synthesizer chords flesh out the vista, relatively empty by Kassav standards, and the biguine-style bass of George Decimus jumps wildly. The song rises to a climactic finish with a swooping, repeated strings melody which owes much to the seminal 'chamber' cadence of Malavoi.

From 1983 Kassav built on their success. Each new LP is a fresh configuration which includes at least one song which further expands zouk's ambience as well as spotlighting traditional as well as avant-garde instruments. Over the last few years, however, they have shifted the emphasis of their sound. Ka drums have all but gone – drum- and bass-machine arrangements increasingly do the business. While some Antillean zoukers have steered even further into this territory – Eric Cosaque's latest LP is, excepting horns, totally electronic zouk – many of the big bands on the islands – for example Experience 7 and Batako, and in Paris, Gazoline – have continued to develop ka-rooted zouk.

This does not mean that Kassav have moved further away from their African roots. It is only that these most primary elements have been further redefined and moulded to serve the requirements of creatively thirsty musicians and, perhaps more important, the needs of dancefloors around the African-peopled world.

The most recent Decimus/Désvarieux LP, *Gorée*, highlights the new approach – a new level of sophistication for zouk. On this record Kassav seem to be using a musical shorthand. They move through ideas at a dizzy pace – the moment the listener has hooked on to a rhythm or melodic pattern, it is gone, to be replaced by another momentary design. Their sources have also become more eclectic than ever. Kora ends the title track and Cameroonian bassist Michel Alibo delivers a sprightly makossa bass on 'Mwen Envi Ou'.

Arguably, Kassav have attained the most developed pastiche in the world of displaced African music retentions. And in the same way that makossa and soukous are watching and absorbing zouk methods, Kassav too are scrutinizing recent African developments. The African-music swap shop has never been healthier, busier or more imaginative, a bitter irony for the half of the continent which is on the verge of starvation.

In an interview with the magazine *African and Reggae Beat* in summer 1986, Jacob Désvarieux expands on the swap-shop idea.

When you listen to our music it is a mixture of African and European musics. There were Spanish here [on Guadeloupe], then English, then French . . . it's a mixture of all of that. In the music of Kassav sometimes the piano player plays in a Cuban style, the bass plays funk and the guitar highlife. So you see you have a lot of things. It's like when you see the people on the street, to say exactly where they came from . . .[1]

Zouk in 1987 seems to be spiralling in at least three directions while the shadow of Kassav hovers over all: the ka-heavy, cadence-soaked power drive of Batako, Sartana and Gazoline; the lighter, slower, melodic chic-zouk of Simon Jurad, Gilles Floro, Jocelyn Beroard and Lazair; the state-of-the-art electronic pillaging of Ronald Rubinel and Kassav.

The last two groupings, typified by Lazair and Rubinel, could be coined new-wave zouk. Lazair's new LP *Move* follows on from their debut *Yche Man Man* – the most popular record in the Antilles in 1985. The deceptively simple sound is built up around Dominique Gengoul's excellent multi-tracked guitar. It owes as much to Kimoko Dally or Syran Mbenza from Zaire as to Coupé Cloué.

Another notable chic-zouk record is Jocelyn Beroard's *Siwo*. Its paces move from slow to fast, its moods from the orchestrally vast to the intimacy of a single-guitar accompaniment. Jocelyn's dreamy, fluid voice deals out a pumping disco zouk on the title track, then conjures a folklorique feel on 'Kaye Manman' – aided by Naimro's wonderful accordionized synthesizer, ka drums and flute.

On the heavier, electronic end, Ronald Rubinel's latest release, *Zoulou*, is almost too much of a mélange to believe. He has travelled as far into technical and rhythmic pluralism as he can go without ditching zouk's urgency or governing constitution. The chant vocals are by Aurlus Mabele from the Congo, Kichar Kilesa from Zaire and R. Cabral from Senegal; the guitars from in-demand soukous session musician Ringo Star. The tempo is hectic, the mix dense, clammy and claustrophobic. It is as if Rubinel is programming a maelstrom of ideas and concepts that no longer are owned or claimed by one style, or one land; he is on a rhythmic collision course.

Despite all these creative searches to push back the boundaries of rhythm, zouk's initial mission hasn't been completely swamped. O. Ramon Pyrme's 'Biguinement Votre' is respectful and unadorned and 'Défoulement' runs through a succession of Caribbean beats – merengue, Haitian and Antillean cadence, biguine, compas and soca – all held together by ka drum breaks, extra percussion and beat box. Zouk's mission, to build a radical new music out of Antillean, Caribbean and European elements has come round full circle here. The mission certainly has only just begun.

ZOUK AND AFRICA

In an interview with *Blues and Soul* magazine, Zairean singer and guitarist Souzy Kasseya said, 'We've never really had our own percussion. So it's necessary to go elsewhere: to the Antilles, to Nigeria. And why not? They've been getting stuff from us all the time. They've borrowed our rhythms, our guitar sounds, our melodies. They may not have much to offer us in the way of melody, but they've certainly got percussion.'[2]

By 1987, the marriage of African and Antillean music had reached unforeseen levels of fruitfulness as musicians from Francophone west and central Africa, most notably Zaire and Cameroon, embraced the new zouk sound, and Antillean artists looked to Africa for further inspiration.

The new sound, as notable as much for its high technology, bristling percussion and good-time 'tropical' feel, threw the spotlight on a number of musicians who had adapted, with more or less ease, to the new imperatives. From the Côte d'Ivoire, Daouda, with his *Gnama Gnama Sentimental*, called in top zouk musicians and translated the soukous of his earlier *Le Sentimental* into a lavish and hi-tech production. Woya achieved similar results with little outside help. Among the Paris-based Zairean musicians, Kanda Bongo Man brought a heavy zouk feel into his 1987 album *Lela Lela*, and went to work with a group of Kassav musicians on the successful album *Zouk Time*. Bopol applied zouk technology, arrangements and percussion to one of his best-known songs, 'Helena', while his fellow-Quatre Etoiles colleagues took similar steps, Syran Mbenza forming the zouk-influenced band Kass Kass, Nyboma teaming up with fellow-Zairean star Pepe Kalle to release an album whose inspiration, and some of its guitar lines, came clearly from Kassav. But the music made its biggest impact on artists from Cameroon: people like Sam Fan Thomas, Moni Bile, Alexandre Douala, Georges Dickson, Toto Guillaume and Aladji Toure. For them, zouk offered more than rich percussion and new technology: the fusions went beyond outside trappings to create a sound that drew equally on the African and the Antillean heritage.

One of the key figures in the great coming together of African and Antillean artists is Jean-Claude Naimro, a member of Kassav, who has played keyboards and produced arrangements for many of the African artists based in Paris. One of his early influences was a Zairean band, Rico

Jazz, who settled in Martinique in 1967. 'It was the first time I had heard African music,' he said early in 1987. 'Yet it seemed familiar to me. It wasn't so different to our own music; and this made it easier, later on, to play keyboards with African musicians.'³ The interest that Rico Jazz created was later rekindled in Martinique, and the Caribbean generally, by two huge Cameroonian hits, Sam Fan Thomas's *Makassi* album, featuring 'African Typic Collection' and Bebe Manga's 'Amie', which stimulated a number of cover versions. Naimro first worked with African artists in 1980; spending two years with Manu Dibango's back-up band and joining Miriam Makeba on tour before becoming massively in demand as a session player.

Kassav's founder, Jacob Désvarieux, shared Naimro's early experience of Africa, living in Senegal as a child. These influences, augmented by frequent and ecstatically received tours of west and central Africa, have had a shaping effect on the Kassav sound. 'At the start,' says Naimro, 'we'd just put in African rhythms to break the zouk a bit. We did it later on the *Gorée* album. But they weren't particular rhythms. We didn't say, "Let's take something from Zaire or Cameroon." We just composed a song and said, "Let's put it in an African way." It wasn't something that was prepared in advance.'⁴

A 1981 album, *To Guy*, with Cameroonian guitarist and singer Toto Guillaume, and a range of albums, including the 1980 *Roots Relations*, in which Naimro joined together with Cameroonians Jules Kamga, Vicky Edimo and Claude Vamur from Gabon, signalled the start of Naimro's session adventures with top African artists. The most notable, for him, have been Guillaume, and Aladji Toure, a fellow-Cameroonian bass player and producer. Out of these collusions have developed a strong new sound in which Cameroon bass and vocal styles are as prominent as the Antillean rhythm flavours and hi-tech zouk arrangements. 'For us, the bass is the motor of the song,' says Naimro. 'When you have a bass line that is typically African, the whole song becomes African – and when we use such patterns, they come from Cameroon. It's easy to pick up ideas from there. The music is commercial, and you have many many Cameroonians working in Paris.'

A strong percussion sound provides a further link between the Kassav sound and Cameroonian makossa. As Naimro explains, the heart of zouk is the ti-bois, a bamboo slit-drum, which is laid sideways and beaten with sticks. Live, Kassav still play the drum. In the studio, the ti-bois sound is re-created on a drum machine. Similar log drums are played in many parts of Africa, traditionally to tap out short messages and warnings. In

Cameroon, the log drum features prominently in the work of Sam Fan Thomas and other new-look makossa artists.

The popularity of zouk leaves Naimro with mixed feelings. For some artists, he feels, zouk has sunk to little more than a commercial formula; there is much borrowing but little originality. Others, though, and he cites Regine Feline and Ronald Rubinel, have used zouk, and African music, as the springboard for new, creative fusions. Despite the success of Kassav in Africa, and the zouk craze which has engulfed African pop both at home and in Europe, there seems little sign of a permanent takeover. In Zaire, Naimro notes a strong resistance to outside music. 'It's a special country,' he explains. 'People there don't pick other people's music. They play their own. In Cameroon, everyone goes for international music, but in Zaire, they don't want to be too European. They want to keep to their music, to keep it strong. It's a good thing — but it's a paradox too: they can become weak if they don't change.'

INDUSTRY
AND
DIASPORA

THE RECORD INDUSTRY

AFRICA

The Western exploration of Africa, begun in the fifteenth century, was still going strong 500 years later. Only the people had changed – and their motives. In 1912, Mr J. Muir, an official with the Gramophone Record Company, later EMI, packed his bags and steamed his way down the west coast of Africa in search of suitable places to start a record industry. He was deeply pleased with what he saw, especially in Sierra Leone. 'The native of Freetown is well-educated and, like all west African Negroes, is extremely fond of music,' he wrote back to company headquarters in Hayes. 'It would, I feel sure, repay you if you could let one of the various English trading houses stock our goods.'[1]

In Ghana, he was equally enthusiastic. Here was a large country whose wealthy plantations, mines and ports, sizeable towns and European populations suggested a lucrative market.

Muir singled out several large trading companies who might be persuaded to take the Gramophone Company's product: the African Association, Swanzy's, Millers, Patterson Zachonis. All were based in Britain and all had grown fat on exporting to stores in Africa. What could make better sense than to follow through with wind-up gramophones, ten-inch records and needles from London?

There was no lack of material to choose from. The Gramophone Record Company had produced its first records in 1894 and had continued to pump on to the market a varied selection of classics, operas, marches and music-hall songs. Others were having the same thoughts. By 1925,

Columbia signed a deal with the Niger Company of Liverpool to distribute their goods down the coast from Senegal to the Congo.

But selling British records, either to African businesspeople, teachers and administrators, or to colonial rulers, was only part of the plan. The second step was to record Africa's abundant local music as a way of building up sales in the continent's rapidly expanding towns.

In 1903, the Gramophone Company had bought controlling shares in a second company, Zonophone, as a way of penetrating the overseas markets. Five years later, they built a plant in India and, in 1912, Zonophone staff set off to record local artists in South Africa, India and China.

Zonophone's catalogue was one thing – a mixture of operas, 'extra-loud band selections' of military music, concertina selections, hornpipe medleys, 'waltzes from Mr Alex Prince', 'banjo selections from Mr Olly Oakley' and comedy numbers including 'Father Keeps on Doing It', 'The Sneezing Song' and 'Put a Bit of Powder on It, Father Do' – the African recordings, carried out on bulky acoustic equipment shipped in cases from Britain, were quite another. In Johannesburg, Zonophone set up their large acoustic horn in front of a variety of local artists. Their first ten-inch, recorded in 1912 on Zonophone Native records, features the George Goch Mine Natives – a large, male choir dressed, like some early Ladysmith Black Mambazo, in leopard skins, holding spears and singing Shangaan melodies, for the most part unaccompanied, occasionally with 'native piano accompaniment'. A second choir, made up of Swazi chiefs, mixed hymns – 'Rock of Ages', 'What a Friend We Have in Jesus' – with warrior and praise songs; while a Zulu artist, J. Selby-Msimang, recorded a string of Aesop's fables and eulogies.

Choral music was especially popular with South Africa's middle classes – many of whose members had attended mission schools, sung in church choirs and taken part in concerts and festivals. One of Zonophone's earliest records featured the St Cyprian's Choir, dressed in suits, starchy collars and ties with gold watches set in tightly buttoned waistcoats, the women in ankle-length skirts and lace blouses. The Salvation Army band produced three records, brisk affairs enlivened by concertinas, snare drums, bass drums and trumpets. Finally, the wing-collared Abonwabisi Party 'Don't Worry' Entertainers, solo and chorus, headed straight to the suits and gold watches of Edwardian parlour-land.

By 1914, Zonophone had spread its net up through west Africa. Yoruba records appeared, recorded in Nigeria, pressed in Hayes and featuring the bespectacled Reverend J.J. Ransome-Kuti, a forebear of

259

Afrobeat star Fela Anikulapo-Kuti, in a mixture of funeral laments, hymns and patriotic songs, accompanied by a solo piano. Other records attracted equal attention – including a spoken version of the Lord's Prayer, by C.A.W. Pratt, and a selection of 'wrestling ballads' by Shotayo Adeyemi.

The Yoruba recordings sparked off a new wave of recorded music. From Nigeria, the focus shifted to Ghana. George Williams Aingo recorded songs in Fanti, featuring solo and chorus vocals, and, on tracks like 'Ohye Atar Gyen', accordion, drums and castanets. Hymns were popular, with Harry Eben Quashie from Mampong singing to an organ accompaniment but finding time for two additional tracks: 'Sika Mpoano', a 'vocal one-step' sung in Twi with full orchestral backing, and 'Bontofo Pia', a vocal foxtrot again sung in Twi.

The twenties saw a jazz-age boom with large west African orchestras taking their place alongside parlour quartets and solo choristers. There is little doubt about the identity of the most prolific musician of this period: the wing-collared Roland C. Nathaniels, a teacher who had been trained by the Lyons African Mission Society, and whose repertoire ranged from passages from the Catholic Benediction ceremony – 'Tantum Ergo Sacramentum' and 'O Salutaris Hostia' – to twenties dance tunes like 'Telephone My Baby', sung in Creole, 'Tell Me So, Miss Earle' and a foxtrot called 'Dreams of Cape St Paul'. By the late twenties, Nathaniels had released a set of well-known west African dance tunes, known up and down the coast as 'sibi saba' but played possibly for the first time on piano. These included 'Cheerio Fofo', 'Wobe Mayo' and 'Gbenyata', released, according to Zonophone, for 'the vast interest of west Africa, especially the Gold Coast, where the dances originated'.[2]

The range of Zonophone's records is massive, from traditional songs in modern and traditional formats, to Western dance-band and vocal parlour music, even political speeches made by a Gold Coast chief, Nana Sir Ofori Atta, who travelled to London's Zonophone studio for the occasion. By the end of the twenties, records had appeared in Hausa, Ewe, Creole and 'Coast English', with hymns in Ibo from J.D. Thomas; Negro spirituals, traditional songs and 'vocal gallops' on piano, organ and mouth organ from Ghanaian Harry E. Quashie; Yoruba songs on guitar from Domingo Justus; Efik piano and organ hymns from William Etam and Paul Burnett, and Kru records, featuring chorus, drum and castanet, from Liberia. At the far end of the elite spectrum, the Gold Coast Quartet put on their colonial wing collars and black suits and waistcoats and, under the direction of Mr Bruce Gibbon recorded, to piano accompaniment,

'Abie and Susie', 'I Come from the Gold Coast', 'Flow Merrily Flow', and, by an amazing colonial sleight of hand which showed how far the new elite took their models from the West, 'The Coon's Lament'.

The last word goes to the prodigious R.C. Nathaniels. In 1931 he cut a ten-inch single with a back-up of piano, clarinet, guitar, castanet and cymbals. It was called simply 'Highlife'.

EAST

By now, a recording industry was starting up in east Africa, where Gramophone Company officials toured the coast looking for suitable markets. In 1921, Sidney Sheard set off on an east-coast tour.

The music scene was flourishing. From Uganda to Tanganyika and Kenya, Indian music, recorded and pressed at the Gramophone Company's Bombay factory, was in vogue. In Mauritius, with its large Indian population, Sheard saw further possibilities for local record sales and suggested that head office ship out the Zonophone equipment.

Five years later, a second company man made the trip, and noted the growing competition in the area: Decca, Columbia and Brunswick records were on sale in many of the stores. Opera was doing well and Indian music, particularly in Hindi, Punjabi and Gujarati, was popular with the expatriate trading community living and working in east Africa. In 1926, the Gramophone Company had sold 42,714 Indian records in Kenya alone and dealers began to press for a greater variety, recorded in Swahili and local languages. Indigenous music was in demand.[3]

'It is my experience,' wrote a second company representative, P.B. Vatcha, 'that though the natives have got no tunes, or any such thing in their singing, whatever they sing, people go mad for it. Especially among those natives, there is a dance known as the gomo which is well worth recording.'[4]

The Gramophone Company representatives had already toured Uganda and found all the signs of a flourishing potential market. Pushbikes were in evidence, people wore linen suits and local stores, Whiteways and Mengo Planters, were full of record players. All that was needed was a supply of records to go with them. 'The music here is unlimited,' wrote Vatcha in 1926. 'New songs are always being composed and there are many artists.'[5] The Buganda population also showed a strong interest in Negro spirituals and other black American music, Frank Crummit's 'Billy

Boy' being extremely popular. The only problem was that Odeon already seemed to have captured the market. The Gramophone Company turned elsewhere.

Although east Africa lacked 'native' records in any great quantity, there were two strong traditions to draw on. The first was the abundant Christian church music, sung in local languages throughout east Africa. 'The missions,' wrote a third company man, Mr H. Evans, 'have already performed prodigious feats in training native converts to sing church music and they really sing extremely well and show much musical appreciation.'[6] The second was a form of African-Muslim music popular along the coast and called taarab. The taarab orchestras, with veiled and jewelled female singers and fez-topped men playing guitars, lutes, trumpets and clarinets, enjoyed a widespread popularity based partly on their use of Swahili, a dominant trading language that was spoken up and down the coast and inland as far as the Congo. Swahili music, although restricted at that time to taarab, could perhaps form the basis of a new, inter-ethnic form. The Gramophone Company moved in.

The first session took place in Nairobi in 1928, followed by two more in 1929 and 1930. The pressure was building up as Odeon from Germany, Pathé from France, and Columbia all went ahead with their own sessions, to corner the Swahili market.

At a recording session held at the Uganda Bookshop, Kampala, Odeon cut twenty-four titles, eleven of them from high-school choirs sung in Luganda, the remaining twelve church music sung in Swahili. The former sold out, the latter bombed. In Portuguese East Africa, Odeon recorded music sung in local languages and played by instruments ranging from marimbas to mbira, harps, percussion and xylophones.

Columbia's Swahili sessions in Zanzibar produced a string of marching-songs, a record of the Zanzibar national anthem and Swahili versions of 'Good King Wenceslas' and 'The First Noël' from the choir of St Andrew's College.

Pathé took matters further, bringing a group of Mombasa musicians – guitarists, violinists, trumpet and clarinet players – to Marseilles for a session. After quarrelling broke out among the various bands, the session was cut short. Eighty-six tracks were cut, none of which sold in any quantity.

This confusion was in some ways typical. There was little time for preparation or rehearsal, and a number of artists crop up singing the same songs on different labels.

The Gramophone Company's own recordings produced mixed reactions. The 1928 sessions, giving fifty-six titles in all, sold well. By 1930, though, poor material, competition from the other companies, and weak recordings – marred by quarrels between the musicians in the studio – reduced the appeal.

The company seems to have come unstuck. The local music they regarded as 'crude, connected mainly with dances'. Even taarab seemed too restricted. One possible answer lay, according to Mr Evans, in grafting local music on to other familiar styles, heard throughout centres of migration in southern and central Africa, possibly on to American 'Negro' music, already selling well in the Congo and other parts of east Africa. The fusion of east African 'native' and other 'allied' musics could create a marketable sound. Indeed, this is precisely what did happen – but only in the forties and fifties, when Latin American, later Congolese music played a large part in the development of east African pop.

Mr Evans may have been prophetic, but his far sight had little appeal for the Gramophone Company. At the end of a long, meticulous report sent back to headquarters in London appears a mysterious note. It reads simply 'No action'.

SOUTH

Through its early industrialization, and the size of its European population, South Africa became an early focus for record-company attention. By the turn of the century, the Gramophone Company had a branch in Cape Town and in 1904, the formation of British Zonophone led to the later recording of Zulu choirs, vocal groups and, by the end of the twenties, records in Xhosa and Sesotho alongside the Zonophone collections of dixieland, waltzes and Sousa bands, and Afrikaans piano and vocal music.

In 1929, Columbia staked a claim to the local scene, appointing Herman Polliack as their dealer. The company were keen to break into local recording and wrote regularly to Polliack, who by now was convinced that 'native' and Afrikaans recordings were imperative. Columbia wanted a lorry; Polliack found one, with the right dynamo for recording in out-of-the-way places. As regarded remuneration, this was soon settled: many of the artists were not known and had not made records before; Polliack explained, 'They would not in the ordinary way be able to command high fees.'[7] The recordings duly went ahead in 1929.

A year later, Gramophone Company men toured the country and reported good prospects. One record shop, Tybam in Durban, was already doing a large trade in Indian and Zulu records; they held a royal appointment with the King of the Zulus, keeping two rooms aside for his use.

'I am of the opinion that native records will play a very important part in the future,' wrote a Gramophone man. 'It is quite possible they will sell better than Afrikaans records. The natives are taking to the gramophone. Our new cheap portable will be a valuable asset in this direction.'[8]

The quality of the music seemed to take European listeners by surprise.

> One night, two men and two other natives came to Mackay Brothers, the distributor's stores, with a pianist. We found the quartet extremely good. I seriously considered trying to make an arrangement to bring these boys to Hayes for recording – the more so as they assured me that they can sing in Shangaan and Xhosa as well as their own language – Sechuana – but I decided against this.[9]

Other South African artists would make up for this missed opportunity. By the early thirties, Reuben Caluza's Zulu Choir, with its repertoire of tap dancing, choral work and orchestral dance numbers, came to Britain to record, releasing a number of titles including 'uBungca' or Oxford bags.

Other companies pitched in. Brunswick made a series of their own 'native' recordings; in 1931 Gallo, then a small local company, set up the country's first recording studio and later employed Griffiths Motsieloa as a talent scout. A stream of recordings followed, from Zulu traditional songs to accordion music. Later came the jazzier sounds of Lemmy Special and new varieties of kwela music, the guitar work of George Sibanda and, also from Bulawayo, a drinking-song called 'Skokiaan' which was first recorded by the Cold Storage Commission of Southern Rhodesia, and later sent in three different versions into the American charts. As a sign of his commercial bravura, the owner, Eric Gallo, also put out a series of African records, captured by his 'A and R' man Hugh Tracey in the early fifties.

While smaller companies followed Gallo's lead, the larger ones went the way of large companies everywhere and amalgamated. In 1931, Columbia and the Gramophone Company merged to form the largest single record company in the world. Electrical Musical Industries, or EMI, controlled fifty factories worldwide and a group of significant trademarks that would include HMV and Columbia, later Parlophone and Odeon. The stage was set for the second great scramble for Africa.

WEST

At times, 'scramble' seemed the only appropriate word to describe how the companies operated. When Decca wanted someone to start their operations in west Africa in the fifties, they chose the blimpish figure of Major Kinder, a representative of Longman Green, the publishers, who had the advantages of knowing the area, being on the spot and wanting to do something with his spare time.

Kinder was a larger-than-life figure, an acquaintance of the Decca founder, Sir Edward Lewis, and in many ways the epitome of the colonial Briton abroad. Outdoors, he would carry a small towel with which he constantly mopped his brow. Held up in slow traffic, he would jump from his chauffeur-driven car and thump the bonnet of the car in front, abusing the African driver in the coarsest of terms. On tour between Ghana and Nigeria, he would travel first-class on the liner; in hotels he would insist on being served by two wine waiters and two food waiters. Up country, his car would be carried over streams and rivers by local bearers.

Kinder's financial arrangements were no less exotic and exploitative. At the start, he claimed 1d. commission for every record imported and sold in his area. By the late fifties, Decca were shifting over 1,000,000 records a year; his earnings rivalled those of the chairman of the company. He was soon bought out.

The first west African highlife records go back to 1927, when the Zonophone EZ series released 78s by Sam, the composer of 'Yaa Amponsah', and other Ghanaian musicians. The Decca West Africa series charted the continuing highlife boom of the forties and fifties, relying on the traditional practice of sending sound engineers out to west Africa. The tapes would then be brought back to London; the pressed records were shipped out to the west coast three or four months later.

Among their rivals EMI continued to record throughout the thirties and forties, while Parlophone set up, in the late thirties, their own Parlophone International West African records, featuring the prolific Sam, with his 'J. Sam Trio', the Kpagong Band from Accra, two singing bands run by Larteh and Yaw Ofori, and a set of guitar records from 'The African Guitarist', H.K. Williams.

In the fifties, Decca went further and built studios on the spot — first in Accra, later Lagos. Philips followed suit, leaving EMI rather wrong-footed. In the past, they had relied on the big trading stores to sell their products. Now they relied on them for recording as well. In 1949 they signed an agreement with the United African Company (UAC). The latter agreed to scout for local artists, record them in their own studios and pass on the tapes to be pressed and released under the HMV label. In 1952, the UAC opened a small studio twenty miles from Accra, usable only at weekends. Two years later, they built a larger one in Accra and erected a sizeable board which read: 'HMV Recording Studio, Distribution for the Gold Coast, the United Africa Co Ltd'.

The arrangement proved disastrous. Throughout west Africa, the company's sales of vernacular recordings slumped. In 1956, Nigerian sales stood at 119,073. Two years later they had fallen to 44,002, and by 1959 to 12,591. In Ghana, annual sales fell from 345,122 units in 1956 to 68,853 two years later. In 1960, UAC, who cared less about local music than imports, lost interest altogether, leaving the market in the hands of Decca and Philips.[10]

The growth of nationalism and the first wave of African independence sent further tremors through the European business community. Record companies looked for new ways of safeguarding their interests. EMI top brass noted the new situation as 'unfortunate', but they reluctantly had to come to terms with it.

Ironically, as the colonial administrators moved out, businesses moved in, imposing new forms of control. Companies like Guinness and Dunlop ditched the old trading-house networks, building regional headquarters on the spot. In Ghana, record companies found themselves dealing with a new generation of hard-nosed African music dealers. By the mid-fifties, Mr K. Badu, a wealthy member of the Ashanti royal family, threatened to upset the whole European recording scene by building the new Ambassador Studios in Kumasi. Other Ghanaian producers set up their own labels but, lacking finance, were forced to deal with the old companies as before. H. Teymani's first release was E.K. Nyame's 'Onim Dii Fo Kokodrufo Kwame Nkrumah', recorded by the United Africa Company in Accra. In Kumasi, A.K. Brobbey launched his BRB Specials, featuring Dr K. Gyasi and his band. Gyasi's work — a mixture of highlifes and mambos — also featured on Brobbey's BKB series.

In Nigeria, new producers proved crucial to the network of artists and outlets established by the big companies in the fifties and sixties.

In the east, C.T. Onyekwelu, a leading trader in African records, had been issuing his own records since 1951, sung in Yoruba, Efik, English and Ibo and pressed by Decca. He also distributed HMV's Blue Label records from east Africa. Josy Fajimolu had a large catalogue of vernacular records, pressed by Philips in Holland, while the most successful dealer in the north, Chief Tabansi, pressed his records with UAC and promoted them through two music vans which toured local towns and villages.

The arrival of independence put new pressures on the companies: to adapt, to come to terms with the new Africa, and, in some cases, to group together to fight the new developments. At Hayes, EMI worried about copyright problems and the end of the old system of royalty-free down payments. 'Most traditional tunes have now been worked out,' noted an official in 1954. 'The recent recordings are tunes composed for the occasion. But there is no thought of publishing them as sheet music. It might easily happen that acts were passed to protect African composers in a way that might not suit us.' The EMI man then suggests that the UAC engineer legislation before the possibilities occur to an 'African barrister', and recommends that 'the copyright department at Hayes discusses the matter with UAC and Decca'.[11]

By 1960 change was in the air. Decca decided to concentrate their operations in Lagos. With their new studio at Henshaw House, they were able to record all the year round, rather than twice a year, with visiting engineers.

The company's greatest success was with the Yoruba market, through apala star Haruna Ishola and juju king I.K. Dairo. But they also recorded Ibo highlife acts, including E.C. Arinze and Charles Iwegbe and the Archibolts and, between 1964 and 1967, they built up a substantial market for Ghanaian bands such as E.T. Mensah's Tempos and the Broadway Dance Band.

For four years, Decca virtually controlled the Yoruba market. Philips established themselves in Onitsha, through a deal with C.T. Onyekwelu, and built up a strong repertoire of eastern highlifers, including Rex Lawson and, later, Chief Stephen Osita Osadebe. In 1964, EMI decided to move in. Until then, the company's one African branch was in South Africa, the rest of their business being carried out by large trading houses or local distributors. Now they came north.

A site was chosen in Jos — a strange choice, being 700 miles away from the nearest port and the country's main marketplace, Lagos. There were reasons for this. The staff were coming from South Africa. Jos was on the same altitude – around 6,000 feet above sea level – and would no doubt provide the right weather conditions.

EMI's arrival caused a local shake-up, as top Decca artists, I.K. Dairo and Haruna Ishola, left to join the company. 'I reached for my contracts file,' says Mike Wells, Decca's man in Lagos. 'It was empty.'[12]

By 1966, Wells himself had joined EMI, helping set up a new studio in Lagos. Already he had taken part in one technical innovation – the arrival of the first 45s in Nigeria. Their appearance caused dismay. People preferred the old, larger 78s. To demonstrate their strength, Wells would put the new singles down on the road and run over them with his van.

At Decca, Wells had been selling Jim Reeves, Kitty Wells and other Western or 'sentimental' artists, as they were known. By 1964, the early Stax recordings, especially the work of Booker T and the MGs, had pushed Western music on to the Nigerian marketplace in quantities never seen before. 'I got fed up with being asked for the Beatles, and having to say, "Sorry, we've only got the Rolling Stones,"' says Wells. By 1966 he was with EMI in Lagos.

The same year saw the start of the Nigerian civil war, a catastrophe which also had a distastrous effect on the Nigerian music scene. Many of the well-established bands split up, as their members returned to their home regions. In Jos, eastern staff at EMI's factory either fled or were killed during the Ibo massacres. In Onitsha, the Philips factory was reduced to rubble after federal troops had discovered there records praising the Biafran leader, General Ojukwu.

Decca used the opportunity to put the screws on Philips, their pressing agents in Nigeria. According to their contract, Philips would supply finished pressings at 2s. each. Decca insisted on the deal, factory or no factory, and Philips were forced to press the records in Holland and fly them back to Nigeria for the original, but now ridiculously inappropriate, sum.

EMI shifted its plant from Jos to Lagos and, when the war ended, concentrated on their most popular artists, Fela, Sonny Okosuns and the northern poet el Haji Shata Katsina. In the east, the once thriving music scene that had established itself around Onitsha slowly reappeared, and with it, a new brand of music, heavy, progressive sounds, pioneered by bands like Cloud 7 and the Funkees. Decca kept its grip on the Yoruba market, boasting Ebenezer Obey, with a mass of juju, apala and waka singers among its top sellers.

Decca's success was unsurprising. By the late sixties, they had signed virtually all of Ghana's top highlife acts, from E.T. Mensah and the Tempos Band to the Messengers and the Stars of Ghana, plus a selection of top Nigerian artists, including I.K. Dairo, the celebrated juju star. Aside from juju and highlife, the company picked up on most of the major west African trends, from merengues to calypso, and local roots forms. The Ghanaian Dynamite Eryco Jazz Band recorded Congolese numbers, including 'Chauffez' (cha cha) 'Cathy' (cara cara) and 'Rosita' (rumba). Ali Ganda's 'Africa Wants LBJ' and 'Nigeria is a Republic' reflected the calypso rage of the sixties, while 'Kinshasa Carrefour de l'Afrique' and 'General Yakuba Gowon' brought Kalle's African Jazz into the Decca fold.

Roots music, free of electric guitars, constituted an equally large proportion of the Decca catalogue. Haruna Ishola, the apala star, remained one of Nigeria's top-selling artists; Salliah, the Sierra Leonean accordionist, played Mende songs and proverbs, his records appearing alongside those of Nigerian singers and percussionists specializing in waka, sakara and agidigbo music performed by outfits like the Guinea Special Band.

Equally revealing is the variety of repertoire produced by individual artists. Ebenezer Obey is credited with several 'juju/highlife' numbers, while fellow-Nigerians Julius O. Araba and his Afro Skiffle Group covered juju, highlife, merengue and toy motion, a variant of juju. Pop bands like the Black Santiagos covered 'Twist and Shake' while the Gambian Super Eagles covered just about everything in sight. Their *Viva Super Eagles* album included soul numbers, pachanga, bolero and merengue, even a reworking of 'Hey Jude'. For Mike Wells, though, Fela was, and to a certain extent remains, the most exciting figure on the scene. His occasional obscenities, a cover showing two naked bodies, caused offence, but the music and the personality were unique. 'He was far and away the best African musician and personality I'd met,' says Wells. 'Only later, with the politics and the wives did he go "bush". In those days, he was an inspiration. He was handsome and the music was magnificent.'

Despite this, Fela's music never sold in the huge quantities notched up by Dairo, Obey, even Bongos Ikwue. His appeal lay more with the younger age groups in society, for whom Fela was like an early incarnation of the Sex Pistols.

In the sixties and seventies, the big companies remained convinced that west Africa was the place to be. Their aim was partly to sell their international product, from Jim Reeves to Tamla Motown artists and the Beatles; partly to build up local artists, whose work they could then sell across Africa. And partly to keep a presence. Just in case . . . 'There was a growing feeling among the majors that something big was going to come out of Africa,' says Wells. 'The fact that when it did come it could hit them on the head and they wouldn't notice, was neither here nor there.'

A number of Africa's most talented acts could easily have broken through on the world market but were held back by the indifference of the major companies – either on the spot or further away, at head office.

'The number of times we came to EMI in London with repertoire,' says Wells. 'EMI had a man in their headquarters in Manchester Square who was meant to look after the odds and sods. We sent samples, we brought samples. Nothing. That Fela record [*Fela's London Scene*]. They did the most awful sleeve you could think of. He looked a parody of a black. You could just see the whites of his eyes. It was so cheap and nasty. The promotion was nil. It was disgraceful. Sonny Okosuns could have done something. So could the Lijadu Sisters and Bongos Ikwue. But no one at Manchester Square was interested. It's easy for me to be critical, because I was living with the music and it was my repertoire. I had people like Sonny Okosuns selling fifty or sixty thousand albums and saying, "Mike, what, for heaven's sake, is EMI going to do for me?" They'd read that Decca had done something with Obey or something like that. "I've been with you for ten years and what's happened? Nothing!"'

NAIROBI SOUNDS

In east Africa, as in the west, the scene had been largely dominated by the trading companies. The African Mercantile Company spread HMV as well as Capitol, MGM and Mercury records through Kenya, Tanganyika and Uganda. They were also responsible for recording local musicians, whose work was released under the HMV Blue Label. Despite this, the company proved unsuccessful at marketing local music. And faced with competition from the local Jambo Company and Indian dealers, they gradually gave up their east African recordings.

Others stepped in: Capitol Music Stores and African Gramophone Stores. The music in the fifties was strictly acoustic. The HMV Blue Labels, designed for the African market, carried works by acoustic stars like Edouard Masengo and Funde Kondi. Capitol Music produced its own records, while the African Gramophone Stores, with its AGS Boys Band, led by John Mwale, produced a range of highly successful African-twist records.

Kenya developed as a focus of record-company interest as attempts to set up an Opel gramophone factory in Uganda failed, largely through lack of local repertoire. The Tanganyikan industry was restricted to one film studio.

The early company men carried out their business with an air of merchant adventurers. 'We used to go out with the ferrograph machine into the bush,' says Mike Andrews, now head of AIT records, Nairobi, 'and record all different dialects. We'd call some bloke over and he'd sing right there by the side of the car, with the machine running off the car battery.'[13]

Despite the interest in local material, Kenya became a crossroads for music from every quarter: from Europe and South Africa where, in the fifties, sax jive and pennywhistle music was distributed by companies like Capitol Music Stores. Later they went on to sign an exclusive deal with OK Jazz throughout east Africa. And so, it appears, did many other companies.

The love of import music – which stemmed from the refusal of the elite to value anything considered 'local' – grew throughout the sixties. Congolese music had already flooded the area. By the time the civil war broke out in the Congo, musicians from that area fled to east Africa in considerable numbers. For local record companies, it was a matter of beating the boom or joining it by recording Congo repertoire from musicians living in east Africa. The Congolese boom continued throughout the sixties; only in the seventies did tastes change in any dramatic way. The change registered at Mike Andrews's AIT records, set up as a subsidiary of the Lonhro company.

Up to that point, Andrews had concerned himself with bringing in South African and international material, which he handled on an agency basis. In the early seventies, Andrews's A&R man was Patrick Kanindo, one of the most dynamic figures on the music scene, and it was Kanindo, later a minister in Kenya, who was largely responsible for the boom in Luo music that followed.

Kanindo's achievement was prodigious. He virtually discovered D.O. Misiani and Shirati Jazz, plus other bands like the Koweri Boys Band and Ngori Sound. At full capacity he was said to produce as many as twenty singles a week, up to 400 numbers a month. With the main bands, every musician would then bring out singles under their own names as well. By

271

1973, the Nairobi sound was big in east and west Africa, and the Zaireans were starting to show signs of its faster and harder beat in their own rumba music.

There was only one problem: overproduction. One melody was taken and flogged to death. 'It was pure money,' says Andrews. 'To hell with the royalties or the image. It was just: "Into the studio. We've recorded X amount. Please pay us."'

Andrews himself showed no great knowledge of the music. 'I wouldn't have known if it was good or bad,' he says. 'But I knew when it sold.' Sales were sometimes brisk. A good single would shift 20,000, some as many as 50,000. And when Tanzanian jazz boomed, sales went higher still. Afro Jazz and Western Jazz, singing Swahili over Zairean guitar rhythms, could notch up sales of around 200,000 copies. Although the benga boom burnt itself out, Kanindo continued to work with the Luo bands; AIT took up with Orchestre Super Mazembe and Super Wanyika, many of the musicians coming from Zaire or Tanzania.

By the mid-seventies, the company was still using techniques that the large companies would have turned their noses up at. 'When we started the benga stuff,' says Andrews, 'a chap would go round with a portable player on the back of his bike. If the number was hot, a group would gather round to pay a couple of shillings to hear the record.'

Since then, the Kenyan music scene has found itself in considerable difficulties. In part, these stem from the lack of a single, identifiable national music, offering the prospect of sustained commercial development; in part from the proliferation of home taping and home-made cassette albums, which divert money away from the companies. In other countries, where pressing facilities don't exist, artists release their work on cassettes quite legitimately. Elsewhere, cassettes are pirated. 'From one single, in the 1970s, we might expect to sell 20,000 copies,' says Andrews. 'Now it would do 2,000. That's partly because of cassetting, partly due to the economic situation. The population has doubled. The GNP is down and the workforce has stayed the same. The breadwinners simply don't have the cash for luxuries.'

The experience of larger companies in Kenya has been mixed, to say the least. Polygram, who had bought up the old East African records plant in the late sixties, had a virtual monopoly of record pressing in the whole of east Africa. At one time it was their most profitable factory in the world.

In 1976, EMI set up a local subsidiary, EMI (Kenya) to handle international products and record local artists. The move went badly wrong. A local partner was found to be pocketing most of the profits. The concern was wound up.

The following year, CBS set up a base in Nairobi and built a large studio which, according to some, proved too large for Kenya's needs. 'The musicians there are at the four-track stage,' says EMI's Mike Wells, now with Serengeti records. 'There was none of the complexity of an Obey or a Sonny Okosuns.' The result: CBS lost money.

Today, CBS's involvement with local artists is small. The company mainly market international music or push other African artists like Anna Mwale, from Zambia. One exception was the singer Sammy Kasule, who recorded an English version of the popular 1983 hit 'Shauri Yaku', which was released on CBS in Scandinavia and America. Apart from that, the company's presence seems largely symbolic.

Polygram and AIT still operate, alongside a host of small independent labels producing Kenyan music in major regional languages. But the overall picture is one of decline. 'In the early seventies, Nairobi had eight-track facilities, and three pressing plants,' says Bavon Wayne-Wayne, a producer and musician. 'It was a vibrant, massive scene. Today the studios are gearing themselves up to do commercials. No one bothers with anything else.' The arrival of disco music delivered a further blow. 'There are no night spots left. It's all disco. Things wouldn't be so bad if local bands were playing the disco music, but again, all the records have been released under licence. Local bands really have no equipment, and the young musicians, who you'd expect to be coming up with lots of new stuff, leave for Tanzania, where it's all coming back to life.'[14]

Wayne's partner, Zembi Okeno, elaborates. 'There is so much talent in Kenya. Really big talent . . . But the young people don't get a break. Look at the big companies. I doubt if they have a single Kenyan on contract.'[15] 'Piracy is only one reason,' explains Wayne. 'The fact is that the music industry has no interest in local musicians. Two years ago, someone got as far as getting the government radio station to agree to ban all kinds of local music. We took a delegation to the President to get it reversed. The reason for this apathy is simple. It's a lot easier for the companies to get licences for stuff that's already been recorded in Europe and other parts of Africa, bang out the records and sell them. Why should they bother to record local bands? They're just not interested.'

CENTRAL AFRICA

The growth of a strong African sound can be traced, with far greater success, to central Africa, and an industry which grew up in the Belgian Congo in the fifties and sixties.

In the early days, recording was largely in the hands of Belgian or Greek traders, who imported records from the large European companies such as the Paris-based Pathé Marconi, and did a little recording of local music on their own. A Greek businessman, Geronomidis, the head of the N'Goma record company, produced the first record by a Congolese musician – Antoine Wendo's 'Marie Louise', in 1948. The record, like all of N'Goma's later material, was pressed in Paris.

By the mid-fifties, the Congolese recording scene had grown alongside the rapidly expanding electric-music scene, centred in Leopoldville, now Kinshasa, and other urban centres. Benator Frieres, with his Opika label, and Willie Pilgrims, who opened his Ecodis factory in the mid-fifties, were among the first to sign up local artists.

Other European companies were keen for a slice of the cake. EMI representatives were impressed, in the early fifties, by what one describes as the 'constantly developing purchasing power of the native and the expanding electrical power which is going to have a big effect on radio sales'.

The Congolese market, it was estimated, could give sales of half a million 78s per annum with substantial LP sales and a potential boom in vernacular 45s, suited to the 'jukebox possibilities' of Leopoldville.[16]

For the major overseas companies, the problem was getting hold of the right people on the spot. There was no lack of candidates. N'Goma, by the mid-fifties, was pressing around 800,000 records a year in France. Opika, who also pressed in France, had opened new studios in the fifties, catering, with other Leopoldville recording units, for a flurry of small labels, such as Essengo, Efa and Vita. Among the outsiders involved, Philips had made virtually no impact while Gallo had stirred up some interest with their east and South African recordings.

After various false starts, EMI settled for a deal with a Greek label owner, Antonopoulos, whose Loningisa and Essengo labels could guarantee a steady flow of local music that could be sold across Africa. Antonopoulos could also promise wide sales for EMI records and equipment shipped in from London. By the late fifties, the deal had borne fruit – and EMI's Columbia label was carrying Essous, Dr Nico and other top Congolese artists throughout west Africa. 'The exciting Essengo rhythm', said the record sleeves.

The record companies had not been slow in picking up on the new sound. Their thinking is reflected in a document circulated around EMI in 1958. It was called 'A New Approach to Africa'. 'The African is already asking for quality,' it asserted. 'The "star" and the "craze" are in the offing. At present there is a demand for 78s but urbanization is bringing electricity to more and more middle-class and artisan Africans.'[17]

The concept of the recording 'star' — on a continent where, for the most part, musicians remained working members of the community, gripped the companies. But their wilder expectations failed to materialize. EMI and Pathé seized on the Congo as a source of material to sell throughout the rest of Africa. Their early efforts were hampered by confusion. Pathé started with African Jazz but seemed unable to work out whether 'Mr Kabasele' was a manager, a musician or both. EMI showed a keen interest in Franco, but their efforts to arrange an exclusive deal foundered when it became clear that Franco, and many other local artists, had already entwined themselves in a complicated web of local contracts. At one stage the tussle for OK Jazz involved EMI, Philips, Essengo and Epanzan Makita, while in east Africa, Associated claimed local rights.

Despite their aggressive launch in the Congo, EMI lagged behind Decca's west and central African operations. By the mid-sixties, Decca controlled sixty per cent of the French West Africa market, leaving EMI's share at around fifteen.[18]

NEW MOVES

The mid-sixties saw new developments: the Africanization of major foreign companies in Zaire, the rise, at the end of the decade, of new local companies such as Veve to challenge the dominance of earlier Greek- and Belgian-owned outfits, and the furthering of the concept of the 'star', the producer and career development generally.

High-profile entrepreneurs and producers became a regular part of the scene; some purely for commercial reasons, others making a valuable contribution to musical development. One of the most important promoters and producers in Ghana in the 1960s and 1970s, Faisal Helwani, became active in the mid-1960s, organizing gigs for local musicians and visiting artists from other parts of west Africa. One of his earliest, and most prominent, liaisons was with Fela Kuti. As the decade progressed, Helwani grew increasingly involved with the promotion of local bands and music – bucking the then prevailing fashion for copyright music in Ghana spearheaded by such artists as Sierra Leonean bandleader Geraldo Pino and Super Eagles. Helwani concentrated his attentions on local dance-band highlife outfits like the Black Santiagos, the Barbecues and the Black Beats, turning Accra's Odeon cinema into a regular showplace for the bands. At the Odeon, Helwani resurrected the unusual practice, previously introduced by Guy Warren after his return from the USA, of staging sit-down concerts as opposed to stand-up dances.

In 1969, Helwani opened his first club, the Napoleon, in Accra and put together his first band, Hedzolleh Soundz. His idea was to stem the tide of imported copyright music by building up an outfit that would deal in contemporary, but traditionally based, Ghanaian music. Hedzolleh's music was built on folk rhythms like adowa and kpanlogo and played on a mixture of flutes, acoustic and electric guitars, trap drums and extensive traditional percussion.

The formation of Hedzolleh coincided with the appearance in Ghana of Hugh Masekela. In Accra, Masekela stayed with Helwani and jammed with Hedzolleh at the Napoleon – a dynamite combination. Trumpeter and band then set off for gigs in Lagos and the USA, where they received tremendous acclaim from club audiences. Soon however, the relationship between Masekela and Helwani soured, with the latter unhappy about the high profile Masekela was receiving compared with the also-ran status of Hedzolleh, who were generally perceived as little more than Masekela's backing band. Hedzolleh, though, sided with Masekela in the dispute and in 1974 Helwani returned to Ghana.

Back in Accra, Helwani set up other bands in the Hedzolleh mould – notably Bassa Bassa Soundz and Bunzu Soundz, the latter fusing rock with guitar-band highlife. He also embarked on an ambitious programme of record productions for Decca West Africa, using the Decca studios in Lagos. Eventually, Decca cancelled the deal. The then policy of Nigerianization was to blame, suggests Helwani, while others have said that a cartel of Western-owned major labels, worried at the growing threat represented by Helwani's independent efforts, manipulated the Nigerianization policy to stifle him.

In 1977, Helwani helped set up the first Musicians Union of Ghana, dedicated to safeguarding musicians and independent producers against the dominance of labels like Decca, EMI and Phonogram. One of the union's first priorities was the introduction of proper recording contracts and improved royalty structures for local musicians.

In 1979, Helwani set up his own recording studio, producing among other projects the first new album to be recorded by E.T. Mensah in over ten years. His intention was to produce a catalogue of African records that could be sold across Africa and overseas – but he was frustrated by the lack of an import licence, which made it impossible for him to bring in the tapes and raw materials he needed. Currently, Helwani operates out of Liberia, where he records a large number of west African artists for local cassette-only release, while laying plans for another attempt at taking African music into the overseas market.

In Nigeria, the boom and the development of new studios attracted foreign interest with visits from Paul McCartney and Ginger Baker, and heralded new possibilities for Nigerian musicians. Among the newly prosperous juju musicians, Sunny Ade went on to form his own company, while Ebenezer Obey underlined his own position in the community by becoming a director of Decca West Africa.

Countries lacking Nigeria's ready supply of mineral wealth found the going harder. In Ghana, an economic slump put an end to the import of vinyl, instruments and spare parts for the handful of deteriorating studios.

Tanzania suffered an unlikely combination of a thriving, largely government-sponsored music scene and a virtual absence of recording facilities. Bands either played live over the radio – relying on listeners to make their own tapes, some of which might then be pressed into records in Malawi – or left for the thriving Kenya studios.

Of the smaller countries, Zimbabwe's studios remained for the most part in European hands, a number of local artists like Oliver Mtukudzi sending vocal tapes to South Africa to have the backing added; while Gabon, Congo Brazzaville and Togo have seen the rise of new, top-class studios, ranking with the Côte d'Ivoire in their ability to attract top talent from west and central Africa.

For all this abundance of talent, a large question mark hangs over the future of an African recording scene that has been severely eroded by economic depression. Even in the richer countries, records are becoming a luxury. The Kenyan situation has already been described. The pattern repeats itself through large, richer countries like Nigeria, where Sunny Ade talks of local pirates with rooms full of recording equipment in their inner-city Lagos houses, to Sierra Leone, where the record shops offer single records which are taped for the customers.

Despite its obvious social value in bringing cheap entertainment to the less well-off African citizens, piracy has caused considerable alarm among the artists affected. Ade's own response has been to drop the prices of his records to a level slightly above that of the bootlegs, to issue new albums with win-a-car lottery tickets inserted in them and, on a more institutional level, to channel his effort and that of other artists, such as Prince Nico and Sonny Okosuns through PMAN: the association of Nigerian performers, musicians and artists which is calling for greater government help in the fight against the pirates.

ABROAD

African musicians have been leaving home and travelling overseas in search of enhanced career opportunities for many years, but what was once a trickle of more or less isolated individuals has changed in recent years into a steady stream moving from all parts of the continent to Britain, mainland Europe and North America. When the Nigerian percussionist Ginger Johnson came to London in the 1940s to join Edmundo Ros's dance band, he was one of a tiny handful of African musicians active in the city. Today, many more African musicians are more or less permanently based in Britain, augmented by a floating group of temporary residents in the country to complete specific short-term projects such as concert appearances or recording sessions. The same is true in France, Germany, Holland, Belgium, Switzerland, the USA and Canada.

But if the extent of migration has increased in recent years, the reasons behind it remain the same. On the one hand, African musicians feel frustrated by the limited technological and career opportunities available to them at home; on the other they realize that any ambitions they have to move on to the stage of the global entertainments business must be realized from the West rather than from Africa – with the possible exceptions of Fela Kuti and Sunny Ade, no African musician has yet made a substantial impact on the international music scene without first basing him/herself in Europe or North America (and Fela's international breakthrough was preceded by lengthy periods of residence in Britain and the USA). Manu Dibango, Hugh Masekela, Osibisa, Miriam Makeba, all have been obliged to migrate to the Western centres of the music business, and until Africa is equipped with the same technological and communications facilities as the industrialized West, that necessity looks likely to remain.

The rate of migration by African musicians over the past twenty years has increased by a series of bursts which have followed perceived (but often, sadly, imaginary or temporary) increases in the acceptance of African music in the West. Osibisa's emergence in Britain in the late 1960s accelerated the number of Ghanaian and other west African musicians moving to the country. The worldwide success of Manu Dibango's 'Soul Makossa' in the early 1970s, alongside Miriam Makeba's North American breakthrough, led to another burst of migration. More recently, Sunny Ade's high-profiled marketing attack on the USA and Europe (via Island records) has brought about another dramatic upturn. Ghanaian journalist Kwabena Fosu-Mensah has noted that in the period 1983/4 there were some thirty-five albums released by the Ghanaian diaspora in the West, while at the same time there were more Ghanaian records available in London than there were in Accra. The same pattern continues to be true in 1987, not only for Ghana but for many other western and central African musical worlds.

While there is no doubt that the audience for African music has grown substantially in the West over the past twenty years, it is still a long way from breaking through into the mainstream of popular music – a fact that often comes as a rude shock to African musicians migrating to Europe or North America. Encouraged by the successes of Osibisa, Dibango, Makeba and others, many of these musicians have arrived in the West anticipating a ready acceptance by the popular-music audience and the record business which caters to it. The reality which greets them, however, is otherwise – record contracts with all but tiny specialist labels are practically impossible to secure, and the opportunities for regular live appearances which could support the musician while he or she pursues that contract remain sorely limited. Sooner or later the musician realizes that all the previous successes of African musicians in the West have been essentially unconnected flashes in the pan, novelty breakthroughs which have not resulted in a substantial mainstream audience for their music.

It is hard, particularly for the African musicians themselves, to determine why this should be so. Throughout Africa, Western popular music – especially that of Britain and the USA – has huge followings, sensitive to the changing fads and fancies of the Western pop-music audience and in many instances sharing them. When Cliff Richard gave way to the Beatles and the Stones in Britain in the early 1960s, the same was true throughout Anglophone Africa. When Michael Jackson established himself as the biggest phenomenon in Western pop in the 1980s, it was only a matter of months before he'd found similar acceptance in Africa. It is no exaggeration to say that every major development in Western pop music since the 1960s has found a huge and enthusiastic audience in Africa. Why then should African music itself, which has always been an important root of Western popular music, not enjoy a similar mirror-image welcome?

Putting aside the point of view which holds that the popular-music audience in the West is irredeemably more conservative and insular than its counterpart in Africa, an observation which contains a great deal of truth, a number of reasons suggest themselves. The most credible of these are the language barrier, the nature of the Western record business and the difficulty of the African musician being able to work within it, and the structural racism of a music industry which shies away from anything seen to be different, dangerous or 'foreign'. None of these factors on its own provides a convincing answer to the problem, but taken together they represent a massive roadblock on the path of African music's breakthrough.

The theory that is most commonly advanced to explain African music's ghettoization within a limited specialist audience in the West concerns language. This is given credence by the fact that those African artists who have gained the biggest Western followings either sing in one of the varieties of the English language (Fela Kuti, Osibisa) or offer music that is primarily instrumental (Hugh Masekela, Manu Dibango). True, Miriam Makeba has found success with African-language lyrics, but these have often been perceived by her Western audience as 'novelty' songs, while Makeba's repertoire has always included a considerable amount of English-language material. Sunny Ade's Western success in the early 1980s would seem to disprove this language-barrier theory, but it by no means completely demolishes it: Ade's massive media profile during this period was not matched by equally huge record sales, and many of the people acquiring his records were either members of the specialist music audience or media/record business people who obtained them as totems of chicness rather than valued listening experiences. A couple of years on from Ade's 'breakthrough', his audience has shrunk to a residual specialist following, while he has never achieved a major album success in the West (much less the all-important singles-chart hit).

Further credence is given to the language-barrier theory when one looks at Fela Kuti's breakthrough in Africa itself in the early 1970s. Almost alone among African pop musicians at that time, Kuti began to record almost exclusively in Krio, sometimes referred to as 'broken English', as opposed to the tribal languages used by most of his colleagues and competitors. While these latter artists found their appeal limited in the main to members of their own tribal groupings, Kuti's records found an enthusiastic following throughout west Africa, particularly in Anglophone areas where Krio was the lingua franca. It was a deliberate and inspired initiative on Kuti's part, and one that did not in any way diminish the 'Africanness' of his music.

Opponents of the language-barrier theory point to the success of Zairean and South African music among Western audiences. But this success is limited exclusively to the specialist music audience, for whom impenetrable lyrics may well be a plus factor rather than a hindrance. Indeed, members of this audience can regularly be heard opining that they'd rather not understand the literal meaning of lyrics by such artists as Franco, on the grounds that their translated banality would spoil enjoyment of the music.

It must be said, moreover, that common sense insists that African music's failure to find a substantial mainstream audience in the West must in large part be due to language factors. The average member of the Western pop-music audience, dispassionately identified by the business as a fifteen-year-old shop assistant in Woolworths, wants to understand the lyrics of the records he or she listens to – even if those lyrics are endless and mundane variations on the themes of lost or found love.

Alongside the hurdles of language and lyrics, African musicians looking for acceptance in the West need to understand and deal with an entertainments industry that is infinitely more complex and demanding than those that they may be used to in their home countries. Not only is the structure of this industry difficult for an outsider to comprehend and penetrate, its attitudes to music and musicians differ widely from those of the record business in Africa. Whereas the African record business, even today, is concerned with simply recording and releasing a succession of records into what remains a seller's market, the European and North American industry is massively more competitive, and is obliged to employ sophisticated marketing, sales and production techniques as each label and its artists fights for market share and media exposure. Ironically, this had led to a situation in the West where the musician him/herself has become decreasingly important to the music business. It is the accountant and the marketing person rather than the creative spirit who directs the activities of individual labels, and record-company personnel are speaking only partly in jest when they say 'The only thing wrong with the music business is the musician.'

To make a lasting impact on the Western pop mainstream then, the African musician arriving in London or New York has first to learn how the record businesses in those cities work, and then persuade them to work on his/her behalf. It would be hard to overstate the scale and difficulty of this task. Trustworthy and able management must be found, the arcane intricacies of copyright, royalty and contractual law understood, technologically awesome studio and recording techniques mastered, broadcast and print media persuaded to support the musician's output. At the same time, the musician is very likely having to deal with the pressing problem of economic survival in an alien environment: somehow generating enough cash to secure housing, food and clothes.

Meanwhile, of course, the newly arrived African musician is running up against the subtle yet profound structural racism which permeates British society and all its institutions, and from which the record business is no exception. Even in record companies which specialize in black forms of popular music, it is rare in Britain (though less so in the USA) to find black executives. The same is true in the media world. The musician is constantly having to deal with executives, journalists and radio DJs who understand very little about African music and culture, and who may also actively look down on black people. It is axiomatic in mainstream magazine publishing, for instance, that a black face on the cover will actually diminish sales of that issue (unless the face is of that tiny handful of black stars, like Michael Jackson and Diana Ross, who are no longer perceived as 'exclusively black') – and whether that perception is true in prejudice rather than in fact the end result for the African musician is the same. Similar scenarios pertain in the world of radio and TV. Equally importantly, while record companies are willing to invest large amounts of time, effort and cash in the long-term career development of white pop artists, they are less inclined to do so on behalf of black ones – whom, even in the latter half of the 1980s, they continue to regard primarily as, at best, 'one-hit wonders'. Happily, this is no longer as true in the USA as it is in Britain, and as artists like Prince, Michael Jackson and Diana Ross continue to generate huge cash flows throughout the international entertainment business, attitudes among the British arm of that business can be expected to change for the better.

In combination, the language barrier, the nature of the Western record business and racial attitudes represent a major obstacle to the mainstream acceptance of African music in the West. Indeed, for the present, they can be said to preclude that acceptance. If African music is to make a lasting and substantial impact overseas it will have to follow an alternative route, identifying positively-inclined specialist audiences and reaching them via specialist and smaller labels who share those enthusiasms.

This process has already begun with a handful of small labels issuing African music as a labour of love, sometimes a labour of commerce. Among them, DiscAfrique made considerable impact by releasing the Bhundu Boys' *Shabini* album, under licence, in 1986. Healthy doses of radio play plus enthusiastic and endless live shows took the album to the top of the independent charts, and made the Bhundu Boys the first African band of the 1980s to penetrate the pop and rock market.

The Asona label, set up by Anthony Roberts, played a major part in forging a brand of funk, occasionally soca-influenced, highlife, geared specifically to British tastes. Thomas Frempong's *Aye Yi* album set the standard, with its roots rhythms, splashes of yaa amponsah guitar, and vocals from one of Ghana's top singers.

GlobeStyle proved more diverse, adopting the slogan 'Worldwide – Your Guide' to bring a range of global sounds to British ears. The label, set up in 1985 by Roger Armstrong and Ben Mandelson, formerly of Orchestre Jazira, has released music from the Antilles, Israel, Colombia, salsa from New York, a set from the Super Rail Band of the Buffet Hotel de Gare de Bamako in Mali, and a series of effervescent soukous albums from Kanda Bongo Man, Pablo Porthos, Tchico et les Officiers of African Music and the Choc Stars.

In 1986, Armstrong and Mandelson set off for Madagascar, where, with the aid of Sony digital equipment, they recorded a range of pop, folk and traditional musics, which were later released in two gatefold-sleeved albums. 'Our criteria for inclusion on GlobeStyle are simple,' says Mandelson. 'It comes down to: "Do I like it? Would I want to buy it?" There's no feeling that: "This ought to go out as a service to mankind." For me, the best African stuff, on our label, has been the Choc Stars. After the clean Paris productions, with their layers of drums and guitars, Choc Stars sound completely different. They're like Zaiko: rougher, far more of a beat group.'

Such enthusiasm is shared by a range of other companies, some large, some small, who have played an important part in bringing African music to a wider public.

ISLAND

When Island records signed Sunny Ade for a three-album deal in 1981 it seemed to many lovers of African music that a breakthrough was at hand. The death of Bob Marley had left a vacuum that could, it was argued, be filled by the world's first African superstar.

The fact that Marley's songs were in English, and that his music was soaked in the hooks and flavours of Western pop and soul, counted for little in the optimism that followed the deal.

A mountain of television and press coverage followed, which tended to obscure the fact that Island had no wish to create a new, African, Bob

Marley. Instead they approached the African project in a low-key way: with a couple of twelve-inch singles that would be launched with little or no publicity. The media ballyhoo came only later.

Island's interest in Africa went back to the 1970s, when they attracted a roster of African session musicians, including Ghanaian sax man Ray Allen and percussionist Speedy Aquaye, and released an album by Ghanaian trumpeter Eddie Quansah. Then their interest faded. It was revived at the end of the decade by the singer Robert Palmer, a friend of Island boss Chris Blackwell, and, over the past ten years, an ardent follower of juju music. Island had already released, on their US imprint, two volumes of traditional and pop music from Togo. Palmer now suggested to Blackwell a series of African releases and Blackwell followed through.

The first release in Island's low-budget, no-fuss, left-field African Series came with a twelve-inch single entitled 'Bo Mbanda', from Zairean bass guitarist Pablo Lubadika Porthos. For Island this was a leap into the unknown. They had little knowledge of Africa or its music, and even less of Pablo Lubadika Porthos. They were content to follow their ears, and those of British guitarist Ben Mandelson, who stepped in as an A&R adviser and album compiler.

The ears pointed to Paris, where a healthy African-music scene had developed, and in particular to the Salsa Musique label whose owner Richard Dick had built up a sizeable roster of artists, all living and working in Paris. Island signed a deal for a batch of the label's material — and showed strong interest in Sam Mangwana's *Maria Tebbo* album, but the asking price proved too high.

After the Porthos single, a compilation of Richard Dick material from Zaire, Senegal and other Francophone countries appeared under the title *Sound d'Afrique*. The album received good reviews and, with little promotion, sold over 9,000 copies. Island were amazed. It seemed that they had, almost without thinking about it, hit a market. The future of the African Series looked bright.

At that point, French producer Martin Meissonnier approached the company. He'd been involved in African music for ten years, and had worked with a number of artists including Fela Kuti. He suggested that if Island were serious about African music they should sign an African artist directly to the label, rather than just license material from Paris. Three artists were suggested: Sunny Ade, Ebenezer Obey and Sandra Isadore, who had recorded with Fela and whose late-1970s album *Upside Down* had scored a big Nigerian hit. On Blackwell's insistence, the project narrowed down to one artist, Sunny Ade.

Ade's Island debut album, *Juju Music*, was recorded in Lome, the capital of Togo, and released in 1982 to fulsome reviews. Indeed, critical and commercial response was so positive that Island were persuaded to change their African-music strategy. What had started as a left-field, specialist venture became an altogether more aggressive, bigger-budget marketing operation. Sunny Ade, it was discovered, was a regular visitor to London, a man of considerable 'sus' and charm. Island decided to put money into promoting Ade and his African Beats in the same way that they'd promote any other potentially top attraction. Suddenly, Sunny Ade had arrived, headed straight at the mainstream album market.

In 1983, Ade and the African Beats arrived in London to start work on a second album and to sell themselves to the British public. Their first concert of the 1980s – they had played to Nigerian audiences in London in the previous decade – took place at the London Lyceum in January 1983. The promoters had been worried by poor advance sales. On the night, crowds besieged the theatre. Police had to be called to hold them back. Five hundred people had to be turned away. 'It was one of the greatest gigs I've ever seen,' says Island's press director Rob Partridge. 'We had no idea what a juju gig was like and here it was – a weird cultural mix. Most of smart Nigeria had turned out, alongside rastas and the London set. It was a superb show and the reviews were astonishing.'[1]

So were sales. *Synchro System* sold 14,000 copies in a week – roughly the same as *Juju Music* had sold in six months. But despite this, a number of problems had appeared. The main one was lack of radio airplay. If Ade had written three-minute songs, in English, matters might have been different. But neither he, nor Island, was prepared to compromise.

Tours of Europe and America followed. The concerts were packed, the reviews excellent. Ade appeared in a film directed by Robert Altman, received glowing testimonials from Stevie Wonder and played second on the bill to the Police in Canada.

Ade's third album marked a change of style. *Juju Music* and *Synchro System* had both reworked a number of older tracks, well-known to Nigerian listeners. With *Aura* Ade went into the studio with no songs prepared. What he did have, though, was an idea of what the new album should sound like. 'Ninety per cent of what you heard on the radio at that time was produced like Michael Jackson,' explains producer Meissonnier. 'It's a question of sound rather than rhythm. So we really wanted to have this modern technology applied to juju music.'

The album, which featured Stevie Wonder's harmonica playing on the title track, sounded tighter, more concentrated and self-consciously modern than any of Ade's previous work. It was tailored for massive mainstream success, but it bombed. *Aura* sold a disastrous 5,000 copies. 'We concluded that people who had been intrigued by juju music bought the first two albums,' says Rob Partridge, 'but then their interest faded.'

The failure of *Aura* left Island with a serious problem. To go forwards would have meant a further massive investment in large and expensive world tours. Lack of radio play was a lesser problem – other Island bands, like the Wailers and, more recently, U2, had built up their reputations from live shows, rather than airtime. But with Ade the issue was different, and more difficult. He lacked a readily identifiable audience. At the start, Island had had no idea of the market for juju music. Later it emerged that the audience was small, largely white, with a small West Indian interest. While Jamaican music in Britain was rooted in a strong West Indian community, the numbers of record-buying Africans living in the country was minute.

The last straw came with a change in Island management. In 1984, Dave Robinson, the founder of Stiff records, was taken on as managing director. Robinson's ears were more attuned to the successful sounds of Frankie Goes to Hollywood than the commercially limited appeal of juju music. After three albums, Ade's contract was allowed to lapse.

So what went wrong? At the time of the break-up, it was suggested that Island had wanted Ade to produce a funkier, more commercial sound. Island deny this. 'The first we heard of Ade's albums was when he brought us the finished tapes,' says Rob Partridge. 'Any changes in the music would have to come from Ade himself.' There was also talk of high studio costs for *Aura* and of Ade's dissatisfaction with what he saw as poor accommodation during his lengthy American tour.

To Island, the problem was one of strategy. 'There's a terrible tendency to start things as left-field projects, where they can operate profitably and then, as soon as the optimism increases, to try to push them into the mainstream,' says Partridge. 'You then have to spend an awful lot of money and you have to sell many more records to return your investment. Suddenly it becomes unprofitable.'

The concentration on Ade took Island's attention away from its more heartening success: the African Series, which in the early days had spawned two compilations, *Sound d'Afrique* and *Sound d'Afrique 2: Soukous*, and two singles from Pablo Porthos. But the company hasn't given up hope. 'African music isn't a trend,' says Partridge. 'It's not a Two-Tone. It's a large continent with a lot of artists. They're not all going to suddenly stop and start playing R&B. Given the right conditions and the right records, I'm sure it will happen again. Island hasn't abandoned its plans to release African records.'

EARTHWORKS

Of all the African-music labels operating in Britain, Earthworks has the strongest identity, as a company associated with the music of Zimbabwe and South Africa.

'It's the area I know best,' says Jumbo Vanrenen, a South African emigré who founded Earthworks with his wife Mary. 'Also it's a very neglected area. We've always been able to get Zairean music and stuff from Nigeria, Ghana and Senegal – but South Africa and Zimbabwe are two areas that have received little exposure.'[2]

The Vanrenens started Earthworks in 1982. For eleven years before that, Jumbo had worked at Virgin records – where, as A&R man, he dealt with Jabula and Dudu Pukwana, plus later arrivals like Rip Rig and Panic and Public Image, and launched the reggae Frontline series. In the early 1980s, he set up the recording of Orchestre Makassy in Kenya – a move that marked Virgin's hesitant entry into the African scene proper. He also helped introduce kora music to Britain by releasing a Virgin album by the Konte family from The Gambia.

Earthworks' own policy is more direct. Their first release, a twelve-inch single entitled 'Love' from the London-based Orchestre Jazira, proved unsuccessful. From then, the Vanrenens set up a succession of licensing deals to bring African music to Britain. The first was with AIT Records in Kenya, who supplied tapes for the *Viva Zimbabwe* and *Zulu Jive* compilations plus a set by Kati Eliclean Namanono. The second was with Rough Trade, who established Earthworks as their African-music division. With Rough Trade's backing Vanrenen planned a series of South African releases from Amaswazi Emvelo to the Mahotella Queens and Ladysmith Black Mambazo. The plan stalled when Rough Trade, who had given their support to the cultural boycott of South Africa, pulled out, blacking a Phezulu Eqhudeni album which had already been pressed.

Earthworks turned to music that was more acceptable, releasing albums by Orchestre Virunga from Kenya, A.B. Crentsil from Ghana and a single from Shina Williams from Nigeria. The relationship with Rough Trade continued with two Thomas Mapfumo albums, *Mabasa* and *Mr Music*. In

1984, tired of merely putting out other companies' material, Earthworks went into production – choosing first Tony Allen then Dele Abiodun and Souzy Kasseya – and releasing South African choir Ladysmith Black Mambazo on their own, rather than through Rough Trade.

Jumbo Vanrenen is unrepentant about his attitude to the boycott. 'I see the cultural boycott as a one-way thing,' he says. 'Something that starves white South Africans of their creature comforts. But to obstruct the flow of information from black South Africa is negative. It doesn't do the struggle any good. When you're talking about the struggle you're talking about information and music is information.'

Speeding up the flow is one of Earthworks' aims. The other is to put at least some money back into developing countries and the people who make the music. This may involve buying tapes from record producers in South Africa and other sources whose business set-ups can't be fully checked. But Vanrenen is undeterred. 'It's like that with reggae. You'd set out not to deal with a producer who has a dodgy reputation, but if his music is the best, what do you do? You can't control the circumstances in which the music is made. You hear a good record, which may have sold thousands. Then you hear that the artist was ripped off. That doesn't stop you enjoying the music.'

Earthworks' music policy is geared to the dance market. Dele Abiodun and Tony Allen supply a solid groove. Abiodun's album was recorded at the Decca Lagos studio – the best anywhere for juju music – and the tapes were mixed at the Addis Ababa studio in London. The policy is to leave the music clear and concise. 'I don't want to change anything,' says Jumbo. 'Things went wrong with Sunny Ade because he changed so radically that he lost both his ethnic market and his specialist market. My aim is to keep the feel of Africa but to present it clearly.'

Partly through choice, partly through lack of finance, Earthworks avoids big-name producers. Vanrenen dismisses Bill Laswell's work for the Celluloid label as imposing a foreign, New York sensibility on to African music. On an Earthworks album, all the innovations come from the musicians themselves.

Souzy Kasseya is a case in point. Vanrenen was impressed by his single 'Le Téléphone Sonne' and put it out on twelve-inch. Kasseya then recorded an album, *The Phenomenal*, that showed an even stronger grasp of the two traditions – European and African – and a willingness to lay strong melodies over a dance groove.

The main problem for Earthworks is selling the groove to a European audience fixated on funk and pop. 'At the moment, African music has no clear message or style,' says Vanrenen, 'and style is important. Maybe Papa Wemba will change that.'

As far as messages go, Earthworks' biggest success is likely to be Thomas Mapfumo. Where most African artists take jazz, funk or Latin as their external reference points, Mapfumo's roots are in rock. In full flow, the music has the intensity of a rock concert, and that common, if not immediately obvious, link with a sizeable section of the Western audience could prove crucial.

Mapfumo's British tours, in 1984 and 1985, attracted considerable media attention and the sales of his 1985 album *Mr Music* looked promising. But they fell far short of Earthworks' other ventures, notably the *Zulu Jive* and *Indestructible Beat of Soweto* albums, the latter marking Vanrenen's first joint project with fellow South African, Trevor Herman. Sales of over 5,000 copies pointed the label into a new direction – away from artists, tours and egos and towards the releasing of compilation albums.

In 1987, Vanrenen took a further step forward. A deal with Virgin records established a new Earthworks/Virgin label, and with it a projected annual flow of ten compilation albums from Africa, the Caribbean and Latin America. In July, while working on his first Virgin compilations, he was taken on by Island records to head their black-music section.

'The work that has gone on over the past five years is beginning to have an impact,' he says. 'We'll see the benefit over the next few years, particularly with artists from southern Africa who have a strong grasp of the pop medium. In Britain, promoters for live gigs can now guarantee an audience. People know they can come along and get bowled over.'[3]

STERNS

It started in the 1950s with a small shop, Sterns, selling toasters, kettles, lightbulbs – and African records – in London's Tottenham Court Road. The stock was small. Many records appeared from suitcases, brought in by Nigerian and Ghanaian businessmen passing through town. They were sold, at high prices, to the African community and a few English enthusiasts, many of whom were attracted from the nearby University of London and the School of Oriental and African Studies.

By the early 1980s, Sterns was catering for a new, 'hip' audience. It attracted disc jockeys like John Peel, musicians like Ian Dury, plus new African-music freaks stirred into action both by Island's signing of Sunny Ade and the general feeling that Africa's time had come.

The original owners retired in 1982, after thirty-odd years in the business. Sterns was reopened, with drumming, singing and dancing, the following year and with three new owners: Don Bayramian, a businessman; writer Charles Easmon; and Robert Urbanus, who had worked as a researcher in Ghana in the mid-1970s. Apart from selling records – buying from source rather than suitcases this time – the new owners moved into production on a somewhat tentative basis.

Their first signing, Hi-Life International, a London-based band specializing in highlife, soukous and agbadza, released their debut album, *Travel and See*, in 1983. The results were of mixed quality: strong melodies making up for patchy production and raw vocals. Sterns then moved into juju music. Rather than wait for the right artist to come along with finished tapes – as they had done with Malcolm Ben, the African Brothers and Eric Agyeman – they decided to travel. Don Bayramian went to Lagos and, having already been impressed by Segun Adewale's album *Ase*, contacted Adewale and signed him to Sterns. His album, *Adewale Play for Me*, appeared in 1984 and provided a powerful antidote to the moves Ade was making with Island. Whereas Island were concentrating on a single artist, Sterns, by virtue of their expanding catalogue of African releases, were able to put the music into context. For Urbanus, the difference was important. 'Ade was seen as an isolated and exotic phenomenon,' he says. 'He was promoted through a media circus like any other pop act.'[4]

Sterns' approach was different. Many of their releases – particularly in the highlife field – were aimed well away from the new African 'hipocracy' towards Sterns' traditional west African market. There was little attempt to push the music, to try to generate chart success.

The label took chances, however. 'Trina 4', a twelve-inch single from Nigerian singer Onyeka, mixed Afro reggae with a blast of bagpipe music. And with the debut single 'Come to Africa' – released well after their first album – Hi-Life International were produced by the celebrated dub producer Dennis Bovell. The experiment failed – largely, thinks Urbanus, due to poor material. For the subsequent album, the band produced themselves, in a straight, gadget- and dub-free fashion. The timing was also against the Bovell–Hi-Life link-up. 'The band had to be squeezed in between sessions that Bovell was doing with Orange Juice,' says Urbanus. 'There was no time to listen and reflect.'

As with most small companies, finance was crucial. Sterns had the choice – to put a great deal of money and promotion behind one single, in the hope of chart success, or serve the existing market, after the fashion of small jazz labels. 'Our aim is to bring out good-quality music and just hope the market improves,' says Urbanus. 'If you haven't really got the money to gamble on a big promotion, you might as well forget it.'

But this hasn't stopped Sterns from building up their own roster of musicians. In the beginning it included Hi-Life International and Segun Adewale. In late 1984, the company signed Somo Somo, a soukous band set up by Mosese Fan Fan, a former guitarist with OK Jazz who had been working in Tanzania. At first, Sterns were doubtful about the idea of backing a Zairean band when there was so much good soukous music coming in from Paris. But with their album *Somo Somo*, released in 1985, Somo Somo were able to stake out their own territory – creating a sound that had enough bass and bluster for the London market, and a guitar style whose speed and hardness carried east African, possibly even South African, flavours, reflecting Fan Fan's own time in Kenya and Tanzania.

At the same time, the company kept their options open, releasing an album of straight kora music from The Gambia. Sterns make few concessions to the ephemerally popular.

The Somo Somo connection continued into 1986 with a second album, *Paris*, which abandoned the earlier adrenalin for a smoother, more comfortable rumba sound. Fan Fan recorded the album in Paris, switching his regular line-up for a group of session musicians. Among them was Pablo Porthos, whose bass lines were later reworked, to greater effect, by Herman Asafo-Agyei, of Native Spirit.

One of Sterns' greatest successes has been its 1986 *African Moves* compilation, which included tracks from Somo Somo, Segun Adewale, Ebenezer Obey, Tabu Ley and the African Brothers, and offered a useful introduction both to their own catalogue and to three of the African sounds that had made an early impression in the UK: highlife, juju and soukous. Their increasingly keen nose for the hottest African music in Paris led them, in 1987, to release the debut album from Kass Kass and Salif Keita's extraordinary, hi-tech *Soro*.

'We feel that a regular market has now established itself,' says Robert Urbanus. 'It will develop like jazz or blues or salsa, selling well enough for a company to put out its own releases or stuff under licence, and make a living – although no one will be riding round in a Rolls.

'To get into the singles chart was a silly idea. If it happens, it will happen accidentally or through one of the companies who have enough money to hype that sort of thing. The main thing with our sort of market is to get a good distribution and the right radio play.'[5]

OVAL

As a disc jockey and the co-owner of an independent label producing African music, Charlie Gillett should be in a unique position to discover what the public wants and to provide it for them – or so it might seem. The truth, however, is more complex. Gillett's releases on his Oval label – one kora album, two soukous singles from the London-based African Connexion, two funk–highlife crossovers recorded in Berlin and an Afro–soca mix – have been aimed at the mainstream rather than the specialist market, but despite positive media response have not sold well enough to cover their production costs.

The problem is partly one of exposure. At the outset, Gillett decided that any company selling African music had to start in the clubs. Once a single had aroused dancefloor interest, radio play and a wider public could be hoped for. African music, though, has a curiously hard time in clubland. The occasional twelve-inch single – Sunny Ade's 'Synchro System', Kabbala's 'Ashewo Ara' – created a flicker. For the rest, the going is perilous.

Gillett's first shot at releasing an African record came in 1984. At that time, he was hosting Capital Radio's Saturday-evening show, 'A Foreign Affair', which gave him an hour a week to expose African and other 'Third World' music. Among the steady stream of tapes sent in, the best was from African Connexion, a sparkling soukous number called 'C'est La Dance' which had 'strong melody, a structure and a good groove'.[6] Oval put the single out, followed by George Darko's 'Highlife Time', a more commercial song that Gillett felt would break into the clubs with greater ease. Both singles failed, selling around 1,500 copies each.

At the start, Gillett had little idea of the exact audience for African music and was content to follow the instincts that had led him to associations with Ian Dury, Lene Lovich and Dire Straits. 'The difficulty is that I'm not a normal businessman,' he points out. 'I know that over the years if I get enthusiastic about something, the rest of the world eventually catches on. The trouble is my timing, it's hopeless. I may be six months out, or ten years.'

Despite the apparent naïveté of his approach, Gillett has massive enthusiasm and a sharp ear for the commercial sound. An album from the German-based Ghanaian band Kantata, *Asiko*, proved one of the more memorable 1980s crossover sounds. African Connexion's follow-up to 'C'est La Dance', 'Dancing on the Sidewalk', mixed a strong melody with an upbeat cavacha sound and a pronounced funk backbeat. Both bands managed to mix the straight funk beat into more intricate webs of African rhythm – but not, it would seem, in a way to satisfy funk fans or African enthusiasts.

But for Gillett, this remained the way forward. From the late 1970s, American bands had gradually returned percussion to the fore. And given the skill with which most African guitarists play around the main beat, the scene was set for a blending of rhythm patterns, held together by the hi-tech lash of the Simmons electronic drum.

'So far, no one's really been able to pull it off,' says Gillett. 'The Sunny Ade album *Aura* was possibly trying to do that, but it didn't sound very good. The principle was there – polyrhythms around an electronic drum – but the songs weren't very strong.'

In 1985, Oval moved further into the mainstream with a single from Bosca Banks, former drummer with African Connexion. But the problem of the right sound remained. For Gillett, Oval releases must sound good alongside American funk and Banks's single, despite its strong Western feel, was still heard as 'ethnic' by the club DJs around the country who received the promotional mailout.

Oval's production policy is simple. With George Darko and Kantata, the songs arrived as finished tapes. The crossover sound was already established. With African Connexion and Banks, Gillett worked within strict limits – choosing economical studios, avoiding big-name producers and trusting the artists to keep a grip on their own material and the sound they wanted. The result is a straight, reasonably 'natural' sound with no attempt by Oval to channel the music into a new direction.

'It's not a sound or a style we're after,' says Gillett. 'It's an approach, and it's very much do-it-yourself.'

And the end result? 'It must be able to sit alongside American funk. Which is another way of saying that it must emphasize the second and fourth beats in the bar.'

Finally, though, the funk won. In 1985, Oval shared in an international pop hit as the publishers of Paul Hardcastle's song '19', that went on to sell over three million copies worldwide, some four years after Oval had begun working with Hardcastle by releasing his singles by his groups Direct Drive and First Light. For once, it had not hurt Gillett to be ahead of his time.

As a DJ, Gillett continues to play African pop on his Capital show, later renamed 'A World of Difference' to encompass a wider spread of world music. As he juxtaposes African beats against the 'square' dance patterns of American rock and funk, and the sinuous rhythms of salsa and soca, he hopes to enable London musicians and audiences to feel comfortable with words they can't understand and dance beats they never tried before. 'For me,' he says, 'this music follows on naturally from Dire Straits and the Police, and it's just a matter of time before the rest of the world catches on. There will be African equivalents to Lionel Ritchie, Mark Knopfler and Bob Marley, who learn how to provide the world with what it wants while retaining their own individuality. But nobody knows when this will happen'.'

By 1987, the answer seemed to be 'soon'. Gillett had already changed direction by releasing an album of contemplative kora, guitar and balafon music from Malian singer Jali Musa Jawara, a brother of Mory Kante. After his interest in funk beats and polyrhythms, he was looking for a 'purer African sound'. 'In France and Germany, music with a substantial Western element goes down well,' he explains. 'Toure Kunda is a good example. British audiences seem to prefer African musicians who play a more African sound. It seems, unfortunately, as if Paul Simon can get away with a crossover where an African musician can't.'[7]

The success of the Bhundu Boys bore out Gillett's belief in the attraction of a 'purer' African sound. By now, the larger companies had started to change their thinking. Shortly after the Earthworks link-up with Virgin, WEA asked Gillett to bring them music from his own areas of interest; the target sales per album would be 100,000. 'It sounds a lot,' he says. 'And it's a target few African artists beyond Sunny Ade and Manu Dibango have achieved. But if you think of selling 20,000 in the UK, 50,000 in the States, 10,000 in Holland and a further 20,000 in Germany, well, it's possible.'

Robert Cray's success in bringing his own brand of blues to a massive new market bears out Gillett's point. By March 1987, Cray's *Strong Persuader* had reached the American top ten album charts, selling over 500,000 copies. 'The fact is that if the big companies put the same weight behind gifted "specialist" artists like Sipho Mabuse as they do behind something supposedly commercial, the music will take off.'

THE BRITISH SCENE

One of the first African musicians to make an impact in Britain was Ambrose Campbell, a guitarist from Lagos who came to London in 1940. Campbell's band played regular gigs in the West End, and an annual show at the Architectural Association in Bedford Square. By 1944 he had formed his West African Rhythm Brothers and was playing to a clientele of African barristers, diplomats, military personnel and businessmen at Club Afrique in Wardour Street. As the *West African Review* put it, Campbell played 'traditional airs' and used a set of drums borrowed from London museums.

The same newspaper charts other momentous events in the early penetration of African music into London: the arrival of E.T. Mensah and his introduction to the stage of the Royal Festival Hall in 1955 by local jazzman Chris Barber; the presentation of Ghanaian Rans Boi singing highlife and calypsos at the Piccadilly Club in the West End in 1956.

For the past forty years, Britain has had a regular community of African musicians working in city clubs, playing either African music or whatever was fashionable at the time. The rock bands who flourished in the late 1960s nodded briefly in the right direction: Gasper Lawal worked with the Rolling Stones, Ghanaian sax player Ray Allen with Traffic. In the world of peace and love, Africa enjoyed a brief, token status.

But if the hippy scene's dalliance with African music offered only the briefest and most self-consciously 'ethnic' of introductions to the wealth of music in Africa itself, it did at least open the door to the first tentative flowering of a British (or perhaps, London) African-music scene. By the early 1970s, the specialist listener who knew where to look could find plenty of sustenance. Fela Ransome Kuti (as he then was) and Ebenezer

Obey were the biggest names in the record racks at Sterns (to the left of the hairdryers and in front of the torch batteries), the Iroko and Roundhouse live-music venues put on regular African-music gigs, and there were at any one time at least six African-orientated bands in the London area – the most deserving of memory being Ginger Johnson's African Drummers, Lord Eric and Agor Mmba, Dudu Pukwana's Spear, the Funkees, Noir and Osibisa. Bands based in Africa itself also visited fairly regularly, playing in the main at dances organized by expatriate social groups (but open to anyone who cared to come along).

Of the various African bands based in Britain, it was Osibisa who looked – briefly – as though they might put their continent's music permanently and substantially on the British map. There can have been few 'progressive rock' fans of the late 1960s/early 1970s who weren't familiar with the band's first album for Island records – and its introductory message about 'criss-cross rhythms that explode with happiness'. Between 1969 and 1972 it really did look as though Osibisa might make it into the mainstream of British pop music in a big way – their albums continued to notch up sizeable sales and their hugely infectious live performances won over many fans to the spirit of Africa. By 1974, however, when the band enjoyed their biggest singles-chart success with 'Who's Got the Paper, I've Got the Match', it was clear that – novelty hits aside – African music was destined to remain on the British sidelines, at least for the foreseeable future.

By the late 1970s, most of the school of 1969 British-based African bands other than Osibisa were inactive. Ginger Johnson had returned to Nigeria, where he intended to set up as either a farmer or a tourist entrepreneur or some combination of the two. Tragically, he wasn't used to the heat of his homeland any more, and died of a heart attack shortly after arriving back there. The Funkees and Noir had taken the high road. Lord Eric, now with Sugumugu, could still be found working the ill-paid, but much-needed, circuit of political benefits, community benefits and children's play schemes. Dudu Pukwana was still keeping on, blowing his heart out in small clubs and colleges, and even getting recognition on the international jazz-festival circuit. And Osibisa were Number One in Poland, kept youthful by the criss-cross rhythms that explode with happiness.

The renaissance of interest and activity in African music in Britain today, in the mid- to late 1980s, seems to have developed quite independently of that first early-1970s flush. By 1982, a rush of new bands had appeared. London saw the creation of the Ivory Coasters and

OK Jive, a mixture of Kenyan and British musicians playing a cross between pop and benga music. Orchestre Jazira aimed at a sound which drew on African and European elements. Kabbala and Native Spirit fused African rhythms with funk. Super Combo came back to life after a period of inaction and, with African Culture, became popular for their Sierra Leonean highlife and rumba. African Connexion mixed soukous with a dash of funk. Alpha Waves and Hi-Life International led the Ghanaian bands, while Orchestre Somo Somo, later Taxi Pata Pata, contributed to a growing Zairean presence, along with Bushmaster, who mixed the Zairean sound with makossa from Cameroon. While most South African musicians based in London concentrated on jazz, Shikisha turned to vocal music and township mbaqanga. George Lee, with his band Anansi, plugged with some success into the jazz-funk circuit. In Hull, My Private War flourished briefly with a spirited mixture of benga and pop, while the Bristol-based Graffi Jazz played makossa and songs by Prince Nico.

The following account takes a closer look at those African-music bands active in Britain in the 1980s whose work can be heard on record. Despite the enthusiastic specialist audience for the music, by the early 1980s it was clear that African musicians hoping to break their music in Britain faced an uphill, almost mountainous, task. Although the press and television might give occasional coverage to well-known artists, such as Fela and Sunny Ade, who were based in Africa, those who had set up shop in Britain were relegated to the periphery, surviving, for the most part, on small-company record deals and a set of promoters the bulk of whose running costs came from the late Greater London Council and other official or semi-official bodies.

But it wasn't all gloom. In 1982 *The Face*, a British music and fashion monthly, pronounced on a likely new trend. 'African Pop Gets Its Turn' ran the headline. The feature that followed announced that: 'Hopes for a major "salsa boom" seem to have diminished recently, despite sell-out London concerts by Tito Puente and Celia Cruz . . . So someone else's music falls prey to the whims of UK musicians and punters, and all things point to African pop as becoming *the next big thing* [their italics].'[1]

For a small number of African-music enthusiasts, *The Face*'s assessment, albeit negative, seemed eminently logical. Rock music, in its more excessive 1970s form, had come and gone. Punk had given way to the equal excesses of the 'new romantics', leaving a gaping hole, to be filled by what? African music was new and danceable. It was attracting the attention of successful artists from Adam Ant to Brian Eno and Robin Scott of M. It seemed easy to believe *The Face*'s somewhat snide assertion that the 'big push from the bush' was at hand. One of the first bands to receive the kind of media attention normally reserved for chart-orientated British pop bands was Orchestre Jazira, a large multi-ethnic, Ghanaian and British outfit based at the Jenako Centre in Hackney. For an African band, Jazira's approach was unorthodox; for a British record company it would later prove impossible to market. Rather than stick to a ready formula, playing highlife, soukous or Afro-funk, Jazira branched out on their own. They had a large, shifting membership with a sound to match. Of the early members, Isaac Tagoe had started drumming classes for the Inner London Education Authority in 1974. Singer Martin Nii-Moi had worked with E.T. Mensah, the king of highlife, between 1969 and 1973, while guitarist Folo Graff joined the band after playing Afro funk and cultural music at home in Freetown, Sierra Leone. The line-up also included a handful of British musicians, notably Ben Mandelson who had first heard African music on acoustic records by Jean Bosco Mwenda and later gone on to study benga music in Kenya. Before joining Orchestra Jazira, Mandelson had played lead guitar with Howard Devoto's Magazine.

From the start, Jazira set out to offer something different. 'We weren't aiming to be a highlife band,' recalls Mandelson. 'We were looking for a new direction and finding that new direction caused considerable pain.'[2] Because Jazira worked on a co-operative basis, conflicts were perhaps inevitable. The band soon developed strong tensions between the traditionalists, favouring a roots approach, and the progressives, who wanted to take Jazira's music into new, uncharted waters. These tensions would later resolve themselves into one of the more interesting albums of the early 1980s.

After making unsuccessful approaches to Island and other major companies, Jazira signed a singles deal with the newly formed independent Earthworks label, run by Jumbo and Mary Vanrenen. The first single, 'Love', backed by 'Dedevi', came out in 1982, offering a mixture of Zairean guitars, blustering horns and a middle section whose melody and rhythms came from a Ga festival of twins held each year in Accra. The approach made sense, mixing accessible English lyrics with Ghanaian roots material. 'We were sending a message to our fellow-Ghanaians,' says Martin Nii-Moi, 'to say that African people here in Europe were still remembered at home.'[3] The B-side used a 12/8 rhythm, the agbadza, which is associated primarily with Ghana's Ewe people. (Although it is played in similar forms throughout west Africa and has also been played in modern, electric form by such bands as Hedzolleh and

Basa Basa Sounds, both of whom made their names at Accra's Napoleon club in the 1970s. Isaac Tagoe explained Jazira's policy as follows: 'A lot of people call our music highlife. But that's quite wrong. Highlife is just one rhythm and we use a whole lot more, everything from nagla, from the northern region, to kpanlogo, a street music played by the Ga people in Accra when there's a full moon. We take the rhythms and write our own songs around them. We mix Ghanaian and Western music without losing the Ghanaian touch.'

Like other African bands, Jazira ran into problems trying to convince record companies and, by extension, the wider public, of the merits of their approach. As Opata Azu, the original bass player, explained, 'Our music was different. It was hard to pin down, to identify, to sell . . .' For some of the band, the difficulties stemmed from a deeper source. 'The companies always play safe,' says Folo Graff. 'I came from one of Britain's first colonies, Sierra Leone. We read about the history of Western music. In church we had hymns, the rest of the time classical music: Handel, Beethoven, Mozart. We knew that the Europeans enjoyed music the same as we did. But here, we have to talk politics, struggle, fights, ask people to come and record us. At the same time, we find record companies have exploited African music in their own way. They see great musicians and say, "If we can get it today at a cheaper rate, we'll take these people." They talk about the language barrier, but that didn't stop them taking the rhythms from us . . .'[4]

It's hard to ignore the frustration and anger in Graff's words. They are as true today as they were four years ago. Little has changed. By 1983, however, Jazira had signed a three-year deal with Beggars Banquet and were looking for a more coherent commercial statement. To create this, they called on Akie Deen, a Sierra Leonean producer based in London. Deen was a dynamic, somewhat elusive man who had made his name in west Africa largely through his work with fellow-Sierra Leonean Bunny Mack, a studio band called Wagadougou, and the creation of a glossy, highly danceable Afro-soca sound that he christened discolypso. For Jazira, Deen created a smooth, mainstream sound. The second single, 'Sakabo', released in 1983, mixed Deen's soca trademark and a polished production with hard bass lines into a nagla rhythm from northern Ghana. In its English lyrics, 'Sakabo' dealt with a situation common in African families, the choice of a career for the sons. As Tagoe explained, 'When the colonialists came to Africa, people were made to believe that their own music was bad. Because of Christianity, if you played cult music, they'd give it discouraging names like juju. The attitude spread to other areas. Everyone had to get white-collar, European jobs. That's why I wrote the song. If parents asked the kid "what job", and he said "musician", he wouldn't have come back into the house. They'd have thrown him out. You had to become a doctor, a lawyer, a white-collar worker, that's all. We feel that because Africa was being underdeveloped, we were given white-collar jobs we didn't need. Instead, the land could have been cultivated, and other forms of technology developed. But what actually happened was that everyone became a boss.'

As a reflection of this cultural dilemma, the band's approach took on a new depth. Rather than displaying African music for a Western market, Jazira worked back to their roots, trying to connect with patterns that had been stamped on and dislocated during colonial times. Highlife, to them, was a recent, colonial product. 'We're trying to bring back the confidence that people lost during those days,' says Tagoe. 'The music that we lost during colonialism. We're bringing back the traditional music, the pride in these lost things.'

From the outset, Jazira was a multi-racial band, combining a Ghanaian rhythm section with a European, all-woman horn section, European drummer and African and European guitarists. But they dismissed any suggestion that the music was being diluted. The key to Jazira, as Graff pointed out, lay in the rhythm section, with its armoury of congas, bells and talking drums. When Jazira wrote songs, they worked the rhythm over and over, developing melody and instrumental parts as offshoots of the rhythm patterns. The nationality or background of the rest of the band was irrelevant. As long as the rhythm machine was working, Jazira functioned.

The band's 1984 album, *Nomadic Activities*, proved a shock. The cover was symbolic. A long string of musicians walking across a desert ridge – in real life, a Surrey gravel pit previously used for a Paul McCartney video. Ben Mandelson's colonial pith helmet and baggy shorts struck a jarring note; his unfolded map symbolized a curious lack of direction. The uncertainty continued with the album itself. Interviews with the band at the time revealed strong tensions. 'We quarrel all the time,' said Folo Graff. 'The essence of Jazira is that there never was a common line, just friction between our differences.' Later, Graff admitted that he felt 'mentally crucified' in the band. He had pushed for a collective album, one to which all the members would contribute equally. The result would reflect the different experiences inside the band. 'I wouldn't say that we were playing African music,' he explains. 'It's just Jazira, a band. It's not African or European. It's made up of different people, some of them from Africa, but our total output is from individuals.'

Graff's individuality came over most strongly in an unsettling number called 'Mr Lulle', a song the band had previously played on percussion and xylophones at a health festival in the Savoy Hotel. Rather than follow the usual practice and work the song out in performance, Jazira took the spiky, unnerving song, with its melody that seemed to have sprung direct from a hand piano, straight into the studio. It remains the album's strongest track. The rest of the numbers veered between roots rhythms, arranged Jazira-style, and the irreverent, occasionally zany touch. Mandelson's 'Winnipeg My Leg', with its Turkish feel and flaying violins, represents the furthest flight into cloud cuckoo land. At the other extreme, the album included the plodding 'Sakabo', and a version of Graff's stage favourite, 'Money', sung in what he calls his Andy Williams voice and fading into a traditional adowa rhythm. Tagoe's beautiful lullaby 'Adowa' offered a moment of calm in an otherwise jostling array of music.

For all its inventiveness, *Nomadic Activities* received a cool reception. People were confused by the variety, the shift of moods. As Mandelson explained: 'The record company would have felt easier with an all-night party record. The full Jazira bit. We just tried to choose things that showed different aspects of the band, to show another dimension.' The worst fault, it seems, was to dispense with the 'happy' sound that had been one of the hallmarks of African pop in Britain since Osibisa days. *Nomadic Activities* with its British setting, British producer, and London-based performers was less of an African dance album, more of a cosmopolitan mixture, which sounded moody, complex and, for public and record company alike, too difficult to handle. 'African bands aren't meant to sound like that,' said Mandelson. 'If "Mr Lulle" had been given to Teardrop Explodes, no one would have batted an eyelid.'

Problems with Beggars Banquet bedevilled the band. Shortly before the album's release, the label had decided to release 'Happy Day' as the single, rather than the band's own choice, 'Mr Lulle'. According to Mandelson, the projected B-side, written by Graff and featuring violin, horns and percussion, disappeared mysteriously at company headquarters. When the band's contract expired, the company chose not to renew it.

Over the next three years, Jazira slowly unwound, as the membership thinned. Folo Graff, one of the key people in forging the Jazira sound, left, followed by Mandelson, drummer Nigel Watson and singer Martin Nii-Moi. The sax players, Jane Shorter and Sophie Hellborg, joined Mory Kante's band in Paris, leaving Jazira to play the club circuit under the continuing leadership of founder member Isaac Tagoe.

Jazira's occasionally self-conscious approach raised the whole question of adaptation, and how far African music needed reworking and structuring for a British audience. An alternative answer to this problem came from the London-based soukous band Orchestre Somo Somo. Where Jazira functioned as an unwieldy co-operative, with everyone pooling ideas, Somo Somo's direction stemmed from one man, Zairean guitarist Mose Se Sengo or 'Fan Fan', and the soukous music that had made him well-known across Africa.

Fan Fan came to London in 1980. It was an unusual move. Most Zairean musicians wanting to push their music in Europe chose Paris or Belgium, both of which have large communities from their former central African colonies. For Fan Fan, London was more important. 'Since I started, the monopoly of world music rested with London,' he says. 'If something sells in London, it sells throughout the world. Paris is nothing. There are masses of Zairean musicians there, many African stars. But not one of them is in the world charts. London is more important for me, but it's tougher as well. If I can achieve something, it'll be easier for the musicians that come afterwards.'[5]

The role of ambassador sits easily on Fan Fan. Born in Kinshasa in 1944, he started his career with a youth band called Ricem Jazz, in 1962, followed by a short stint with Zairean pop singer Pierre Rassin. He then switched to Jazz Baron, where he played alongside guitarist Bavon Marie-Marie, one of the founders of new-wave rumba in Zaire. 'It was the start of the belle epoque,' he recalls. 'Jazz Baron was Bavon's first band. We'd play the whole night, and well-known musicians, like Michelino and Sam Mangwana, would come and play with us.' He goes on to describe how Bavon Marie-Marie left to join Orchestre Negro Succès. Franco provided the instruments. 'That's how the whole youth music started.' Other musicians left Jazz Baron. Some joined Vox Afrique, which then became Festival du Maquisards. Initially, Fan Fan stayed with Jazz Baron, before moving to Orchestre La Revolution, which split up after two years through the rivalry of its two singers, Kwamy and Mujos.

In 1967, Fan Fan joined Zaire's top band, OK Jazz. He made his mark both as a guitarist and a writer of songs like 'Djemelase' and 'Mongando' and others that Sam Mangwana would later sing with the band after his departure. He played on some of Franco's best-known recordings, including 1973's 'Marceline', sharing solo duties with bandleader Franco.

In 1977, Fan Fan and a number of other OK Jazz musicians, including vocalist Youlou Mabiala, now one of Congo Brazzaville's top stars, and

Franco's right-hand man, Lutumba Simarro, decided to make some clandestine recordings under the name Orchestre Mi. 'Franco was furious,' says Fan Fan. 'Around that time he was convinced that the musicians who had come from Congo Brazzaville were out to break up OK Jazz. He was determined that the Congolese musicians should leave. So Youlou went. I was mortified. Because I was Zairean, I was allowed to stay. It was unjust, so I left too.'

Shortly afterwards Fan Fan, along with Youlou Mabiala, formed the first Orchestre Somo Somo. It was an ill-fated move. The band lacked instruments and had to borrow them. Then Youlou was involved in a car crash. He needed money and persuaded Franco to readmit him to OK Jazz, where he became, once again, the star attraction. Fan Fan himself was invited back, but refused. 'It would have been shameful,' he says. He sought the advice of Joseph Kabasele, the founder of African Jazz. 'He advised against it,' says Fan Fan. 'He said I'd look ridiculous.' So Fan Fan decided to leave Zaire. He travelled first to Zambia, staying there till 1978. The following year he left for Tanzania, where he ran into an old friend, the fellow-Zairean Mzee Makassy. At that time, his band, Orchestre Makassy, was in disarray. Fan Fan's arrival gave them a new lease of life and the band went on to record the original, highly plaintive version of Fan Fan's theme tune, 'Mosese 2000'. The song later appeared as 'Mosese' on Makassy's *Agwaya* album recorded for Virgin records in 1982, by which time Fan Fan was in Kenya.

'For me, OK Jazz was the belle epoque,' says Fan Fan. 'In Kinshasa, life was easy. When I left, everything changed. During my travels, I met different people with whom I had little rapport. It was difficult to adapt. In Zambia, for example, the musicians were nothing like the Zaireans, although the situation improved in Tanzania and Kenya. The problem was not that the musicians copied Zairean music, but that they copied it so badly.' In Kenya, he met up with Robin Scott, whose group M had previously had a hit with the single 'Pop Music'. They worked on two singles, 'Jalenga' and Fan Fan's own composition 'Africa'. Scott suggested that Fan Fan travel to Britain to launch his career. By 1984, Fan Fan was playing with Mwana Musa in his London-based African Connexion, and later set up a new chapter of Somo Somo.

London had an interesting effect on Fan Fan's music. He remains to this day a classic rumba guitarist, immersed in the rhythms and guitar styles made famous by OK Jazz. Franco remains for him a kind of idol, and through him he traces a direct line back to the old roots guitarist, Bowane, who introduced a strong element of folklore into the Zairean acoustic rumba. 'Franco inherited his style from Bowane,' he explains. 'It's the same thing. Franco simply modernized the music. When Wendo played the guitar it was pure accompaniment. With Bowane it was different. He was one of the first people to play a solo style.'

Although Fan Fan remains a purist at heart, his band, Somo Somo, soon developed a London style that replaced the sweetness of the old music with a rush of fast, muscular new arrangements. The first album, *Somo Somo*, crystallized the new sound with a hectic pace, repetitive and stinging guitar lines, and a mass of blurting saxophones, whose punch and attack suggested some mid-sixties soul review. 'I wanted to make a music that moved,' says Fan Fan. 'At home, I could always count on the slow rumba. But in Britain, the whole temperament is different. People need something they can dance to.' The result was a new, breakneck soukous, one updated folk rhythm on 'Jammy Jammy', and a new version of 'Mosese 2000', brought to life with a roaring tempo and some abrasive sax playing from Stuart Boardman and John Glyn on baritone.

The shift on Somo Somo's 1986 follow-up, *Paris*, was remarkable. Where the London album had expressed the brash, experimental side of Fan Fan's music, he now set out to produce an album that would have greater appeal for the Zairean community living in France. To achieve the necessary sound, Fan Fan left Somo Somo behind, and recorded with a group of session men in Paris. Among them was Jean Papy, one of Zaire's best session singers, and a group of musicians who had made their names with Tabu Ley and Jean Bokelo. After the hectic pace of the first album, Paris offered a sweeter, more polished mixture of soukous and slow rumba, Fan Fan's preferred style, while the band later went on to release a dub version of the closing track 'Poleni'.

A number of other bands followed Somo Somo's approach, and stayed within the broad confines of well-known musical styles. A prime west African example comes from Hi-Life International, who mixed Ghanaian dance-band highlife with occasional soukous tracks. The band came together in 1982, around guitarist Kwabena Kwarteng; Kofi Adu, one of London's best kit drummers; bass player Herman Asafo-Agyei; and trumpeter Stu Hamer, who had played with a string of jazzmen including Dizzy Gillespie. For Kwarteng, who wrote all the tracks on the band's debut album, *Travel and See*, highlife, with its Western feel and jazzy horn arrangements, was an obvious choice. Its lowly status in Ghana, where the old big bands had long since lost their following to the rootsier guitar bands, made little difference. Britain was a new market, and the music was nothing if not accessible.

Travel and See came out on the Sterns label in 1983. It was distinguished by strong melodies, a stand-out being 'Salaam Alekum', an Islamic greeting already immortalized by Dr Nico in the late 1960s. If not exactly breaking barriers, Hi-Life seemed anxious to shake them slightly. They incorporated soukous and agbadza into the mix, plus 'Salaam Alekum', which was written in Hausa, a language spoken throughout west Africa. Despite this, the album was marred by poor vocals, which a roomful of echo did little to camouflage.

The under-produced first album gave way to the polished *Na Wa for You*, which was released in 1985, shortly after Hi-Life's debut single, 'Come to Africa'. The band's approach had changed. After a straight presentation of west African music, they were ready for something more adventurous. The single, written by Herman Asafo-Agyei, had a heavier funk feel, with pronounced bass and straighter percussion. Dennis Bovell, who had produced a number of London-based reggae and pop bands, plus a live Fela set from Amsterdam, took over the production, creating a spacey dub feel, laced with sudden echo and flurries of brass. The expensive new production took the band into new areas, but nowhere near the charts. On the album the band produced themselves, creating a natural, unfussy sound for a group of songs that ranged from highlife-funk to soukous and the middle-of-the-road pop of Stu Hamer's 'Seventeen'. Fusion music – the linking of African forms with pop or funk – raises strong passions. When Ghanaian artists like George Darko cross highlife with funk or soca, as in 'Moni Palava', it is a reasonable bet that true highlife lovers will dismiss the results as a sell-out, or see it as a distortion imposed from the outside by European record companies. Hi-Life International see their own musical progress in a different light. Herman Asafo-Agyei recalls that Bovell was chosen as a way of updating the band's sound and linking it up with parallel developments in pop and funk. 'The industry's always on the look-out for new material,' he explains. 'A producer adds a new dimension. He's in touch with all the new technology. If you want to stay with the traditional, that's fine, producers aren't necessary. But if you want to get in touch with what's happening, they can do that. Even then the music doesn't necessarily change. It's still African, and will continue to be. If you can put in a Linn drum, it doesn't necessarily change the music. It simply updates it, enabling the musicians to compete with the demands of the music industry. That's why we called in Dennis Bovell.'[6]

On the subject of fusion, Herman is equally clear-sighted. 'When people attack African musicians for bringing funk into their music, they fail to take into account the society that the musicians grew up in. I started listening to music in Ghana's disco age. Life in Accra was no different from life in London. It was every bit as fast. My whole generation listened to Santana and James Brown. I still like to listen to rock guitar. It's infuriating when someone tells me what sort of artist he feels I should be. What he's really saying is, "You guys just keep to African music. Play it the way we want. If we want to listen to funk, we'll buy a Cameo record." This ignores the musician's true interest, which is to reach as wide an audience as possible.'

By 1986, Hi-Life had seen a number of changes. Trumpeter Frank Williams had left to set up his own band, Kintone. Stu Hamer left, along with bass player Herman Asafo-Agyei, whose funk-oriented band Native Spirit, formed in 1986, provided a touring band for Ghanaian highlife singer Pat Thomas. Charles Kodjo, a singer with Ghana's famed Ramblers Dance Band, took over lead vocals.

By then it seemed as if the band, like Orchestre Jazira, had passed through their experimental phase and fallen back on the tried and tested. For other bands and musicians though, the jostling of styles and sounds became a permanent way of life as the search for a winning formula continued. One of the most adept at reworking African sounds for a predominantly British audience was Mwana Musa, the Sierra Leonean founder member of African Connexion. The band's debut single, 'C'est La Dance' came out on Oval records in 1984, mixing straight pop melodies into a crisp Zairean soukous. On the two subsequent singles, Musa created a stronger funk feel, using a hard Linn drum beat for the Zairean-flavoured follow-up, 'Dancing on the Sidewalk', and opting for straight funk vocals, with Zairean guitars and a chanted African introduction for the more commercial 'Tell Mandela'.

Mwana Musa's skill at switching the genres reflects a long knowledge of the British scene, his work with London-based reggae and funk bands and his own perception of the way African music is going. 'Getting the right blend is the thing,' he says. 'For me, it's relatively easy. Like other members of African Connexion, we've all lived in the West. It's like a chemical experiment. We know exactly what we want and we can put it together to get that result. Most African musicians have been running away from their roots. We've worked hard to keep our identity. We haven't compromised, just put the music in a new form so that other people can get into it.'[7]

The mixture of African music with Western technology is vital if the music is to survive – in the West at any rate. Musa singles out highlife stars like C.K. Mann and Osita Osadebe, people whose music has suffered simply because they are unable to update it, put it into a broader, international context. 'It has to adapt,' he insists. 'We can't go on reading the old books. Music advances with time. Some people say the music has to stay "African". I think it will always be African. But it has to go forward. I introduce new patterns and rhythms, and work with musicians like Ray Carless, from Jamaica, and British producers like David Toop and Steve Beresford. It's the only way forward.'

African Connexion take soukous, from Zaire, as their starting-point. Zairean music was always popular in Sierra Leone, and Musa grew up in Freetown on a late-1960s diet of Franco; Dr Nico, a particular favourite in Sierra Leone; Tabu Ley; Orchestre Negro Succès, later Orchestre Veve and Bella Bella. Fourteen years after leaving Sierra Leone, he still looks on the Zaireans as great innovators. 'They'd sooner compromise than lose their music. In the 1970s, the Zaireans introduced echo, phaser, repeater and phlangers into the music. It may have held it back artistically, but the music still sold.' As an example of Zairean flexibility, he cites the Quatre Etoiles' 'Mama Iye Ye', a Paris rerecording of a track made famous by Orchestre Bella Bella in the early 1970s. 'They changed the rhythm slightly, mixing the Zairean beat with a reggae feel, which comes through in the bass lines and the chopping rhythm guitar. But it's still a recognizable Zairean sound.'

Like most Zairean bands, African Connexion developed their own dance, the kwanza kwanza, which featured in 'C'est La Dance'. The track remains one of Musa's favourites, along with 'E Siddon Pan Am', the B-side of the follow-up, 'Dancing on the Sidewalk'. 'On that one, the guitar just flowed,' he says. 'The rhythms criss cross each other, while the vocal carries on. Tee-Jay, the guitarist, is playing something different. The lead guitarist, Len Jones, just holds the beat. Listen to "E Siddon Pan Am", and "C'est La Dance". They're almost identical except that "E Siddon" is more controlled. "C'est La Dance" is wild . . .' With the second single, African Connexion moved from soukous to a second, faster Zairean beat, the cavacha, a tighter, funkier drum sound. 'We used the funk drop beat,' he explains. 'But everything about the guitar was African. The whole idea was to make the music faster and more furious.' Cavacha held important associations for the band, being the beat that gave Orchestre Shama Shama a massive cross-African hit of the same name, and helped launch Zaiko Langa Langa as Zaire's top and wildest youth band. British sales of African Connexion's version proved disappointing and in 1985, African Connexion and Oval parted company.

The lack of success proved puzzling. The blame, Musa feels, lies partly with African musicians living in London who prefer to fight among themselves than to approach the music business in a united, purposeful way. And partly with the companies who, as Paul Simon's *Graceland* shows, can deal with African music when it is presented by a well-known artist, but not by the artists themselves. 'There seems to be a policy of keeping black musicians out of the scene,' he explains. 'Possibly because they represent a threat to the livelihood of white bands. Rather than sign on black bands, they take a few musicians and mix them into other bands. It's a way of saying "We keep control". Most black musicians know it. They want to break away but can't. The answer, I feel, is for black musicians to come together, to set up our own companies, or at least to work out a compromise with other companies so that we can get our own stuff out. But we can't at the moment operate independently. We need white record manufacturers as much as they need us, perhaps more. And we also need access to the media.'

By 1985, it became clear that African Connexion had other problems beyond lack of media access. Always heavier on individual rather than corporate talent, the band started to disintegrate. After a trip to Sierra Leone, Mwana Musa re-formed African Connexion and, with Carless, Toop and Beresford, set up Sidewinder records, with the aim of creating 'a new phase in African recording'. Using a selection of equipment that included a Roland and Yamaha DX7, Musa aimed at rhythmically accessible sound based less on electric guitars, more on what he calls 'that mysterious African feel, a combination of woodblock and marimba, the pre-guitar sound that brings our past into the present'.[8] The marimba sound, heard on 'Dancing on the Sidewalk', and the 1986 'Tell Mandela' was already winning favour with other African artists, among them Hugh Masekela, who put it to good use on 'Don't Go Lose It Baby', and Tabu Ley and M'Bilia Bel, who applied something similar to 'Cadence Mundanda' from the *Keyna* album.

Other African Connexion members went their separate ways. Otis Thompson, an outstanding singer, left to form his own Afro-soca band, Sayinoh, later releasing the cassette album *Welcome*. Bosca Banks, the drummer, recorded a soca-flavoured single, 'We'll be Together', for Oval. By this time, guitarist Abdul Tee-Jay had already left to form his own band, African Culture. In many ways, Tee-Jay's own initiative proved the most interesting. By the time African Culture had formed, he had already recorded two singles. 'Salima' and 'Agooda Medley' explored a rich vein of Sierra Leonean street music. Since the early 1960s, the country had been dominated by Congolese rumba beamed up the coast by Radio Brazzaville, and played by local bands. It was fashionable, but inaccurate, to claim that Sierra Leone, like other Zairean 'satellites', had no music of its own. Tee-Jay's London productions pointed away from the Zairean rumba and Afro-soca, the favourite crossover material for Sierra Leonean musicians, and back to a deeper, indigenous sound. The Agooda Society is the name given to a young people's cultural association which holds open-air dances and celebrations in the capital, Freetown. The chief instrument connected with the society is the dumbu lekun, a frame drum. For his own medley, Tee-Jay took a selection of agooda songs which had been well-known since the 1940s, and added guitars, trumpet and keyboards to a vigorous vocal line supplied by Liberian Miatta Fambouleh.

Apart from his early interest in agooda music, Tee-Jay also came under the spell of electric guitarists like the Zairean Dr Nico and a local musician, Freddie Greene, an early member of the top Sierra Leonean band Super Combo Kings. His parents disapproved, and smashed the first guitar that he bought. Finally his mother bowed to the inevitable, and produced an electric guitar with which Tee-Jay and two friends, the National Combo, would invade the stage when other Freetown bands were playing. In the early 1970s, Tee-Jay studied economics in America and joined a top-40 funk band, Spice, before arriving in Britain and joining Mwana Musa and Otis Thompson in Masala Kotoko, an early forerunner of African Connexion. The band recorded at Eddy Grant's north London studio, releasing the merengue 'Dis World', before breaking up, Thompson going on to record 'My Woman', and Tee-Jay working as a session man for Sierra Leonean producer Akie Deen.

After leaving his next band, African Connexion, Tee-Jay released a further song, 'Okoti Movement', part of a live album recorded at the Bass Clef club in London, and continued his exploration of Sierra Leonean rhythms. Among them were the matoma beat, played by the Limba people, and featured in a song called 'Ro Manke', and two further songs, 'African Girl' and 'Teti', based on the milo jazz percussion music of Freetown. Although African Culture also played soukous, Tee Jay remains rooted in street music and the early guitarists who brought it into their repertoire. 'These palm-wine musicians, men like Ebenezer Calendar – one of the first people to mix guitar and milo jazz – they were the true pioneers, just like the old blues musicians. They'd drink, smoke, and weren't serious. But they were the real originators, like the griots.'[9] The argument about roots and authenticity is one that has dominated discussion about a disparate range of musics, from traditional jazz to rhythm and blues and reggae. With African music, the discussion continues. A crossover sound like Hugh Masekela's *Techno-Bush* or George Darko's *Hi-Life Time* is seen as a dilution, something that takes away the spirit of the original sound. Yet there is no denying the ability of the crossover to attract a different, and wider, audience. The best example comes from France, where Toure Kunda reached sales of 100,000 for their *Sambala* album. In Britain, the Ghanaian Afro-funk band Kabbala achieved a notable success with their single 'Ashewo Ara' in 1982. Kabbala's natural constituency lies in clubland where their adaptation of funk to Ghanaian roots rhythms has won them a relatively large following. 'Ashewo Ara' was based on a music peculiar to eastern Ghana, the rhythm being beaten out by tailors on tobacco tins. The flipside, 'Voltan Dance', linked a jazzy horn-and-guitar arrangement to a rhythm of the Volta region. From there, Kabbala recorded three glossily commercial singles, from the chanted 'Yamba Osei' to the cooler 'Get Back to Summer' and 'What Love is'. Despite attracting the attention of several large companies, the band lacked what they most needed, an album deal. This they attribute to caution on the part of the companies. 'Once Island had finished with Sunny Ade, no one wanted to know,' says founder member Michael Osapanin.

On record, Kabbala sound like an instant crossover. Yet their musical direction took years to cement. Michael and his brother Isaac Osapanin came to Britain in 1964 as students. He played intermittently over the next ten years, forming Double U with his brother. 'We'd been bashing away for years,' he recalls. 'We'd do free gigs and even hired clubs to perform there. I thought there must be something wrong somewhere. So I spoke to Isaac, who was doing engineering at the time, and he agreed to pack it up so that we could concentrate on this thing properly.'[10] Their direction changed slowly. In the early days, Osapanin had been playing highlife, classical and jazz. He now looked around for a new direction. 'Back in Ghana, highlife was for the educated classes. But we couldn't do traditional music. That was too "uneducated". During Nkrumah's cultural revolution all that changed. It was from there that we took our inspiration, to go back and work with the occult music, connected with the funerals, birth and initiation ceremonies, and various occult practices.'

Kabbala's current music illustrates the paradox, which purists find hard to swallow, that a modern, polished and Western-sounding music can be strongly, possibly *more* strongly rooted in traditional music than older forms. 'The great thing about Kabbala,' says Michael Osapanin, 'is that someone from Accra will listen and say "Kpanlogo". Someone from the north will say, "These guys are playing our music." While others will recognize adowa and konkomba. What we're really doing is going back to the source of the music. The Europeans enjoy the sound, the Africans identify the region. It combines the lot. The most important thing is that it does go to the roots. You'd have to go to the villages, not the cities, to hear what we're playing.'

The Osapanin brothers, with their polished funk sound, were just two of the musicians who have played and recorded in London. Ray Allen came out of the great highlife bands of the day and found himself in the strange sideline position of playing sessions with well-known rock and jazz bands. In Ghana, Allen is remembered as a veteran of the great Uhuru Dance Band. By the 1970s he was playing with Hi-Tension, Traffic and Jim Capaldi. In 1978, he turned back to Africa and founded Ojah, a London highlife and jazz outfit. This evolved a year later into Alpha Waves, which featured Kofi Adu on drums and Will Stallybrass on guitar. The band's repertoire, which included versions of old classics like 'Yaa Amponsah' and 'Give Me Your Heart', breathed the fragrance of golden-age highlife. But a lack of live performances gradually sapped the band's momentum.

George Lee is another highlifer whose roots go back to west Africa of the 1950s. To the jazz-funk audience, Lee is best known for his 1984 hit 'Sea Shells'. The idea of a club full of people dancing to the sax sound of a man who was playing bebop and highlife thirty years ago affords him a certain wry amusement. Lee's first musical inspiration came from the old palm-wine guitarists and the dance bands of the 1950s, led by E.T. Mensah. 'When he was playing, I'd jump the fence to see him,' he recalls.[11] But it was Tricky Johnson, Mensah's guitarist, who gave him his first tuition. At school, Lee had learnt the fife. Under Johnson's tutelage, and inspired by his vast collection of 78s, he switched to saxophone. He was later dubbed 'the man who came out of the bush playing bebop'.

Lee's first break came with the Star Aces, who were playing at a wake. 'The alto player went to the toilet,' says Lee. 'The players were shouting "Hey, George, come on." I got up on stage, started playing and could hear the crowd saying "The band is sweet today-O." The guy came out of the toilet and left.' From there Lee went to Accra, where he joined the Delta Dandies. 'They were all Nigerian in those days,' he says. 'Few of them were playing highlife, just mambo and jazz. In fact, what they were really doing, was playing African music without realizing it, thinking they were borrowing it from somewhere else.' After the Delta Dandies, Lee joined the Alkot Dandies, toured Nigeria, then returned to Ghana where he joined Louis Armstrong and leading Ghanaian musicians for a tour of the country. He left for Britain in 1962 and spent the next twenty-two years playing jazz and funk, returning occasionally to Ghana. In 1984, he toured Mozambique with Chris McGregor and his Brotherhood of Breath, and later set up a studio in Swaziland.

Lee's music draws on various sources, but the rhythms remain African. 'What do you expect of me as a Ghanaian?' he says. 'I play jazz but most of my compositions are typically Ghanaian. As for roots, what do you mean? All I know is that every country has certain authentic rhythm structures and it's up to the musician to make use of whatever he's exposed to, whatever he feels strongly about.'

Lee's own 'rhythmic structures' remain a 'trade secret'. Agbadza is part of it, he explains, plus other Ewe rhythms which give the foundations for a set of jazz and funk top lines. The finished work comes over as a fusion, a welding together of sympathetic elements.

At the other extreme we find an artist like Eddie Edem, who follows a tradition of Nigerian highlife music that stretches back to the 1930s. The root of Edem's dance-band style lies in the itembe street music played by the musicians of the Efik people on a set of square-framed samba drums and shekeres. 'It's heavy cultural stuff,' says Edem. S.S. Peters was one of the first people to introduce the guitar into itembe music. His greatest hit, 'Canaan Canaan Calabar', was later covered in dance-band style by E.T. Mensah, while Ambrose Campbell, the Nigerian bandleader, produced a similar cover. In the 1970s, Iyang Henshaw and Kingsley Bassey continued the Efik highlife tradition, although both men are now dead: Henshaw of a heart attack, Bassey in a motor accident.

Edem started work as a merchant seaman with the Elder Dempster line, whose ships sailed between Britain and the coast of west Africa. By the early 1950s, he had jumped ship and settled in London, where he worked as a trumpeter in Ambrose Campbell's band. 'In Nigeria, I was put off the trumpet,' he says. 'It sounded dry, and lacked soul. It was mostly played by people in the brass bands. But when friends played me records by Clifford Brown, I changed my mind.'[12] After leaving Campbell in the early 1960s, Edem worked with African theatre groups and the free-jazz People's Band and, in 1973, Steel and Skin. Like George Lee, he had spent a long time playing other people's music. The period ended in 1983 when Lee guested on 'Row Your Boat', a highlife EP recorded by Edem and his new band, Foreign Exchange. Apart from the itembe-highlife sound, heard on the title track, Edem also reworked a set of deeper cultural rhythms associated with the Ekpe secret society. The sound was directly linked to the society ceremonial. As Edem explains, the Ekpe society, at full strength, operated a form of local government, laying down and enforcing laws governing private and public behaviour, even civic responsibilities. 'If the society said "clean the streets", everyone cleaned the streets,' he explains. A masked dancer, accompanied by singers and percussionists, represented the society's public face: his job being to impress or reprimand the local citizenry. Edem's Efik rhythms have their own distinctive dance movements. 'Our style is unique,' he says. 'The movement is like a wave. We move the body in a smooth, fluid sort of way.' No such fluid movements attended Edem's own career. Faced by a lack of money and management, Foreign Exchange, like a number of other London-based African bands, achieved little in the way of popular recognition.

In France, the mixture of musicians from Africa and the French West Indies, and the resultant mixture of styles, has been one of the great developments of the 1980s. In Britain, progress towards a black music linking Africa and the West Indies has been slow. But some notable first shots have been fired, among them producer Dennis Bovell's work with Hi-Life International and his production of a live album from Fela Kuti. A small group of African musicians have also bridged the two communities with a sound that embraces African and Caribbean rhythms. Producer Akie Deen developed his 'discolypso' sound, which hit its peak with his studio bands like Wagadougou and Sierra Leonean singer Bunny Mack, and found its biggest market in west Africa. Fellow-Sierra Leoneans Otis Thompson and Bosca Banks, both former members of African Connexion, created their own highly accessible variations: Thompson recording 'My Woman', and 'Let Me Love You', plus a cassette album with his band Sayinoh; Banks releasing an Oval single 'We'll be Together', which later featured on the Street Sounds label's *New Sounds of Africa* album.

Further fusions developed around Ghanaian singer Thomas Frempong, who arrived in London in 1982. In Ghana, Frempong had built up a considerable reputation for his work with Dr K. Gyasi, the highlife doctor and promoter of a new form of Ashanti music, 'sikyi highlife', in the mid-1970s. After leaving Gyasi, Frempong produced the solo album *Sasakroma*, and toured Britain with Eric Agyeman and A.B. Crentsil in a new band called Highlife Stars. While playing with highlife singer A.K.

Yeboah at a party in Barnet, north London, he came to the attention of fellow-Ghanaian record producer Anthony Roberts, who promptly signed him to his Asona label. Roberts's idea was to take Frempong away from the 'roots' sound into a more accessible crossover mould. Their first collaboration, *Aye Yi*, 1985, was originally written as a sikyi album, with minor chords and plaintive harmonies. But what came out bore little relation to the original concept. The finished album nods in several different directions, from roots to modern crossover. The opening title track mixes the traditional yaa amponsah guitar rhythm with hi-tech Linn drums and programmed studio sound. The second track, 'Odo Pa', uses scratched guitars and rapid percussion rhythms to create a virtual soca track. 'Since 1983 highlife has changed,' says producer Anthony Roberts. 'People like George Darko and Kantata have developed a new sound, in which the rhythms and drum patterns are increasingly European.'[13] The injecting of a central, hard funk beat into a network of finely balanced African rhythms goes back beyond Darko and Kantata to the pioneering figure of Pat Thomas and his milestone album *1980*. Since then a range of other artists, from King Sunny Ade to Bembeya Jazz, have embraced the electro sound, using it as an addition to an existing electric band. Frempong went further, towards total programming, with his 1986 *Anansi Shuttle* album, where the percussion, bass and keyboards were largely synthesized. The content of the album continued along the lines established by *Aye Yi*. Frempong kept one sikyi track, the bulk of the rest falling into the new crossover style laid down, perhaps with greater success, on the previous album. The album also included two dub tracks.

Frempong's approach sets him at odds with many of his Ghanaian colleagues, from whom London offers pressing facilities for albums that have already been recorded and put on master tapes in Ghana or the Côte d'Ivoire. For many, the system of the multiple release still obtains. Where royalties are virtually non-existent, the musician relies on a heavy output, maybe three or four albums a year, selling them for single sums to a number of small record labels. Career development goes by the board. Frempong, with his single-minded producer, releases one album a year, and works from an analysis of other developments in the British market. 'It's essentially a marketing problem,' says Roberts. 'And we're faced with a mass of people who, at the moment, don't really want to know about African music. Our aim is to Europeanize the music, while keeping the lyrics in Twi. But the most important thing is to show that you like and respect your own music. It's no good putting out rubbish and trying to sell that. We've got to respect our music, and develop it. Only then can we expect other people to enjoy it properly.'

Roberts's view finds echoes among other African musicians living in Britain. As refugees from apartheid, South African musicians have been coming to Britain since the 1960s, among them such talents as Dudu Pukwana, Julian Bahula of Malombo, and Lucky Ranku. With the exception of sax player Dudu Pukwana who shortly after his arrival released a kwela album, the musicians have played jazz.

One of the few groups to show interest in the mbaqanga, regarded as a humbler, low-class music by some, is Shikisha, an all-woman trio whose repertoire stretches from the gumboot dance to traditional Zulu Shangaan and Sotho music set to electric backing tapes. The band comprises Julia Mathunjwa, who started her career singing in a Zulu version of *Macbeth*, Betty Hlela and Nomsa Caluza, both of whom worked with the Dima Sisters, a warm-up act for the celebrated Mahotella Queens.

The three musicians came together in *Ipi Tombi*, a mid-1970s South African musical berated in the West for its cosy view of South Africa. When the musical toured Europe all three left, but more out of boredom than dislike of the controversy that accompanied the production. Since then they have recorded one single, released in South Africa, and returned home once, to find their own brand of mbaqanga sadly out of fashion. In the South Africa of the 1980s, electro funk has gripped the youth, creating new stars such as Brenda and the Big Dudes, Sipho Mabuse and Margaret Singana. Shikisha went looking for Mahlathini, the top bass groaner, but he was nowhere to be seen.

South African mbaqanga has had a further influence on Sanko, a Lesotho band who came to Britain shortly after the release of their debut album, *Sankomota*. Sanko's history goes back to 1976 when, under the name Uhuru, or Freedom, they crossed into South Africa, and were promptly deported, partly because of their name, partly because of their lyrics. The route south has been well trodden: South Africa attracts large numbers of migrant workers from Lesotho, and Johannesburg studios do steady business with the Lesotho music recorded by migrants in Johannesburg and offering nostalgic reminders of a largely rural way of life that the migrants have left behind. 'At home, there is virtually no modern music,' says lead guitarist and vocalist Frank Leepa. Sanko's prototype takes Lesotho's traditional choral music, retracing its strong harmonies and melodies on a modern — sax, guitar and keyboards — line-up. The music has a strong mbanqanga, and at times, jazz, flavour, but its heart still lies in the old choral harmonies.

Sanko's urge to modernize and repackage a traditional music strikes a chord with the large majority of African bands who see their heritage not as an unchanging, frozen entity but as something that changes, and re-establishes itself in a range of new fusions and crossovers. For Kintone, a band made up of South African and Caribbean musicians, South African jazz provided the starting-point for an album, *Going Home*, and a 1986 single 'State of Emergency', which recasts the root music in a variety of tones and moods. The album presented a soft, at times reflective edge; the single was altogether harder and more demanding. For saxophonist Frank Williams, the music may be fusion, but it has lost none of its African qualities. 'Music changes all the time,' he says. 'Even traditional music doesn't stand still. It's alive, it changes. If it doesn't, it's a music in the doldrums, something that everyone repeats, contributing nothing.'

The failure of African bands to cut across commercially comes as no surprise in some quarters. Kwesi Owusu, of the poetry and music collective African Dawn, explains, 'Many African musicians in Britain are like factory workers. The company decide how to produce the music and how to distribute it. African musicians become the wallflowers of the system.'[14] African Dawn's response has been to take the process into their own hands by creating their own label, and a sound that brings together traditions kept apart in colonial times. For African Dawn, a strong umbilical link draws together rap and dub poetry, the public commentaries of the Trinidadian calypso singers and the work of the African griots. Their own aim is to cross the colonial frontiers, bringing together disparate rhythms, from calypso to roots west African percussion, and instruments like the kora, mbira and atentenben drums, not normally heard together.

The dislocation of African culture, first experienced during slavery and colonial rule, continues today through the indirect arm of big business. 'It's the companies who label and classify us,' says Owusu. 'But African artists are now refusing this. First and foremost we represent a majority tradition. Pierre Akendengue is not just a musician. He's a poet as well. There are a whole lot of people, from the Last Poets to Gil Scott-Heron, who have worked in the same tradition. It's a mainstream African tradition. What we're doing with African Dawn is to offer cultural resistance to this worldwide white definition . . .'

For Stuart Boardman, a founder member of the Ivory Coasters and later sax player with Somo Somo, the problem lies largely with record-company timidity. 'When anything new happens, they're always frightened, at first, and try to avoid it,' he says. 'No one really wants to be at the mercy of something they can't control or understand. So they fight shy.

Commercial acceptance only comes later, when the companies learn how to copy the music and produce their own "plastic replicas". We had it with the punk scene: the market was flooded with pseudo-Sex Pistols. Even Tin Pan Alley was churning out punk songs.'

Though the Ivory Coasters were in the vanguard of the early 1980s British-based African-orientated band scene, they never themselves regarded the band as wholly and exclusively part of it. Stuart Boardman explains: 'We've never, even when we were working hardest on learning African music, tried to sell ourselves as an African band, whether we've had one African in the line-up, no Africans or three Africans. We're not an African band because most of us aren't Africans, none of us lives in Africa, we don't play in Africa and our music reflects, I think, living in London. I mean, I might prefer living in Zaire, but I don't. So we're not trying to defend anything, we're definitely not purists. All we're trying to do is play something we enjoy.'

Dave Draper expressed a similar sentiment when describing the origins of the Coasters in a 1982 interview. 'The African connection wasn't planned. We first started playing it when we were stuck for material a couple of years ago. We heard some records and liked it and thought, "OK, we'll do a bit of that." It grew from there. I got into African music myself because I was bored with rock, and started checking out the international folk section in my local public library's record department.'

The acuity of these sentiments notwithstanding, the Coasters turned out some of the most stimulating and innovative 'African' music of their era. Particularly memorable in their set were the mutant-African numbers 'Mungaka Makossa', 'The Bongo that Ate Pik Botha' and 'Scatter' (the latter, loosely based on Fela Kuti's 'Everything Scatter', inspiring Claude Deppa to flights of indescribable, aberrant beauty). Other outstanding band originals included 'High Times' and 'Soma'.

The Coasters' refusal to be pigeonholed as 'An African Band' exacerbated the difficulties they found, early on, in acquiring a recording deal with an established British label – and was a factor in their decision to record and release through their own label, Politone.

'In looking at the difficulty we've found in finding a deal,' explained Boardman, 'you have to start with the way record companies see African pop music in general. They see it essentially as a curiosity, in the same way they used to see Jamaican music. Occasionally something would get released, but it was a curiosity, a novelty thing. They weren't attempting to turn anyone into a major international recording artist. It's the same with African music now [1984]. I mean, Island have done a good job promoting Sunny Ade, but they are patently not interested in anybody else, neither African artists nor artists living over here.

'On top of that, we have a problem because we're not an all-African band in terms of personnel, so we don't fit into the "Ethnic Curiosity" picture. And even the clothes they like wearing – like Claude, who's lived here eight years, wears the sort of clothes anyone else in London might wear. He'd feel daft going onstage in African gear just to impress somebody.

'At the same time, record companies don't see us as being commercial enough, a straight pop band. Of course, they may be right about that – but obviously, we don't agree. We believe we play music that can sell, if it's promoted.'

Optimism, sometimes misguided, has been one of the hallmarks of the African scene in Britain. In 1982, Boardman explains, Jazira received a lot of attention but fell down when poor marketing failed to break their music outside a small, largely self-contained market of African-music fans. The same fate befell Somo Somo, who remained very much the property of the African scene. 'The music has got to be directed at a far bigger audience than is happening at the moment,' he explains. 'There's a whole independent market out there, people who buy New Order and Wall of Voodoo albums and who keep up with the indies charts and are interested in a wider range of music than the large companies offer. The problem is that at the moment they just don't know about African music. The small labels have got to want to sell more records.'

Boardman takes a realistic view of the limitations of African pop. Only a small proportion could ever be considered top-twenty material. The rest keeps its appeal for the dancefloor, where it offers a ready dance music for a small-club crowd turning increasingly to electro, hip hop, salsa and other sideline musics.

Much of the impetus comes from the enthusiasm of the disc jockeys, one of the best known being Dave Hucker, who played his first gig at London's Sol y Sombra club in March 1982. Originally Hucker was a Tamla Motown enthusiast. He then listened to American blues, followed by ska and early reggae, before hearing his first African record, Fela Kuti's *Lady*, in 1975. 'I got it from a computer operator who'd been working in Nigeria,' he recalls. 'It was fantastic, revolutionary. I'd never heard anything like it. The only possible point of contact was James Brown. Fela sounded a bit like him at times. Maybe James Brown sounded a bit like Fela – whichever way you want to look at it.'

Hucker was not alone in his interest. He was joined by a small section of British clubgoers who were looking for new, fresh forms of dance music. 'The thing was that people had outgrown their interest in American dance music,' he explains. 'In the 1970s, soul had been a fringe music. But by the time I opened at the Sol y Sombra, it was middle-of-the-road. The whole of the top ten was soul. Everyone was playing it. So people were prepared to open their minds a bit. Up to that point we'd had old soul, R&B, a Latin splurge. People had tried everything and were now looking further afield. They were aware that there was other music.'

By now, a significant change had taken place in the structure of London's clubs. The original set-up, where the owners hired resident disc jockeys to play non-stop disco music, gave way to a host of independent nights, where the clubs were hired out to budding entrepreneurs who then called in disc jockeys with esoteric music tastes, and small cliquish followings, often no more than a group of friends or hangers-on. It was not unusual to find a London club like Gossips resounding to rhythm and blues one night, rockabilly the next, followed by ska and reggae and jazz and psychedelia.

One of the earliest beneficiaries of the new system was John Armstrong, who started a 'Roots with Zoots' night at London's Beat Route in 1981. Four years later, he was playing Afro-Cuban and Latin music at the Bass Clef in Hoxton. Armstrong notes three distinct trends in African music: the Zairean which, along with Antillean and Latin music, appeals chiefly to the dance audience, the 'Arabic' vocal sounds from Mali, Guinea, Senegal and The Gambia, which, along with rai music from Algeria and taarab from east Africa, appeals to the 'folk roots' crowd. Finally, South African mbaqanga and jazz attracts a mixture of the politically aware and people interested in rhythm and blues. Armstrong himself sees a strong link between South African and American music. 'The township sound has a distinct 1950s American feel,' he says. 'You get the same exploitation of the artists by the studios, the same vitality, the same interest in new dance crazes.'

The most influential of these has been the mabone, a South African township rhythm that goes back at least to 1973 with Noise Khanyile's '2 Mabone 6 Mabone', and possibly further. The craze came from the Gallo studios, where it was created by Robert Bopape, and a studio band featuring Marks Mankwane (guitar) and producer West Nkosi (bass). Mabone itself means headlight, the idea being, in Armstrong's words, that 'the more of a dude you were, the more lights you had on your car'. The light, with its attendant dances, and the stabbing, unforgettable bass line, underpinning township sax or violin lines, have spawned a host of hits, from 'Jive Mabone' by the Mahotella Queens to 'Jive Mabone 800', by Mr Singo, 'Seven Mabone', a new version by West Nkosi, 'Last Mabone' by John Mzizi and, in 1985, possibly the hardest and heaviest of all, 'Two Mabone' by Nkosi's studio band, the Makgona Tsohle Band. When the former Sex Pistols manager Malcolm McLaren used the rhythm for his *Duck Rock* album (1982), Nkosi hit back with the perfect answer record: 'Hula Hoop Jive' from a band called Kataki. In Britain, 'Hula Hoop Jive', with its English dance instructions, became a popular number both with Hucker and Armstrong, its popularity bolstered by its rare import status. Other fashions came and went. At one time, Hucker was playing three versions of the cross-African hit 'Shauri Yako', the original, by Nguashi N'Timbo, and two covers, one by Orchestre Super Mazembe and a Kenyan disco-version, popping electro drums and all, from Sammy Kasule. A run of Latin records with African names, including 'El Watusi' and 'Bantu' provided a further link, while Armstrong cites the South African 'fruit jive' tracks, which produced 'The Pineapple Jam' by Jozi, and Mr G's 'Avocado Pear Juice' sung in a curious mixture of English and Afrikaans.

In presenting new dances and fashions, the disc jockeys are doing little more than reflecting what is already happening in Africa. When a new style is 'created' in Britain, the issue becomes more complex. Juju music, the first African sound to receive widespread promotion in Britain, had limited appeal for the clubs and it was only when Dele Abiodun introduced a straight electro drum on his *Confrontation* album that the music became more attractive. In Armstrong's words, it didn't work as a dance music, but 'it was something that people could talk, drink or wiggle their hips to . . .'

Hucker largely passed juju by, concentrating his early efforts on highlife music, then soukous. Many of the subsequent attempts to put a heavy funk beat into African music leave him cold. 'The Western beat is all too often an impediment,' he says. 'It shows down the rhythm, giving a sluggish, slovenly feel. George Darko's "Hi-Life Time" was half-half, neither one thing nor the other. The electro beat was far too prominent. You can use that sound properly, but you shouldn't become a slave to the American sound. I'm totally opposed to this "rhythmic imperialism", which reduces music to sub-disco.' Among the exceptions, Hucker singles out Hugh Masekela's 'Don't Go Lose It Baby', the *Benediction* album by Franco and Michelino, which introduced electro drums but avoids the central funk beat, and 'Marguerita' by a Côte d'Ivoire band, Woya. 'They use the electro sound properly, to give a hard modern edge; it's a completely different sound from the traditional guitars, brass and keyboards,' he explains. 'But the original feel of the music is still there.'

Bill Laswell, the New York producer whose work with artists like Fela and Mandingo marked out a new electro–Africa 'collision', draws Hucker's especial contempt. 'He should have been locked up and not allowed near a mixing-desk.'

Changing production values have made a lasting impact on modern music, whether African, European or otherwise. For Armstrong, the danger lies not so much in the imposition of a simplified and alien rhythm pattern, but in the overall loss of sound quality. 'African music is becoming too formularized,' he says. 'The same thing has happened to rock and roll. Listen to an early Little Richard or Hank Ballard. Those guys really knew what they were doing when they recorded sound. It's a lost art. Listen to modern pop. It has a fantastic sound, but it's the sound of the studio, not the sound of the music. The same is happening with African and Antillean music, all of which runs a similar risk of over-production.' As examples, Armstrong points to recent Paris recordings by Empire Bakuba which sound fine on a sound system, but bear little relation to the live sound of modern Africa. Zaiko Langa Langa take a different approach, with a rougher sound that captures the intensity and the spark of the actual performance.

Although Hucker and Amstrong both play African music, their range of interests extends wider, reflecting the current cross-fertilization taking place in black dance music. Armstrong's playlist of music from the Caribbean, South and Central America suggests that the old divisions of African and Latin are slowly becoming redundant, and that we should be talking about 'tropical' music instead. Hucker makes the same point with publicity materials that pinpoint 'music from two continents and several assorted islands'. The tropical mix-up has already produced a number of African–Antillean crossovers, including Bopol's 'Helena' which mixes soukous and zouk, and Moni Bile's first 'new-look makossa' hit, 'O Si Tapo Lambo Lam', which marries biguine with Cameroonian music. Many of the Afro–Antillean mixes come from Paris, with its large, multi-ethnic bands of session artists. The same process is taking place in New York, where salsa artists turn out soca and Trinidadians turn their attention to soca–merengue mixtures.

For the disc jockey, such eclecticism signals a new approach to dance music, in which one culture meets another on equal terms. Hucker illustrates the global nature of modern music with a set of rhythm clusters that allow him to switch from American to African and Antillean tracks without missing a beat. Using the standard two turntables, he can move from a pure percussion and marimba track by South African roots band Amampondo to a brassy soca follow-up like 'Tarshika' from the Trinidadian Crazy Kalico Band. An earlier mix combined the voice of Martin Luther King, with a rhythm track from Grand Master Flash, before fading into Shina Williams's 'Agboju Logun', while James Brown's 'Do the Hustle' segued into Fela's 'Open and Close'.

Whether or not the tropical mix will leave the clubs and go mainstream is hard to say. For Armstrong, the stumbling-block is the standard British fear of dancing – watching and talking are the preferred modes – plus a curious ambivalence towards tropical music generally. On the one hand, the British have always embraced 'happy-sounding' tropical music, calypso in particular, while shying away from harder sounds like reggae. 'You can hear calypso at a barrister's garden party,' he says. 'You won't hear [hardcore rap-reggae artist] Shinehead.' On the other hand, the record-buying public react strongly against any music that sounds too 'sweet'. And in Africa, 'sweet' is a widespread term of praise. 'Anglo-Saxon youth culture has been brainwashed by the diminished 7th and minor mode Mississippi blues,' he claims. 'That's why Youssou N'Dour, and the "Arabic" sounds are so popular. They're seen as working from a blues base. We link into it because we don't like major chords or happy-sounding sweet stuff. The reason is mainly historical. The first black music we heard was rock and roll. Then R&B. So we think a hard melody is one that has flattened thirds and sevenths.'

The best example came from Bob Marley, whose early work for Island took a light, almost gospel sound into a world inhabited by minor chords, riffs and doomy sax solos, and album-cover imagery composed of radical chic, drugs and an attitude of studied cool and defiance. It seems worlds away from the packaging and promotion given to most current African artists. But if it worked for Marley . . .

DISCOGRAPHY

King Sunny Ade and His African Beats, *The Message* (Sunny Alade). Peerless juju, looking to the future as well as the roots of the traditional Yoruba praise song. From 1981. Pure magic.

King Sunny Ade and His African Beats, *Synchro System* (Island). The most satisfying of Ade's albums for Island, carefully balancing Western and Nigerian elements. The straightened and strengthened beat made it the first juju album (1983) to generate easy dancing on British floors.

Adeolu with the Western Toppers Band, *12 Original Highlife Compositions* (Decca West Africa). Swaggering sixties highlife from a Nigerian bandleader who made the switch from agidigbo to guitar music.

Segun Adewale and His Superstars International, *Adewale Play for Me* (Sterns). The loose rhythms and regulation slide-guitar licks of Adewale's early juju given a relentless, heavy power punch and tagged yopop (aptly nicknamed kick-and-start music).

Admiral Dele Abiodun and His Top Hitters Band, *It's Time for Juju Music* (Leader). A mixture of hi-tech juju, straightened out with electro drums plus, on side two, all the subtleties and shifts of the adawa king at his best.

African Brothers Dance Band, *Ena Eye A Mane Me* (Afribros). A crucial introduction to the music of one of Ghana's top guitar bands. Includes the classic 'Ebi Te Yie', from the early sixties.

African Brothers International, *Agatha* (Makossa). Classic guitar-band music from Ghana's top band.

Various, *African Music* (Vertigo). A Dutch compilation from 1983 that includes tracks from Prince Nico, Victor Uwaifo, Celestine Ukwu and other great Nigerian highlife artists.

Eric Agyeman, *Highlife Safari* (Agpogee). A 1981 album featuring one of Ghana's top guitarists and a band made up largely of Sweet Talks members.

Tony Allen with Afrobeat 2000, *NEPA* (MWKS). Hard dance rhythms from Fela Kuti's former drummer. The album includes two Afrobeat dub tracks.

Les Amazones de Guinée, *Au Coeur de Paris* (SLP). A live 1983 set that captures the magical stage sound of Guinea's women's police band.

M'Bilia Bel and Tabu Ley, *Keyna* (Genidia). Effortless vocals and strong melodies from one of Zaire's most popular singers. Composition credits go largely to her mentor Tabu Ley.

Jocelyn Beroard, *Siwo* (GD). Impressive debut album from Kassav's frontline female singer.

The Bhundu Boys, *Shabini* (DisqAfrique). They came, gigged and conquered. *Shabini* took the Bhundu Boys to the top of the independent charts in 1987.

Moni Bile, *O Si Tapa Lambo Lam* (Safari Ambiance). Densely arranged, often stirring, dance music from this Cameroonian singer; earthy vocals set against a precisely arranged horns-and-guitar backdrop. A classic of the new-look makossa.

Alpha Blondy, *Apartheid is Nazism* (Sterns). Warm, unfailingly melodic sounds from the Ivoirian singer who has inherited Sonny Okosuns' Afro-reggae mantle.

Bobongo Stars, *Zairo* (RCA). Alternative non-soukous sounds, from jazz to roots, from Zaire's maverick dance band.

Ifang Bondi, *Saraba* (Bellot). In the 1960s and 1970s singer Paps Touray fronted the Super Eagles and dealt in sharp suits, highlife, pop and soul. This minor-keyed (and often melancholic) 1982 foray into Gambian jazz-fusion is underscored by a tough mixture of cultural sounds and rhythms.

Canadoes, *Fine Woman* (Ras). The hardest and most riveting Ghanaian guitar-band album of its year (1984).

Frederick Caracas, *Voulez Vous Venir* (Moradisc). One of spring 1987's most popular zouk sets, with bassist Caracas' title track developing into a sumptuous melange of zouk codes.

Choc Stars *Awa et Ben* (GlobeStyle). Zairean new-wave band plays it relatively loud and rough. From 1986.

Oliver De Coque, *Opportunity* (Olumo). Fresh and appealing Nigerian highlife in the same vein as Prince Nico (and showing Nico's influence in the topline melodies).

A.B. Crentsil, *Tantie Alaba* (ERT) Love and drinking-songs from the top Ghanaian highlife singer and raconteur best known for 'Moses', 'The Lord's Prayer' and 'Adam and Eve'.

Various, *Dance! Cadence!* (GlobeStyle). First British-released cadence compilation, including the early zouk of Georges Decimus plus notable contributions from Eugene Mona and Godzom Son Traditionel.

Daouda, *Le Sentimental* (Sterns). The melodies could be from 'Island in the Sun'. With the exception of the jumpy 'Je Suis Fatigué', the rest of the tracks set Daouda's sweet-edged melodies against a relentless soukous backdrop.

Dark City Sisters, *Star Time* (EMI). A light, beautifully harmonized late-sixties set that marks a transition between the easy swing of kwela and the hardness of latter-day mbaqanga.

George Darko *Moni Palava* (A&B). Darko's best-known British outing, 'Highlife Time', added funk to the mix. The 1986 follow-up mixes soca and pop. The flip side contains three electro-flavoured roots tracks.

Jacob F. Désvarieux, *Banzawa* (GD). From 1983, zouk's earliest dynamic workout, with Naimro's synthesized keyboard sound heralding the hi-tech sound.

Désvarieux/Decimus, *Yelele* (GD). From 1984, a glossy and still mightily impressive Kassav album, including the band's much loved song 'Zouk La Se Sel Medikaman Nou Ni'.

Ernesto Djedje, *Amaguhewou* (SED). The last single from the Côte d'Ivoire's great ziglibithy star. The flip contains news-style street interviews with stars mourning his mysterious death.

Etoile de Dakar, *Tolou Badou Ndiaye* (ET). Mbalax 1980-style: a minimal and spacy prelude to the denser studio sounds of *Immigrés* and *Nelson Mandela*.

Franco et TPOK Jazz, *20ème Anniversaire* (6 Juin 1956–6 Juin 1976) (African, Sonodisc). A classic collection that features many of Franco's best-known vocalists, from Youlou Mabiala to Wuta May.

Franco et Sam Mangwana avec le TPOK Jazz, *Cooperation* (Visa/Edipop). The reunion between Franco and his former star vocalist, features the rousing title track and the lilting 'Loboko Nalitama'.

Thomas Frempong, *Aye Yi* (Asona). Ghanaian highlife, cut in London in 1986. A careful, at times inspiring balance of highlife rhythms and guitar patterns, worked around a central electro drum.

Pier Rozier and Gazoline, *Carerement News* (Moradisc). Though not as innovative as Kassav, or as sweet as Lazair, singer Rozier and band

Gazoline produce a stirring, big zouk sound.

Toto Guillaume, *Makossa Digital* (Sonodisc). An album of occasional brilliance which pushes makossa as far towards the spirit of disco and pop as it can go before becoming something else.

K. Gyasi and His Noble Kings, *Sikyi Highlife* (Essiebons). A reworking of traditional sikyi rhythms into a mournful, minor-key modern highlife sound. The band features Eric Agyeman and Thomas Frempong.

Various, *Independence Special* (ZML). An introduction to many of Zimbabwe's top artists, from Thomas Mapfumo to Devera Ngwena, Zexie Manatsa and Hosia Chipanga and the Balfour Black Diamonds.

Jali Musa Jawara, *Fote Mogobon* (Oval). A well-publicized record since its 1986 British release, *Fote Mogobon* sets Jawara's inspired kora playing against a lyrical and highly accessible guitar, balafon and vocal backdrop.

Various, *Juju Roots: 1930s–1950s* (Rounder). A collection that spans urban Nigerian recorded music, juju and non-juju. Featured artists include Ayinde Bakare, S.S. Peters and Tunde King.

Joseph Kabasele et L'African Jazz, *Homage au Grand Kalle* (Sonodisc). Features the wonderful 'Independence Cha Cha' alongside other sixties material from the father of modern Zairean music.

Kantata, *It's High Time Now* (Asona). A 1986 hi-tech outing from the German-based purveyors of what has become known as 'burger' highlife – from the city of Hamburg.

Mory Kante, *A Paris* (Sacodis). Kora in a modern funk setting. Kante's explorations include Denis Hekimian and other top Paris studio musicians, in a set that includes the popular 'Yeke Yeke'.

Various, *Music of Africa Series Musical Instruments, 6. Guitars 1 by Hugh Tracey* (Kaleidophone). A collection which shows the full excitement and the wide spread of acoustic guitar music in the fifties. The most famous cuts include 'Masanga' and 'Mama Na Mwana' from Jean Bosco Mwenda.

Souzy Kasseya, *The Phenomenal* (ERT). A lush, soft-edged soukous from the singer best known for 'Le Téléphone Sonne', 1985. A pure Paris production, with women back-up singers, Cameroon-style, and lavish horn charts.

Kassiry *Afrika* (PRD) Polished funk, with African flavours, from the Ivoirian hi-tech star. The gatefold sleeve, with a montage of studio hardware and rural African scenes, speaks volumes.

Salif Keita et Les Ambassadeurs International, *Mandjou* (Celluloid).

Keita's classic Sékou Touré praise song receives a vocal performance of unsurpassed passion and intensity. A riveting and unforgettable performance.

Steve Kekana, *Amandla Amasha*. A 1982 set whose six of pop and mbaqanga provides a fitting showcase for one of South Africa's finest male singers.

Ousmane Kouyate, *Beni Haminanko* (Sacodis). A patchy 1982 album from the ex-Ambassadeurs' guitarist features balafon player Djeli Moridian Kouyate on the stirring title track. The ensuing mix of roots and funk palls slightly.

Toure Kunda, *Natalia* (Celluloid). Senegal music at its glossiest. Guests include Bernie Worrel and Foday Musa Suso.

Fela Kuti, *Everything Scatter* (Phonogram). Along with Gentleman, Yellow Fever, Expensive Shit, Kalakuta Show and Zombie, definitive 1970s Kuti. For the 1980s, check *Perambulator* and *Army Arrangement*.

Ladysmith Black Mambazo, *Induku Zethu* (ELP). Recorded well before the Paul Simon connection, the album offers a good introduction to Ladysmith's vocal passion and precision.

Lazair, *Yche Man Man* (Kadence) & *Move* (Kadence). Two albums establishing guitarist Dominique Gengoul and singer Jean Luc Alger as masters of chic-zouk.

Ray Lema, *Medicine* (Celluloid). Synthesized keyboards and drums, plus live guitars, from Zaire's gifted electro-maverick.

Tabu Ley Rochereau et L'Orchestre Afrisa, *Extrait de L'Enrigistrement direct au festival Mondial des Arts Negro-Africains de 1977 au Square Tafawa Balewa et au National Théâtre de Lagos*. From 'Aint no Sunshine' to 'Soweto', a live FESTAC set that confirmed Tabu Ley as Zaire's top, progressive artist. His back-up band is augmented by members of Zaiko Langa Langa.

Mahotella Queens, *Izibani Zomgqashiyo* (EMW). A British release for a 1977 album that shows the power and force of the Queens' music – the indestructible beat.

Miriam Makeba, *The Click Song* (ESP). Makeba's late-fifties American debut includes Zulu traditional songs, 'House of the Rising Son' and a version of 'Mbube', the Solomon Linda classic. A fresh and compelling vocal performance.

Makgona Tsohle Band, *Mathaka Vol 1* (Spades). A 1983 classic that features 'Two Mabone', 'Seventeen Mabone' and other stomping sax and violin jives.

Mandingo *Watto Sitta* (Celluloid). Gambian kora player Foday Musa Suso meets New York electro. Fine playing alongside one of Bill Laswell's more successful productions.

Bebe Manga, *Amie* (SIIS). Along with Moni Bile's 'O Si Tapo Lambo Lam', one of the most important records in the post-1980 rise of Cameroon music. The title track, composed by makossa veteran Ebanda Manfred, von huge acclaim in Africa and the Caribbean.

Sam Mangwana, *Maria Tebbo* (SAM). The title track, covering the whole of side one, rerecords the old acoustic rumba classic. Side two includes a celebration of Zimbabwe's independence. Mangwana at his best.

Samba Mapangala and Orchestre Virunga, *Malako* (ERT). Zairean music through a Kenyan filter; 'Malako' became a cult record with African-music aficionados in the early eighties.

Thomas Mapfumo, *Ndangariro* (ELP). Mapfumo's first British release mixes deep chimurenga music with less intense, good-time tracks such as 'Temerina'. A powerful and compelling performance.

Thomas Mapfumo, *The Chimurenga Singles 1976–1980* (Earthworks). Mapfumo's chimurenga singles earned him harassment and a prison term in the then Rhodesia. Though the lyrics were necessarily coded, there's no mistaking the fervour of the music.

Bavon Marie-Marie, *L'Intrepide* (African). A posthumous release whose silken rumbas and immaculate vocal harmonies have rarely been surpassed. Bumpier rhythms shine through in the sebens.

Hugh Masekela, *Techno-Bush* (Jive Afrika). Great southern African hits, from 'Skokiaan' to 'Grazing in the Grass' and 'Mbube' receive a polished early-eighties sound. Recorded in Botswana, at Jive's mobile studio.

Prince Nico Mbarga & His New Rocafil Jazz, *Music Message* (PNM). Lyrical guitar playing, tough bass lines and some surprising sax solos distinguish otherwise straightahead panko melange of Congolese guitars and highlife.

E.T. Mensah and His Tempos Band, *All For You* (Retroafric). Offers some of ET's greatest songs, including the title track, 'Inflation Calypso' and 'Sunday Mirror'.

Various, *The Nairobi Sound* (OMA). A collection of acoustic and light electric guitar music from Jim Lasco, Daudi Kabaka and John Mwale. Tracks include Fadhili Williams' much covered 'Malaika'.

Obed Ngobeni and the Kurhula Sisters, *Gazankulu* (Heads). Shangaan pop music from South Africa: a mixture of deep vocals and stinging guitars.

Eternel Docteur Nico, *Merveilles du Passe 1963–1965* (African). A selection that shows the range and versatility of Zaire's late 'God of the Guitar'. Tracks include 'Mambo Hawienne' and 'Merengue President' and much solid rumba playing.

Ko Nimo, *Odonson Nkoaa Part One* (Philips). Ghana's roots revivalist at the front of a vibrant percussion and harmony vocal troupe.

Kwame Nkrumah with Jewel Ackah, *Safari and Classical Highlifes* (Pan African). A triumphant return to the basics by Ghanaian highlife guitar veteran Nkrumah, featuring fine vocals from Ackah.

Nyboma et L'Orchestre Les Kamale Dynamiques du Zaire, *Double Double* (Ledoux). One of Nyboma's best albums, which marked his emergence as an international solo artist. He gets as fiery as the Zairean mode allows, concentrating on up-tempo numbers with stinging melodies.

Sonny Okosuns, *3rd World* (EMI). Warm Afro-reggae, plus a range of pan-African themes mark Okosuns as one of the continent's most enduring talents.

Pablo Lubadika Porthos, *En Action* (Salsa Musique). Following the Island exposure via *Sound d'Afrique*. Porthos achieved a higher profile in the UK than back home in Zaire.

Various, *Radio Freedom* (REV). Mbaqanga, choral music, talks and speeches culled from the broadcasts of the underground station of the South African liberation movement, the ANC, and the People's Army, Umkhonto We Sizwe.

The Ramblers Dance Band, *The Hit Sound of the Ramblers Dance Band* (Afrodisia). A showcase for the band's unmistakable two-line vocal harmonies, plus a range of rhythms, from akwete to the kpanlogo, all presented in a lush dance-band style.

Shirati Jazz, *The East African Hit Parade* (Jicco). A 1975 album, released under licence in Nigeria, at a time when benga was rocking Kenya, and countries across west Africa too.

Soukoue Ko Ou, *Vacances* (NR). Pseudonymous Kassav. Sizzling zouk.

Various, *Sound d'Afrique 11 'Soukous'* (Island). Volume one introduced Etoile de Dakar alongside dance music from Zaire and other countries. Here Moussou Doumbia's balafon, flute and kora classic, 'Menebo Nden', is equally prominent in an above-average set of soukous tracks from Zaire, Congo and the Central African Republic.

Various, *Sound of Kinshasa* (Original Music). The album starts with likembe music from Obiza Charles before moving to African Jazz, OK Jazz, African Fiesta and other Zairean bands. A good introduction.

Various, *South African Trade Union Worker Choirs* (Rounder). An album of vibrant choral music which shows the strength and cultural vigour of the workers' movement in South Africa.

Sunsum Band, *Odo* (Love) (Asa). Guitar-band highlife from the top Ghanaian outfit led by Smart Nkansah.

Super Biton du Mali, *Balandzan* (Tan). Synthesizers and rippling guitars from one of the best-known names in modern Malian music.

Super Rail Band of Mali, *New Dimensions in Rail Culture* (GlobeStyle). British release from the band that produced Salif Keita and Mory Kante. A remarkable side two throws Franco guitar licks into the Malian mix.

Super Sweet Talks International, *The Lord's Prayer* (Ofori). Consistently satisfying dance-band highlife from the chief exponents of the genre, with the title track, pulling out all the gospel stops, outstanding.

Philip Tabane and His Malombo Jazzmen, *Man Phily* (PAM). South Africa's unique guitarist fuses traditional music, jazz and much more on a German compilation that includes 'Hi Congo', 'Marabi' and 'Malombo Blues'.

Blissi Tebil, *Ziglibithy – La Continuité* (SHA). In a tribute to the late Ernesto Djedje, Tebil shows himself to be an expert disciple on an album that makes full use of the complex ziglibithy rhythms.

Sam Fan Thomas, *Makassi* (Tam). Features the celebrated 'African Typic Collection' plus a set of tracks in the makassi rhythm that confirm Thomas as one of the Cameroon's great innovators.

Pat Thomas, *1980* (Pan African Records). Formative disco-highlife from one of Ghana's great voices.

Bibi Den's Tshibayi, *The Best Ambience* (Cel). Tshibayi is a Zairean musician based in Abidjan. The album reflects the city's status as a musical crossroads, with a mix that ranges from soukous to Antillean rhythms. An early-eighties fusion that would set the pattern for many of the Afro-zouk albums that would follow.

Nana Tuffour, *Highlife Romance* (Gab). Fresh-faced bubblegum highlife, laced with light reggae rhythms, from the man who went on to record Sikyi Highlife.

Sir Victor Uwaifo and His Melody Maestros, *Sir Victor Uwaifo Big Sound* (Philips). A set that contains 'Akwete', 'Joromi' and other guitar-band classics from the great Nigerian guitarist and singer.

Verckys, *Bankoko Baboyi* (Sonodisc). A selection from Verckys' hugely popular Orchestre Veve. The album covers the years 1969–73 and contains the remarkable authenticity ballad, 'Nakomitunaka'.

Victoria Kings Jazz, *Ikwo Kiri Kwo* (Jicco). Nigerian release of a lively mid-seventies benga outing.

Papa Wemba, *Le Kuru Yaku* (Don Dass). Other Wemba albums may be far more polished and better produced, but the superb, splintery harmonies of 'La Vie Comme Elle Va Bola' command instant attention.

World of Music Arts and Dance, *Raindrops Patterning on Banana Leaves and Other Tunes* (WOMAD Foundation). The first of many fascinating, and, for the most part, better titled WOMAD compilations, this one recalls the heady days of 1982 with a set that features Kanda Bongo Man, the Beat and the Drummers of Burundi.

Tout Choc Zaiko Langa Langa, *Oldies and Goodies 1974–1978* (MGL). Early, new-wave rumba from the band that set off Zaire's youth revolution.

Glossary

Abgaya: a pre-rumba rhythm popular in the Congo

Adaha: Ghanaian brass-band music

Adakam: dance music of the Akan people of Ghana

Adowa: percussion and vocal music of the Ashanti people of Ghana

Afrobeat: term coined by Fela Anikulapo-Kuti to describe his synthesis of west African and black American music

Afro carnival: a bass-heavy style of contemporary music created by Sonny Okosuns

Agbadza: Ghanaian percussion rhythm regularly used in electric bands

Agidigbo: a wooden box with a sound-hole and iron keys (also known as a 'hand piano')

Ajiwere: Islamic music which wakes the faithful during Ramadan and has played a key role in the development of fuji in Nigeria

Akpombo: rhythm from Côte d'Ivoire

Akwete: Nigerian rhythm associated with guitarist Victor Uwaifo

Aloukou: traditional rhythm from Côte d'Ivoire

Ambasse bey: Cameroonian street music whose best-known purveyors include Salle Jean, Jean Ferdinand Dikoto and others

Apala: Nigerian vocal and percussion music popularized by the late Haruna Ishola

Apremprensuah: a Ghanaian 'hand piano' or bass box

Asiko: Cameroonian rhythm

Balafon: west African xylophone

Bata: west African drum

Benga: Kenyan dance rhythm, popular in the seventies

Beni: competitive dance form derived from brass-band music and popular, until the dominance of electric jazz bands, in many east African countries

Biguine: Martinique dance rhythm; European: beguine

Bikoutsi: Cameroonian rhythm

Blues: a slow highlife form, as in Ibo or Ashanti blues

Bodi: women's music of Kenya

Boucher: Zairean and Congolese dance rhythm popular in the 1960s

Box guitar: acoustic guitar

Cadence: dance music from Guadeloupe and Martinique, an influence on zouk

Caretta: 'fancy' dance introduced into Lagos by freed slaves from Brazil and Cuba

Cavacha: Zairean dance rhythm associated with Zaiko Langa Langa in the early 1970s

Chakacha: dance form of taarab music from east Africa

Chimurenga: literally 'struggle' (from the liberation of Zimbabwe) and the name given to the music of Thomas Mapfumo

Claves: pair of resonating wooden percussion sticks

Dansi: ballroom music played on guitar and accordion in turn-of-the-century east Africa

Discolypso: a fusion of African and Caribbean music associated with Sierra Leonean producer Akie Deen and singer Bunny Mack

Dry guitar: acoustic guitar

Fanfare: French for 'brass band', big in Zaire before the guitar bands

Fuji: a popular form of Nigerian music derived from the Islamic festival of Ramadan

Gbegbe: traditional rhythm from Côte d'Ivoire played electric-style by Sery Simplice and other modernizers

Goje or Goge: west African stringed instrument similar to violin

Goumbay: frame drum common throughout west Africa, and a form of music influenced partly by freed slaves, that developed in Freetown, Sierra Leone

Griot: French colonial term to describe a 'jali' (court or peripatetic troubador)

Groaner: South African male singer who takes the deep bass parts in mbaqanga songs

Gwo ka: percussion and street rhythm that has fed into zouk from Guadeloupe and Martinique

Highlife: a form of dance music popular in Ghana, Nigeria and other Anglophone west African countries

Hosho: Zimbabwean gourd rattle

Ingoma ebusuku: form of South African choral music

Itembe: Nigerian frame drum

Jali: court or peripatetic troubador combining role of entertainer and historian

Jamosket: dance rhythm created by Papa Wemba

Jazz: generic name for African dance music that, for the most part, uses horns and electric instruments

Jerusalem: Zimbabwean music played by Oliver Mtukudzi

Jit: Zimbabwean percussion music, as in 'jit jive'

Kara kara: Zairean dance rhythm

Kinsensengoma: dance rhythm associated with Grand Zaiko Wa Wa

Kiri kiri: dance rhythm associated with Dr Nico in the mid-1960s

Konkomba: Ghanaian street music popular in the 1940s (in Nigeria, 'konkoma')

Kora: harp-lute played by Mandinka musicians of The Gambia and Senegal and elsewhere

Kpanlogo: popular percussion rhythm that developed in Ghana in the 1960s, said to be in answer to the twist

Kushaura: lead, or solo part played by Zimbabwean mbira musician

Kusum: Ghanaian northern rhythms played by the Sweet Talks

Kutsinhira: melodic rhythm played by Zimbabwe mbira players

Kwela: South African township pennywhistle music popular in the 1950s

Likembe: hand piano, from Zaire

Lokole: Zairean slit log drum, played on stage by Papa Wemba

Mabone: literally 'headlight', a South African dance craze

Makassi: rhythmic basis of San Fan Thomas's music

Makossa: Cameroonian rhythm

Mangembeu: Cameroonian rhythm

Marabi: South African township music popular in the 1930s and 1940s and an important influence on South African township jazz

Maringa: Sierra Leonean rhythm associated with Ebenezer Calendar

Matindique: rhythm played by Zairean fanfares

Mazurka: guitar style developed by Zairean acoustic musicians, late 1930s onwards

Mbalax: Senegalese percussion music, put into electric form by Youssou N'Dour

Mbaqanga: South African township music popular from late 1960s onwards

Mbira: hand piano of the Shona people in Zimbabwe

Mbube: literally 'lion', the name of a Solomon Linda song, sometimes used to describe South African choral music

Merengue: Latin American dance rhythm

Mi-compose: Zairean guitar style

Miliki: literally 'enjoyment', as in Miliki System (the juju played by Ebenezer Obey)

Milo jazz: Sierra Leonean street music

Mi-solo: Zairean finger-picked electric guitar style

Nagla: percussion rhythm of northern Ghana

Nkuiti: Zairean percussion instrument

Odonson: Ghanaian folk music

Omutibo: Kenyan guitar style

Osibi: music of the Fante people of west Africa

Osode: Ghanaian folk music modernized by C.K. Mann

Owambe: pre-electric form of juju

Ozzidizm: philosophy of Sonny Okosuns

Pachanga: Latin American dance rhythm which enjoyed considerable popularity in Africa from the 1940s and 1950s

Palm-wine: acoustic guitar music, whose name derives from west African bars where palm wine is sold

Panko: dance music associated with Prince Nico

Pata pata: South African township dance of the 1950s

Patenge: small drum played in early Zairean rumba ensembles

Polka pique: Zairean acoustic guitar style

Rai: Algerian popular music

Rumba: Latin American dance rhythms, the dance music of Zaire

Rumba odemba: rumba variation created by Franco
Rumba saccade: 'hot' rumba

Sabar: Senegalese drum
Sakara: Nigerian vocal and percussion music popularized by Yusufu Olatunji
Samba: square frame drum popular in southern Nigeria and of a type found in many parts of Africa. Gumbay drum is the Sierra Leonean equivalent
Sanza: hand piano popular throughout central Africa
Sarenga: Zimbabwean rhythm
Sax jive: South African township dance music which took over from pennywhistle jive in the 1960s
Seben: second and faster section of the two-part Zairean song
Seprewa: Ghanaian lute
Shangara: Zimbabwean rhythm
Shebeen: South African township bar often associated with sale of moonshine liquor
Shekere: West African percussion instrument made out of dried gourd filled with beans or beads
Sibi saba: Ghanaian rhythm from the 1930s
Sikyi highlife: highlife associated with Dr K. Gyasi and his Noble Kings
Simanje-manje: South African dance
Soukous: modern Zairean dance music
Soum: guitar style popularized by Tabu Ley
Soumdjoum: musical style created by Tabu Ley
Sukuma: Zairean dance style, popularized by Verckys
Sukuti: Kenyan percussion rhythm
Sungura: Zimbabwean dance rhythm, based on speeded-up version of Zairean rumba

Taarab: orchestral music from Swahili people of east Africa
Talazo: Nigerian laxative, and name taken, for his music, by fuji star Barrister, as in Talazo Disco
Tama: Senegambian talking-drum
Tam-tam: percussion instrument, a talking-drum
Tchamassi: Cameroonian rhythm usually associated with Andre Marie Tala
Ti bois: wooden log drum played in zouk
Tickey draai: early folk dance popular in South African towns

Tripo: Côte d'Ivoire women's music

Toy motion: early juju variant

Tsaba tsaba: Zimbabwean acoustic guitar music associated with George Sibanda

Tumba: percussion instrument, resembling large conga drum

Waka: form of Nigerian women's vocal and percussion music

Were: an Islamic music influential in fuji

Wundelow: Senegambian dance

Xalam: small Senegambian lyre-like instrument

'Yaa Amponsah': song written by Kwame Asare (Sam), which later gave its name to classic guitar-band rhythm yaa amponsah

Yeki yeki: Zairean dance rhythm popularized by Franco and others

Yopop: style of juju-related music played by Segun Adewale

Zekete zekete: rhythm associated with Zaiko Langa Langa

Ziglibithy: traditional Côte d'Ivoire rhythm updated by late Ernesto Djedje

Zogbo: dance rhythm from Côte d'Ivoire

Zomgquashiyo: mbaqanga style associated with the Mahotella Queens

Zouk: modern hi-tech Antillean music

REFERENCES

URBAN DEVELOPMENT (pp. 3–30)

1. David Coplan, *The Urbanization of African Performing Arts in South Africa* (Indiana University, Phd dissertation, 1980)
2. T.O. Ranger, *Dance and Society in Eastern Africa* (London: Heinemann, 1975)
3. Joseph E. Harrison (ed), *The Recollections of James Juma Mbotela* (East African Publishing House, 1977)
4. Henry Weman, *African Music and the Church in Africa* (Uppsala: Studia Missionalia Upsaliensia, 3 Svenska Institutet for Missionsforskning, 1960)
5. Kazadi Wa Mukuna, *Trends of Nineteenth- and Twentieth-century Music in the Congo-Zaire* (Regensburg: Musikkulturen Asiens, Afrikas und Ozeaniens in 19. Jahrhundert, 1973), p. 267
6. E.G. Parrinder, *Music in West African Churches* (Johannesburg: African Music Society Newsletter, 1956), p. 37
7. Interview with David Rycroft, South Africa, 1964
8. T.O. Ranger, op cit
9. David Coplan, op cit
10. John Collins, *African Pop Roots* (London: Foulsham, 1985), p. 110
11. Quoted in Graeme Ewens, *King of the Congo Sound* (London: Africa Music, September 1983)
12. Chris Waterman, *Juju Roots: 1930s–1950s* (Massachusetts: Rounder Records, 1985) sleevenotes
13. John Collins, op cit

341

14. Interview with CS, London 1985

15. Gerhard Kubik, 'Katanga!' (London: *Africa Beat* No. 3, September 1985)

16. David Rycroft, 'The Guitar Improvisations of Mwenda Jean Bosco' (Johannesburg: *African Music* 2–4, 1961), pp. 81–2

17. John Collins and Paul Richards, *Popular Music in West Africa: Suggestions for an Interpretative Framework* (Goteborg and Exeter: Popular Music Perspectives, the International Association for the Study of Popular Music, 1981), p. 132

18. Interview with CS, London 1986

19. *Nigerian Citizen* (Lagos: 12 July 1951)

20. Bernard Dadie, *Climbie* (London, Ibadan, Nairobi: Heinemann, 1984)

21. J.K. Nyerere, Tanzania National Assembly Official Reports (Dar Es Salaam, 1962), p. 9

22. Cyprian Ekwensi, *People of the City* (London, Ibadan, Nairobi: Heinemann, 1963)

23. Interview with CS, London 1986

24. Willard Rhodes, *African Music Journal* (Johannesburg, Vol. 2 No. 1, 1958), p. 83

25. Interview with CS, London 1987

WEST AFRICA: HIGHLIFE (pp. 33–62)

1. Kwabena N. Bame, *Come to Laugh, African Traditional Theatre in Ghana* (New York: Lilian Barber Press, 1985), pp. 8–14

2. Quoted in John Collins, *E.T. Mensah, King of Highlife* (London: Off the Record Press, 1986), p. 10

3. Interview with Tony Amadi, Onitsha 1986

4. Interviews with CS, London 1986

5. John Collins, op cit

6. Interview with CS, London 1986

7. Interview with Tony Amadi, op cit

8. Interview with CS, London 1984

9. Interview with CS, London 1983

10. Interview with CS, London 1985

11. Interview with CS, London 1987

12. Interview with CS, London 1983
13. Interview with CS, London 1987
14. Interview with CS, London 1983
15. Interview with CS, London 1984
16. Interview with CS, London 1985
17. Interview with CS, London 1982
18. Interview with CS, London 1985
19. Interview with CS, London 1984
20. Interview with CS, London 1987

WEST AFRICA: AFROBEAT AND AFRO-POP (pp. 63–77)

1. Interview with CS, London 1984
2. Tony Addis, interview with CS, London 1984
3. Interview with CS, London 1982
4. Interview with CS, London 1985
5. Interview with CS, London 1984
6. Interview with CM, 'Manu's Afrovision' (London: *Black Music*, May 1978), p. 40
7. Interview with Bob Okenodo, 'The Magnifunk Seven' (London: *Black Music*, December 1974), pp. 22–3
8. Interview with CS, London 1982
9. Interview with CS, London 1982

WEST AFRICA: JUJU (pp. 78–97)

1. Interview with CS, London 1983
2. Interview with CS, London 1983
3. Interview with CM, London 1984
4. Interview with CM, London 1980
5. *Lagos Weekend*, 31 May 1985
6. *Africa Music* (London, No. 13, January 1983), p. 12
7. Interview with CS, London 1986
8. Interview with CS, London 1981

WEST AFRICA: MAKOSSA, MALI AND GUINEA, SENE-GAMBIA, CÔTE D'IVOIRE (pp. 98–133)

1. Interview with CS, London 1985
2. Interview with CS, Paris 1984
3. Interview with CS, London 1985
4. Interview with CS, London 1985
5. Interview with CS, London 1985
6. Keita's uncle, interview with Sylvie Coma and Guy Le Querrec, *France International*, 1985; reprinted *Jazz Magazine*, February 1985
7. Phil Ekwengi, *Disques, Afrique Asie*, 1985
8. Interview with CS, London 1985
9. Interview with CS, London 1985
10. Interview with CS, London 1985
11. Interview with CS, London 1986
12. Peter Bradbrook, 'A Man of the Future' (London: *Africa Beat*, No. 4, 1985), p. 16
13. Interview with CS, London 1987
14. Peter Bradbrook, 'The Magic Mbalax' (London: *Africa Beat*, No. 5, 1986), p. 23
15. Interview with CS, London 1985
16. Interview with CS, London 1986
17. Quoted by Jon Pareles, 'Familial Beat Enlivens Toure Kunda' (*New York Times*, 10 April 1985)
18. Ibid
19. Interview with CS, London 1987
20. Interview with CS, London 1984
21. Interview with CS, London 1986

CENTRAL, SOUTHERN AND EAST AFRICA: ZAIRE

(pp. 135–85)

1. H.H. Johnston, *Journey up the Congo River* (London: Sampson Low, Marston and Co, 1895), p. 297

2. Kazadi Wa Mukuna, 'Congolese Music' (London: Macmillan, *The New Grove Dictionary of Music and Musicians*, Vol. 4, 1980), p. 660

3. David Birmingham and Phyllis M. Martin (eds), *History of Central Africa* (London: Longman)

4. Kwebe-Kimpele, Kinshasa 1985

5. Interview with CS, Kinshasa 1985

6. Citoyen Basunga, Kinshasa 1985

7. Gerhard Kubik, 'Katanga!' (London: *Africa Beat*, Summer 1985), p. 11

8. Anon, *Belgian Congo Today* (Brussels: April 1953), p. 65

9. Interview with CS, London 1984

10. Kwebe-Kimpele, Kinshasa 1985

11. Kolanga Molei, 'Kinshasa, Ce Village d'Hier' (Kinshasa: undated)

12. Interview with CS, Kinshasa 1985

13. Mobutu Sese Seko, 'Discours sur l'Etat de la Nation' (Kinshasa: 1972)

14. Interview with CS, Kinshasa 1985

15. Interview with CS, London 1984

16. Ibid

17. Francis Laloupo, 'Rochereau Tabu Ley, Le Spectacle Continue' (Paris: *Musiki Magazine*, No. 2, 1982), pp. 23–6

18. Interview with CS, Kinshasa 1985

19. Ibid

20. Interview with CS, Kinshasa 1985

21. Ibid

22. Interview with CS, London 1984

23. Ibid

24. Yoka Lye Mudaba, 'Le Phénomène de la Mode à Kinshasa' (Kinshasa: *Zaire Afrique*, September 1983), p. 427

25. *Elima* (Kinshasa: 14 March 1983), pp. 2–4

26. Interview with CS, Kinshasa 1985

27. Interview with CS, Kinshasa 1985

28. Interview with CS, 1985

29. Interview with CS, London 1983, published in *Blues and Soul* (London: October 1984)

30. Interview with CS, Paris 1984

CENTRAL, SOUTHERN AND EAST AFRICA: TOWNSHIP

POP (pp. 186–212)

1. Mbulelo Vizikhungo Mzamane, *The Children of Soweto* (London: Longman, 1982), p. 11

2. Todd Matshikiza, *Drum* (Johannesburg: December 1951)

3. Interview with CS, London 1985

4. Ibid

5. David Coplan, *Labour, Townships and Protest* (Johannesburg: Raven Press, 1979), p. 202

6. Harry Bloom, *King Kong, an African Jazz Opera* (Glasgow: Collins, 1961), p. 7

7. Interview with CS, London 1985

8. Priscilla A. Clark, *Some Effects of Western Influence on Zulu and Xhosa Music (since 1850)* (London: School of Oriental and African Studies, 1984)

9. David Rycroft, 'Zulu Male Traditional Singing' (Johannesburg: *African Music*, 1, 4, 1957), p. 33

10. Mbulelo Vizikhungo Mzamane, op cit, p. 124

11. Interview with CS, London 1987

12. Interview with CS, London 1984

13. Quoted in John Godfrey, 'Dancing with the Devil' (London: *City Limits*, 2 April 1987), p. 13

14. Interview with CS, Birmingham 1987

15. Anthony Sampson, *Drum* (London: Collins, 1956), p. 20

16. Mbulelo Vizikhungo Mazamane, sleevenotes for Jazz Afrika, *Son of the Soil* (Tsafrika records, 1982)

17. Interview with CM (London: *Black Music*, June 1975), p. 50

18. 'Your Weekend' (South Africa: *The Star*, 22 May 1981)

19. Interview with CS, London 1986

20. Interview with CS, London 1987

21. Interview with CS, London 1987

22. Hamilton Malaza, 'Meet Sipho Mchunu and Johnny Clegg' (South Africa: *Nangwane Times*, 7 August 1981), p. 9

23. Interview with CS, London 1987

24. Interview with CS, London 1987

CENTRAL, SOUTHERN AND EAST AFRICA: CHIMURENGA

(pp. 213–25)

1. G.P. Kahari, *The History of the Shona Protest Song: a Preliminary Study* (Zambezia, 1981), p. 89
2. Interview with CS, London 1985
3. Interview with CS, London 1985
4. Alec J. Pongweni, *Songs that Won the Liberation War* (Harare: College Press, 1982), Preface
5. Julie Frederikse, *None but Ourselves, the Masses vs the Media in the Making of Zimbabwe* (London: Heinemann), p. 108
6. Interview with CS, London 1985
7. Sue Steward, interview with Thomas Mapfumo in *Echoes* (London: 15 December 1984), p. 8
8. Interview with CS, London 1985
9. Ian Anderson (Guildford: *Folk Roots*, October 1985), p. 28
10. Tinos Guvi, 'Oliver Mtukudzi Says It All' (Harare: *Prize Africa*, Vol. 11, No. 11, November 1984), p. 10
11. John Peel, 'Five Zimbabweans' (London: *Observer*, 1 June 1986)
12. Interview with CS, London 1986
13. Interview with CS, London 1986
14. Interview with CS, London 1987

CENTRAL, SOUTHERN AND EAST AFRICA: KENYA AND TANZANIA (pp. 226–39)

1. Aziz Salim, London 1986
2. John Storm Roberts, *Songs the Swahili Sing* (New York: Original Music) sleevenotes
3. Interview with CS, London 1985
4. Aziz Salim, London 1986

5. Zembi Okeno, interview, CS, London 1985
6. Interview with CS, London 1987
7. Interview with CS, London 1987
8. Interview with CS, London 1987
9. Interview with CS, London 1987

ZOUK'S GRAND PLAN FOR GLOBAL DISCO DOMINA-TION AND ZOUK AND AFRICA (pp. 240–53)

All interviews with Charles de Ledesma, London 1987
1. Gene Scaramazzo, *Africa and Reggae Beat* (Los Angeles: Vol. V, 5/6, 1986), pp. 49–51
2. *Blues and Soul* (London: October 1984)
3. *Blues and Soul* (London: February 1987)
4. Interview with CS, London 1987

THE RECORD INDUSTRY: AFRICA (pp. 257–78)

1. J. Muir, Report, EMI archives, Hayes, Middlesex, 1912
2. Zonophone catalogue, EMI archives
3. EMI archives
4. P.B. Vatcha, letter to the Gramophone Company, 1926, EMI archives
5. Ibid
6. H. Evans, report on a tour of Kenya, Uganda, Tanganyika, Zanzibar and Portuguese East Africa, May–July 1893, EMI archives
7. H. Polliack, letter, EMI archives
8. S.H. Sheard, letter to the Gramophone Company, Hayes, 1930
9. Ibid
10. EMI archives
11. A trip to the Gold Coast and Nigeria, 1954. EMI archives
12. Interview with CS, London 1985
13. Interview with CS, London 1985
14. Interview with CS, London 1986

15. Interview with CS, London 1987
16. Letter, EMI archives
17. 'A New Approach to Africa', EMI archives
18. Interview with CS, London 1985

THE RECORD INDUSTRY: ABROAD (pp. 279–95)

1. Interview with CS, London 1985
2. Interview with CS, London 1985
3. Interview with CS, London 1987
4. Interview with CS, London 1986
5. Interview with CS, London 1987
6. Interview with CS, London 1986
7. Interview with CS, London 1987

THE BRITISH SCENE (pp. 297–324)

1. Sue Steward, *The Face* (London: No. 25, May 1982), p. 24
2. Interview with CS, London 1984
3. Interview with CS, London 1982
4. All quotes from interviews conducted in London, CS, 1982 onwards
5. Quotes from interviews with CS, London 1985, 1986
6. Quotes from interviews with CS, London 1984
7. Interviews with CS, London 1984, 1986, 1987
8. Interviews with CS, London 1986
9. Interviews with CS, London 1985
10. Interviews with CS, London 1982
11. Interview with CS, London 1984
12. Interview with CS, London 1986
13. Interview with CS, London 1987
14. Interview with CS, London 1985
15. Interview with CM, 1984
16. Interview with CS, 1987, all quotes

INDEX

Note: page numbers in bold type refer to main entries; page numbers in italic refer to illustrations